BEYOND SANCTUARY

BEYOND SANCTUARY

The Humanism of a World in Motion

Edited by Ananya Roy and Veronika Zablotsky

With Leisy J. Abrego, Gaye Theresa Johnson, and Maite Zubiaurre

DUKE UNIVERSITY PRESS
Durham and London
2025

© 2025 DUKE UNIVERSITY PRESS
This work is licensed under a Creative Commons
Attribution-NonCommercial-NoDerivatives 4.0 International
License, available at https://creativecommons.org/licenses/
by-nc-nd/4.0/.
Printed in the United States of America on acid-free paper ∞
Project Editor: Michael Trudeau
Designed by A. Mattson Gallagher
Typeset in Minion Pro and Futura by Westchester Publishing
Services

Library of Congress Cataloging-in-Publication Data
Names: Roy, Ananya editor author | Zablotsky, Veronika editor
author | Abrego, Leisy J. editor author | Johnson, Gaye Theresa
editor author | Zubiaurre, Maite editor author
Title: Beyond sanctuary : the humanism of a world in motion /
edited by Ananya Roy and Veronika Zablotsky, with Leisy J.
Abrego, Gaye Theresa Johnson, and Maite Zubiaurre.
Other titles: Humanism of a world in motion
Description: Durham : Duke University Press, 2025. | Includes
bibliographical references and index.
Identifiers: LCCN 2024054861 (print)
LCCN 2024054862 (ebook)
ISBN 9781478031987 paperback
ISBN 9781478028772 hardcover
ISBN 9781478060949 ebook
ISBN 9781478094340 ebook other
Subjects: LCSH: Humanitarianism—Europe | Humanitarianism—
United States | Emigration and immigration | Refugees—
Europe | Asylum, Right of—Europe | Xenophobia—Europe |
White nationalism—Europe | Race discrimination—Europe |
Refugees—United States | Asylum, Right of—United States |
Xenophobia—United States | White nationalism—United States |
Race discrimination—United States
Classification: LCC BJ1475.3 . B496 2025 (print)
LCC BJ1475.3 (ebook)
DDC 201/.76—dc23/eng/20250521
LC record available at https://lccn.loc.gov/2024054861
LC ebook record available at https://lccn.loc.gov/2024054862

Cover art: "La Casa de los Puntos Rojos / The Red-Dotted
House," artistic installation by Álvaro Enciso, in collaboration
with Maha Benhachmi, Eliza Franklin-Edmondson, Miranda
Hirujo-Rincón, Xiuwen Qi, and Maite Zubiaurre / Filomena
Cruz, southern Arizona desert, 2021. Credit: Maite Zubiaurre /
Filomena Cruz.

Open access was made possible by support from the Ideas and
Organizing project at the UCLA Luskin Institute on Inequality
and Democracy funded by the Marguerite Casey Foundation.

CONTENTS

ix   FOREWORD

        Sanctuary Politics and the Role of the University in the Time of Trumpism

        Ananya Roy and Maite Zubiaurre

1   INTRODUCTION

        Beyond Sanctuary
        The Humanism of a World in Motion

        Ananya Roy and Veronika Zablotsky

41   INTERLUDE

        ~~Asylum~~
        At the Borders of Humanitarianism

        Ananya Roy

        PART I. ABOLITION ON STOLEN LAND

45   1   **This Is an Incitement**
             Abolition on Stolen Land

               Gaye Theresa Johnson and Damon Azali-Rojas

59	2	**Beyond the Social Death of Conquest**
		Kuuyam and Healthy Human-Land Kinship(s)
		Charles A. Sepulveda
77	3	**Killing the Dead**
		Genocide and Antiblackness
		Moon-Kie Jung and João H. Costa Vargas
96	4	**From Minneapolis to Dessau, from Moria to Tripoli**
		Breathing, Resistance, and International Pathways of Abolition
		Vanessa E. Thompson
116	5	**Abolition Is My Sanctuary**
		A Love Letter to Freedom
		Lorgia García Peña
131		INTERLUDE
		Abolitionist Praxis
		Bringing Our Imagination to Life
		Veronika Zablotsky

PART II. THE END OF HUMANITARIANISM

135	6	**"Mujer Migrante Memorial (MMM)" and Necro-Art**
		Maite Zubiaurre

| 155 | 7 | **From Camp to Commons**
Infrastructures of Decolonial Solidarity in Europe
Charalampos Tsavdaroglou and Maria Kaika |

| 176 | 8 | **Humanitarian Racism**
Saree Makdisi |

| 196 | 9 | ***trans*/BORDER/*ing***
(an un-play 4 accompaniment)
Amy Sara Carroll and Ricardo Dominguez |

| 214 | 10 | **Postcoloniality, Race, and the Ruse of Asylum**
An Interview with Nicholas De Genova
Ananya Roy and Veronika Zablotsky |

| 231 | | INTERLUDE
Sanctuary and Solidarity
Resisting the US War on Refugees and Migrants
Veronika Zablotsky |

PART III. FREEDOM AND FUGITIVITY

| 235 | 11 | **Fugitive Relation and Errant Social Reproduction**
A Note
Sarah Haley |

| 249 | 12 | **An Oceanic International in Catastrophic Times**
Sharad Chari |

266	13	**Black Mediterranean Freedom Dreams**
		SA Smythe
294	14	**Dispossession and Its Aftermath**
		The Sites of Black and Indigenous Fugitivity
		Kyle Mays
309	15	**Freedom's Revenge, or Toward Liberation**
		Rinaldo Walcott
323		INTERLUDE
		Codeswitch
		The Transborder Immigrant Tool
		Veronika Zablotsky
325		CONCLUSION
		Sanctuary and the Praxis of Solidarity
		Gaye Theresa Johnson and Leisy J. Abrego
341		Acknowledgments
343		Contributors
353		Index

FOREWORD

Sanctuary Politics and the Role of the University
in the Time of Trumpism

Ananya Roy and Maite Zubiaurre

A few days after he was sworn into office in 2017, President Donald J. Trump issued an executive order titled "Enhancing Public Safety in the Interior of the United States" (January 25, 2017). Targeting "sanctuary jurisdictions," it focused on the "interior enforcement" of immigration laws and claimed that these jurisdictions, by sheltering "removable aliens," had "caused immeasurable harm to the American people." In the United States, the sanctuary designation refers to local governments that limit the cooperation of local law enforcement with federal immigration authorities. Trump's order sought to withhold various kinds of federal funds from such sanctuary jurisdictions. A few days later, another executive order followed, this one blocking travelers from seven Muslim-majority countries from entering the United States, and suspending the resettlement of Syrian refugees.[1] Dubbed the "Muslim ban," it was engineered by Trump strategist and white nationalist Stephen Bannon, who views the West as under assault by "Islamic fascism" (Shane 2017). Framing this "crisis" in terms of a supposed clash of civilizations, Bannon hails the "two historic victories of Christian forces over Muslim attackers" during the Middle Ages and calls for similar "actions" (Shane 2017). This is the significance of the question posed by Bannon to Jeff Sessions, Trump's first attorney general, during the presidential campaign: "Do you believe the elites in this country have the backbone, have the belief in the underlying principles of the Judeo-Christian West, to actually win this war?" (Blumenthal and Rieger 2017).

Trump's executive orders set into motion a series of lawsuits against the federal government by prominent sanctuary cities such as New York City, Chicago, and San Francisco. Pledging defiance, the mayor of Boston declared that as a last resort he would use city hall to shelter undocumented immigrants (Irons and Guerra 2017). Protracted legal battles also unfolded regarding the constitutionality of the Muslim ban. But the juridical limits of sanctuary also became quickly apparent. With varying degrees of "noncooperation" with federal immigration authorities, sanctuary jurisdictions do not prevent the detention and deportation of undocumented immigrants, and as Paik (2017) has shown, in many instances they deny protection to various criminalized categories of migrants. Indeed, in previous work (Roy 2019), we have argued that sanctuary jurisdictions must be understood as a technology of what Walia (2013) has called "border imperialism," specifically a management of interiorized borders through liberal governance, one that entails the consolidation of the police state. While the white nationalism of the Trump regime framed the problem of sanctuary in relation to civilizational conflict, sanctuary is also a problem of liberal democracy. It raises this profound question: *What are the terms of protection through which liberal democracies recognize and include racial others?* In turn, such a question requires that we situate the question and problem of sanctuary in the long arc of what Rodriguez (2021, 1, 3, 6) terms "white reconstruction," in which "white fascist statecraft" is part of a "historically persistent, continuous, and periodically acute logic of reform, rearticulation, adaptation, and revitalization." White nationalism and liberal democracy are entangled rather than opposed. Indeed, hegemonic formations of sanctuary and refuge, those that center the West as the place of hospitality, are exemplars of what Rodriguez (2021, 17) calls "*multiculturalist white supremacy*," "institutional rearticulations of liberal and neoliberal multiculturalism" that consolidate and strengthen "the logics of anti-Blackness and racial-colonial dominance." They evade and obscure the grounds of dispossession that constitute migration regimes.

The problem of sanctuary soon came to haunt our university campuses. At our university, the University of California, Los Angeles, as at many others, students, staff, and faculty, while aware of the tenuous protections afforded by this juridical category, demanded the declaration of sanctuary. But administrators and gatekeepers were quick to reveal the complicities of liberal governance. We, Ananya Roy and Maite Zubiaurre, remember a particularly tense meeting with the leadership of our Academic Senate at which we were reminded that the declaration of the University of California as a sanctuary jurisdiction would jeopardize federal research funding—for example, to the "big science labs." Especially insidious was the argument that sanctuary jurisdiction would threaten, and possibly stall, the crucially important flow of federal funds for students in financial need, such as Pell Grants. Insidious because it was accurate. Accurate because such colonial logics of division—undocumented students versus low-income "eligible" students—animate and reproduce racial capitalism.

The problem of sanctuary is also then the problem of the university as an institution of racial capitalism, raising a question: *Who enjoys sanctuary on stolen land?* Many of our universities are land-grab institutions that have consolidated their financial and territorial power through the state-organized theft of Indigenous land and through ongoing processes of gentrification, policing, and displacement (Baldwin 2021; Lee and Ahtone 2020). Many of our universities are actively involved in practices of border imperialism, producing the algorithms, maps, and databases that facilitate militarized borders as well as detention and deportation. It is thus that Michele Lancione, in exposing the collusion between Frontex, the EU border agency, and the Polytechnic of Turin, where Lancione is professor of economic and political geography, writes of how "the violent and expulsive apparatus of the European Union [seeks] to legitimise itself, to clothe itself with scientific objectivity, to reduce everything to a technical issue that reproduces its evil by turning it into a passing of documents between hands." The Stop LAPD Spying Coalition, an abolitionist organization based in Los Angeles, appropriately terms this "academic complicity" and calls instead for "academic rebellion." The postracial university is especially proficient at legitimizing academic complicity through liberal governance, specifically the politics of recognition, from land acknowledgments to DEI (diversity, equity, inclusion) bureaucracies. Sanctuary, as problem and limit, thus leads us to this fraught question: *How do we dismantle and disrupt the settler logics of possession on which the imperial university is founded?* Through radical love, Lorgia García Peña argues in chapter 5 of this book, noting that "what is needed in the university is not inclusion nor reform but abolition." All through this book, we thus return to the question posed by Sarah Haley in the "Abolition on Stolen Land" convening,[2] a question that Gaye Theresa Johnson and Damon Azali-Rojas take up in chapter 1 of this book as incitement: "How does abolitionist refusal show up in your life?"

This book is our effort to take on the problem of sanctuary while being located within, against, and beyond the university. In the wake of Trump's election, we (Ananya, Veronika, Leisy, Gaye, and Maite), the editors of this book, embarked on a critical, historical, and transnational inquiry of sanctuary through a collective scholarly endeavor, the Mellon Foundation Sawyer Seminar "Sanctuary Spaces: Reworlding Humanism," housed at the UCLA Luskin Institute on Inequality and Democracy.[3] Adapting to the difficult circumstances of the COVID-19 pandemic, and along with graduate student researchers, institute staff, and artists-in-residence, we invented virtual spaces and modes of convening around three themes that are also the scaffolding of this book: "Abolition on Stolen Land," "The End of Humanitarianism," and "Freedom and Fugitivity." Our intent was always to (re)organize knowledge in accompaniment of struggle. Tomlinson and Lipsitz (2013, 9) remind us that accompaniment is "both a commitment and a capacity that can be cultivated." We arrive at the critical inquiry of sanctuary with commitments to accompaniment. We undertake this inquiry with the firm belief that such inquiry can expand the capacity for accompaniment.

In the essay "Research as Accompaniment: Reflections on Objectivity, Ethics, and Emotions," Abrego (2024, 38) writes, "We cannot fully distance ourselves from the structures that produce violence; intellectualizing is not the end goal. Instead, we are deeply committed to people's wellbeing just as much as, and often more than, to the advancement of a field. We are aiming to be in accompaniment." Abrego's scholarship has actively involved serving as a pro bono expert witness in US asylum cases. Accompaniment is evident in the award-winning documentary film *Águilas / Eagles*, co-written, co-directed, and co-produced by Maite Zubiaurre, which, like the broader scope of Zubiaurre's necro-art, militantly refuses the invisibility of migrant death.[4] In the concluding essay of this book, Gaye Theresa Johnson shares how she enacted pedagogical praxis in the context of the Trump regime, teaching students how to accompany social movements and impacted communities, often while they themselves faced and resisted illegalization and endangerment. Veronika Zablotsky co-founded the Abolition Beyond Borders Collective with Vanessa E. Thompson and Daniel Loick to co-organize Germany's first large-scale prison, police, and border abolitionist movement summit "Racial Capitalism, Crisis, Abolition" in June 2023, which emphasized cross-cutting solidarities, internationalist struggle, transformative justice, and movement-based (un-)learning beyond the academy.

In such work, the university as we know it cannot be kept intact. In anticipation of Trump's inauguration and the executive orders that swiftly followed, Ananya Roy, in her role as founding director of the UCLA Luskin

Institute on Inequality and Democracy, organized a national day of collective action titled "Teach. Organize. Resist."[5] Through artistic practice, musical performance, teach-outs, manifestos, assemblies, and more, January 18, 2017, became a day of education about, and protest against, white nationalism in the United States and beyond. Instead of a demand for the juridical protections of sanctuary, such academic rebellion was a prefigurative politics. While aimed at Trump's statecraft, it was, as is this book, one piece of a long and persistent struggle to reorganize knowledge in order to expand the capacity for disruption and accompaniment. The scholars who have come together in this book are on the front lines of such struggle. It is from the impossible space of the university as solidarity that we take up the problem of sanctuary as the ethico-political demand of a world in motion.

Coda

This manuscript is headed to publication amid the genocide of Palestinians in Gaza perpetrated by the Israeli state. More than ever, the Palestine exception—that liberals defend academic freedom and condemn mass killing except in the case of Palestine—is acutely evident in the universities of the West. Palestine is being rendered unutterable through the criminalization of solidarity. Even humanitarian reason, of which we are deeply critical in this book, is suspended in the case of Palestine. At our university, the University of California, Los Angeles, we find ourselves facing colleagues who would like to ban all speech, assembly, protest, and teaching regarding Palestinian liberation, even going so far as to equate those actions with supporting "terror." On both sides of the Atlantic—the territory of this book—colonial amnesia and imperial presentism have come together in the weaponization of antisemitism. From legislatures to boardrooms to classrooms, right-wing and liberal interests are mobilizing this accusation against those who dare historicize and criticize the Israeli nation-state and Zionist ideology. We are inspired by the endurance of Palestinian resistance, by the thousands of people flooding city streets across the world demanding an end to the genocide and occupation, by movements and unions that recognize that what is at stake is the global history of dispossession and displacement and therefore our collective liberation. Refaat Alareer (2014), the Gazan poet, scholar, and teacher, assassinated by Israel on December 7, 2023, had asserted that "Gaza writes back." We hope that this book, first conceptualized amid Trumpian ascendancy and now completed amid the US- and Europe-backed genocide in Gaza, is one such act of writing back.

As we undertake the final copyedits and review of this manuscript, news arrives of Trump's second electoral victory and imminent return to power. Promising mass deportations and the denaturalization of US citizens, a triumphant Trump is set to consolidate the fascist restructuring of US democracy. Our book is a disruption of this arc, insisting on a world that must be made beyond liberalism, beyond humanitarianism, and beyond sanctuary.

NOTES

1. Executive Order 13769 of January 27, 2017: "Protecting the Nation from Foreign Terrorist Entry into the United States," *Federal Register* 82, no. 20 (February 1, 2017). To bypass court orders, it was replaced by Executive Order 13780 of March 6, 2017, which imposed severe travel restrictions on citizens of North Korea, Syria, Iran, Chad, Libya, Yemen, and Venezuela. The latter order was permanently extended by Trump's Presidential Proclamation 9645 but revoked by President Joseph Biden on his first day in office, January 20, 2021.
2. The Abolition on Stolen Land convening is available to view at https://challengeinequality.luskin.ucla.edu/abolition-on-stolen-land-with-ruth-wilson-gilmore.
3. The materials of the Sanctuary Spaces endeavor are available to view at https://challengeinequality.luskin.ucla.edu/sanctuary-spaces.
4. *Águilas / Eagles* is a 2021 documentary film by Kristy Guevara-Flanagan and Maite Zubiaurre.
5. The publication *Teach. Organize. Resist.* can be read at https://escholarship.org/uc/item/8bp6r8qg.

WORKS CITED

Abrego, Leisy J. 2024. "Research as Accompaniment: Reflections on Objectivity, Ethics, and Emotions." In *Out of Place: The Power of Positionality in Socio-Legal Research*, edited by Lynette Chua and Mark Fathi Massoud. Cambridge: Cambridge University Press, 36–56.

Alareer, Refaat. 2014. *Gaza Writes Back: Short Stories from Young Writers in Gaza, Palestine*. Charlottesville, VA: Just World.

Baldwin, Davarian. 2021. *In the Shadow of the Ivory Tower: How Universities Are Plundering Our Cities*. New York: Bold Type.

Blumenthal, Paul, and J. M. Rieger. 2017. "This Stunningly Racist Novel Is How Steve Bannon Explains the World." *Huffington Post*, March 4, 2017. https://www.huffpost.com/entry/steve-bannon-camp-of-the-saints-immigration_n_58b75206e4b0284854b3dc03.

Irons, Meghan, and Cristela Guerra. 2017. "Walsh Rails Against Trump, Calls Immigration Actions 'Direct Attack.'" *Boston Globe*, January 25, 2017. https://www.bostonglobe.com/metro/2017/01/25/walsh-says-boston-will-use-city-hall-itself-last-resort/UtZrLHENkQvEC1fTjgs7bP/story.html.

Lee, Robert, and Tristan Ahtone. 2020. "Land-Grab Universities." *High Country News*, March 30, 2020. https://www.hcn.org/issues/52-4/indigenous-affairs-education-land-grab-universities.

Paik, Naomi A. 2017. "Abolitionist Futures and the US Sanctuary Movement." *Race and Class* 59 (2): 3–25.

Rodriguez, Dylan. 2020. *White Reconstruction: Domestic Warfare and the Logics of Genocide*. New York: Fordham University Press.

Roy, Ananya. 2019. "The City in the Age of Trumpism: From Sanctuary to Abolition." *Environment and Planning D: Society and Space* 37 (5): 761–78.

Shane, Scott. 2017. "Stephen Bannon in 2014: We Are at War with Radical Islam." *New York Times*, February 1, 2017. https://www.nytimes.com/interactive/2017/02/01/us/stephen-bannon-war-with-radical-islam.html.

Tomlinson, Barbara, and George Lipsitz. 2013. "American Studies as Accompaniment." *American Quarterly* 65 (1): 1–30.

Walia, Harsha. 2013. *Undoing Border Imperialism*. Chico, CA: AK.

INTRODUCTION

Beyond Sanctuary

The Humanism
of a World in Motion

Ananya Roy and Veronika Zablotsky

Thinking the West Otherwise

In March 2023, the Promise Institute for Human Rights at the University of California, Los Angeles, hosted an official visit by Soledad García Muñoz, special rapporteur on economic, social, cultural, and environmental rights of the Inter-American Commission on Human Rights. The request for such a visit had come from the Los Angeles Community Action Network (LA CAN), a Black liberation movement organization located in Skid Row, the city's downtown neighborhood where mass homelessness has been concentrated and contained. Noting the "serious homelessness crisis in the western United States," LA CAN's petition argued that "the situation of unhoused people in Los Angeles is a violation of human rights under the Inter-American human rights framework."[1] During the visit, a public hearing was held in Ananya's classroom at UCLA. Unhoused comrades who were part of a class on spatial justice testified through narrative, analysis, and art about the forms of criminalization, illegalization, discrimination, and dehumanization they face in Los Angeles. Unfurled behind the row of presenters was a banner inspired by ACT UP's activism during the AIDS pandemic: "If I die unhoused—forget burial—just drop my body on the steps of L.A. City Hall," which served as a reminder of the social murder underway in US cities, including in those that are known for their liberal governance.

This was not the first time that international rapporteurs had borne witness to the state-led displacement and disappearance of poor and unhoused communities in the United States. A 2018 report by Philip Alston, the UN special rapporteur on extreme poverty and human rights, noted that conditions in LA's unhoused encampments were worse than those in refugee camps and that the local government relied on criminalization "to conceal the underlying poverty problem." Indeed, the language most often used to describe the state of mass homelessness in Los Angeles is "humanitarian crisis" (Levin 2023). In Ananya's class on spatial justice, which brought together university-based scholars with movement intellectuals and unhoused comrades for a yearlong "lab for liberatory projects," such transnational frameworks served as important methodologies for a defamiliarization of the rehearsed repertoires of state violence: evictions, encampment sweeps, sit-lie bans, human caging disguised as care, interminable waiting, permanent displaceability. The participants of this class came to reframe the necropolitical zone of the First World homeless camp in relation to other spaces of death by design, notably border regions of impeded passage and lethal non-assistance such as the US-Mexico border, the external borders of the European Union, and the Mediterranean Sea. Together they read the report by Balakrishnan Rajagopal, UN special rapporteur on the right to adequate housing, on "domicide," "the systematic and deliberate mass destruction of homes during violent conflict" (Rajagopal 2022, 4). Conceptualizing the United States as being in a perpetual state of violent conflict, rooted in settler conquest and legacies of slavery, they reinscribed mass homelessness, and its criminalization, as domicide. Inspired by E. Tendayi Achiume's (2019) powerful call to view unauthorized global migration as a process of decolonization, they came to see the unhoused encampments where our comrades reside and organize as decolonial spaces of forced mobility. Indeed, the connections were everywhere, threaded through the bodies and memories of those gathered in the class. As the class studied the search for missing migrants in the Arizona desert, a space of forced and deadly crossings, one of the class participants, Sandra, broke down in tears and shared the two crossings she had made there as a child. Sandra is a key protagonist in Reclaiming Our Homes, a movement of unhoused mothers to occupy vacant state-owned houses. That deadly desert haunts her, always.

But while the vocabulary of discrimination and the remedy of rights were omnipresent, the class struggled with two questions: To whom were the displaced and unhoused to present a petition of discrimination and a demand for justice? Whom were those cast out into the world to charge with domicide? The class itself was already a refusal of liberal governance and its systems of aid and care. Like the ruse of asylum, such systems perpetuate containment, surveillance, separation, and carceral supervision and never deliver on the promise of domicile, of home. Unhoused encampments, migrant detention centers, and refugee camps are part of the same global geography of displacement and disappearance, managed through the twinned logics of non-assistance and humanitarianism. What, in such a world, is sanctuary? When thinking simultaneously from the streets of Los Angeles, where five unhoused persons die each day, from Sandra's route through the Arizona desert, from the migrant detention center where other unhoused comrades have been held before making their way into the perpetual state of violent conflict that is the United States, it becomes evident that sanctuary is not going to be found in international human rights or in juridical protections. Sanctuary laws in California have repeatedly made peace with the police state and sacrificed to deportation those illegalized migrants deemed less worthy. The insistence that global institutions bear witness, the accounting of death and domicide, the demand for the right to remain and the right to return, and the legal battles against criminalization and discrimination are important, but ultimately they were incommensurable with the intention for the class to be a lab for liberatory projects. Instead, class participants came to see their work as forms of being and knowing that emanate from being cast out in the world. Such too is the collective endeavor that is this book.

Our Mellon Foundation Sawyer Seminar, "Sanctuary Spaces: Reworlding Humanism," and this subsequent book constitute a project that foregrounds the necropolitical spaces and routes of forced mobility in a postcolonial world. Conceptualizing the territories of Europe and the United States as a fractal geography of camps and crossings, we are especially concerned with modes of humanitarianism that govern and manage the suffering and resistance that racial capitalism produces, keeping abjected subjects in a state of permanent displaceability. In such a world, sanctuary is a site of incommensurability. As a technology of liberal democracy, sanctuary is the West's promise to include and protect racial others. This promise, though, lays bare the problem of the racial other in a postcolonial world. Who is the migrant, refugee, asylum seeker, border crosser in relation to the (never) welcoming West? Such relationalities are unrecognizable within humanitarian reason, which can offer only conditional (and often carceral) protection but never liberation. Sanctuary as humanitarian reason is an essential part of "the story of humanism," which inevitably is told as a "European coming-of-age story" (Scott 2000, 197). Sylvia Wynter (2003, 260) reminds us that the imperative here is "securing the well-being of our present ethnoclass (i.e., Western bourgeois) conception of the human, Man, which overrepresents itself as if it were the human itself." Those cast out into the world are incommensurable with Man. It is thus that the problem of sanctuary—its unfulfillable promise—is the problem of the West. It is in the face of such incommensurability that we undertake the seemingly impossible: the collective dreaming of freedom under conditions of fugitivity; the making of abolition as a rehearsal for life (as argued by Ruth Wilson Gilmore in our "Abolition on Stolen Land" convening)[2] on stolen land and in the wake of stolen lives; the assertion of solidarity in the face of incalculable loss of life, displacement, and disappearance. Drawing on intellectual traditions that demand a rethinking not just of humanitarianism but also of humanism itself—the Black radical tradition, Indigenous studies, postcolonial thought, and critical refugee studies—this book is an effort to think (from the West) otherwise, beyond sanctuary. It is therefore also an effort to think the West otherwise.

Genealogies of Sanctuary

This book takes up sanctuary as keyword rather than juridical category. While the imperative for this endeavor emanates from Trump's US presidency and the assault on sanctuary jurisdictions, we do not limit ourselves to an analysis or defense of such policies and legal tussles. Instead, we wish to present the complex genealogies of sanctuary and expand the capacity for liberatory meanings and practices of sanctuary, while simultaneously marking the limits of sanctuary. For the purposes of sanctuary as keyword, we follow Raymond Williams (1983, 24) to understand keywords as "a crucial area of social and cultural discussion, which has been inherited within precise historical and social conditions and which has to be made at once conscious and critical." Here we focus on two genealogies of sanctuary, each of which also takes us to the limits of sanctuary as inclusion and protection. The first is the religious histories and meanings of sanctuary, and the second is the call for sanctuary as cosmopolitanism.

Our intention is not to solidify these genealogies but rather to reworld them through a critical interrogation and reimagination of sanctuary, one that learns from and accompanies migrant movements. We use the term "migrant movements" to indicate the ethico-political demands of a world in motion and to foreground forms of revolt and mobilization by migrants and their demands for justice. Migrant movements are connected to many other struggles against displacement and dispossession. To this end, the chapters are filled with key interlocutors and concepts that might not otherwise feature in a book on sanctuary—Fanon, Wynter, antiblackness, Palestine, abolition, coloniality, death, marronage, freedom, kinship, liberatory love. These serve as "a normative discursive space." We borrow this phrase from Scott's essay "On the Very Idea of a Black Radical Tradition." By "a *normative discursive space*," Scott means "not merely a descriptive but also an *argumentative* space in which what is at stake are *claims* on the moral-political present" (2013, 1). As we consider the conjuncture at hand, we situate our inquiry in two dominant migration regimes, the United States and Europe, where sanctuary has taken on new urgency in recent times. Reinscribing Europe through the modality of the Black Mediterranean, and reinscribing the United States through the modality of stolen land, we consider the moral-political present within the long history of global racial capitalism.

The Sacred

Sanctuary is often understood to be a religious (Christian) practice. Indeed, in present times, one could argue that since there is no codified right to resist colonization and imperialist war-making within secular law, whether in the United States or in Europe, religion has been produced as the only site of legitimate solidarity action with refugees and migrants. US sanctuary movements have often relied on faith-based claims. In Europe, sanctuary congregations "petition" state administrations to uphold or expand their biopolitical mandate of protection. Furthermore, the 2011 Charta of the New Sanctuary Movement in Europe echoes Bartolomé de las Casas's "In Defense of the Indians" when it grounds its politics of welcome and hospitality "in the conviction that God loves the strangers and that in them we encounter God" (Resolution of the Annual Meeting of the German Ecumenical Committee on Church Asylum, October 2010). We pay attention to this genealogy while marking its limits by foregrounding militant Black, Brown, and Indigenous horizons of sanctuary as practical abolition.

Etymologically, the word *sanctuary* denotes a holy place or altar where, in the Christian tradition, fugitives could take shelter from persecution. The Old Testament of the Bible designates "cities of refuge," where those who had unintentionally committed manslaughter could find protection from "blood avengers" (Quant 2015). Amid the legal pluralism of medieval Europe, the practice continued, albeit contested, to offer protection to persons facing prison sentences and debtors. With the consolidation of modern state power, ecclesiastic immunity was disestablished by decree in most European contexts (Tomba 2019). In the Americas, sanctuary traveled as a colonial technology that became imbricated with "genocide and forced removal of Indigenous peoples, the transatlantic slave trade, and other forms of persecution and unfreedom that marginalized groups suffered under European colonialism" (Villarreal 2019, 51). Since the Spanish colonial period, Indigenous people were made "refugees in their own homelands" and forced to congregate in Christian missionary compounds as "spaces for protection" against presumably "external spaces of violence" of which they were constitutive (Villareal 2019, 44, 47). The Indigenous historian Aimee Villareal offers a "counternarrative" of "mobile and intertribal sanctuary place-making in the Americas" that forged "Indigenous and African sanctuaryscapes," beyond the reach of the Christian church, in "regions of rebellion" (Villarreal 2019, 45, 51). The "deep historical memory" of Indigenous resistance to displacement and enclosure inscribes sanctuary as a "form of collective action against injustice" that offers an "alternative vision of solidarity and belonging" (Villarreal 2019, 64).

As a challenge to dominant accounts of sanctuary as a predominantly Christian or European tradition, our anthology is guided by anticolonial genealogies of "practical abolition" and "black fugitive sanctuary" (Haro and Coles 2019, 662) within landscapes of pan-Indigenous resistance to removal, enclosure, and dispossession. We foreground sanctuary as an "ethicopolitical mode of being" and "transformative power" forged through the "disruptive hospitality politics of [Black and Indigenous] fugitives" (Haro and Coles 2019, 656, 666). And we are attentive to the emergence of "new" sanctuary movements on both sides of the Atlantic since the 1980s, often inspired by Central American liberation theology, a syncretic set of doctrines and principles that "weaves together Indigenous Central American and Christian cosmologies" (Mei-Singh 2021, 80).

In the United States, asylum seekers from Guatemala, El Salvador, and Honduras introduced sanctuary to churches, synagogues, and then cities. As Renny Golden and Michael McConnell write in their "people's history" of that moment, Central American refugees arrived as truth-tellers and political agents who "obliterate[d] the imperial vision" of the West (Golden and McConnell 1986, 5, 4). From the perspective of the movement, Golden and McConnell acknowledge the "inherent racism that judges newsworthy any risky act undertaken by whites" but routinely leaves out solidarity action by Black and Brown mutual aid networks and communities, such as a "declaration of sanctuary" issued by Operation PUSH in Chicago (Golden and McConnell 1986, 5).

Across Europe, significant anti-imperialist and feminist mobilizations played a key role in moving congregations to shelter refugees against deportation orders. Memories of antifascist resistance gave moral and political force to the idea of sanctuary, while theological arguments were oftentimes elaborated after the fact.[3] In the United States, sanctuary workers on trial cast their work as civil initiative, "one in which individuals carry out just laws their government is ignoring and misinterpreting" (Coutin 1995, 553). Rather than a philosophy of welcome to suffering strangers, the sanctuary movement of the 1980s was a framework of transnational obligation and responsibility meant to challenge Western imperialism. It is thus that Section 1 of San Francisco's City of Refuge Ordinance, for example, passed in 1989, stated: "The people of the United States owe a particular responsibility to political refugees from El Salvador and Guatemala because of the role that the United States military and other war related aid has played in prolonging the political conflicts in those countries" (Ridgley 2008, 79).

It is important to note the limits of such sanctuary politics and practices. Despite the radical commitments of anti-imperialism, antifascism, and international solidarity that animated the sanctuary movements of the 1980s in Europe and the United States, sanctuary policies have narrowed to what Nicholas De Genova, in an interview for this book (chapter 10), calls the "ruse of asylum." At present, as shown by Paik (2017, 2020), the structural violence of border imperialism is most forcefully challenged by self-organized refugee and migrant justice movements, which have built significant platforms and visibility since the 1990s. For example, as an anticolonial politics that resists the criminalization of people on the move, Black "border feminism" (Barry 2021, 39) denounces all too facile appeals to a shared humanity and insists upon actualizing them in practice. This, as Paik (2017, 16, 18) notes, is sanctuary as a "mode of resistance," one that is necessarily abolitionist in its refusal of the criminalization of migrants and all other people "cast as illegal, terrorist, criminal, expendable," and thus cast out into the world.

The Cosmopolitan

Another vision for sanctuary comes from French philosopher Jacques Derrida. In 1995, the Council of Europe and the European Parliament adopted a charter for "cities of asylum" that had been drafted by the International Parliament of Writers (IPW). Prompted by the fatwa against Salman Rushdie, who was elected the first president of the IPW, and the assassination of writers in Algeria, the charter declared that cities that joined the network would provide "persecuted intellectuals" with asylum, including housing and access to municipal services. It is interesting to note that in the "declaration of independence" that Rushdie drafted in 1994 for the IPW, he presents a vision of a borderless world: "Writers are citizens of many countries.... The art of literature requires, as an essential condition, that the writer be free to move between his many countries as he chooses, needing no passport or visa, making what he will of them and of himself" (Council of Europe 1995). What if we were to replace the word "writer" with "migrant"? Derrida does just that in his 1996 speech to the IPW and in the subsequent essay "On Cosmopolitanism" (2001). Insisting that "*ethics is hospitality,*" he argues that cities must protect the "foreigner in general, the immigrant, the exiled, the deported, the stateless or the displaced person." Drawing on Levinas, Derrida (1999, 45) is in fact challenging the distinction between host and guest, proprietor and visitor, concluding that "hospitality thus precedes property" (see also Dikeç 2002). As Carroll (2006, 822) writes, "What makes hospitality in its most radical, implacable sense, therefore, possible is not possession but a radical dispossession." In advancing a radical ethics of hospitality, Derrida pushes against the limits of Kantian cosmopolitanism. Kant, Derrida (1997, 21) argues, formulates hospitality as "the right to visitation," not "right of residence." Right of residence, for Kant, "must be made the object of a particular treaty between states" and is thus "dependent on state sovereignty." Derrida (1997, 3–4), on the other hand, makes a distinction "between two forms of the metropolis: the City and the State," with the city of refuge or "free city" as one that "transforms and reforms the modalities of membership by which the city belongs to the state." It is "above nation-states," declares Derrida (1997, 9). But it must be asked: Where is the free city, this space of sanctuary? In Derrida's vision of sanctuary, the answer to this question is Europe.

In *Monolingualism of the Other*, Derrida (1998, 15) writes of his sudden loss of French citizenship, repositioning himself, as Baring (2010, 258) notes, from "French Algerian, a European in Algeria ... [to] Franco-Maghrebian, meaning a French citizen who by birth was North African, an Algerian in France." Derrida (1996, 16) eventually regains his French citizenship, writing: "The state, to which I never spoke, had given it back to me." But Algeria remains for Derrida, as Damai (2005, 89) argues, the "other of Europe," and "the other is granted a place only in relation to Europe." Silent on the matter of colonialism, Derrida conceptualizes radical dispossession as a universal condition, one to which he can lay claim when subjected to the loss of citizenship by the French state. His cosmopolitanism is protected from "racial terror," a phrase we borrow from Gilroy (1993, 73) to indicate the structured violence of postcolonial modernity. And his free city can only be in the place that is organized as Europe in the world, as Reason. In a footnote written in 1963, the year after Algerian independence had been won, Derrida makes the argument thus: "A bit like how the anti-colonialist revolution can only liberate itself from a *de facto* Europe or West in the name of transcendental Europe, that is, of Reason, and by letting itself first be won over by its values, its language, its technology, its armaments; an irreducible contamination or incoherence that no cry—I am thinking of Fanon's—could exorcise, no matter how pure and intransigent it is" (quoted in Baugh 2003, 240; see also Baring 2010, 257). In other words, it is only Europe that can grant sanctuary to those constituted as the racial other of Europe. In an essay on "a European public," El-Tayeb (2008, 655) notes how Derrida and Habermas came together in 2003, despite their profound differences, to condemn the Iraq War and present a united call for "new European political responsibilities beyond Eurocentrism." As El-Tayeb notes, they were united by the idea of "Europe having to save the world," which is an idea that relies on what El-Tayeb calls "colonial amnesia."

In ongoing writings on humanitarian reason, Fassin (2005, 376) argues that "the recognition of refugee status by European nations appears as an act of generosity on the part of a national community toward a 'suffering stranger . . . rather than the fulfillment of a political debt toward 'citizens of humanity.'" It creates "the illusion of a global moral community" (Fassin 2013, 37). By constituting sanctuary as a problem, we draw attention to the ways in which humanitarian reason serves to uphold racial-colonial logics of detention, deportation, and even death. What does it mean to plead sanctuary on the basis of (recognized) suffering? Who has the power to grant such recognition? The power of recognition and reconciliation, as Danewid (2017) argues, lies with "white innocence," a term that Wekker (2016) has mobilized to explain Dutch culture and its structured denial of racial-colonial violence. Scrutinizing frameworks of hospitality toward the suffering stranger that stretch from Derrida to Butler and that are premised on dispossession and precariousness as common ground for all, Danewid (2017, 1682) concludes that this is about "saving Europe for itself": "By erasing Europe's colonial past and its neo-colonial present—and with that, the responsibility that Europe bears for the bodies on its shores—the migrant's status as a stranger is secured. This enables the European subject to re-constitute itself as 'ethical' and 'good,' innocent of its imperialist histories and present complicities."

In deliberate contrast, the Black Mediterranean Collective presents migration, specifically the Black Mediterranean, as "a powerful ethical-political demand" (Danewid et al. 2021, 17; see also Hawthorne 2022). In this book, we hold such present histories in clear view while paying attention to the specificities of the conjuncture at hand, including particular formations and deployments of border discourse, policy, and technology. In doing so, we seek to shift the question of sanctuary from the recognition of suffering to fugitivity and mobility in response to this ethico-political demand of a world in motion.

The colonial relationalities of Europe, on which Derrida is silent, remain activated in these present times. In chapter 13 of this book, SA Smythe writes of the election of Giorgia Meloni, leader of the neofascist party Brothers of Italy, as prime minister of Italy. Stoking fears of a "great replacement," Meloni has called "for a naval blockade against migrants" (Horowitz 2022). In a seeming response to the election, Pope Francis warned Italians against "raising walls against our brothers and sisters, which imprison us in solitude" (Roberts 2022). Of course, the walls were raised well before Meloni's ascendance to power. As Charalampos Tsavdaroglou and Maria Kaika argue in chapter 7, the containerization of migrants as bare life makes evident the (neo)colonial apparatus that is the European refugee management and asylum system. But as Smythe reminds us, Meloni's intensification of migrant surveillance and detention goes hand in hand with the expansion of extractive ventures and plans in Africa, dressed up as development. In this vein, the United Kingdom's deportation agreement with Rwanda was called a "Migration and Economic Development Partnership." If Derrida's cosmopolitanism delivers us to the threshold of Europe, then we must be attentive not only to Africa in Europe but also to Europe in Africa.

The Ruse of Sanctuary

Embedded in Western liberal democracies, sanctuary must be understood as a distinctive technology of state power. And it is within, against, and beyond such state power that migrant movements have organized the practical abolition alluded to earlier in this chapter and which we will take up again in the next section through a focus on fugitivities and mobilities. In this section, we ask: what is the nature of the administrative and governmentalizing power that is sanctuary?

In chapter 10, Nicholas De Genova foregrounds "the ruse of asylum," analyzing how the European asylum system is designed to deny rather than grant asylum. De Genova argues that "what on its surface appears to be about a humanitarian commitment on the part of European countries and the larger European Union, a humanitarian commitment to protecting and welcoming and receiving refugees—that asylum regime has as its very predictable and durable material outcome the production of *rejected* asylum seekers." De Genova notes that this "machinery for . . . rejection" engenders a "conversion from the once-hallowed figure of 'the refugee' to the more derisive figure of 'the migrant.'"

There are many aspects to the ruse of sanctuary, including the externalization of borders, which ensures that migrants do not reach European shores or cross the borders of the United States. Indeed, these borders produce death by design. After decades of relative porousness, the present-day US-Mexico border is a massively surveilled and militarized zone of extralegal violence, heightened exploitation, and mass detention of asylum seekers who have no access to legal counsel and are held in privately run and Immigration and Customs Enforcement–administered detention camps across remote areas of the United States. Since 1994, US Customs and Border Protection has officially deployed a border enforcement strategy known as "Prevention Through Deterrence," which pushes border crossers away from urban ports of entry into the Sonoran Desert. As Amy Sara Carroll and Ricardo Dominguez note in chapter 9, this has gone hand in hand with the redirection, by the US Drug Enforcement Administration, of "hemispheric narcotics routes through the Greater Mexican corridor." In this calculated way, the desert is weaponized as a "natural barrier to passage" that masks the "workings of social and political power" (De León 2015, 28)—as exposed by "Hostile Terrain 94,"[4] an exhibition by the Undocumented Migration Project that geolocates the remains of thousands of migrants—represented by over 4,000 handwritten toe tags on a wall map—who died in the Sonoran Desert of Arizona since the mid-1990s.

Maite Zubiaurre, in chapter 6, shares "Mujer Migrante Memorial," an art installation that brings the lives and deaths of migrant women who have died in the Arizona desert since the 1990s to the neighborhoods of Los Angeles. For those who survive the deadly crossing, policies such as the "Migrant Protection Protocols," initiated by the Trump administration and informally known as "Remain in Mexico," deny the right to petition for asylum in the US. Instead, migrants are returned to Mexico and made to endure the long and uncertain wait for an asylum hearing. Carroll and Dominguez show that the border is also virtual, with technology companies such as Palantir and Anduril anchoring a global network of security and surveillance.

The externalization of borders is long at work in Europe as well. Since the 2014 revocation of the Mare Nostrum program of the Italian coast guard, which extended over 150 kilometers into Libyan waters, the European Union's external border police, Frontex, patrols only five kilometers off the Italian coast under joint maritime command with NATO vessels. At the same time, civilian search and rescue missions are being disallowed and criminalized. The disastrous effects of this are compounded by the 2017 Italy-Libya Memorandum of Understanding that outsourced so-called pushback operations—illegal within the EU's own fundamental human rights framework—to the Libyan coast guard, a pseudo-governmental organization that does the EU's border imperialist bidding with boats and surveillance technologies provided by Italy. If not outright left to die at sea, those who are rescued by NGO vessels are frequently denied the right to disembark and arrive on European shores (Tazzioli and De Genova 2020). As documented by the Border Violence Monitoring Network, thousands of migrants are routinely pushed or pulled back into Libyan, Turkish, or international waters, resulting in over 60,620 documented refugee deaths as of June 2024 (UNITED for Intercultural Action n.d.).

During the COVID-19 pandemic, furthermore, public health and hygiene returned as motifs of border enforcement against migrants on both sides of the Atlantic. Ports of arrival in Italy, Malta, and Greece, for example, were declared "unsafe" for asylum seekers and closed in the name of "protection" (Tazzioli and Stierl 2021). With the political decision to establish an EU-wide resettlement scheme in December 2023, efforts to further restrict the arrival of "illegitimate" asylum seekers—those who are deemed "economic migrants" from presumably "safe" countries of origin or those who arrive by way of non-EU countries deemed "safe"—are well underway. Planned changes to the Common European Asylum System (CEAS) will result in the routine detention of asylum seekers—including families with children—in EU-funded camps across and beyond Europe as a "mechanism of partitioning" to funnel "admissible" refugees into "institutionally forced . . . channels of mobility" while "disrupting, decelerating and diverting migrants' autonomous movements" (Tazzioli and Garelli 2018, 4, 2, 3). By normalizing "fast-track" deportations, Europe's "asylum compromise" sanctions illiberal bordering practices that reveal the hypocrisy of any remaining liberal pretense of benevolence and protection by countries such as Germany and France.

The European border regime on the African continent is also responsible for outright massacres such as in June 2022 at the Morocco-Melilla border fence (Bremner 2023) and at other EU-adjacent land borders. In 2021, the Polish-Belarusian border, for example, was infamously turned into an "exclusion zone" in which asylum seekers from Syria, Afghanistan, and elsewhere were left to freeze in subzero conditions and met with military force until a physical border wall was completed in July 2022. In contrast, Ukrainian citizens who fled after the Russian invasion of February 2022 were granted an automatic three-year right of stay in the Schengen Zone, free transportation, and access to employment, schooling, healthcare, and social services. Notably, for the first time after the "long summer of migration" of 2015 (Kasparek and Speer 2015), Europe's self-proclaimed culture of "welcome" was reinstated on the implicit premise of Ukrainian assimilability to whiteness—as a product of selective inclusion rather than a historical given (Godzich 2014)—while Ukrainians of color and racialized international residents fleeing Ukraine were delayed, detained, and pushed back by soldiers and border guards. In response, coalitions of Black and Brown community groups and mutual aid networks in the European interior such as the Tubman Network in Berlin and the Black Is Polish Collective in Warsaw created alternative solidarity infrastructures, coordinated private accommodations for new arrivals, provided legal support, and offered access to basic healthcare. Equal rights for all refugees emerged as a demand of organized noncitizens and international students from Ukraine who rallied behind the hashtag #EducationNotDeportation while facing legal limbo and extreme vulnerability to exploitation.

The ruse of sanctuary also works through the interiorization of borders—for example, in the role of migration regimes as labor regimes and the subordination of labor through the ever-present threat of detention and deportation. De Genova's substantial scholarship on border regimes, including the important essay "Migrant 'Illegality' and Deportability in Everyday Life," shows how the systematic illegalization of migration serves as the linchpin of exploitative labor regimes, especially in the United States (De Genova 2002, 419).

Vanessa E. Thompson, in chapter 4, draws attention to mobilizations in France, such as those by the Gilets Noirs (Black Vests), illegalized and irregularized migrants. Thompson writes: "Inspired by the Gilets Jaunes (Yellow Vests) movement while critiquing their lack of attention to the question of superexploitation and the migration regime, the Black Vests put a focus on the conditions of undocumented racialized workers that occupy the lower strata of the workforce and bear the primary brunt of the expansion of the French carceral anti-state state . . . and its deportation regime." Thompson urges us to take up the question of borders within an analysis of racial capitalist "surplusification."

Indeed, the ruse of sanctuary can be understood as the management of surplus populations. It is against such a ruse that there is, as Thompson highlights, "the multiplicity of strategies of resistance of working-class, working-poor, stateless, and surplus folks." In chapter 12, Sharad Chari focuses on precisely such an archive of struggles, specifically "oceanic archives of struggle," including maritime strikes as collective organizing. Through "human oceanography," Chari connects various "imaginations and instruments of struggle, including the maritime origins of the strike, struggles for the abolition of the transatlantic slave trade . . . Third World lawyering on the determination of the Law of the Sea, and emergent critiques of oceanic ecocide." In inviting us to think about the "oceanic international," Chari reinscribes oceans of deadly crossings as the "planetary 'storm' of multiple struggles," toward the horizon of "planetary sanctuary."

It is to this (im)possibility of crossings that we now turn. We do so with close attention to the many registers of rebellion against surplusification and ecocide, including those that are often illegible in the rosters of racial capitalism. In chapter 1, Johnson and Azali-Rojas remind us of Nick Estes's intervention in the "Abolition on Stolen Land" convening of the Sanctuary Spaces Sawyer Seminar. Estes foregrounds "the deep relationships of land" that "Indigenous caretakers have with the living world" and which "are not counted as productive," the forms of "land defense and water protection [which] are undervalued but necessary for a planet teetering on collapse" (UCLA Luskin Institute on Inequality and Democracy 2020b).

Crossings: Fugitivities and Mobilities

Our book is concerned with a world in motion, one in which fugitivities and mobilities are both structured by, and disrupt, cartographies of global racial capitalism. "The business of a border is, in fact, to be crossed," argues Achille Mbembe (2018), in an essay on the control of movement. Such control, Mbembe notes, is about "the capacity to decide who can move, who can settle, where and under what conditions." In a key essay titled "Migration as Decolonization," E. Tendayi Achiume, professor of law and former UN special rapporteur on contemporary forms of racism, challenges the notions of state sovereignty that underpin today's migration regimes, specifically the exclusion of economic migrants. Achiume (2019, 1509) puts forward "a theory of sovereignty that obligates former colonial powers to open their borders to former colonial subjects" and that views "economic migrants as political agents exercising equality rights when they engage in 'decolonial' migration." This attention to colonial relationalities shifts the question of sanctuary and refuge to that of transnational reparations and what Mbembe (2018) calls "the redistribution of the earth." What lies ahead, Mbembe argues (2019, 16), is "a creeping para-genocide, or imagining together different ways of reorganizing the world and redistributing the planet among all its inhabitants, humans and non-humans."

We are concerned with sanctuary as an ethico-political demand that insists on the redistribution of the planet while also marking the limits of sanctuary as such a demand. For as Moon-Kie Jung and João H. Costa Vargas remind us in chapter 3, there is no means of charging genocide in a world structured through antiblackness. Analyzing *We Charge Genocide: The Crime of Government Against the Negro People*, the 1951 landmark human rights treatise of the Civil Rights Congress, which exposed the many forms of racial terror against Black people in the United States, they take us to the limits of the law and other institutions of national and international justice, notably liberal democracy. Their analysis reminds us that there is incommensurability between "the overwhelming historical and contemporary evidence of democracy's own enabling of Black social and physical death" and the "prodigious confidence in democracy's self-correcting abilities . . . [to] project an improved future." As Jung and Vargas argue, if "Black Human" is "a foundational and perpetual oxymoron" because the "concept of the Human . . . is parasitic on Black lives," then so is the possibility of sanctuary in the "empire-state."

If Mbembe writes of a time of "creeping para-genocide," this book is being completed at a time of genocide in Gaza. South Africa's case to the International Court of Justice charging the state of Israel with genocide makes it clear that such violence is not a singular moment. Its application to the court places "acts of genocide in the broader context of Israel's conduct towards Palestinians during its 75-year-long apartheid, its 56-year-long belligerent occupation of Palestinian territory and its 16-year-long blockade of Gaza" (International Court of Justice 2023). It is instructive to note the rejection of South Africa's case against Israel by European powers that are themselves perpetrators of genocide. As the Namibian government reminded Germany on X: "On Namibian soil, #Germany committed the first genocide of the 20th century in 1904–1908, in which tens of thousands of innocent Namibians died in the most inhumane and brutal conditions. . . . Germany cannot morally express commitment to the United Nations Convention against genocide, including atonement for the genocide in Namibia, whilst supporting the equivalent of a holocaust and genocide in Gaza."[5] In an essay titled "Reparative Futurities," Zoé Samudzi (2020) draws our attention not only to the genocide committed by Germany against the Nama and Ovaherero people in present-day Namibia but also to Germany's role in "the Ottoman genocide against ethnic Armenian, Assyrian, and Greek Orthodox communities." Samudzi notes that while the German parliament has recognized the Armenian genocide, this is consistent with recognition and even reparation being reduced to a "singular harm rather than a commitment to address and repair the structure of colonial violence within which that harm was and is situated." As Samudzi writes, "The imperial time scale renders colonial genocide and violence to a past because we are all now post-colonial." Writing in the time of the Gaza genocide, we set aside the language of humanitarian crisis and the longing for what Jung and Vargas call a "planetary common sense." Indeed, Samudzi (like Jung and Vargas in this book) raises the challenge with the charge of genocide in a postcolonial world: "Inherent to the politics of recognition is some ushering into whiteness: the affirmation of genocide is, crudely, an extension of and assimilation into an always Eurocentric *humanity* through a frame of event uniqueness no matter the identity of the victims." The denial of genocide, then, with its state-orchestrated variants of denialism (Altanian 2024), symbolically repeats and materially continues the genocidal process of erasure from the juridical humanity (Esmeir 2014) that is protected by the UN Convention on the Prevention and Punishment of the Crime of Genocide. We return to this dilemma of recognition in the final section of this chapter, where we wrestle with the concept of humanism and our aspiration of reworlding humanism. Here, we turn to fugitivities and mobilities that disrupt and trouble humanitarian reason and the modalities of recognition and inclusion. We argue that such crossings constitute what Samudzi calls "a grammar of futurity" and take us beyond sanctuary.

Take, for example, the African Mobilities initiative led by South African scholar and architect Mpho Matsipa and its exhibition "This Is Not a Refugee Camp" (Wolff Architects 2021). Seeking to challenge the logics of developmentalism and humanitarianism through which African mobilities are often understood, the exhibition positions itself as a counter-cartography of mobility. Matsipa argues that it is crucial "to destabilize Global North preoccupations with the spectacle of black death as the principal signifier of African mobility as well as the preoccupation with the large numbers of people from Africa, Asia, and Eastern Europe moving to the centers of global capital" (Matsipa and Simone 2020). Counter-cartographies of mobility are also present in the US-Mexico borderlands. An example is the ongoing work of the Electronic Disturbance Theater 2.0 (EDT 2.0), an artivist collective that, in collaboration with the migrant solidarity groups Border Angels and Water Station Inc., developed the mobile app Transborder Immigrant Tool (TBT), which supplies GPS location data and poetry—conceived by the group as a "geo-poetic-system"—to guide border crossers to safety along migrant routes in the Sonoran Desert. In chapter 9, Amy Sara Carroll and Ricardo Dominguez of EDT 2.0 draw on "trans/BORDER/ing," a cross-genre and transmedia play, to suture divided geographies and to destabilize both "aid narratives and regimes of visualization that privilege surveillance and capture."[6] In conversation with the Sanctuary Spaces Sawyer Seminar, EDT 2.0 mobilizes an undocumentary aesthetics to challenge "hierarchies of personhood and movement" and reimagine witnessing after neo/liberal humanitarianisms. In chapter 9, they repurpose "the ubiquitous Mylar blanket of the detention center" as a "poem-quilt" that "maps Gloria Anzaldúa's 'third country,'" thereby separating "syllables, not families." Carroll and Dominguez write: "In the break: my 'Lar,' a Roman spirit of the home, proxies a continental higher law doctrine for the 2020s, undocumenting histories of the vanishing present."

Such counter-cartographies of mobility are part of a broader repertoire of spatial practices that reinscribe sanctuary through alternative relationalities of solidarity. From migrant squats to refugee strikes to cross-border solidarity action networks, they are part of the global history of revolt, engendered by those cast out into the world. As highlighted by Charalampos Tsavdaroglou and Maria Kaika (2020), grassroots migrant housing projects are a vitally important counterpoint to the institutionalized housing within which migrants are contained and managed in Europe. They show how refugees burned down the infamous Moria camp on Lesbos in Greece, thereby defying the "police cordon of isolation," and created makeshift settlements to take care of one another (Tsavdaroglou and Kaika 2022a, 235–36). Other spatial practices have entailed squatting in abandoned buildings in the urban core of cities such as Athens (Tsavdaroglou and Kaika 2022b). In fact, squatting entered the repertoire of migrant justice movements in the 1960s, inspired practices of church asylum in Europe, and continues to provide autonomous solidarity accommodations and community centers for political education and activism, all in stark contrast to the isolation of state-run refugee camps. As Lafazani (2018, 896), a member of the former City Plaza squat in Athens, puts it, these housing commons must be understood "as an occupied place and not a housing institution that belongs to the state or to any nongovernmental organizations." Connecting migrants and locals, these autonomous solidarity projects challenge the "border between host and hosted" (Lafazani 2018, 896). Thus, in their chapter for this book, Tsavdaroglou and Kaika interpret such self-organized housing as a remaking of the urban commons through "infrastructures of decolonial solidarity."

In Germany, the self-organized refugee strike movement organized caravans and occupied public squares to resist and draw attention to the colonial violence of the European asylum system. Over the cold winter months of 2012, an empty former school building in Berlin was transformed into the "Refugee Strike House," an autonomous center for political education and sanctuary place-making. During a solidarity visit, Angela Y. Davis affirmed that "the refugee movement is the movement of the 21st century" (Bergt 2017). In 2022, Davis was invited back by International Women* Space, a feminist antiracist collective which formed at the Refugee Strike House to oppose all forms of sexualized violence. As part of a weeklong festival to commemorate the ten-year anniversary of the occupation, she discussed the refugee resistance movement as a crystallization point of intersecting liberation struggles—from Germany to the United States, Brazil, Palestine, Kurdistan, and Iran—while emphasizing the active leadership and resilience of displaced women of color, including queer and trans women of color, at the forefront of these movements (International Women* Space 2022).

On both sides of the Atlantic, cross-border solidarity action networks such as No Border Assembly and No One Is Illegal broaden the horizon of sanctuary beyond church asylum or liberal logics of hospitality by "challenging the nexus among border regimes, Western imperialism, and neoliberal capitalism" (Maira 2019, 139). As noted by Sunaina Maira, "Abolitionist sanctuary . . . links border violence to carcerality, neoliberal capitalism, white supremacy, settler colonialism, and fascism" (Maira 2019, 140). Through direct action and social media campaigns such as Voices from Moria, #saytheirnames CommemorAction, and Solidarity with Refugees in Libya, autonomous migrant solidarity organizing in postcolonial Europe contests migrants' dehumanization in camps and prisons while aiming to achieve freedom of movement for all as a form of "grassroots democratic web-weaving oriented toward . . . collective well-being" (Haro and Coles 2019, 657).

While autonomous solidarity networks are criminalized for accompanying those who seek to arrive and to remain in a desired destination (Mudu and Chattopadhyay 2017; Dadusc and Mudu 2020; Stierl 2019), defense attorneys and human rights lawyers who assist asylum seekers face "politically motivated legal harassment" (Amnesty International 2019). Some, like Nicole E. Ramos, director of the binational legal advocacy organization Border Rights Project of Al Otro Lado, were placed on no-fly lists by the US Department of Homeland Security for advocating on behalf of asylum seekers in Tijuana.[7] Engaging in solidarity action with refugees and migrants produces corridors of solidarity (Kubaczek and Mokre 2021) that sanctuary activists link to the nineteenth-century Underground Railroad (Golden and McConnell 1986), which facilitated the escape of fugitives from slavery in the United States.

At present, the Indigenous cross-border activism of groups such as Kumeyaay Defense Against the Wall, the O'odham Anti Border Collective, and the Beyond Borders Caucus of the Red Nation, a pan-Indigenous liberation organization, links anticolonial resistance to decolonial visions of migrant justice through grassroots solidarity and immediate aid to border crossers, many of whom are themselves Indigenous persons fleeing political persecution in Central America and elsewhere. In 2018, the Red Nation Beyond Borders Caucus joined an occupation of the Tornillo-Guadalupe Port of Entry, on Rarámuri territory, in opposition to the Trump administration's policy of family separation and the detention of unaccompanied minors. "Settler nations have no right to say who does and doesn't belong," they argued, nor "to detain, deport, and kill people fleeing violence" (Alvarado, Lira-Pérez, and Cruz 2019).

To prevent the partition, militarization, and desecration of their homelands, the Kumeyaay people have blocked access roads and construction equipment for the US border wall. In September 2020, Amber Ortega and Nellie Jo David, two young women of Hia-Ced O'odham and Tohono O'odham descent, were arrested by the US Border Patrol for resisting the destruction of Quitobaquito Springs, a protected site of profound spiritual significance to the O'odham people that had been slated to make way for a ten-meter steel border wall. By putting their bodies on the line—which crossed *them* in the first place—Indigenous communities resist colonial border violence and assert Indigenous sovereignty, which "stands for: caretaking and creating just relations between human and other-than-human worlds on a planet thoroughly devastated by capitalism" (Red Nation 2021, 7–8).

Acquittals in the high-profile cases of Indigenous border resister Amber Ortega and Scott Warren, a No More Deaths volunteer who faced twenty years in prison for providing shelter, food, water, and medical care to two undocumented men (Ingram 2020), rested on the Religious Freedom Restoration Act of 1993. Even if framed in liberal terms, and thus depoliticized as "belief," "practices of sanctuary tending to individual and collective well-being" (Haro and Coles 2019, 658) pose an ethico-political demand that cannot be fully domesticated. Outside of the federal courthouse in Tucson, Ortega affirmed Hia-Ced and Tohono O'odham sovereignty: "This is our land. . . . We, today, again defended our culture, our ways, our songs, our locations, our mountains, our sacred sites. Today was a victory for our people" (Dominguez 2022).

Inspired by Indigenous land and water defense, the focus of migrant justice movements has notably shifted from bids for citizenship rights and inclusion to frameworks of decolonization and anticapitalist critique (Walia 2013; Walia 2021). On unceded Wet'suwet'en territory just north of the present-day US-Canada border, for example, refugee activists have participated in "several delegations to Indigenous blockades, while Indigenous communities have offered protection and refuge for migrants facing deportation" (Walia 2012). Such experiments in decolonial solidarity displace the liberal binary of church and state by rejecting both terms as colonial technologies of control and dispossession that are incommensurate with Indigenous modes of governance and "relational futures" (Yazzie 2018).

On the other side of the Atlantic, solidarity action transforms the Black Mediterranean into a "sea of struggle" (Stierl 2016) to intervene in the necropolitics that is Europe. To force states to account for the practices and policies that lead to migrants' deaths, projects such as Forensic Oceanography, a research-based collaboration between Lorenzo Pezzani and Charles Heller, scrupulously reconstruct and collect evidence to build legal cases against responsible parties that fail to render assistance despite distress calls by migrant boats at sea (Lynes, Morgenstern, and Paul 2020). Following Sharpe (2016, 59), we interpret counter-cartographic endeavors such as those of Forensic Architecture, a research agency directed by Eyal Weizman, as "wake work . . . that might counter forgetting, erasure, the monumental, and that ditto ditto in the archives." In doing so, we are especially attentive to Black fugitivity (Sojoyner 2017) and marronage as "creative and emergent methods of life-building . . . the valuation of Black life amidst a world that saw Afro-descendant populations as completely devoid of humanity" (Bledsoe 2017, 30, 32).

Reworlding Humanism

When we wrote the first draft of this introduction, the world was riveted by the search effort for missing billionaire tourists on the *Titanic*-bound submersible that ultimately imploded in the deep Atlantic. For a brief moment, the contrast between this rescue and the abandonment of migrants crossing the Mediterranean became starkly visible, especially as hundreds—from Pakistan, Egypt, and Jordan—died with the sinking of a fishing trawler off the coast of Greece. For a brief moment, the global media deemed these migrant deaths to be "preventable," noting that the gatekeepers of Europe watched the distress but did not assist (Stevis-Gridneff and Shoumali 2023).[8] Not only are such drownings commonplace, with De Genova (2018) stating that the Mediterranean has become a mass grave, but also those providing nongovernmental assistance are subject to criminalization and punishment. This lethal non-assistance, which governs the Black Mediterranean and other zones of deadly crossings, includes the invisibilization of death, rendering lost lives into those that cannot be remembered and mourned. Indeed, following the argument presented by Jung and Vargas in chapter 3, we can think of this as "genocide beyond genocide." They write: "If genocide is the murder of a people, it is, for Black people, the murder of an already murdered 'people'—or, more precisely, the murder of a *nonpeople of nonpersons*."

In the essay "On Difference Without Separability," Denise Ferreira da Silva explains how Europe's "refugee crisis" is structured through a "racial grammar" disguised as "cultural difference": "For in the tale of the dangerous and undeserving 'Other'—the 'Muslim Terrorist' disguised as (Syrian) refugee and the 'starving African' disguised as asylum seeker—cultural difference sustains statements of uncertainty that effectively undermine claims for protection under the human rights framework, thereby supporting the deployment of the EU security apparatus" (Ferreira da Silva 2016, 57). Indeed, as De Genova (2016, 76, 82) argues, Europe's "migration question" is now refracted through the "Muslim question," positioning migrants as potential terrorists and threats to national security and thus beyond recognition. Genocide beyond genocide is on our minds as we write the final version of this introduction amid the unfolding genocide in Gaza, which is carried out as openly as it is being denied. Indeed, critical scholars of genocide are now grappling with the "futility of genocide studies after Gaza" (El-Affendi 2024) due to seemingly discarded normative commitments to prevention.

The expensive and elaborate search for the *Titan* submersible generated a fleeting moment of global shame for the sanctioned sinking of migrant ships, and in some media platforms of the West, the lives lost in these forced crossings were humanized. A black-and-white photograph of Thaer Khalid al-Rahal circulated widely. In it, al-Rahal tightly hugs his four-year-old son, Khalid, who is suffering from leukemia. Fleeing the war in Syria, the family lived in a Jordanian refugee camp for a decade, where the Office of the United Nations High Commissioner for Refugees (UNHCR), the UN refugee agency, would not fund an urgently needed bone marrow transplant for Khalid. Risking near-certain death, al-Rahal boarded the fated fishing trawler with the intent of making it to the shores of Europe, where he hoped to earn money for his son's treatment (Loveluck et al. 2023).

We could fill this book with such humanizations, telling the stories of countless al-Rahals. Theirs is the ethico-political demand of a world in motion. But we are acutely aware of the limits of this "planetary moral commonsense." Whom are we to charge with genocide for the hundreds of lives lost in this latest crossing? Humanitarian reason governs abjection but does not intervene in the structured and sanctioned violence that casts abjected subjects out in the world—what we call domicide. Humanitarian reason reproduces racial-capitalist surplusification, proliferating a global geography of containment and containerization. Saree Makdisi, in chapter 8, appropriately coins the term "humanitarian racism," exposing the hypocrisies of celebrity humanitarian interventions. In such governance, humanitarian reason sorts valued and devalued lives, deserving and undeserving refugees, good and criminal migrants. But, as Makdisi shows, there is more. As in the case of Palestine, humanitarian racism whitewashes present forms of settler colonialism and ethnic cleansing through the metonymical identification of the Zionist project with global values of democracy, tolerance, and human dignity. Such transactions, cast in the discourse of human rights, uphold the moral standing of the West, especially the United States, as the keeper of humanitarian reason. To disrupt such metonymies, it is necessary, as Melanie Yazzie (2015, 1007) reminds us, to build solidarity across "interlocking, transnational, and hypermilitarized forms of settler colonialism." Of the Diné Bikéyah campaign for solidarity with Palestine, Yazzie (2015, 1007) notes: "The campaign understands that Palestinian liberation requires the liberation of Indigenous and other oppressed peoples from occupation by Israel's collaborator and guarantor, the United States."

Our conceptualization of sanctuary spaces takes seriously such practices of solidarity and liberation in a world of social death, or what Smythe (2018) terms the "wet cemetery." We grapple with Gilroy's (2021, 122) provocation that "a new and urgent articulation of . . . planetary humanism" can emerge from the "humanizing gestures" of "human salvage, naming, and burial" that in turn emerge "from the deadly waters of the Mediterranean." But also at stake is how we understand such death. To this end, we grapple with Saucier and Woods's (2014, 62) understanding of the Black Mediterranean as "an old and repressed issue that haunts and composes the European project and modernity itself." In their critique of migration and border studies, they situate the deadly crossings of the Mediterranean within the "accumulated violence against black people globally" (Saucier and Woods 2014, 55). In doing so, they challenge "Western humanism's conception of violence as contingent," noting that it is a mistake to interpret border violence as "a punishment for a transgressive act" (Saucier and Woods 2014, 60). Instead, such violence is precisely what Sharpe (2016, 13) calls "living in/the wake of slavery." As the Black Mediterranean Collective argues, the crisis of the Mediterranean "is not the state of exception . . . but a state of repetition of the subjection of Black life through the same old means: borderless apparatus of surveillance, containment, captivity, forced displacement, forced labor, the slave markets, and dehumanization" (Lombardi-Diop 2021, 4). In this book, we take up the Black Mediterranean as a conceptual framework that makes possible an understanding of such subjection and repetition while also being attentive to the reemergent geopolitics of exclusion and expulsion that bring a diversity of migrant lives into deadly crossings from old and new war zones. Whether or not such diverse migrant lives should be understood as Black life is a matter of debate and leads us to the consideration of antiblackness. Here it is worth keeping in mind Stuart Hall's (2005, 442) reminder of how, why, and when the term *Black* comes to reference "the common experience of racism and marginalization," of when it even becomes "the organizing category of a new politics of resistance, among groups and communities with, in fact, very different histories, traditions and ethnic identities." Writing to mark "the end of the innocent notion of the essential black subject," Hall (2005, 444) emphasizes "that 'black' is essentially a political and culturally *constructed* category, which cannot be grounded in a set of cultural or transcendental racial categories and which therefore has no guarantee in nature."

As we discussed in the section "Genealogies of Sanctuary," we are acutely aware that dominant conceptions of sanctuary as asylum and protection rest on the tenets of Western humanism. But such humanism is constituted, as Jung and Vargas remind us in chapter 3, through antiblackness. Antiblackness, Jung and Vargas (2021, 3) note, "is a profoundly 'antisocial' condition," one that consigns the racial other to what Patterson (1982) has famously called "social death" and thereby negates the social as "common ground for all." What is sanctuary for those subjected to social death? What human rights can be ascribed to those marked as (Black) nonbeing? Our work in this book entails the reworlding of sanctuary through what Kelley (1999, 1048) has called "black revolt." Smythe (2018), inspired by Kelley, reinterprets the Black Mediterranean as "a variegated site of Black knowledge production, Black resistance and possibilities of new consciousness." Such is a "mobile commons" (Papadopoulos and Tsianos 2012), elaborated by "fugitive planning" (Harney and Moten 2013).

The concept of reworlding takes us to postcolonial critique. The problem of sanctuary is also a problem of Western thought. As Ananya Roy has argued in previous work (Roy and Ong 2011; Roy et al. 2020), the reworlding of disciplines is a refusal of Eurocentrism as well as a rehistoricization and reconceptualization of the histories and futures that are narrated and consolidated under the sign of the West. It is a counter to what Spivak (1985, 247) pinpoints as the "worlding of what is today called the Third World." Such worlding is pithily captured by Spivak (1985, 247) in the opening lines of her iconic essay on archival inheritances: "Two years ago, when a conference with the title 'Europe and Its Others' was proposed by the Sociology of Literature Group at Essex, I made some pious remarks about an alternative title, namely, 'Europe as an Other.'" What is sanctuary if we understand Europe as an other rather than as a place of asylum for Europe's racial others? Spivak continues by noting that the proposed revision implied that "a critique of imperialism would restore a sovereignty for the lost self of the colonies so that Europe could, once and for all, be put in the place of the Other that it always was." Rejecting this reversal, Spivak argues that "if instead we concentrated on documenting and theorizing the itinerary of the consolidation of Europe as sovereign subject, indeed sovereign and subject, then we would produce an alternative historical narrative of the 'worlding' of what is today called 'the Third World.'" Our critical interrogation of sanctuary, and thereby of Western humanism, is precisely such an analysis. As Mignolo (2015, 108) writes, "the problem of the Human is . . . in the *enunciations* of what it means to be Human." In the universal grammars of Western humanism, in enunciations such as humanitarianism and cosmopolitanism, who is recognizable as human? In other words, the problem of sanctuary is the problem that is the West.

Here we return to Gilroy and what, following Wynter, Gilroy (2018, 19) terms the "creative re-enchantment of the human." In a rather surprising move, Gilroy (2018, 19) draws inspiration from Europe's sanctuary cities where "solidarity activities" both "pressurize" and "bypass government power." Our book is filled with such examples, from migrant squats to migrant revolts. These are for Gilroy (2018, 14, 16) "a vernacular energy" that has the potential for a "reparative humanism," a "planetary humanism." The question at hand, Gilroy (2018, 19) argues, is "whether we perceive the vital, vulnerable cargo of this and other wrecked boats as human rather than as infrahuman," reduced to "objects among other objects." The equally difficult question at hand is whether this is a form of postcolonial restitution: "More is indeed being recovered from the waves than wreckage and corpses. Europe's relationship with its own shrinking civilization is at stake in the decision to intervene as well as in the later lives of the survivors" (Gilroy 2019, 19). Is the creative re-enchantment of the human possible without the creative re-enchantment of Europe? Here it is worth considering what Gilroy writes prior to the previous passage: "a wider struggle to re-enchant humanism by endowing a stronger sense of *reciprocal* humanity in Europe's proliferating encounters with vulnerable otherness." What is sanctuary when we refuse benevolent gestures of protection and insist upon reciprocity? But what then are the limits of reciprocity in a world of genocide beyond genocide? Here we return to Spivak's argument about the limits of reworlding Europe. In an interview with Wynter about "the re-enchantment of humanism," Scott (2000, 153) puts forward the notion of "embattled humanism." Wynter expresses enthusiasm for the term: "You know that you cannot turn your back on that which the West has brought in since the fifteenth century. It's transformed the world, and central to that has been humanism. But it's also the humanism against which Fanon writes [in *The Wretched of the Earth*] when he says, they talk about man and yet murder him everywhere on the street corners. Okay. So it is that embattled [humanism], one which challenges itself at the same time that you're using it to think with." This is the reworlding of humanism at work in this book.

The reworlding of humanism requires, as Rinaldo Walcott elaborates in chapter 15, "a different order of knowledge." As Mbembe (2018) argues, "The western archive does not help us to develop an idea of borderlessness. The western archive is premised on the crystallisation of the idea of a border." In this book, we do not seek a resolution of humanity/humanism but rather take it up as a question. For after all, as Hartman (1997, 5) reminds us in the landmark book *Scenes of Subjection*, the discourse of humanism is "double edged"; for those relegated to social death, it means seizing upon "that which had been used against them and denied them." Our intent is not the recovery of humanism but rather the reinscription of the Western archive through fugitivities and mobilities, revolt and freedom. We focus on a world in motion that must be understood as "living in/the wake of slavery" (Sharpe 2016, 15). To this end, Walcott claims the idea of freedom, or "freedom's revenge," as a way of undoing "Euro-American white supremacist logics of what it means to be human, to be a life-form, to be speciated." Refusing the ruse of liberal democracy, Walcott reminds us that "those institutions marked as democratic manage unfreedom." As we have already argued earlier in this introduction, this is the ruse of asylum, the ruse that is sanctuary, and the ruse that is the West. Instead, Walcott imagines an "untethering" for which the "only name . . . is decolonization," or "freedom beyond humanism."

We follow Walcott in refusing the renovation of Western humanism and its institutional scaffolding of liberal democracy and humanitarian reason. Instantiations of freedom beyond humanism are evident in the fugitivities and mobilities, the Black revolt, the oceanic strikes and struggles, the migrant squats, and the cross-border solidarity initiatives that we study and accompany in this book. If the prominent philosophers of Western humanism have felt at home in the world, dwelling securely in realms of freedom, then we are concerned with forms of being and knowing that emanate from being cast out in the world. When unhoused comrades in Los Angeles living in street encampments assert the right to remain and demand the right to home, when anticolonial migrant justice movements such as No One Is Illegal assert the right of stay, the freedom to move, and the right to return, they unsettle the "bare humanity" of human rights as critiqued by Hannah Arendt. Once a stateless person is "forced outside the pale of the law" (Arendt 1962, 286), they are turned into an "outlaw by definition" (283) and "set outside human jurisdiction" (Agamben 1998, 82)—a condition that Agamben theorizes as the "sovereign exception" (82). By taking "exception from the exception" (Bargu 2017, 5), migrant movements unsettle the grounds of dispossession and disrupt (neo)colonial border regimes. The humanity invoked by such rights discourses is not that of universal Man but rather of those rendered illegal and beyond recognition.

Walcott reminds us that freedom beyond humanism is not a singular endeavor but rather one of "multiple theoretical routes." Walcott writes: "The critique provided of Euro-American humanism is not one in search of a space, a gap, or a position to enter it, but rather one that demolishes its edifice. What these thinkers have in common is not a theoretical unity but a political project that writes us toward freedom beyond Euro-American humanism." In this book, we take up the reworlding of humanism through such multiplicity and what might in fact be incommensurability. Take, for example, the closing event of the Sanctuary Spaces Sawyer Seminar. Titled "Freedom and Fugitivity," this online convening featured Saidiya Hartman along with Aisha Finch, Tiffany Lethabo King, Kyle Mays, and Sarah Haley.[9] A key line of conversation and debate was Hartman's (1997, 5) argument that "the recognition of humanity and individuality [can act] to tether, bind, and oppress" and that this can take place "through notions of reform, consent, and protection," as was the case with "benevolent correctives and declarations of slave humanity." Indeed, in our Sanctuary Short ~~Enclosure~~: *Geographies of Refusal*, Tina Campt refuses the imperative of humanism, reworlded or otherwise, and foregrounds refusal as a key modality of Black feminist thought and practice (UCLA Luskin Institute on Inequality and Democracy 2021d).[10] "Refusal," Audra Simpson (2017, 19) argues, "is an option for producing and maintaining alternative structures of thought, politics and traditions away from and in critical relationship to states." Simpson, also featured in this Sanctuary Short, exposes the "ruse of consent" that underpins the politics of recognition and reconciliation, or what Gooder and Jacobs have dubbed the "postcolonial apology." As Gooder and Jacobs (2000, 229) point out, "The apology becomes a lifeline [for settler subjects] through which a legitimate belonging in the nation may be restituted." Sanctuary, asylum, and refuge, as enacted by the West, must be understood as different forms of the postcolonial apology. The ruse of sanctuary is the ruse of consent. Simpson (2017, 19) argues that the "ruse of consent" must be understood as "a technique of recognition and simultaneous dispossession ... for Native people, this ruse of consent marks the inherent impossibility of that freedom after dispossession, a freedom [that] is actually theft."

Our book and the related Sanctuary Spaces Sawyer Seminar foreground ways of knowing and being that transform colonial relationalities into radical relationalities of kinship. We do so, as Sarah Haley argues in chapter 11, by paying attention to how such histories and relationalities "operate, of course, *without sanctuary*." And in this way, they defy "the violence of normative humanism produced by the historical archive through a practice of creative social reproduction that entails inhabitation, confrontation, elusion, and intuition." Haley emphasizes, "Although there is no sanctuary on the page, Black creative life undermines the terror of Western humanism and charts possibility in its beyond." As Tiffany Lethabo King (2019, 12) argues, "Specific forms of Black abolition and Native decolonization interrupt ... liberal (and other) modes of humanism ... [and] offer new forms of sociality and futurity."

One example is "No Ban on Stolen Land," a powerful Indigenous-led rallying cry of the migrant justice movement (Monkman 2017). When the Trump administration passed its infamous Executive Order 13769 in 2017, also known as the "Muslim ban," Melanie Yazzie, one of the founders of the Red Nation, joined a spontaneous protest led by Indigenous organizers and communities at the Los Angeles airport. In an interview we conducted with her in 2021 for the Sanctuary Short ~~Asylum~~: *At the Borders of Humanitarianism*, Yazzie described the intervention as one that asserts "legal and political orders of belonging... that predate the United States" and that provide "an imaginary of... how we might... be able to relate to the rest of the world differently than the United States does."[11] Yazzie noted the protest was an "Indigenous hospitality and an Indigenous welcoming" that disrupts US empire, including the settler-colonial narrative of the United States as a "nation of immigrants" (UCLA Luskin Institute on Inequality and Democracy 2021c).

In chapter 2 of this book, Tongva and Acjachemen scholar Charles Sepulveda presents kuuyam as a decolonial possibility of hospitality on Indigenous terms and land: "Kuuyam is an Indigenous theorization that disrupts the dialectic between Native and settler through a Tongva understanding of non-natives as potential guests of the tribal people, and more importantly—of the land itself" (Sepulveda 2018, 41). Kuuyam, the Tongva word for "guests," is a framework that "disrupts the view of land and people as domesticable and instead understands place to be sacred and as having life beyond human interests" so that "settler colonialism can eventually be abolished" (Sepulveda 2018, 40). Expanding on his crucial intervention at the opening event of the Sanctuary Spaces Sawyer Seminar, titled "Abolition on Stolen Land" and featuring Ruth Wilson Gilmore, Charles Sepulveda lays out the imaginative intersection of abolition and decolonization: "Both decolonization and abolition are not simply seeking an end result. Instead, they are continuous creative processes: an imagining of life beyond prisons and the theft of land" (UCLA Luskin Institute on Inequality and Democracy 2020b). We thus follow Sepulveda to propose a radical retheorization of sanctuary as kuuyam, an insistence on the rematriation of land and an invitation to form strange kinship(s) against "the social death of conquest."

In their concluding chapter for this book, Gaye Theresa Johnson and Leisy J. Abrego reimagine sanctuary "in the inspired intersections of migrant imaginaries, prison abolition, and Land Back." Building on visions and practices of fugitivity and marronage, they are concerned with a "praxis of solidarity" that refuses both the criminalization of sanctuary by white nationalism and the depoliticization of it by liberal recognition. Kyle Mays, in chapter 14, situates solidarity in "sites of Black and Native fugitivity." In a seminal essay that has deeply influenced this book, "Abolitionist Futures and the US Sanctuary Movement," A. Naomi Paik (2017) shows how organizers have been building this praxis of solidarity. In subsequent work, Paik (2020, 5) argues that the convergence of these various struggles is forging "an abolitionist approach to sanctuary."

We want to be clear that the question of sanctuary in the US empire-state and in Europe is a fraught one. This book is not a blueprint for radical sanctuary but rather is an accompaniment of global revolt toward liberated life-ways (Gilmore 2022; Abrego 2024). As we have argued all through this introduction, how we think about a world in motion, whether as Chari's "oceanic international" or Mays's "sites of Black and Native fugitivity" or Smythe's *poēsis* of the Black Mediterranean or Walcott's (2021, 65) conceptualization of the "black aquatic" as a "hauntology of contemporary claims of black subjectivity." But the difficulty—indeed, incommensurability—of sanctuary in the empire-state leads us also to the question of land, or rather to land as relationality. What is sanctuary on stolen land? What is an abolitionist approach to sanctuary on stolen land? Accompaniment, as a methodology for abolitionist research partnerships (Mei-Singh 2021, 79), entails a "position of co-resistance based on a commitment to decolonial Indigenous futurity." As Johnson and Azali-Rojas argue in chapter 1, to imagine and enact abolition in the empire-state of the United States requires acknowledgment and repair of community and land relationships upon which the carceral system is imposed. Mays explicitly addresses this question of land, writing: "The paradox I want to explore entails calls for reparations and decolonization, specifically the question of land. As we move toward the aftermath of settler colonialism and white supremacy, we might critically interrogate the meaning of justice, freedom, and reparatory justice. We must think as creatively and judiciously as possible regarding Black freedom and its relationship to Indigenous sovereignty." For Mays, kinship is a speculative tool for visualizing a future in the aftermath of settler colonialism and white supremacy. Mays reminds us that "centering land is also about kinship—and it is through kinship that we might find solidarity."

And so the question of sanctuary has brought us to kinship. Inspired by Smythe's Black register of *poēsis*, we understand kinship as "a metaphysical paradox in which black life is possible," "an otherwise orientation that does not look to any state for recognition but considers coalitional practices . . . via the Mediterranean's seascape, peripheries, and stories/storytellers on the move rather than national European borders and the economics-driven valuation of human life." We can understand this to be a queering of kinship, one that insists upon relationality beyond and against heteropatriarchal and colonial-racial social structures. Smythe asks us to dwell on this question: "Who, that is to say, is 'we' at all?" Our book takes up this question as "a love letter to freedom," which is Lorgia García Peña's lyrical analysis in chapter 5 of the twinned endeavors of abolition and sanctuary. Thinking with bell hooks and insisting upon abolition as love, García Peña challenges us to do more/other than "write about death, dispossession, violence, oppression, domination, patriarchy, capitalism." "The unloving world in which we racialized, colonized, otherized peoples have come to exist is the norm," García Peña reminds us. How do we write/dream/make otherwise? In the essay "On Plantations, Prisons, and a Black Sense of Place," Katherine McKittrick (2011, 953–54) gives us "a cautionary tale," writing that the "intellectual work of honoring complex racial narratives that name struggles against death and a black sense of place can be, paradoxically, undermined by the analytical framing of racial violence." McKittrick calls for "plantation futures—the insistence that spaces of encounter, rather than transparent and completed spaces of racism and racist violence, hold in them useful anti-colonial practices and narratives." The condition of "un-breathing" that Vanessa Thompson foregrounds in chapter 4 is precisely such a practice, "a political device for struggle . . . [with] a long history in anti-colonial critique." This is, as Thompson notes, following Fanon, "combat breathing" in a world in which "the impossibility of breath . . . is an effect of colonial state violence, dispossession, and expropriation." This is, in Thompson's words, "a breathing that is characterized by living under the conditions of occupation and war."

In reimagining sanctuary as the ethico-political demand of a world in motion, as strange relationalities of kinship created through fugitivities and mobilities, our book strives to be more than the condemnation of an unloving world. Sepulveda argues that "the logic of conquest deployed throughout the Americas can be reduced to a single word: *possession*." García Peña draws our attention to a very different kind of possession, that of *montarse*, which in Afro-Caribbean religions "refers to the act of the dead taking possession of a living person's body to share truth." In this book, we write from and about the necropolitical zones of the empire-state—the unhoused encampment, the container camp, the deadly oceans, the racially segregated *banlieue*, the desert that does not give bodies back—but we do so through *montarse*, to insist upon freedom beyond sanctuary.

NOTES

1 The petition was disseminated by the UCLA Promise Institute for Human Rights.
2 The convening "Abolition on Stolen Land" can be viewed at https://challengeinequality.luskin.ucla.edu/abolition-on-stolen-land-with-ruth-wilson-gilmore.

3 This is evident from interviews with sanctuary activists in Berlin, collected in the oral history archive "40 Years of Church Asylum" available at https://portal.oral-history.digital/en/catalog/collections/21894753. See also Mitchell and MacFarlane 2022.

4 The participatory art project "Hostile Terrain 94" is documented at https://www.undocumentedmigrationproject.org/hostileterrain94.

5 The tweet is available at https://twitter.com/NamPresidency/status/1746259880871149956.

6 The convening "trans/BORDER/ing" can be viewed at https://challengeinequality.luskin.ucla.edu/trans-border-ing-the-aesthetics-of-disturbance-and-undocumentary-flight.

7 As part of the online conversation "Sanctuary & Solidarity: Resisting the U.S. War on Refugees and Migrants," Nicole E. Ramos speaks about her advocacy work with Al Otro Lado, available at https://challengeinequality.luskin.ucla.edu/sanctuary-solidarity-resisting-the-us-war-on-refugees-and-migrants/.

8 The online mapping platform "Watch the Mediterranean Sea" monitors deaths and migrants' rights violations at the maritime borders of the EU, https://watchthemed.net. Its volunteer-run Alarm Phone project fields and redirects migrants' distress calls to coast guards, documenting cases of non-assistance and alerting civilian search and rescue in the entire Mediterranean and the Aegean Sea. More information is available at https://alarmphone.org/en/.

9 The convening "Freedom and Fugitivity" can be viewed at https://challengeinequality.luskin.ucla.edu/freedom-and-fugitivity-event.

10 The film Enclosure: Geographies of Refusal can be viewed at https://challengeinequality.luskin.ucla.edu/freedom-and-fugitivity.

11 The film Asylum: At the Borders of Humanitarianism can be viewed at https://challengeinequality.luskin.ucla.edu/the-end-of-humanitarianism.

WORKS CITED

Abrego, Leisy J. 2024. "Research as Accompaniment: Reflections on Objectivity, Ethics, and Emotions." In *Out of Place: The Power of Positionality in Socio-Legal Research*, edited by L. Chua et al., 36–56. Cambridge: Cambridge University Press.

Achiume, Tendayi E. 2019. "Migration as Decolonization." *Stanford Law Review* 71 (6): 1509–74.

Agamben, Giorgio. 1998. *Homo Sacer: Sovereign Power and Bare Life*. Stanford, CA: Stanford University Press.

Alston, Philip. 2018. *Report of the Special Rapporteur on Extreme Poverty and Human Rights on His Mission to the United States of America*. New York: United Nations.

Altanian, Melanie. 2024. *The Epistemic Injustice of Genocide Denialism*. London: Routledge.

Alvarado, Hope, N. Lira-Pérez, and Nicolás Cruz. 2019. "No Están Solos! You Are Not Alone! A Report on the Child Detention Facility in Tornillo, Texas." *Red Nation*, January 2022. http://therednation.org/no-estan-solos-you-are-not-alone-a-report-on-the-child-detention-facility-in-tornillo-texas-2.

Amnesty International. 2019. "'Saving Lives Is Not a Crime': Politically Motivated Legal Harassment Against Migrant Human Rights Defenders by the USA." AMR 51/0583/2019. https://www.amnesty.org/en/documents/amr51/0583/2019/en.

Arendt, Hannah. 1962. *The Origins of Totalitarianism*. Cleveland and New York: Harcourt, Brace and Company.

Bargu, Banu. 2017. "The Silent Exception: Hunger Striking and Lip-Sewing." *Law, Culture and the Humanities* 18 (2): 1–28.

Baring, Edward. 2010. "Liberalism and the Algerian War: The Case of Jacques Derrida." *Critical Inquiry* 36 (2): 239–61.

Barry, Céline. 2021. "Schwarzer Feminismus der Grenze: Die Refugee-Frauenbewegung und das Schwarze Mittelmeer." *Femina Politica*, 2:36–48.

Baugh, Bruce. 2003. "Sartre, Derrida and Commitment: The Case of Algeria." *Sartre Studies International* 2:40–54.

Bergt, Denise Garcia. 2017. "Angela Davis: The Refugee Movement Is the Movement of the 21st Century." Vimeo. https://vimeo.com/229530582.

Bledsoe, Adam. 2017. "Marronage as a Past and Present Geography in the Americas." *Southeastern Geographer* 57 (1): 30–50.

Bremner, Matthew. 2023. "The Melilla Massacre: How a Spanish Enclave in Africa Became a Deadly Flashpoint." *Guardian*, August 23, 2023. https://www.theguardian.com/world/2023/aug/29/the-melilla-massacre-spanish-enclave-africa-became-deadly-flashpoint-morocco.

Carroll, David. 2006. "Remains of Algeria: Justice, Hospitality, Politics." MLN 121 (4): 808–27.

Council of Europe. 1995. "Report on the Charter of Cities of Asylum." https://rm.coe.int/report-on-the-charter-of-cities-of-asylum-2nd-session-strasbourg-30-ma/16808becac.

Coutin, Susan. 1995. "Smugglers or Samaritans in Tucson: Producing and Contesting Legal Truth." *American Ethnologist* 22 (3): 549–71.

Dadusc, Deanna, and Pierpaolo Mudu. 2020. "Care Without Control: The Humanitarian Industrial Complex and the Criminalisation of Solidarity." *Geopolitics* 27 (4): 1–21.

Damai, Puspa. 2005. "Messianic-City: Ruins, Refuge and Hospitality in Derrida." *Discourse* 27 (2–3): 68–94.

Danewid, Ida. 2017. "White Innocence in the Black Mediterranean: Hospitality and the Erasure of History." *Third World Quarterly* 38 (7): 1674–89.

Danewid, Ida, et al. 2021. "Introduction." In *The Black Mediterranean: Bodies, Borders, Citizenship*, edited by Gabriele Proglio et al., 9–28. Cham, Switzerland: Springer.

De Genova, Nicholas. 2002. "Migrant 'Illegality' and Deportability in Everyday Life." *Annual Review of Anthropology* 31:419–47.

De Genova, Nicholas. 2016. "The European Question: Migration, Race, and Postcoloniality in Europe." *Social Text* 34 (3)(128): 75–102.

De Genova, Nicholas. 2018. "'Crises,' Convulsions, Concurrences: Human Mobility, the European Geography of 'Exclusion,' and the Postcolonial Dialectics of Subordinate Inclusion." *Parse* 8 (Autumn). https://doi.org/10.70733/l4vk1g2rtohs.

De León, Jason. 2015. *The Land of Open Graves: Living and Dying on the Migrant Trail*. Oakland: University of California Press.

Derrida, Jacques. 1998. *Monolingualism of the Other, or the Prosthesis of Origin*. Translated by P. Mensah. Stanford, CA: Stanford University Press.

Derrida, Jacques. 1999. *Adieu to Emmanuel Levinas*. Translated by P. A. Brault and M. Naas. Stanford, CA: Stanford University Press.

Derrida, Jacques. 2001. "On Cosmopolitanism." In *On Cosmopolitanism and Forgiveness*. Translated by M. Dooley, 1–23. New York: Routledge.

Dikeç, Mustafa. 2002. "Pera Peras Poros: Longings for Spaces of Hospitality." *Theory, Culture, and Society* 19 (1–2): 227–47.

Dominguez, Carina. 2022. "Hia-Ced O'odham Woman Acquitted in Border Wall Protest." *Indian Country Today*, January 22, 2022. https://indiancountrytoday.com/news/hia-ced-oodham-woman-acquitted-in-border-wall-protest.

El-Affendi, Abdelwahab. 2024. "The Futility of Genocide Studies After Gaza." *Journal of Genocide Research*, January 18, 2024, 1–7.

El-Tayeb, Fatima. 2008. "The Birth of a European Public: Migration, Postnationality, and Race in the Uniting of Europe." *American Quarterly* 60 (3): 649–70.

Esmeir, Samera. 2014. *Juridical Humanity: A Colonial History*. Stanford, CA: Stanford University Press.

Fassin, Didier. 2005. "Compassion and Repression: The Moral Economy of Immigration Policies in France." *Cultural Anthropology* 20 (3): 362–87.

Fassin, Didier. 2013. "The Predicament of Humanitarianism." *Qui Parle* 22 (1): 33–48.

Ferreira da Silva, Denise. 2016. "On Difference Without Separability." In *32nd Bienal de São Paulo—Incerteza Viva Catalogue*, edited by J. Volz and J. Rebouças, 57–65. São Paulo: Fundação Bienal de São Paulo.

García Peña, Lorgia. 2022. *Translating Blackness: Latinx Colonialities in Global Perspective*. Durham, NC: Duke University Press.

Gilmore, Ruth W. 2023. *Abolition Geography: Essays Towards Liberation*. New York: Verso.

Gilroy, Paul. 1993. *The Black Atlantic: Modernity and Double Consciousness*. Cambridge, MA: Harvard University Press.

Gilroy, Paul. 2018. "'Where Every Breeze Speaks of Courage and Liberty': Offshore Humanism and Marine Xenology, or, Racism and the Problem of Critique at Sea Level." *Antipode* 50 (1): 3–22.

Gilroy, Paul. 2019. "Agonistic Belonging: The Banality of Good, the 'Alt Right' and the Need for Sympathy." *Open Cultural Studies* 3:1–14.

Gilroy, Paul. 2021. "Antiracism, Blue Humanism and the Black Mediterranean." *Transition* 132:108–22.

Godzich, Wlad. 2014. "Sekond-Hend Europe." *boundary 2* 41 (1): 1–15.

Golden, Renny, and Michael McConnell. 1986. *Sanctuary: The New Underground Railroad*. New York: Orbis Books.

Gooder, Haydie, and Jane M. Jacobs. 2000. "'On the Border of the Unsayable': The Apology in Postcolonizing Australia." *Interventions* 2 (2): 229–47.

Hall, Stuart. 2005. "New Ethnicities." In *Stuart Hall: Critical Dialogues in Cultural Studies*, edited by Kuan-Hsing Chen and David Morley, 442–51. New York: Routledge.

Harney, Stefano, and Fred Moten. 2013. *The Undercommons: Fugitive Planning and Black Study*. Oakland, CA: AK.

Haro, Lia, and Romand Coles. 2019. "Reimagining Fugitive Democracy and Sanctuary with Black Frontline Communities." *Political Theory* 5:646–73.

Hartman, Saidiya. 1997. *Scenes of Subjection: Terror, Slavery, and Self-Making in Nineteenth-Century America*. New York: Oxford University Press.

Hawthorne, Camilla. 2022. "Black Mediterranean Geographies: Translation and the Mattering of Black Life in Italy." *Gender, Place and Culture* 30 (3): 484–507.

Horowitz, Jason. 2022. "Giorgia Meloni Wins Voting in Italy, in Breakthrough for Europe's Hard Right." *New York Times*, September 25, 2022. https://www.nytimes.com/2022/09/25/world/europe/italy-meloni-prime-minister.html.

Ingram, Paul. 2020. "Feds Drop Case Against No More Deaths Volunteer Scott Warren." *Tucson Sentinel*, February 27, 2020. https://www.tucsonsentinel.com/local/report/022620_warren_charge/feds-drop-case-against-no-more-deaths-volunteer-scott-warren.

International Court of Justice. 2023. "Application of the Convention on the Prevention and Punishment of the Crime of Genocide in the Gaza Strip (South Africa v. Israel): Institution of Proceedings, December 29." https://www.icj-cij.org/case/192/institution-proceedings.

International Women* Space. 2022. "Angela Davis Speaks at Oranienplatz." October 20, 2022. https://iwspace.de/2022/10/angela-davis-o-platz.

Jung, Moon-Kie, and João H. Costa Vargas. 2021. *Antiblackness*. Durham, NC: Duke University Press.

Kasparek, Bernd, and Marc Speer. 2015. "Of Hope: Hungary and the Long Summer of Migration." *Border Monitoring*, September 9, 2015. https://bordermonitoring.eu/ungarn/2015/09/of-hope-en.

Kelley, Robin D. G. 1999. "'But a Local Phase of a World Problem': Black History's Global Vision, 1883–1950." *Journal of American History* 86 (3): 1045–77.

Kubaczek, Niki, and Monika Mokre. 2021. *Die Stadt als Stätte der Solidarität*. Vienna: transversal texts.

Lafazani, Olga. 2018. "Homeplace Plaza: Challenging the Border Between Host and Hosted." *South Atlantic Quarterly* 117 (4): 896–904.

Lethabo King, Tiffany. 2019. *The Black Shoals: Offshore Formations of Black and Native Life*. Durham: Duke University Press.

Levin, Sam. 2023. "Los Angeles Unhoused Population Reaches 75,000 amid Humanitarian Crisis." *Guardian*, June 29, 2023. https://www.theguardian.com/us-news/2023/jun/29/los-angeles-county-homelessness-unhoused-population.

Lombardi-Diop, Cristina. 2021. "Preface." In *The Black Mediterranean: Bodies, Borders, Citizenship*, edited by Gabriele Proglio et al. Cham, Switzerland: Springer.

Loveluck, Louisa, Heba Farouk Mahfouz, Elinda Labropoulou, Siobhán O'Grady, and Rick Noack. 2023. "They Knew the Boat Could Sink. Boarding It Didn't Feel Like a Choice." *Washington Post*, June 24, 2023. https://www.washingtonpost.com/world/2023/06/24/greek-migrant-boat-victims.

Lynes, Krista, Tyler Morgenstern, and Ian Alan Paul. 2020. *Moving Images: Mediating Migration as Crisis*. Bielefeld: transcript.

Maira, Sunaina. 2019. "Freedom to Move, Freedom to Stay, Freedom to Return: A Transnational Roundtable on Sanctuary Activism." *Radical History Review* 135: 138–59.

Matsipa, Mpho, and Abdoumaliq Simone. 2020. "#Inoperable Relations, African Mobilities 2.0." July 14, 2020.

Mbembe, Achille. 2018. "The Idea of a Borderless World." *Africa Is a Country*, November 11, 2018. https://africasacountry.com/2018/11/the-idea-of-a-borderless-world.

Mbembe, Achille. 2019. "Bodies as Borders." *From the European South* 4: 5–18.

McKittrick, Katherine. 2011. "On Plantations, Prisons, and a Black Sense of Place." *Social and Cultural Geography* 12 (8): 947–63.

Mei-Singh, Laurel. 2021. "Accompaniment Through Carceral Geographies: Abolitionist Research Partnerships with Indigenous Communities." *Antipode: A Journal of Radical Geography* 53 (1): 74–94.

Mignolo, Walter. 2015. "Sylvia Wynter: What Does It Mean to be Human?" In *Sylvia Wynter: On Being Human as Praxis*, edited by Katherine McKittrick, 106–23. Durham, NC: Duke University Press.

Mitchell, Katharyne, and Key MacFarlane. 2022. "Sanctuary Space, Racialized Violence, and Memories of Resistance." *Annals of the American Association of Geographers* 112 (8): 2360–72.

Monkman, Lenard. 2017. "'No Ban on Stolen Land,' Say Indigenous Activists in U.S." CBC, February 2, 2017. https://www.cbc.ca/news/indigenous/indigenous-activists-immigration-ban-1.3960814.

Mudu, Pierpaolo, and Sutapa Chattopadhyay. 2017. *Migration, Squatting and Radical Autonomy*. London: Routledge.

Paik, Naomi A. 2017. "Abolitionist Futures and the US Sanctuary Movement." *Race and Class* 59 (2): 3–25.

Paik, Naomi A. 2020. *Bans, Walls, Raids, Sanctuary: Understanding U.S. Immigration for the Twenty-First Century*. Berkeley: University of California Press.

Papadopoulos, Dimitris, and Vassilis S. Tsianos. 2013. "After Citizenship: Autonomy of Migration, Organizational Ontology and Mobile Commons." *Citizenship Studies* 17 (2): 178–96.

Patterson, Orlando. 1983. *Slavery and Social Death: A Comparative Study*. Cambridge, MA: Harvard University Press.

Quant, John F. 2015. "Asylum." In *The Oxford Encyclopedia of the Bible and Law*, edited by Brent A. Strawn. Oxford: Oxford University Press.

Rajagopal, Balakrishnan. 2022. *The Right to Adequate Housing During Violent Conflict: Report of the Special Rapporteur on Adequate Housing*. New York: United Nations.

The Red Nation. 2021. *The Red Deal: Indigenous Action to Save Our Earth*. New York: Common Notions.

Ridgley, Jennifer. 2008. "Cities of Refuge: Immigration Enforcement, Police, and the Insurgent Genealogies of Citizenship in U.S. Sanctuary Cities." *Urban Geography* 29 (1): 53–77.

Roberts, Hannah. 2022. "Migrants Must Be Welcomed, Pope Francis Says on Italy Election Day." *Politico*, September 25, 2022. https://www.politico.eu/article/pope-francis-migrants-welcome-italy-election-2022.

Roy, Ananya. 2019. "The City in the Age of Trumpism: From Sanctuary to Abolition." *Environment and Planning D: Society and Space* 37 (5): 761–78.

Roy, Ananya, and Aihwa Ong, eds. 2011. *Worlding Cities: Asian Experiments and the Art of Being Global*. Chichester: Blackwell.

Roy, Ananya, Willie J. Wright, Yousuf Al-Bulushi, and Adam Bledsoe. 2020. "'A World of Many Souths': (Anti)Blackness and Historical Difference in Conversation with Ananya Roy." *Urban Geography* 41 (6): 920–35.

Samudzi, Zoé. 2020. "Reparative Futures: Thinking from the Ovaherero and Nama Colonial Genocide." *Funambulist*, June 29, 2020. https://thefunambulist.net/magazine/reparations/reparative-futurities-thinking-from-the-ovaherero-and-nama-colonial-genocide-by-zoe-samudzi.

Saucier, Paul Khalil, and Tryon P. Woods. 2014. "Ex Aqua: The Mediterranean Basin, Africans on the Move and the Politics of Policing." *Theoria: A Journal of Social and Political Theory* 61 (141): 55–75.

Scott, David. 2000. "The Re-Enchantment of Humanism: An Interview with Sylvia Wynter." *Small Axe* 8:119–207.

Scott, David. 2013. "On the Very Idea of a Black Radical Tradition." *Small Axe* 40:1–6.

Sepulveda, Charles. 2018. "Our Sacred Waters: Theorizing Kuuyam as a Decolonial Possibility." *Decolonization: Indigeneity, Education and Society* 7 (1): 40–58.

Sepulveda, Charles. 2020. "To Decolonize Indigenous Lands, We Must Also Abolish Police and Prisons." *Truthout*, October 13, 2020. https://truthout.org/articles/to-decolonize-indigenous-lands-we-must-also-abolish-police-and-prisons.

Sharpe, Christina. 2016. *In the Wake: On Blackness and Being*. Durham, NC: Duke University Press.

Simpson, Audra. 2017. "The Ruse of Consent and the Anatomy of 'Refusal': Cases from Indigenous North America and Australia." *Postcolonial Studies* 20 (1): 18–33.

Smythe, SA. 2018. "The Black Mediterranean and the Politics of Imagination." *Middle East Report* 286:3–9.

Sojoyner, Damien M. 2017. "Another Life Is Possible: Black Fugitivity and Enclosed Places." *Cultural Anthropology* 32 (4): 514–36.

Spivak, Gayatri C. 1985. "The Rani of Sirmur: An Essay in Reading the Archives." *History and Theory* 24 (3): 247–72.

Stevis-Gridneff, Matina, and Karam Shoumali. 2023. "Everyone Knew the Migrant Ship was Doomed. No One Helped." *New York Times*, July 1, 2023. https://www.nytimes.com/2023/07/01/world/europe/greece-migrant-ship.html.

Stierl, Maurice. 2016. "A Sea of Struggle—Activist Border Interventions in the Mediterranean Sea." *Citizenship Studies* 20 (5): 561–78.

Stierl, Maurice. 2019. *Migrant Resistance in Contemporary Europe*. London: Routledge.

Tazzioli, Martina, and Nicholas De Genova. 2020. "Kidnapping Migrants as a Tactic of Border Enforcement." *Environment and Planning D: Society and Space* 38 (5): 867–86.

Tazzioli, Martina, and Glenda Garelli. 2018. "Containment Beyond Detention: The Hotspot System and Disrupted Migration Movements Across Europe." *Environment and Planning D: Society and Space* 38 (6): 1009–27.

Tazzioli, Martina, and Maurice Stierl. 2021. "'We Closed the Ports to Protect Refugees': Hygienic Borders and Deterrence Humanitarianism During Covid-19." *International Political Sociology* 15 (4): 1–17.

Tomba, Massimiliano. 2019. "Sanctuary as Anachronism and Anticipation." *History of the Present* 9 (2): 217–32.

Tsavdaroglou, Charalampos, and Maria Kaika. 2022a. "Refugees' Caring and Commoning Practices Against Marginalisation Under COVID-19 in Greece." *Geographical Research* 60 (2): 232–40.

Tsavdaroglou, Charalampos, and Maria Kaika. 2022b. "The Refugees' Right to the Centre of the City: City Branding Versus City Commoning in Athens." *Urban Studies* 59 (6): 1130–47.

UCLA Luskin Institute on Inequality and Democracy. 2020a. *Sanctuary and Solidarity: The U.S. War on Refugees and Migrants*. Featuring Hope Angelique Alvarado, Brendan Cassidy, Jennifer M. Chácon, Juan B. Mancias, Nicole Elizabeth Ramos, and Veronika Zablotsky. August 28, 2020. https://

challengeinequality.luskin.ucla.edu/sanctuary-solidarity-resisting-the-us-war-on-refugees-and-migrants/.

UCLA Luskin Institute on Inequality and Democracy. 2020b. *Abolition on Stolen Land*. Featuring Nick Estes, Ruth Wilson Gilmore, Sarah Haley, Gaye Theresa Johnson, Ananya Roy, and Charles Sepulveda. October 9, 2020. https://challengeinequality.luskin.ucla.edu/abolition-on-stolen-land-with-ruth-wilson-gilmore.

UCLA Luskin Institute on Inequality and Democracy. 2021a. *trans/BORDER/ing: The Aesthetics of Disturbance and Undocumentary Flight*. Featuring Amy Sara Carroll, Ricardo Dominguez, SA Smythe, Maurice Stierl, Veronika Zablotsky, and Maite Zubiaurre. February 19, 2021. https://challengeinequality.luskin.ucla.edu/trans-border-ing-the-aesthetics-of-disturbance-and-undocumentary-flight.

UCLA Luskin Institute on Inequality and Democracy. 2021b. *Freedom and Fugitivity*. Featuring Aisha K. Finch, Sarah Haley, Saidiya Hartman, Tiffany Lethabo King, Kyle T. Mays, and Ananya Roy. June 11, 2021. https://challengeinequality.luskin.ucla.edu/freedom-and-fugitivity-event.

UCLA Luskin Institute on Inequality and Democracy. 2021c. A̶s̶y̶l̶u̶m̶: *At the Borders of Humanitarianism*. Featuring E. Tendayi Achiume, Fatima El-Tayeb, Denise Ferreira da Silva, Alicia Gaspar de Alba, Nicholas De Genova, Mpho Matsipa, and Melanie K. Yazzie. https://challengeinequality.luskin.ucla.edu/the-end-of-humanitarianism/.

UCLA Luskin Institute on Inequality and Democracy. 2021d. E̶n̶c̶l̶o̶s̶u̶r̶e̶: *Geographies of Refusal*. Featuring Tina M. Campt, Camilla A. Hawthorne, Saree Makdisi, Dylan Rodriguez, Audra Simpson, and Rinaldo Walcott. https://challengeinequality.luskin.ucla.edu/freedom-and-fugitivity.

UNITED for Intercultural Action. n.d. The Fatal Policies of Fortress Europe. Accessed February 10, 2024. https://unitedagainstrefugeedeaths.eu.

Villarreal, Aimee. 2019. "Sanctuaryscapes in the North American Southwest." *Radical History Review* 135:43–70.

Walcott, Rinaldo. 2021. "The Black Aquatic." *Liquid Blackness* 5 (1): 64–73.

Walia, Harsha. 2012. "Decolonizing Together: Moving Beyond a Politics of Solidarity Toward a Practice of Decolonization." *Briarpatch*, January 1, 2012. https://briarpatchmagazine.com/articles/view/decolonizing-together.

Walia, Harsha. 2013. *Undoing Border Imperialism*. Chico, CA: AK.

Walia, Harsha. 2021. *Border and Rule: Global Migration, Capitalism, and the Rise of Racist Nationalism*. Chicago: Haymarket.

Watch The Mediterranean Sea. n.d. Accessed November 21, 2024. https://watchthemed.net.

Watch The Med Alarm Phone. n.d. Accessed November 21, 2024. https://alarmphone.org/en/.

Wekker, Gloria. 2016. *White Innocence: Paradoxes of Colonialism and Race*. Durham, NC: Duke University Press.

Williams, Raymond. 1983. *Keywords: A Vocabulary of Culture and Society*. New York: Oxford University Press.
Wolff Architects. 2021. "African Mobilities Exhibition." *ArchSA*, no. 100. https://issuu.com/sundaytimesza/docs/asa_june-july2021/12.
Wynter, Sylvia. 2003. "Unsettling the Coloniality of Being/Power/Truth/Freedom: Towards the Human, After Man, Its Overrepresentation." *CR: The New Centennial Review* 3 (3): 257–337.
Yazzie, Melanie. 2015. "Solidarity with Palestine from Diné Bikéyah." *American Quarterly* 67 (4): 1007–15.
Yazzie, Melanie. 2018. "Decolonizing Development in Diné Bikéyah: Resource Extraction, Anti-Capitalism, and Relational Futures." *Environment and Society* 9:25–39.

INTERLUDE

~~Asylum~~

At the Borders of Humanitarianism

Ananya Roy

We invite readers of this book to view the Sanctuary Short *Asylum: At the Borders of Humanitarianism*.[1] Filmed amid a global pandemic, each Sanctuary Short is a conceptual conversation with scholars whose work illuminates the colonial relationalities and histories of dispossession that constitute the grounds of migration and asylum in the liberal democracies of the West. ~~Asylum~~ exposes the global systems of liberal governance that structure and manage exclusion through maintaining lethal borders and furthering the relationship between extraction and migration. In the Sanctuary Short, Mpho Matsipa reminds us that the mobility of certain "unwelcome" bodies, those "who are supposed to remain in place"—"the fact that they're moving"—produces the "crisis" of migration. This in turn engenders the cosmopolitan responsibility that Fatima El-Tayeb (2008, 655) critically analyzes: Europe must save the world.

Europe arrogates to itself this duty to save while producing the very crisis of displacement that becomes visible as global migration. By foregrounding "moving in the world in a body that is raced," Matsipa asks us "to conceive of enclosure and borders as something that is actually embodied." Alicia Gaspar de Alba (1987, 5) thus writes, "La frontera lies wide open, sleeping beauty.... In that body of dreams, the Mexicans swim for years, their fine skins too tight to breathe. Yo también me he acostado con ella, crossed that cold bed, wading toward a hunched coyote." Refusing humanitarian reason, we follow migrants and migrant justice struggles to reworld la frontera, that body of dreams, through demands for decolonization. This is nothing less than "a reconstruction of the world," Denise Ferreira da Silva (2014, 82) reminds us: "To reclaim, to demand the restoration of the total value the colonial architectures have enabled capital to expropriate from native lands and enslaved black (and African) labor."

NOTE

1   The Sanctuary Short ~~Asylum~~: *At the Borders of Humanitarianism* can be viewed at https://challengeinequality.luskin.ucla.edu/the-end-of-humanitarianism.

WORKS CITED

El-Tayeb, Fatima. 2008. "The Birth of a European Public: Migration, Postnationality, and Race in the Uniting of Europe." *American Quarterly* 60 (3): 649–70.

Ferreira da Silva, Denise. 2014. "Toward a Black Feminist Poethics." *Black Scholar* 44 (2): 81–97.

Gaspar de Alba, Alicia. 1987. "La Frontera." *Bilingual Review / La Revista Bilingüe* 14 (1–2): 5.

PART I

Abolition on Stolen Land

This Is an Incitement

Abolition on Stolen Land

Gaye Theresa Johnson and Damon Azali-Rojas

We are a living people that the US government has determined are no longer living tribal nations. For the government and most settlers, the theft of our lands and Tongva life are complete. I am here to request that you do not listen to their racialized historical fantasies.

Charles Sepulveda

Racism without race is a choice. Taught, of course, by those who need it, but still a choice. Folks who practice it would be nothing without it.

Toni Morrison, *God Help the Child*

Colonization is not over. We begin with this instruction from Professor Charles Sepulveda, one of the speakers on a panel convened in 2020 as part of the Mellon-Sawyer Seminar, titled "Abolition on Stolen Land."[1] In the same frame, we invite a relevant renunciation: Toni Morrison once credited her limitlessness as a Black writer to her rejection of the white critic, real and imagined. Over decades of writing that attended to racism's deadly social and spiritual consequences, she maintained that race itself was "nothing without the racist." Following Morrison's (2015, 143) keen insight, we are reminded that the construction of "private property" is nothing without the racialized fantasy of manifest destiny—the child of the doctrine of discovery. We are reminded that the concept and promise of "law and order" is nothing without the systematic criminalization of poor people and people of color. Considering Sepulveda's and Morrison's invitations in the same frame, we refuse the limits of colonial critique—both imposed and internalized—that hinder the co-creation of radical democratic futures. In so doing, we discern what we already have as foundational to the world we want to build. Knowing what we have and who we are widens the scope of our understanding, sharpens our tools of analysis, and—perhaps most pertinent here—delimits our dreams for what is possible. When we affirm that colonization is not over, we likewise dismiss any impulse to dilute this argument for those refusing to bend their efforts toward liberation. Abolition on stolen land is a struggle maintained in a highly dynamic and contradictory context, yet there are tools of discernment and future world-making that we inherit from centuries of revolutionary predecessors.

We note here that the panelists themselves—Indigenous Land Back and abolition scholars Charles Sepulveda, Nick Estes, Ruth Wilson Gilmore, and Sarah Haley—all work in theory and in action to refuse the multiple projects and legacies of settler colonialism and racial capitalism. In their collective commitments, sourced in movement work and dynamic public intellectualism, they inspire us into more radical imaginings vis-à-vis material strategies for thinking and acting.

In this introduction, we focus on the places where panelists visibilize the contradictions and possibilities of repairing community and land relationships upon which the carceral system is imposed. We affirm our duty to care for the earth and to refuse the inevitability of the carceral regime and the multiple settler-colonial projects intended for our demise. Finally, we extend an invitation to accountability—a refusal to accept words over action. Knowing refusal only goes so far, we offer a series of incitements inspired by this panel of scholars.

Preliminarily, we wish to foreground our reflections in some thoughts about the intrinsic relationship between practices of resistance, intellectual traditions, and discernment, a connection underscored by the panel.

In this volume's introduction, Professors Roy and Zablotsky remind us that "the collective dreaming of freedom under conditions of fugitivity . . . [and] the assertion of solidarity in the face of incalculable loss of life" are practices of resistance that require serious commitment and study. Indigenous and Afro-diasporic epistemologies and ontologies rooted in resistance and solidarity have done more than inspire revolution and transformation worldwide; they have also shaped significant intellectual traditions across the disciplines. The political underpinnings of Indigenous studies, feminist and gender studies, critical refugee studies, and the struggle and study sourced in the Black radical tradition and Black feminism are premised on our refusal to accept that colonization is complete, as well as our rejection of the naturalization of the multiple projects of racial capitalism. Professors Sepulveda, Estes, Haley, and Gilmore remind us that it is our political duty to maintain this refusal, yet not without an engagement with the practices of discernment forged out of necessity and as the foundation of material strategies of rebellion. Reckoning with the reality of an abolitionist struggle that takes place on stolen land is to reject the fictions of a postcolonial world; to reject these fictions is to discern the discursive tricks used to sustain them; and to create action out of discernment is to organize an alternative future.

Discernment has always been necessary for understanding our realities and mounting resistance to our subjugation. Centuries of situated experience and study create an attunement to the tactics of dispossession hiding in the colonial logics of "civilization" and the tactics of market domination in the promises of "sanctuary" and "freedom." The traditions of marronage, fugitivity, espionage, subversion, strikes, and legal challenges in Black and Indigenous histories worldwide demonstrate the results of moments and processes of discernment—namely, as practices of refusal and negotiation, in which we have resisted the genocidal premises of our presumed inferiority and disposability. While genocide and enslavement are supposedly past, each panelist shows us how the underlying negations of Black life and Indigenous sovereignty live on. We are still fighting. We are still subverting, sabotaging, undermining, lobbying, loving, allying, analyzing, discerning, and regenerating paths to a future that is organized on different terms. The settler-colonial project is not complete. We now highlight reflections from each panel presentation.

Reflection #1: On the Anticolonial Vision of Abolition

Charles Sepulveda: *"'I am alive' and 'We are still here' are radical [declarations] because we are the survivors of centuries of racial colonial terror. We are a living people that the US government has determined are no longer living tribal nations. For the government and most settlers, white supremacy is what allows land theft and prisons to exist. Land Back and 'abolish prisons/ police' are not metaphors but are visions of a world that we want to be in. A world that benefits everyone; white supremacy is not permanent."*

What does it mean to center an explicitly Indigenous, anticolonial abolitionist analysis of the carceral system? Sepulveda urges us to pay attention to Land Back and abolitionist activists and scholars who are working with histories—documented and inherited—of overlapping revolutionary paradigms among Black, Indigenous, and Afro-Indigenous people. These perspectives have been forged over time from the experience of violence against Black, Indigenous, and Afro-Indigenous people that "have been constituted through colonial relations and white supremacy." In her study on carceral redlining, Rai Reece (2020) helps us to understand that the making of white settler nations "relied upon the destabilizing of Indigenous sociopolitical systems in tandem with the implementation of the legally sanctioned practice of Black slavery through social control, displacement and incarceration." So it is first to understand that while Indigenous displacement and antiblackness are often viewed through distinct historical lenses, there is much to be learned about the resultant revolutionary strategies and identities that emerge from studying them in the same lens. Studies by Rai Reece (2020), Tiya Miles (2015), Kyle Mays (2021; also chapter 14 in this volume), and others have shown that the racialization of Black and Indigenous peoples was and still is a central organizing feature of the nation-state (we will add here the construction of illegality related to the dehumanization of immigrants from the southern border of the United States), especially through the specter of incarceration (since Black, Indigenous, and immigrant people are the most incarcerated of any). These revolutionary perspectives emerge not only from violent oppression but also from survival, imagination, creativity, and a resolve to do more than survive inside these contexts. These and other scholars' and activists' most powerful interventions are uncovering stories that were never meant to be heard, ones that direct us to source our understanding of freedom through the experiences and teachings of Black women, Indigenous people, and Afro-Indigenous people. As the inheritors of these visions, movement leaders in abolition and Land Back can work to center anticolonial analyses.

The Abolitionist Convergence is an organizing committee on Wendat, Seneca, and Mississauga lands. It is a collaboration of artists, activists, academics, and people who have direct experience with the carceral system and have worked and struggled against incarceration, detention, deportation, and settler colonialism in various ways.² For them, an anticolonial, abolitionist perspective is one that directs us to defund and dismantle the punitive, carceral structures characteristic of settler-colonial society, and to turn instead to Indigenous knowledges as a guide to how to create and sustain good relations with each other. "As Ojibwe Elder Art Solomon explains, 'We were not perfect, but we had no jails . . . no old people's homes, no children's aid societies, we had no crisis centers. We had a philosophy of life based on The Creator, and we had our humanity.' An abolitionist future, then, must center the stories of this land as essential to collective flourishing and care" (Toronto Abolitionist Convergence 2020). Reclaiming the history of Black and Indigenous mutual care and awareness is one way to unmask and disrupt white supremacy, to renew and deepen solidarity with one another in deeply intertwined struggles, and to engage in mutual invitations to anticolonial, revolutionary creation of vital political realities and affinities. Professor Mays reminds us that Indigenous Africans who were stolen and sold in the Americas worked to retain their inherent Indigenous identities, similarly to how displaced Native tribes forced onto reservations far from their ancestral territories retained their tribal identities. Heeding Mays's caution against romanticizing relationships between Black and Indigenous people over time, we recall his argument that "the relationship between African and Indigenous people can be understood in three words: collaboration, conflict, and controversy" (Mays 2021, xvii). As Mays and Sepulveda imply and as we have often seen in coalitional movement-building, there is no promise of ease in the struggle to reclaim land and abolish prisons, to manifest a vision of a future that is more than metaphor. Yet as Sepulveda reminds us, we are survivors of centuries of racial colonial terror, and to be alive is to know that white supremacy is not permanent. When scholars and activists make statements such as "We can give land back," "Abolish the police," or "We can exist without prisons," some listeners are perplexed, others are afraid, and some will argue that it is not possible. Mays's work reveals well-established patterns of Afro-Indigenous collaboration and solidarity. He shows that Black and Native people have become mutually aware and active in social struggles to make meaningful changes in their own conditions and to make the world we live in a more just place.

Thinking through Sepulveda's statements, we are inspired to consider both Land Back and "Land Black"—specifically, reparations. How can Black people be compensated for centuries of forced labor in a way that isn't used to deny Indigenous claims? How do we place "Land Black" movements side by side with Land Back movements?

This leads us to our first set of incitements:
To create real alignment and deep solidarity for both Black and Indigenous reparations is hard and sustained work. Black and Indigenous peoples need to be in relationship to do so. In order to be in relationship there needs to be:

> *Education on the similarities and uniqueness of our historical struggles.* This means understanding the connections between how the settler state has used similar—though not identical—means to exclude, dispossess our peoples of land, and eviscerate our human rights.
> *Trust.* This means deep, human work by Black people on their anti-indigeneity; deep work by Indigenous peoples on their antiblackness.

Reflection #2: Unambiguous Acts of Poetry

Nick Estes: "[There are some things that] are unequivocal. . . . The same thing could be said of the term 'Land Back,' right? . . . It can't be co-opted, it can't be taken back. The government of Canada is not going to have a reconciliation session around returning land to Indigenous people, because we know that as an impossibility under the current system. And I think about this in terms of how when there's a failure to even articulate demands and aspirations to the system itself, [then] it fails to even co-opt them on the basic level, [and the result is that] you get things that are unequivocal, unambiguous actions, that would be considered acts of poetry. And I would consider the burning down of the Third Precinct an act of poetry. It's not going to be co-opted by this particular moment in time. Or by the neoliberal restoration that is embodied in candidates such as Joe Biden."

Estes reminds us that there is poetry in rebellion, particularly when we are able to use the resources and expressions of our own traditions to deflect surveillance and even understanding by those in power. As he invokes the burning of the Third Precinct in Minneapolis, allegedly by protesters, in the wake of George Floyd's murder, Estes offers an example of an action whose intention cannot be misread. Further, Estes encourages us to read governing institutions' tepid messages of performative regret about genocide and dispossession as an explicit pronouncement of the intention to do absolutely nothing in the service of reconciliation. Estes points in example to the failure of the Canadian government to engage in serious conversations around Land Back. He discerns this inaction as an action, one that is part of the ongoing disappearing of structural brutalization and dispossession, all part of Canada's violent foundations and present.

Estes's encouragement to look to unequivocal and unambiguous actions reminds us of a similarly instructive period. Reconstruction in the United States was a drama of Black, Indigenous, and worker resistance under competing regimes of white nationalist ideologies. These ideologies were fueled by industrial expansion and genocide, and their consequences were most dire for Black and Indigenous people. "Emancipation" for most of our people meant Black Codes, convict leasing, Indigenous dispossession and displacement, broken treaties, and containment—state mechanisms of oppression meant to be permanent and hereditary. But emancipation cannot be seen as a fixed moment in history, since Black people had been rebelling since the moment they were forced into captivity. Cedric Robinson (1997, 71) wrote that once enslaved people discerned that the North would not bend to the South's demands, slave insurrections broke out in Mississippi and Virginia, and there were an additional twenty-five conspiracies in Arkansas, South Carolina, Louisiana, and Kentucky. Escaped slaves in the Lower and Upper South deserted plantations and endeavored to move toward the nearest Union forces (he notes, for example, that of the 112,000 slaves in Missouri, 22,000 had escaped by 1862). There is no ambiguity in this poetic and large-scale fugitivity. It remains one of the most poetic articulations of refusal. Black collective discernment deduced that the conscience of white America would never be capacious enough to abolish slavery; since freedom was as close as it would ever be, it would have to be seized. There was no proclamation or platform. Yet mass fugitivity could not be co-opted by the projects of white nationalism in 1860.

Just as there was power in the unarticulated demands and aspirations of freedom-seeking Black people in the late nineteenth century, there is power in protecting information about the spirit and intention of Black Lives Matter and Land Back movements, which send poetic and unequivocal messages of rebellion that cannot be co-opted or misinterpreted. The burning of the Third Precinct can be characterized in many respects as a poetic "diagnosis" of authority: following Lila Abu-Lughod (1990) and Robin D. G. Kelley (1994), we see these unambiguous articulations of refusal as a reading of changing structures of power.

There are many examples of unambiguous challenges to the carceral regime and of actions that are unequivocal critiques against racial capitalism. Gathering these challenges into the collective memory and actions of our struggle for abolition on stolen land is fundamental to understanding not only the path forward but also that this path includes the poetry of rebellion, and sometimes violence.

Professor Estes's reference to the poetics of unambiguous articulations leads us to consider the role of poetry and the expressive arts in movement-building and collective understanding of the political moment. Activists whose principal organizing medium is art—its practice, creation, and expression in movement spaces—have a central role in the history of organizing that is both undeniable and fundamental. Our second set of incitements emerges from this history: center the cultural expressions of freedom seekers in movement work. Below, we have added models of artivist movement building in Los Angeles.

> Meztli Projects "is an Indigenous based arts & culture collaborative centering Indigeneity into the creative practice of Los Angeles by using arts-based strategies to support, advocate for, and organize to highlight Native and Indigenous Artists and systems-impacted youth." (https://www.meztliprojects.org)
>
> Contra-Tiempo "is a bold and multilingual Los Angeles–based activist dance theater company, dedicated to transforming the world through dance—building community, facilitating dialogue, and moving audiences to imagine what is possible." (https://www.contra-tiempo.org)
>
> Creative Acts "is an organization that seeks to transform urgent social justice issues through the revolutionary power of the Arts; to heal trauma, build community, raise power, and center the voices of those who are or have been incarcerated." (https://www.creativeacts.us)
>
> Tina Orduno Calderon is a "Culture Bearer of the Gabrielino Tongva, Chumash, Yoeme & Chicana descent." (https://www.tinaordunocalderon.com)
>
> The Crenshaw Dairy Mart "emerges from an investment in abolition, modes of accessibility in art practice, and weaving community solidarity through new memories." (https://www.crenshawdairymart.com)
>
> Self Help Graphics and Art "fosters the creation and advancement of new art works by Chicana/o and Latinx artists through experimental and innovative printmaking techniques and other visual art forms. We are an organization rooted in community; and

since 1973, have been at the intersection of arts and social justice, providing a home that fosters the creativity and development of local artists. We establish international collaborations and partnerships nation-wide and create world-wide cultural exchanges." (https://www.selfhelpgraphics.com)

LA Community Action Network's "team of community artists addresses important social justice issues and fosters healing through music, art, performance, and creative expression." (https://cangress.org)

Mujeres de Maiz is "a prolific women's ARTivist (artist + activist) and wellness collective, combines traditions of feminist, LGBTQ, and civil rights activism with indigenous practices to create sacred spaces within diverse communities." (https://www.mujeresdemaiz.com)

Tía Chucha's Centro Cultural's mission "is to transform community in the Northeast San Fernando Valley and beyond through ancestral knowledge, the arts, literacy and creative engagement." (https://www.tiachucha.org)

Eastside Café (https://www.instagram.com/eastsidecafela)

Sepia Collective believes the imagination is the tool for creating limitless futures, and fosters spaces where people can come together to build and create. (https://www.sepiacollective.com)

Hijos del Sol creates opportunities, inspires children and youth, and builds community in the Salinas Valley through visual and multicultural arts experiences. (https://www.hijosdelsol.org)

Fabian Debora is the Executive Director of Homeboy Art Academy, and is inspired in this role to continue to serve greater Los Angeles area and beyond through his art. (https://www.fabiandebora.com)

Indigenous Directions uses "Indigenous cultural protocols and ways of looking at the world to guide theater and film making/writing." (https://www.indigenousdirection.com)

Raices Cultura gathers "like-minded people to work together toward shared goals leading to the strengthening of personal agency and the development of community-focused activism." (https://www.raicescultura.org)

Dancing Earth "creates contemporary dance and related arts through global-Indigenous and intercultural relationships centered in ecological and cultural diversity for creativity, health, and wellness." (https://www.dancingearth.org)

> Studio 526: The People Concern is a "leading provider of, and advocate for, evidence-based solutions to the multi-faceted challenges inherent in homelessness and domestic violence." (https://www.thepeopleconcern.org/studio-526)

Reflection #3: Abolition on Stolen Land Is Intersectional

Ruth Wilson Gilmore: *"This compels us to come to the conclusion that if abolition must be green, it must be red. And if abolition must be red, it must be international. Abolition is an elaboration of what I call very small-c communism without a party. Although I wish some days we had party discipline, I do believe we can prevail with the combination of groupings organized to redistribute and secure material and symbolic real resources . . . that means giving back stolen land. It means making private property in land an impossibility. It means following the Red Nation Statement."*

Professor Gilmore returns us to the politics and practice of discernment by brilliantly connecting workers' rights, abolition, climate justice, and internationalism. She is speaking in a context that many environmental justice and abolitionist organizers recognize: the work of the Prison Policy Initiative has shown that "one-third (32 percent) of state and federal prisons are located within three miles of federal Superfund sites, the most serious contaminated places requiring extensive cleanup" (Sawyer and Wagner 2022). Professor Gilmore knows that as abolitionist work addresses environmental racism, it reveals broader issues of racial and economic inequality, particularly since most prisons are sited on toxic land. Toxic prisons are sited on toxic land that is also, in nearly every instance, located near or in low-income communities of color. Critical Resistance, the Campaign to Fight Toxic Prisons, and other collectives began organizing around this issue in the 1980s and 1990s. These groups are part of the "combination of groupings organized to redistribute and secure material and symbolic real resources" to which Gilmore is referring as an elaboration of "small-c communism," which in turn can and must facilitate the possibility of anticolonial internationalism. It is a model for the kind of connectivity we need if we are indeed to follow the Red Nation Statement, which declares, "We stand with and move with the people, as we move with the earth."

Organizing demands action in a way that creates accountability for multiple and simultaneous dispossessions, and to our communities as people deserving of human rights. This is what Gilmore reminds us we can and must do, by elucidating the connections between climate justice, internationalism, Land Back, and abolition.

Our Incitements: The Settler-Colonial Carceral Project

> Demand a path to abolish prisons. The 1976 book *Instead of Prisons: A Handbook for Abolitionists* describes a plan to shrink the carceral footprint. It includes changing people's thoughts about incarceration as a fix for the problems of racial capital; advocating for a moratorium on prison and jail construction; adopting strategies to decarcerate (reduce prison and jail populations); and extricating ourselves from the false safety net that prisons promise to be, among other things. Prisoners and organizers have created strategies for abolishing prisons. Listen to them.
> Repatriate the land back to its original caretakers. Professor Sepulveda argues, "With the control of our lands, not dominated through white supremacy, we can collectively abolish the prison and through the abolition of prison, Native people can regain their lands." Give the land back, and Indigenous abolitionists will determine a just process and outcome.

Reflection #4: The Role of Public Intellectuals in Abolition Politics

Sarah Haley: *"Do you want a bigger prison, a better prison, a prison on an island, in a city, in a country, a prison with a nursery, or music, or pink jumpsuits, or, or, or . . . The intellectual and political foundation for our current moment, in which abolition is in some hugely productive ways more salient, more saturated in public consciousness, is about [Ruth Wilson Gilmore's] longstanding abolitionist refusal and that of Critical Resistance and others in the face of persistent reformist calls to accept and embrace prison as a natural fact of life. . . . Black feminist refusal [rejects] the project and prospect of stolen people on stolen land and [works to create] landscapes of abolitionist revival [and] decolonial possibility?"*

Professor Haley helps us to understand the role of public intellectuals in abolition politics: to craft a politics of what is possible, and to maintain focus on bringing as many people into that vision as we can, empowering them to think and act critically. This is in the face of the naturalization of prison as a "fact of life," which reveals one of the most important challenges we have: to imagine freedom outside of carceral regimes, and to imagine what we will do with the freedom we envision.

Bernice Johnson Reagon (1983, 359) wrote about the need for taking the time "to try to construct within yourself and your community who you would be if you were running society." But she cautions that once we begin to invite others to work with us in this space, coalition work is not comfortable: "It is some of the most dangerous work you can do. And you shouldn't look for comfort. Some people will come to a coalition and they rate the coalition on whether or not they feel good when they get there. They're not looking for a coalition; they're looking for a home. You don't get fed a lot in coalition. In a coalition, you have to give, and it is different from your home. You can't stay there all the time. It is very important not to confuse them—home and coalition."

Because this work must be done in community, we cannot conclude that it will be everything we need or everything we want. As academics, we must also attend to the reality of coalitional politics and demonstrate through both word and experience what it means to do so. Too many students and scholars have been led to romanticized community work and just outcomes in such a way that any discomfort or strife makes them turn away from the real work that needs to be done.

Reagon invited us to imagine what we could do if we were running society. When there is community, there is less fear and less *to* fear. But it is not easy, and it is not a substitute for home. This is why these conversations must be grounded in reciprocity and community, not floating in a liminal space where there can be no roots. There must be something to plant and something to grow.

We believe that the academy can be a powerful place from which to do the work of abolition and Land Back. But entering into this process is a sacred commitment, and there is much to be learned and unlearned. We return to incitements offered by Charles Sepulveda, who helps us to consider what demands might grow from these understandings: *"If we can acknowledge that [land] was stolen, we can give it back. Like abolition, giving land back is often difficult for people to see as a possibility. If we have any job to do as scholars, I think it's to help people see that it is possible."*

Our Incitements: Academics and Institutions Writ Large

> Make the effort to respectfully learn from and follow the leadership of Indigenous folks on the ground about what they need,

and center their demands and future vision in teaching and writing.
- Make the effort to respectfully learn from and follow the leadership of Black folks on the ground on what they need, and center their demands and future vision in your teaching and writing.
- Make the effort to respectfully learn from and follow the leadership of people who are incarcerated and people who were previously incarcerated, and center their demands and future vision in your teaching and writing.

Conclusion

The mechanisms of white supremacy and settler colonialism put into place to disenfranchise, disempower, and eviscerate Black and Indigenous people still exist. Yet the struggles we have waged from the moment we discerned these intentions have revealed the weaknesses in ongoing discursive and material projects of colonial and carceral terror. Dismissing the white critic, we reclaim the inherent value and right to freedom of the lives of incarcerated and formerly incarcerated people. We do more than acknowledge the unceded territory upon which we write; we write from the position that Indigenous peoples are very much alive, having survived with more than bare life a genocide intended to be pervasive and permanent.

Grace Lee Boggs reminds us that to make a revolution, people must not only struggle against existing institutions; they must make a philosophical and spiritual leap, which includes changing and transforming themselves. As political educators inside and outside academic institutions, we must create active practices of abolitionist refusal, as Sarah Haley demands, and to write and research in a way that undoes the inevitability of prisons and land theft. To do so, we must hear from Indigenous people engaged in on-the-ground work about what they need. We need to ask Black leadership what they need and want. We must ask the incarcerated and formerly incarcerated what they need and want. And to do such things, we must be more than community-engaged. We must put communities—their situated experience, knowledge, and work—first. The role of intellectuals in radical change is important, and yet it cannot exist without deep awareness and work alongside the people whose labor makes these conversations possible. We end with Sarah Haley's incitement, which we believe brings us to the heart of our collective selves: *"How does abolitionist refusal show up in your life?"*

NOTES

1 Video of the panel "Abolition on Stolen Land" is available at https://challengeinequality.luskin.ucla.edu/abolition-on-stolen-land-with-ruth-wilson-gilmore.
2 Information about the Abolitionist Convergence can be found at https://yellowheadinstitute.org/an-indigenous-abolitionist-study-guide.

WORKS CITED

Abu-Lughod, Lila. 1990. "The Romance of Resistance: Tracing Transformations of Power Through Bedouin Women." *American Ethnologist* 17 (1): 41–55.
Kelley, Robin D. G. 1994. *Race Rebels: Culture, Politics, and the Black Working Class*. New York: Free Press.
Mays, Kyle. 2021. *An Afro-Indigenous History of the United States*. Boston: Beacon.
Miles, Tiya. 2015. *Ties That Bind: The Story of an Afro-Cherokee Family in Slavery and Freedom*. Berkeley: University of California Press.
Morrison, Toni. 2015. *God Help the Child*. New York: Knopf.
Reagon, Bernice Johnson. 1983. "Coalition Politics: Turning the Century." In *Home Girls: A Black Feminist Anthology*, edited by Barbara Smith. New York: Kitchen Table: Women of Color Press.
Reece, Rai. 2020. "Carceral Redlining: White Supremacy Is a Weapon of Mass Incarceration for Indigenous and Black Peoples in Canada." Yellowhead Institute, June 25, 2020. https://yellowheadinstitute.org/2020/06/25/carceral-redlining-white-supremacy-is-a-weapon-of-mass-incarceration-for-indigenous-and-black-peoples-in-canada.
Robinson, Cedric. 1997. *Black Movements in America*. New York: Routledge.
Sawyer, Wendy, and Peter Wagner. 2020. *Mass Incarceration: The Whole Pie*. Prison Policy Initiative. https://www.prisonpolicy.org/reports/pie2022.html.
Toronto Abolitionist Convergence. 2020. *An Indigenous Abolitionist Study Guide*. August 10, 2020. https://yellowheadinstitute.org/an-indigenous-abolitionist-study-guide.

2

Beyond the Social Death of Conquest

Kuuyam and Healthy Human-Land Kinship(s)

Charles A. Sepulveda

The logic of conquest deployed throughout the Americas can be reduced to a single word: *possession*. The possession of bodies, lands/waters, souls, and anything else that has meaning or value. The gratuitous terror of conquest and its incomplete, world-altering violence is the past, present, and future of slavery and genocide. Often understood as the enslavement of Black people as chattel and the genocide and dispossession of the Indigenous, conquest functions to possess. The extreme form of possession deployed through conquest destroyed bodies, kinship(s), ecologies, senses of self, nations, tribes, and the human being. Conquest degrades the humanity of Black and Indigenous peoples, destroying to incorporate them into an epistemic system of whiteness. The conquest of California was "spiritual," as San Junípero Serra, the founder and president of California's mission system, called it (Serra and Tibesar 1955, 153). The land/water and Indigenous bodies (and souls) were spiritually possessed by church and state, alienating them from the heritage of their ancestors and their lands. The genocidal conquest of California enslaved Indians (as non-chattel), remaking them as possessions of whiteness, productive for Civilization, and negating their indigeneity. Conquest places Indigenous peoples into a state of permanent displaceability.

Conquest functioned through a social death, in which the sociality and ontology (more than cultures) of California Indians were meant to be completely transformed so that the only meaning for the missionized Indian was in relation to the mission system and subsequent colonial structures—an evisceration of their selves: names, histories, sovereignty, heritage, lands, ceremonial cycles, languages, food systems, and kinship systems, including human-land. Black studies theorist Orlando Patterson explains that social death is a natal alienation in which the slave's social existence does not endure beyond enslavement (1982). The slave in most slaveholding societies was socially dead: desocialized, depersonalized, and detribalized. Nevertheless, social death has implemental limits, and the slave is always resistant to losing their sociality. Orlando Patterson explains that slaves were not free to integrate the experiences of their ancestors into their lives (1982). Despite not having the freedom to do so, the slave continuously resisted by reaching out for relatives in a struggle to reclaim their past and efforts to maintain their culture. For Indigenous peoples, the past includes a healthy environment and a living relationship with the land, a circular, nonlinear futurity intertwining a past that cannot be recuperated with a future that can. Potawatomi environmental scholar Kyle Whyte calls this a "cyclical performance" guided by our ancestors' perspectives to serve as good ancestors for future generations (2017, 160).

In this chapter, I will engage with the structural afterlife of the conquest of California dependent on Native social death, including Native alienation from land. This chapter will utilize my theory of kuuyam, which means "guests" in my Taraaxam ancestor's language.[1] Kuuyam radically imagines place beyond the logic of conquest that moves otherwise from a contrived Native/settler binary. Kuuyam is theorized as an invitation to form kinship(s) previously alienated—beyond the limits of conquest and possession, land dispossession, enslavement, and their structural afterlife. Kuuyam is not a recuperation of an imagined or romanticized Native past but Indigenous protocols for futurity that invite everyone to form non-exploitative relationships with the land, obligating them to begin living as good ancestors. Geographer and abolitionist Ruth Wilson Gilmore calls abolition "life in rehearsal" (2020). Building on Gilmore, I propose kuuyam as a future-focused performance of how to be a human being with consensual relationships with the people of the land and the more-than-human earth. The incommensurability caused by colonialism and racial capitalism is between a Western Christian worldview of the land (including human bodies and souls) as possessable and an Indigenous worldview of the earth as a structure of kinship(s). The earth is a place of sanctuary and remains sacred even when it has been colonized and stolen. To move otherwise, beyond incommensurability and the seemingly impossible dream of freedom under conditions of fugitivity, we must rehearse what it means to be human beings—inseparable from the earth in a sacred relationship.

Logic of Conquest

The European invasion of the Americas and the expansion of empire, otherwise known as Christendom, enacted violence against non-Christian peoples as bodies and souls to possess or exterminate. The logic of conquest brought to the Americas by Europeans was developed over centuries of expansion and war in Europe and with Islam, Judaism, and other non-Christians. The Portuguese first deployed a colonial system rooted in enslavement and conversion in the Canary Islands beginning in 1341. Nearly a century later, in 1434, the Portuguese established a passable route around Cape Bojador to the African continent's west coast and began enslaving and converting the Indigenous population (King 2019). The logic of conquest the Portuguese deployed in Africa was established theologically. The Catholic Church shaped papal law, providing edicts to Portugal and Spain to enslave, make war, convert the pagans, and possess their lands, bodies, and souls.

Slavery is inextricable from conquest vis-à-vis the collective of papal bulls known as the Doctrine of Discovery. For example, the bull *Dum Diversas*, issued by Pope Nicholas V. in 1452, authorized Portugal to conquer Muslims and pagans and possess them in perpetual servitude (Adiele 2017, 312–13). *Romanus Pontifex* (1455), building on *Dum Diversas*, authorized Portugal's colonization of Africa to "invade, search out, capture, vanquish and subdue all Saracens [Muslims] and pagans whatsoever, and other enemies of Christ where so ever placed, and the kingdoms, dukedoms, principalities, dominions, possessions and all movable and immovable goods whatsoever held and possessed by them and to reduce their persons to perpetual slavery" (Adiele 2017, 324). *Romanus Pontifex* is an apostolic declaration of Portuguese ownership of the west coast of Africa. In the bull, Nicholas V encouraged enslavement, as Catholic priest Pius Onyemechi Adiele explains, "expressing hope" that if Portugal "continued to forcefully catch such innocent civilians" in Africa and "deprive them of their freedom as humans," they "might be converted to the Christian faith" (Adiele 2017, 321). Nicholas V wrote that either the enslaved would be converted or "at least the souls of many of them will be gained for Christ" (Adiele 2017, 322).

Romanus Pontifex indicates that Africans were to be possessed, body and soul, for Christendom. Pope Callixtus III followed *Romanus Pontifex* with the bull *Inter Caetera* in 1456, which further solidified the Portuguese right to possess Africa and supported Portugal's economic interests in the slave trade. The bull *Inter Caetera* of 1493, issued by Pope Alexander VI, granted an exclusive right for Spain to the lands "discovered" by Columbus and obligated the conquest to provide instruction in the Catholic faith to the inhabitants, who would be held in subjection and domination in perpetuity.

In every instance of colonialism, from the Canary Islands in the fourteenth century to the west coast of Africa in the mid-fifteenth century and the Americas at the end of the fifteenth and beginning of the sixteenth centuries, the Portuguese and Spanish murdered the Indigenous, made them slaves, dispossessed them of their lands, and converted them to Christianity. The collection of papal bulls known as the Doctrine of Discovery shows that the logic of conquest was not founded on race, separated as Black enslavement and Indigenous genocide/dispossession. Stated differently, the origins of conquest *are* enslavement and genocidal dispossession of non-Christians. Conquest can otherwise be termed possession—possessing everything meaningful and valuable from non-Christians, including their lands, bodies, and souls. Providing further evidence, the *Requerimiento*, first used in 1514 after Africans had already been imported as slaves to the Americas, was read aloud by the Spanish colonizers to new lands.[2] "If you do not [submit]," they ordered,

> I certify to you that with the help of God, we shall powerfully enter your country, and shall make war against you in all ways and manners that we can, and shall subject you to the yoke of obedience of the Church and of their Highnesses; we shall take you and your wives and your children, and shall make slaves of them, and as such shall sell and dispose of them as their Highnesses may command; and we shall take away your goods, and shall do you all the mischief and damage that we can. (Parry and Keith 1984, 290)

The threat of violence and enslavement the *Requerimiento* promised demanded Indigenous acquiescence through submission to church and state. Furthermore, the colonizer blamed those who did not submit "and refuse to receive their lord, and resist and contradict him," for the "deaths and losses which shall accrue" (Parry and Keith 1984, 290). According to the logic of conquest, the fault for the violence against the non-Christians was theirs for not submitting to possession. The *Requerimiento* shows how genocide, land dispossession, enslavement, and property are inextricable from one another in the history of conquest against non-Christians. Racialization, including antiblackness, and its formation beyond a Christian/non-Christian binary would be developed later through colonization and functioned distinctly in place and time, constantly changing (Omi and Winant 1994).

In 1537, Pope Paul III issued the bull *Sublimus Deus*, stating that "Indians" and others "discovered by Christians" should not be "deprived of their liberty or possession of their property." It stated that the Natives were part of the "human race" and should not be denied the faith of Jesus Christ (Pope Paul III 1537). Despite this papal bull, the conquest of Latin America, including California, continued over centuries to enslave and possess Indigenous bodies, souls, land, and anything of value, natally alienating them (wherever they might originate) from their heritage, ancestors, kinship, and relationship with the land. The violence of slavery and dispossession existed beyond both the power of law and the conceptions of the human. Colonization would continue to simultaneously incorporate and eliminate, often through religious conversion. By the time the Spanish invaded California and the first mission was founded at San Diego in 1769, the logic of conquest had been well established as a genocidal project of possessing the Indigenous and their lands and including them into the structure of "civilization" through their conversion to Christianity. According to its founder, San Junípero Serra, the mission system was a "spiritual conquest" authorized by the church and state (Serra and Tibesar 1955, 153). It established twenty-one missions with military force as the point of the spear in the colonization of California to convert Natives to Christianity and expand the empire of Christendom through possession.

The California Missions

The priests, soldiers, settlers, and governance of Alta California entered the territories of diverse Indigenous peoples with many languages, dialects, worldviews, creation stories, and cultures. As non-Christians, the Indians were identified by the Spanish as *gente sin razón*—people without reason. The Spanish knew of their superiority as *gente de razón*—people with reason—or *human*.[3] The primary difference between the two was *gente de razón* acquiescence to Christendom by choice, force, or birth. The Spanish colonized California to expand their empire and prevent the Russian fur trade from becoming further established on the coast. The Spanish colonization of California began with few settlers and relatively small numbers of soldiers and priests. Without the use of large numbers of settlers to establish dominance over the land, the form of conquest utilized by the Spanish depended on the conversion of Indians into productive laborers and their incorporation into the structures of Christian sociality.

gente de razón should not be conflated with "white people," but it is what Black feminist scholar Sylvia Wynter terms a politics of being, "one waged over what is to be the descriptive statement of the human, about whose master code of symbolic life and death each human order organizes itself" (2003, 319). The concept of *gente de razón* structured, in the words of ethnic studies scholar Dylan Rodriguez, "the historical apparatuses of white embodiment as active practices and institutionalizations of sociality" (2020, 8). Within the colonial structure during the time of the mission system (1769–1834), people of color could ascend to embody whiteness through being possessed and incorporated. Through missionization, the Indian was to be alienated from the heritage of their ancestors, their kinship was acknowledged only if sanctioned by the church, and Native alienation separated them from their relationship with the earth. In the words of Wynter, "Given the conception of what it is to be human . . . you had to be seen by them as the negation of what they were. So *you*, too, had to *circumcise* yourself of yourself, in order to be fully human" (Scott 2000, 132). For the Indian to be contained within the sociality of humanness, they had to be extirpated symbolically from the land. Although they would remain racially Indian, the existence of their indigeneity outside the hegemony of church and state had to end so that their only social meaning was within the context of the *gente de razón*, the Spanish Christian conception of the human, or what can be called "civilization."[4]

Gente de razón and *gente sin razón* can be qualitatively understood as separate species, in the words of Frantz Fanon (2004, 5). The human, generated from the logic of conquest, served to wage war and enslave non-Christians. The theological structuring of the world required the extirpation, domestication, and extermination of non-Christians. The two species could not exist simultaneously in the historical creation of the human. All had to submit to, in the words of the *Requerimiento*, "the yoke of obedience of the Church and of their Highnesses" through death or the disavowal of self.

In California, the submission of Indians required conversion to Christianity through their enslavement at the missions. The historians and anthropologists who have studied the mission system have generally agreed that once an Indian was baptized, they were not free to leave. Scholars have debated whether this system was a form of slavery, with most concluding that Indians were not held as chattel and, therefore, were not enslaved. Following

Orlando Patterson, I argue against this limited definition that disavows Indian enslavement by the missionaries. Slavery, according to Patterson, is not dependent on property, and slavery *only* as a system of property fails as a definition (1982, 21). Indians themselves have for centuries understood their "yoke of obedience" to be enslavement, remaking them to embody whiteness through Christianity (Costo and Costo 1987).

Conquest was always rationalized religiously and was never a secular project. While Wynter argues that the logic of conquest today is now "purely secular" (Scott 2000, 165), I would argue that Christianity organized the original project and is perpetually part of the ordering of the world as a racialized, carceral, violent, and disciplinary sociality in which those who do not obey are subject to premature death. Little has changed in the empire-building carried out by nation-states since the founding of Mission San Diego in 1769. Labor continues to be exploited, and those who do not obey and ascend to white life are punished with gratuitous forms of terror and policing. At the same time, those who obey are continuously surveilled and criminalized for behaviors counter to colonial laws, including the United States' notion of freedom and democracy, which serves to maintain global hegemony and power over economies. The term *gente sin razón* is no longer applied. However, the reasoning holds in evaluating who is fully human—only the people who have been incorporated into the sociality of the conqueror.

Furthermore, the undergirding of heteropatriarchy's structuring of the social world of the Americas was first enforced through Christian conquest and continues unabated today. Heteropatriarchy, as a global project, is not secular. Its foundation in the Americas was established through the Christian reordering of the world, delegitimizing women leaders and making female-bodied persons susceptible to sexualized terror. Heteropatriarchy also structures gender as a binary and enforces heterosexuality. To think of gender differently is deemed unnatural, as according to Christianity, the natural order of life is a heteronormative, male and female, patriarchal, and economically productive nuclear family. Patriarchy teaches us proper parenting practices (*mothering*) and structures reproduction as the *fathering* of offspring.

At the California missions, the Franciscan fathers incarcerated baptized Indian women as young as six in *monjeríos* (Castillo 1994). The only release from their maximum-security imprisonment was through a marriage sanctioned by the missionaries. The purpose of the *monjeríos* was to convert Indian women (and their children) and secure their obedience to the structures of heteropatriarchy, domesticating them into productive possessions for Christendom. They were not free to be anything but monogamous, first to God and then to their husband. Likewise, Indian women were forced to be heterosexual and were required to reproduce. Neophyte couples (baptized Indians) who had challenges producing offspring or had miscarriages were subjected to violent and humiliating punishments, including forced inspection of their genitals, being held in the stockade, being whipped, women being forced to carry a wooden doll to mass, and men having to wear bull horns on their heads (Reid and Heizer 1968). Like chattel, the children of missionized women were also possessions of the missionaries and baptized without consent. Children born to neophytes were made slaves from birth. The *monjerios* institutionalized sexual violence, with reports of priests selecting the imprisoned girl or woman of their choice to rape (Miranda 2013, 23–24). The labor of Indians was exploited with gendered forms of work, including being leased out to the presidios (military forts) and private citizens. The payment for their leased labor went to the mission coffers. Conquest was gratuitous terrorism in possession of Indigenous lands, bodies, and souls, enforcing heteropatriarchy in every aspect of the invasion.

Mission San Gabriel

On its founding in 1771, the missionaries and soldiers at Mission San Gabriel were welcomed as kuuyam (guests) by the Taraaxam—"the people." Today, the Taraaxam are known as the Gabrielino. Named Gabrielino by the Spanish through their enslavement at the mission, many now use the endonym Tongva to represent the original people of the Los Angeles basin. Some descendants of the Taraaxam call themselves Kizh, from the domed circular willow houses they lived in. For several days in early September 1771, the Taraaxam gathered building materials and constructed dwellings for the Spanish using the same materials they built their kiyiiy (homes) from, primarily willow and tule. The Taraaxam went out of their way as hosts to welcome the Spanish, even decorating their cots with wildflowers (Palóu and Bolton 1926, 324). Indian actions documented by the priests and soldiers prove their intent to treat the Spanish as guests. The Indigenous protocol of welcoming guests extended to the foreigners to their lands, who through Taraaxam cultural knowledge must have looked like people needing assistance.

In my previous scholarship, I forwarded a theoretical framework named kuuyam, after the Indigenous protocols of welcoming people to our lands as guests, and Taraaxam attempts to form relations with them (Sepulveda 2018). The Spanish settlers were welcomed as guests by the Taraaxam in 1771, not merely as people traveling through, but with the intention to form lasting relations with mutual obligations. In a recent article, education scholars Theresa Stewart-Ambo and K. Wayne Yang differentiate between guests and visitors. They argue that "guests" obligate Indigenous people, while "visitors" do not; as they put it, "*Visit* implies some complicity in colonialism, in harm inflicted, and also refutes claims to permanence and to proprietorship over Indigenous lands." They ask: "What would it mean for a settler speaker of a land acknowledgment to say, 'I am a visitor, and I hope to become a proper guest?'" (Stewart-Ambo and Yang 2021, 34). Stewart-Ambo and Yang build from my use of kuuyam to offer an important reframing of land acknowledgments that move beyond the rote performative use of identifying which tribal nation's lands the speaker inhabits. The framing of the question above helps move non-Natives toward the Indigenous protocol I write about. However, Stewart-Ambo and Yang's framing of visitors relies on the definition of *visit* as temporary despite their simultaneous characterization of visitors as settlers. They define *visit* as "the act of going or coming to see a person or place socially or for some other reason." An alternative definition they provide for *visit* is "to inflict someone" (Stewart-Ambo and Yang 2021, 34). Both definitions of *visit* are acts or events, not permanent or long-lasting forms of settlement and colonialism. As Yang has written elsewhere, the violence of settlement "is not temporally contained in the arrival of the settler but is reasserted each day of occupation. This is why Patrick Wolfe . . . emphasizes that settler colonialism is a structure and not an event" (Tuck and Yang 2012, 34). *Visitor* implies that they will leave. However, even in death, settlers do not leave; their bodies are buried in the land.

The responsibility for the Taraaxam to be hosts exists whether the settler acknowledges us or not. Kuuyam moves beyond land acknowledgments by obligating non-Natives to form relations with land and Indigenous peoples—a performance of life that is otherwise to the structures of conquest. The welcome offered to the Spanish in 1771 by the Taraaxam necessitated reciprocal obligations. Unfortunately, their generosity was not returned in a welcomed way. The generosity provided by the Spanish was in the form of nonconsensual alienation from the worlds of their ancestors through spiritual possession. The Spanish did not attempt to be kuuyam because they viewed the Taraaxam not as equal human beings but as *sin razón*, without reason. In the Spanish worldview, Indians were pagans in need of spiritual teaching. Once they were baptized, as mission apologist Zephyrin Engelhardt explains, they were not permitted to return to a "wild and immoral life; because they bore the indelible mark of a Christian upon the soul which it was not allowed to desecrate" (1912, 265). Soldiers on horseback used dogs to hunt neophytes who escaped. For their fugitivism, Indians were harshly punished with whips and put in stocks, as were those who assisted them.

Soon after the Spanish established Mission San Gabriel, soldiers began raping Indian women and boys. According to San Junípero Serra, the soldiers would use their skills as horsemen and lasso women as they did cattle (Engelhardt 1912, 13). If the men resisted, they would be murdered. The chief of the local Taraaxam village, who had welcomed the Spanish, was killed when he attempted to enforce justice against a soldier who had raped a young Indian woman (Palóu and Bolton 1926, 325). The soldiers cut off the chief's head and put it on a stake outside the mission to visually show the Indians what would happen if they attempted to stop their sexual violence. The Spanish quickly became unwelcome in Tovaangar (the Los Angeles Basin and southern Channel Islands), and the early violence forever affected the relationship between the newcomers and the Natives.

The founding of Mission San Gabriel was not a temporally contained event. It was the foundation of a colonial structure of possession (land, bodies, and souls) that, after more than 250 years, has proven to be a permanent, ongoing, always-changing structure of dispossession. The people living on the lands of the Taraaxam today are not leaving. Therefore, they are incapable of visiting. What needs to change is not their occupation of the land but their relationship with the earth and Indigenous peoples, abolishing the continued logic of conquest that structures possession/dispossession and violence. To begin the long project of abolition, settlers can start understanding themselves as guests, obligating them to the land. Kuuyam is a praxis of relationality forming kinship and responsibility to both human and more-than-human. It is a performance of futurity as good ancestors.

The Multiculturalist Settlement of Los Angeles

Los Angeles's development began with Mission San Gabriel's establishment in 1771 and was followed by the founding of the pueblo in 1781. Tovaangar (the name means "the world") is more than a place. It is a system of knowledge relating people to land and establishing proper protocols and laws for living sustainably with the environment given through creation to the people and all living beings. Tovaangar is ancestral knowledge. Each place, village, mountain, river, spring, valley, rock formation, et cetera had stories associated with it that were spiritual and relational, reciprocally connecting the Taraaxam to land. The meaning of Tovaangar is mutually dependent on language, ceremonial cycles, and sacred history as kinship (Holm et al. 2003). Tovaangar is, as Potawatomi environmental scholar Robin Wall Kimmerer explains, our "identity, the connection to our ancestors, the home of our non-human kinfolk, our pharmacy, our library, the source of all that sustained us" (2013, 17). Taraaxam identity is inextricable from the land. Each village was independent and fundamental to individual and collective ontology. The result of the devastation to the land is severe and overwhelming grief, forever impacting Taraaxam ontology. For the Taraaxam, the ontological trauma is unhealable, and the ancestors' heritage is irrecuperable. This is not dispossession; this is the loss of self. Megacities such as Los Angeles are not places where we can dream of having the settlers leave and recuperate our former ways of life. The settler colonialism of Los Angeles is a permanent presence, necessitating radical change for the future, including the rematriation of land—returning the land to a relationship beyond conquest and heteropatriarchy. Rematriation does not require the removal of people or their indoctrination into Indigenous ways of being.

Forty-four settlers and four soldiers were recruited from Sinaloa and Sonora, México, to establish the pueblo of Los Angeles on Tovaangar. They first traveled to Mission San Gabriel, and then, on September 4, 1781, moved to the Taraaxam village of Yaanga, renaming it El Pueblo de Nuestra Señora la Reina de Los Ángeles del Río de Porciúncula. As historian David Samuel Torres-Rouff writes, the *pobladores* (settlers of the pueblo) entered "an already dense social, political, and economic landscape shaped by increasingly specialized Tongva strategies for environmental management, food production, and trade." The settlers applied their "spatial, racial, cultural, and commercial practices" to Yaanga (Torres-Rouff 2013, 19). Moreover, the change they effected on Yaanga and Yaavetam (the people of Yaanga) depended on the *pobladores'* participation in spiritual domination.

Of the forty-four original *pobladores*, only two were wholly Spanish and, therefore, white. The other forty-two were people of color, with twenty-six having Black ancestry and sixteen having Indian ancestry (Mason 2004). The structure of conquest utilized in settling Los Angeles relied on what Dylan Rodriguez has called multiculturalist white supremacy: "the 'diverse' social subjects (who are also commodified demographic objects)" promiscuously included in the project of white supremacy. They, Rodriguez elaborates, "inhabit the paradigms, methods, and relations of power that constitute the foundational violence of White Being, including but not limited to its conquest, colonial, racial chattel, and neoliberal imperial distensions" (2020, 17). The project of multiculturalist white supremacy selectively includes those who are historically excluded from the power formations of conquest. Spanish colonialism has a long history of including people of color in its project of white supremacy through settlement, containment, policing, coerced labor, evangelism, and forced conversion.

My ancestors include Los Angeles *pobladores* José Antonio Basillio Rosas, his wife, María Manuela Calixtra Hernández, and their children. On California's 1790 census, Basillio is documented as *coyote*—approximately three-quarters Indian and one-quarter Spanish. María Manuela is documented as *mulata*—half Black and half Spanish (Mason 2004). Despite being reported as people of color, they were also documented by the priests at Mission San Gabriel as *razón*—Christianized and possessed by whiteness. They were colonized into the structures of the human without authority over what constitutes humanity, alienated from their histories. Their presence as Los Angeles *pobladores* resulted from their ancestors' social death. Their sociality was only in relation to the sociality of the colonizer who had enslaved them and used their "bare life" for the ascendancy of white Christian life (Agamben 1998; Rodriguez 2020). Black and Indigenous bodies, such as my ancestors, were used to settle California and extend the empire of Spain and Christendom. María Manuela Calixtra Hernández's story of dispossession does not exist, nor does José Antonio Basillio Rosas's. I cannot re-create or recuperate what we lost through their enslavement and dispossession. As Jared Sexton explains, "The loss of indigeneity for Black peoples can be acknowledged only abstractly, and its recovery is lost to history" (2016, 588–89). The same can be said for the indigeneity of the Rosas ancestors. I have no records of their loss, and there is a lack of language to explain their dispossession of self. Despite their absence of subjectivity, their presence in California benefited the Spanish settlement project, the founding of Los Angeles, and the expansion of empire. They were not guests of the Taraaxam; they were the socially dead, whose bare life dispossessed the Yaavetam.

Written in 1781 by Teodoro de Croix, *capitán general* of the Provincias Internas of New Spain, the instructions and regulations for recruiting soldiers and families from México to California included the need for able-bodied men without vices to establish the pueblo. The document states that the pueblo "will be situated in the midst of a numerous population of Gentiles, [who are] docile and without malice but susceptible, like all Indians, to the first impressions of good or bad example set by the Spanish who settle among them aiming to civilize them." The instructions state that the *pobladores* were responsible for providing the Indians with "knowledge of our Sacred Religion, and the Sweet Dominion of our Catholic Monarch" (Parks 1931, 192). In other words, the Indians would be converted and dominated by church and state with the assistance of the settlers. Unmarried men were also instructed to marry Christian Indian women to set a good example for the converted Indians and thus extend the Catholic religion and heteropatriarchy. Historian Antonia I. Castañeda wrote, "To quell the sexual violence, strengthen the population base, and provide models of Christian family life, colonial authorities recruited married soldiers and settlers with families. They also provided incentives of land, animals, and supplies to soldiers who married Christianized Indian women, 'daughters of the country,' and remained in California permanently" (2000, 30). Central to the conquest of California, as elsewhere in Latin America, were gender, sexuality, and the reproduction of family norms.

María Manuela Calixtra Hernández and José Antonio Basillio Rosas's son José Carlos Rosas was born in 1758 in Rosario, Sinaloa, México, and came to California in 1781 with his parents to settle Los Angeles. Three years later, he married María Dolores, a seventeen-year-old Yaavet woman nearly a decade younger than him. The Rosases' marriage formed relations between the *pobladores* and the Yaavetam, but only through the sociality of the colonizer: María Dolores was baptized on the same day as the wedding. Although I would like to imagine a romantic story, I do not have any details of their marriage beyond the instructions to settlers and soldiers to marry Christian Indians, and the incentives they were given to do so. The church documentation does not list her Native name, only her colonized Spanish name, María Dolores. A year after they were married, they had their first child. In 1785, my direct ancestor María Serafina Antonia was born.[5] The officiating priest of her baptism at Mission San Gabriel recorded her ethnicity as *razón*, showing that for all purposes, she was possessed by whiteness, body and soul, negating her indigeneity.

Taraaxam and Yaavetam worlds that existed before Mission San Gabriel and Los Angeles are effectively erased. Their story is not of loss and recovery (although there are efforts to revitalize language and culture) but of loss without recovery or return. When my genealogical investigations have been able to connect me to specific precolonial places, such as Yaanga, many no longer exist. There is no temporal or spatial return for the descendants of the Yaavetam. Our worlds are gone forever. Downtown Los Angeles is built on Yaanga, with shadow-casting skyscrapers such as the Wilshire Grand Center at seventy-three stories and 1,100 feet high. "It is difficult to be Indian under any circumstances," L. Frank and Kim Hogeland write. "Think what it must be like to see a phenomenon like Los Angeles spreading over your meadows and valleys, diverting your rivers, building parking structures on your holy sites, transforming the land that nurtured your ancestors into something unrecognizable" (2007, 93). Still, our love for the land remains vital to who we are, even when the stories of the land can never be told again.

The Taraaxam experienced three waves of colonialism. First was the Spanish conquest, followed by Mexican colonialism and then American colonialism. In each phase, the indigeneity of the Taraaxam was viewed similarly: as something to eradicate and replace. The colonizer exploited Indian labor power and devastated the environment. The city of Los Angeles today is highly racialized. Simultaneously, the bodies of people of color are utilized for the ascendency of white life and the permanent occupation of Tovaangar. The populations of even the smallest immigrant communities in Los Angeles often outnumber the Taraaxam, whose population is less than a few thousand. By contrast, the population of Los Angeles County today, according to the 2020 US Census, includes approximately 5 million Hispanic or Latino people of any race, 2.5 million whites (non-Hispanic or Latino), 1.5 million Asians, 800,000 Black people, 163,000 American Indians or Alaska Natives, and 25,000 Native Hawaiians or other Pacific Islanders. According to the same census, Los Angeles County has a population exceeding 10 million (Los Angeles Almanac n.d.).

To sustain such a large population, the land was domesticated and developed. The colonizers transformed Paayme Paxaayt, the Los Angeles River, from a living riparian ecosystem into a concrete channel for wastewater runoff. Large water projects steal water from elsewhere, including the Owens Valley, to supply water for the city. The Los Angeles Aqueduct, as Tongva scholar AnMarie Mendoza writes, is "a perpetual assault against ancestral waters, indigenous rights and well-being" (2019, 5). The history of legal dispossession, from the founding of the pueblo in 1781 to the continued theft of waters from the Nüümü of Owens Valley, is part of the long history of gratuitous terror inflicted on the land and Indigenous bodies and souls as part of the ongoing conquest of Tovaangar.

Kuuyam as Radical Imaginary

Although centuries of displacement, development, dispossession, and alienation have impaired Taraaxam relationality to Tovaangar, it still serves as the radical imaginary guiding our visions of the future and our relationship with non-Indigenous people and communities (Coulthard 2010, 81). As Yellowknives Dene scholar Glen Coulthard explains, this place-based imaginary "serves as the ethical foundation from which many Indigenous people and communities continue to resist and critique the dual imperatives of state sovereignty and capitalist accumulation that constitute our colonial present" (2010, 82). An otherwise world based on mutual obligation that does not compete with nature but embraces it as part of the community is possible. It begins with a rehearsal of life as good ancestors, guests and hosts, reorienting our worldviews to know that place has spirit and life beyond human interests (Vaughn 2019).

Environmental damage is best understood as the violence of colonial land relations, rather than as pollution or climate change (Liboiron 2021, 6–7). The solution, if there is one, to ongoing environmental harm is not cleaning up the environment or curbing greenhouse gases (although these are critical) but abolishing the logics of conquest that continue to shape our worlds. Formed through the Doctrine of Discovery, Manifest Destiny, and slavery, conquest provided colonizers with the ongoing playbook for gratuitous terror—taking all that has value and assaulting the spirit of people and place. The prison and the devastation of land are different, yet related, outgrowths of conquest wherein land and people are viewed as resources to violently dominate and possess. If abolition is a rehearsal of life, then kuuyam is a performance of transforming human-land kinship(s) and establishing mutual obligation and responsibility rather than exploitation. As a collection of communities, we can radically move beyond exploitation, commodification, and containment. Those living in Los Angeles can channel the knowledge of the Taraaxam, the people who existed prior to conquest, to become kuuyam and learn together how to live more sustainably in gratitude for the beauty of Tovaangar. Kuuyam is a "grammar of animacy," acknowledging the spirit of the more-than-human, gifting us relationality with the land as our teacher (Kimmerer 2013, 57). I use kuuyam, the plural of *kuuy* (guest), to denote that the well-being of individuals is dependent on the health of the whole. Kuuyam invites everyone to radically imagine a future based on mutual obligation, reciprocity, responsibility, and healthy human-land kinship(s). Becoming kuuyam is a way of living in this world for the generations yet to come—as good ancestors—beyond the social death of conquest.

NOTES

1   The name Taraaxam, translated into English, means "the people." For this chapter I choose to use this endonym rather than the more familiar exonym Gabrielino or the endonyms Tongva and Kizh. I have chosen not to italicize the words from the Taraaxam language in this chapter.

2   The first African slaves were imported to the Americas in 1510.

3   In the California mission records of baptism, marriage, and burial, the priests used *razón* to indicate that a person was included in the humanity of the Spanish and the church.

4   I capitalize *Indigenous* as a proper noun when referencing people. *Indigeneity* is a noun denoting relationality to the earth and is lowercase.

5   Serafina Rosas was born on September 2, 1785. The following month, on October 25, Taraaxam leaders Toypurina and Nicolás José led an uprising against Mission San Gabriel.

WORKS CITED

Adiele, Pius Onyemechi. 2017. *The Popes, the Church and the Transatlantic Enslavement of Black Africans, 1418–1839*. New York: Georg Olms Verlag.

Agamben, Giorgio. 1998. *Homo Sacer: Sovereign Power and Bare Life*. 1998. Stanford, CA: Stanford University Press.

Castillo, Edward D. 1994. "Gender Status Decline, Resistance, and Accommodation Among Female Neophytes in the Missions of California: A San Gabriel Case Study." *American Indian Culture and Research Journal* 18 (1): 67–93.

Castañeda, Antonia I. 2000. "Hispanas and Hispanos in a Mestizo Society." *OAH Magazine of History* 14 (4): 29–35.

Costo, Rupert, and Jeannette Henry Costo. 1987. *The Missions of California: A Legacy of Genocide*. San Francisco: Indian Historian.

Coulthard, Glen. 2010. "Place Against Empire: Understanding Indigenous Anti-Colonialism." *Affinities: A Journal of Radical Theory, Culture, and Action* 4 (2): 79–83.

Engelhardt, Zephyrin. 1912. *The Missions and Missionaries of California*, vol. 2, *Upper California*. San Francisco: James H. Barry.

Fanon, Frantz. 2004. *The Wretched of the Earth*. Translated by Richard Philcox. New York: Grove.

Frank, L., and Kim Hogeland. 2007. *First Families: A Photographic History of California Indians*. Berkeley, CA: Heyday.

Gilmore, Ruth Wilson. 2020. "Abolition on Stolen Land." Keynote address for the UCLA Luskin Institute convening "Sanctuary Spaces: Reworlding Humanism," October 9, 2020. https://vimeo.com/467484872.

Holm, Tom, et al. 2003. "Peoplehood: A Model for the Extension of Sovereignty in American Indian Studies." *Wicazo Sa Review* 18:7–24.

Kimmerer, Robin Wall. 2013. *Braiding Sweetgrass: Indigenous Wisdom, Scientific Knowledge and the Teachings of Plants*. Minneapolis: Milkweed.

King, Tiffany Lethabo. 2019. *The Black Shoals: Offshore Formations of Black and Native Studies*. Durham, NC: Duke University Press.

Liboiron, Max. 2021. *Pollution Is Colonialism*. Durham, NC: Duke University Press.

Los Angeles Almanac. n.d. "Racial/Ethnic Composition, Los Angeles County, 1990–2020 Census." https://www.laalmanac.com/population/po13.php (accessed February 1, 2023).

Mason, William M. 2004. *Los Angeles Under the Spanish Flag: Spain's New World*. Burbank: Southern California Genealogical Society.

Mendoza, AnMarie Ramona. 2019. "The Aqueduct Between Us: Inserting and Asserting an Indigenous California Indian Perspective About Los Angeles Water." Master's thesis, UCLA. https://escholarship.org/uc/item/9nn7v9z8.

Miranda, Debora A. 2013. *Bad Indians: A Tribal Memoir*. Berkeley, CA: Heyday.

Omi, Michael, and Howard Winant. 1994. *Racial Formation in the United States: From the 1960s to the 1990s*. 2nd ed. New York: Routledge.

Palóu, Francisco, and Herbert Eugene Bolton. 1926. *Historical Memoirs of New California*. Vol. 2. Berkeley: University of California Press, 1926.

Parks, Marion. 1931. "Instructions for the Recruital of Soldiers and Settlers for California—Expedition of 1781: Teodoro de Croix to Captain Fernando de Rivera y Moncada." *Annual Publication of the Historical Society of Southern California* 15 (1): 189–203.

Parry, John H., and Robert G. Keith. 1984. *New Iberian World*, vol. 1. New York: Times Books.

Patterson, Orlando. 1982. *Slavery and Social Death: A Comparative Study*. Cambridge, MA: Harvard University Press.

Pope Paul III. 1537. "Sublimus Deus." Papal Encyclicals Online. https://www.papalencyclicals.net/paulo3/p3subli.htm.

Reid, Hugo, and Robert F. Heizer. 1968. *The Indians of Los Angeles County: Hugo Reid's Letters of 1852*. Southwest Museum Papers, no. 21. Los Angeles: Southwest Museum.

Rodriguez, Dylan. 2020. *White Reconstruction: Domestic Warfare and the Logics of Genocide*. New York: Fordham University Press.

Scott, David. 2000. "The Re-Enchantment of Humanism: An Interview with Sylvia Wynter." *Small Axe: A Caribbean Journal of Criticism* 4 (2): 119–207.

Sepulveda, Charles. 2018. "Our Sacred Waters: Theorizing *Kuuyam* as a Decolonial Possibility." *Decolonization: Indigeneity, Education, Society Journal* 7 (1): 40–58.

Serra, Junípero, and Antonine Tibesar. 1955. *Writings of Junípero Serra*, vol. 2. Washington, DC: Academy of American Franciscan History.

Sexton, Jared. 2016. "The Vel of Slavery: Tracking the Figure of the Unsovereign." *Critical Sociology* 42 (4-5): 583–97.

Stewart-Ambo, Theresa, and K. Wayne Yang. 2021. "Beyond Land Acknowledgment in Settler Institutions." *Social Text* 39 (1) (146): 21–46.

Torres-Rouff, David Samuel. 2013. *Before L.A.: Race, Space, and Municipal Power in Los Angeles, 1781–1894*. New Haven, CT: Yale University Press.

Tuck, Eve, and K. Wayne Yang. 2012. "Decolonization Is Not a Metaphor." *Decolonization: Indigeneity, Education and Society Journal* 1 (1): 1–40.

Vaughn, Kehaulani. 2019. "Sovereign Embodiment: Native Hawaiians and Expressions of Diasporic Kuleana." *Hūlili Journal* 11:227–45.
Whyte, Kyle. 2017. "Indigenous Climate Change Studies: Indigenizing Futures, Decolonizing the Anthropocene." *English Language Notes* 55 (1–2): 153–62.
Wynter, Sylvia. 2003. "Unsettling the Coloniality of Being/Power/Truth/Freedom: Towards the Human, After Man, Its Overrepresentation—An Argument." *CR: The New Centennial Review* 3 (3): 257–337.

3

Killing the Dead

Genocide and Antiblackness

Moon-Kie Jung and João H. Costa Vargas

Having narrowly escaped Nazi Germany's invasion of Poland in 1939, Raphaël Lemkin circuitously made his way to Durham, North Carolina, by 1941. Sanctuary in the form of a teaching post at Duke University School of Law awaited the indefatigable jurist and activist against genocide, a term he would coin a few years later. During his brief tenure there, he frequently gave speeches around the state to various civic groups, alerting his presumably white audiences of Nazi atrocities taking place in Europe. To his new public, he asked rhetorically, "If women, children, and old people would be murdered a hundred miles from here, wouldn't you run to help? Then why do you stop this decision of your heart when the distance is five thousand miles instead of a hundred?" After his talks, audience members would approach him and echo his earnestness: "I am ashamed that we are standing idle and watching innocent people being slaughtered" (Lemkin 2013, 103, 105). To him and them, undoubtedly congregated in segregated spaces of the blood-soaked Jim Crow South, that the answer to his first question was affirmative went without saying: of course, Lemkin's new acquaintances would intervene to prevent the killing of innocent people nearby. What was required was the geographic enlargement of their moral circle to embrace Jews and other persecuted peoples of Europe.

In his autobiography, Lemkin noted that his first train trip to Durham had had a brief layover in Lynchburg, Virginia:

> And here I saw for the first time, in the rest rooms of the station, the inscriptions "For Whites" and "For Colored." These intrigued me, and I innocently asked the Negro porter if there were indeed special toilets for Negroes. He gave me a puzzled look, mixed with hostility, and did not answer. After seventeen years in the United States I understand now that he must have thought I was making fun of him.
> As the train moved south, I kept thinking about those inscriptions with all the naïvete of a newcomer. (Lemkin 2013, 100)

This contemplation led him to reminisce fondly about the "one Negro in the entire city" of Warsaw, "a dancer in a popular night club, where he pounded the floor with both feet as if to destroy it." This memory immediately pivoted to a wistful comparison: "Everyone enjoyed his dancing and tried to invite him for drinks. A feeling of curiosity and friendliness prevailed toward this lonely black man in Poland. But toward the Jews, I could not help thinking, there was not the same friendliness" (Lemkin 2013, 100). The dancer's supposed loneliness and desire to destroy, despite the friendliness shown him, did not waylay Lemkin's envious reflection, neither in 1941 on the train nor seventeen years later.

Lemkin's relentless advocacy for outlawing genocide, his life's work, culminated in the unanimous passage, in 1948, of the Convention on the Prevention and Punishment of the Crime of Genocide by the United Nations and, by 1950, its ratification by a sufficient number of member states, which notably did not include the United States. A year later, in 1951, expressly leveraging the convention's definition and framework, the Civil Rights Congress (CRC) submitted the aptly named petition *We Charge Genocide* to the United Nations, accusing the United States of committing genocide against Black people. At its heart, "scrupulously [keeping] within the purview of the Convention," the petition catalogued copiously, if necessarily far from comprehensively, the "persistent slaughter of the Negro people . . . on a basis of 'race'" throughout the country, including North Carolina, during just the previous half decade (CRC [1951] 2020, xxvi, 3).[1]

Apparently confident in his understanding of Black people's plight in the United States, having somehow swiftly shed his earlier naivete, Lemkin did not hesitate to weigh in on the CRC initiative. Before drafting the petition, the CRC had polled various prominent organizations and individuals, including Lemkin, on the idea of charging the United States. In his autobiography, William L. Patterson, the CRC petition's editor and main architect, recalled Lemkin's unequivocal reaction: "How an honest person viewing the American scene impartially could come to any conclusion other than that forms of genocide were being practiced in the United States was too difficult for us [the CRC] to see. Professor Lemkin experienced no such difficulty. In a considerable correspondence with me, he argued vehemently that the provisions of the Genocide Convention bore no relation to the U.S. Government or its position vis-à-vis Black citizens" (Patterson 1971, 179).

The CRC's subsequent submission and publication of the petition did not change Lemkin's mind. In a lengthy letter to the editor, he made his view on the topic clear to the readers of the *New York Times*: "By no stretch of imagination can one discover in the United States an intent or plan to exterminate the Negro population, which is increasing in conditions of evident prosperity and progress. . . . The tragically dramatic nature of genocide should not be permitted to be deflated."[2]

Needless to say, Lemkin's perspective prevailed, and among non-Black people, genocide quickly became a heretical notion relative to the Black diaspora. In effect, in this moment of genocide's conceptual emergence in the world, when its meaning was initially molded and shaped, Black people were excluded, even as their predicament clearly met the criteria laid out in the official definition. Ironically but tellingly, in the decades-long struggle to have the US Senate ratify the convention, segregationists of the South took more seriously the possibility of genocide charges being brought against the United States, while liberals insisted on the preposterousness of such an idea; in 1988, the United States finally ratified the convention, but only with a number of caveats—two "reservations," five "understandings," and one "declaration"—attached. At the turn of the millennium, Samantha Power, in her universally heralded book on genocide, still parroted Lemkin and other liberals' rhetoric and de facto definition of genocide: "Although the United States' dismal record on race certainly exposed it to charges of racism and human rights abuse, only a wildly exaggerated reading of the genocide convention left the southern lawmakers vulnerable to genocide charges" ([2002] 2013, 67).

In this chapter, we analyze the case against the United States that the CRC laid out in *We Charge Genocide*, which was as groundbreaking and insightful as it was radical and courageous. We do not, however, belabor the point that it should have been taken seriously at the time. This *historical* exclusion of Black people is too obviously antiblack for further debate.

Instead, through a discussion of philosopher Claudia Card's compelling reconceptualization of genocide as social death, we reconsider the *theoretical* aptness of genocide for the analysis of Black people's plight. In the end, we agree with Lemkin, Power, and others that there is a fundamental incompatibility, but not because the concept would have to be deflated or wildly exaggerated. Rather, genocide misrecognizes antiblackness, Black people's predicament in modernity, by underestimating its depth.[3] It is genocide beyond genocide. We conclude by critically reassessing the CRC's abiding belief in the redeemability of US democracy and calling for the abolishment of this modern world, a world without sanctuary for Black people.

We Charge Genocide is a pioneering and, we insist, yet to be fully acknowledged analytical and political effort. Presenting a radical perspective on racism, its editor, William Patterson, and fellow petitioners, including W. E. B. Du Bois, Claudia Jones, Eslanda Robeson, Paul Robeson, and Mary Church Terrell, backed by extensive and precise research and a well-orchestrated transcontinental political strategy, boldly accused the US state of genocide against its Black citizens.

We admire the initiative's innovative, meticulous, and daring socialist nature. We draw inspiration from the authors' unflinching and courageous ethical commitment and labor to produce such a landmark document that sought to place the multiple and enduring dehumanizing experiences of US Black people on the world stage. We are aware of the fierce and harmful opposition the authors and collaborators—including Jones, Du Bois, Robeson, and especially Patterson, who was eventually incarcerated (certainly due to his allegedly subversive activities)—received from the US government as well as from multiple Black organizations, including the NAACP (Anderson 2003; Horne 2013). For these same reasons—the monumentality of the publication and its accompanying analytical and political efforts—we find the petition a paradigmatic, bold, and precise, if still underexplored and underappreciated, compendium of racism and its manifestations. We agree with Patterson that the petition incites all with a progressive moral consciousness "to think about the broad range of the necessary and political changes to be made by the people" (1971, 204).

We Charge Genocide embodies accumulated Black political genius, particularly as imagined and applied consciously in the preceding decades, marked by deep recession, government-sponsored anticommunism, global warfare, and continued and intensifying violence against Black people. Many of its findings and analyses regarding racism and the state of terror affecting the most vulnerable population, as well as its political guidelines suggesting a combination of popular mobilization and legal action, served as important references for the recrudescing Black freedom struggles of the ensuing decades. It is unsurprising that Patterson, until the fallout over the China question—he was opposed to the "increasingly passionate tie" between the Black Panther Party (BPP) and that country—was a respected elder, a reference point, for those young militants, who affectionately considered him a "Genuine Original Black Panther" (Horne 2013, 201, 196). The petition was on the reading list of the BPP (Horne 2013, 195), and it remained so when one of the authors joined the Los Angeles Coalition Against Police Abuse in 1995, itself run by surviving BPP activists (Vargas 2006, 2018).

Part III constitutes the bulk of the petition, composing nearly 60 percent of the entire text, and lists case after case of violent deaths, bodily and mental harm, and conditions deliberately inflicted to cause the total or partial destruction of Black people between January 1945 and June 1951. Note that these categories correspond to the first three criteria of the UN's definition of genocide. Article II of the UN Convention on the Prevention and Punishment of the Crime of Genocide, adopted on December 9, 1948, defines genocide as

> any of the following acts committed with intent to destroy, in whole or in part, a national, ethnical, racial or religious group, as such:
>
> a   Killing members of the group;
> b   Causing serious bodily or mental harm to members of the group;
> c   Deliberately inflicting on the group conditions of life calculated to bring about its physical destruction in whole or in part;
> d   Imposing measures intended to prevent births within the group;
> e   Forcibly transferring children of the group to another group.
> (CRC [1951] 2020, xii)

As they introduce the evidence, the petition's authors insist on a planetary moral "common sense" that should be scandalized by Black suffering. At the same time, they mistrust the actuality of such common sense and preemptively alert readers that the gathered evidence is only an imperfect and limited translation of an all-encompassing climate of terror Black people experience routinely—that the evidence listed "falls far short of adequately presenting reality . . . [as] the vast majority of crimes against Black people are never recorded . . . , [which is] itself an index to genocide" (CRC [1951] 2020, 57). We are thus presented with a paradox: on the one hand, *We Charge*

Genocide hopes for and demands a global recognition of the permanent state of emergency under which US Black people find themselves; on the other, the petitioners concede that the data they present may not be capable of adequately conveying the intensity, reach, and quality of the phenomenon under scrutiny. It follows that the petition's statement that Black genocide is "a crime . . . manifestly and overwhelmingly true, known to history and notorious to the world" is more of a hopeful plea than an accepted certainty (CRC [1951] 2020, 57).

Hence the petitioners' presentation of evidence that carefully follows the Genocide Convention's definition: analytical precision is employed as a means to render the evidence legible via the juridical rubric of genocide. It is a tall, perhaps unfulfillable, order, as the socially shared symbology that dehumanizes Black people also renders inaccessible and unremarkable their isolation, suffering, and death. In other words, the CRC knows that data on Black suffering are at once remote (given hypersegregation) and filtered through an all-powerful collective unconscious that renders such suffering unexceptional, if not irrelevant.

Substantiation of Article II (a), "Killing Members of the Group," is presented in an extensive yet concise and detached manner. For each calendar year between 1945 and 1951, a large number of cases, about eight per page, are described in short paragraphs of four to ten lines. War veterans, children, women, men, the elderly, entire families: multiple vignettes, one after the other, provide a simultaneous sense of randomness, ubiquity, and systematicity. Paradoxically, the sheer repetition of deaths under circumstances that should be deemed most unjust and reprehensible engenders a sense of ordinariness that is difficult to reconcile with the imperative of demonstrating genocide as a scandalous, horrific, and unacceptable fact. While the petitioners assert that genocide is an overlooked phenomenon authorized by cultural and institutional rules, tacit and explicit, they also want to interrupt the commonsensical acceptance of terror against Black people. Patterson recognizes this tension and challenge, and the recourse to an international forum is an attempt to disrupt the climate of ordinary terror by contrasting it to the country's—and, more specifically, the UN's—alleged democratic and humanitarian convictions, so central in the post–World War II context in which the threats of fascism and mass murder were vivid.

To defamiliarize the country's own production of terror is therefore critical. It is a hopeful move, as on it hinges the entire project of denouncing genocide: either the United States comes to terms with its quotidian brutality against its Black "citizens," or internal intolerance and fascism will prevail and, in the process, endanger the planet. In a minutious exposition of everyday brutality and harm, *We Charge Genocide* holds the mirror up to the empire-state and expects that it will respond by rendering scandalous that which until then was culturally mundane and unremarkable.[4] Given the frequent, direct participation of the police in the deaths and/or the official refusal to investigate and prosecute, these multiple cases also suggest that the death of Black people is consistently sanctioned by law and custom. For example, consider just three cases from 1945:

> *August 15.*—LILA BELLA CARTER, 16 years old, was raped and murdered at *Pine Island, South Carolina*, under circumstances which pointed suspiciously to a white insurance agent. When the young woman's father went to authorities to demand an investigation, he was jailed. Miss Carter's neck and jaw were broken and she had been placed face down in a pool of water in order to give the impression that she had met her death drowning. No action was taken against the rapist.
>
> *September 9.*—MOSES GREEN, Veteran of World War I, was shot to death by two Aiken County law officers near *Elenton, South Carolina*. The officers were deputy sheriffs who were identified. Green was returning from town in his truck and as he stepped out into his own yard he was shot without warning.
>
> *December 23.*—MR. AND MRS. H. O'DAY SHORT and their two small daughters were burned to death two days before Christmas, 1945, in a fire of incendiary origin set by persons who did not want them to move into a "white neighborhood" in *Fontana, California*. The family had received threatening notes and the police told the family that they were "out of bounds." There was no electricity in the [Shorts'] home and neighbors knew that the family was temporarily using lamps. While the Shorts were away, people broke into their home, sprayed the interior with an inflammable chemical, and left. When the Shorts returned, the father struck a match, and the lamp fuel, believed to be kerosene, exploded. All four were fatally burned. (CRC [1951] 2020, 59, 60, 61)

A collective unconscious endorses and renders unremarkable such events. The petitioners are aware of the banality of terror's desensitizing effect on a dominant culture that refuses Black humanity. Yet they have no choice but to press on with the seemingly endless recitation of assassinations, as if their dispassionate presentation will be sufficient to both provoke national and international publics and render compelling the juridical case to the UN.

Regarding Article II (b), "Causing Serious Bodily and Mental Harm to Members of the Group," even though "serious mental harm" is more difficult to demonstrate than "serious bodily harm," the CRC proposes that there is a permanent and ubiquitous state of terror that informs and is furthered by the constant threat and manifestation of violence and lynching. Mental harm—a form of continuous lynching, according to the petitioners—does not depend only on the immediate experience of physical violence. The high likelihood and societal sanctioning of violence also render it terrifyingly effective as a permanent and pervasive symbolic threat. Quoting at length an unpublished paper by Harry Haywood and Earl Conrad, titled "Atrocities Against 15 Million Negro Citizens," Patterson supports their finding that "perennial, hour by hour, moment by moment lynching of the Negro's soul in countless psychological, in myriad physical forms . . . is the greatest and most enduring lynching of all." Haywood and Conrad continue: "This is written into the spiritual hanging of all those millions, it is carved into their daily thinking, woven into their total living experience. They are lynched by the thousands of glances from white supremacists all over the land every day, in discourtesies; insults, snobbery; in all the great events of the total national experience as well as in all the minutest experience" (CRC [1951] 2020, 78).

A veiled threat is also expressed here, which Patterson does not elaborate on but could have been left in the text as a calculated move. If the extensive recitation of harm caused on Black people is unable to sensitize non-Black people, principally whites, perhaps a subliminal threat of Black revolt would work as extra incentive to take *We Charge Genocide* seriously. We say "subliminal" because, in the context of seemingly interminable cases of abuse against Black people, the reference to "chronic rage" can easily be overlooked. Yet, as suggested elsewhere (Alves and Vargas 2019), both a refusal of Black humanity and a proportional fear of Black revolt, exemplified paradigmatically in the Haitian Revolution, primordially inform the collective unconscious and the institutional apparatuses of empire-state formations in the Black diaspora (Vargas 2018). Black rage can thus be consciously overlooked, but it will certainly mobilize subliminally the ever-present collective "fear of a Black planet," to use Public Enemy's apt expression.

Substantiating Article II (c), "Deliberately Inflicting on the Group Conditions of Life Calculated to Bring About Its Physical Destruction in Whole or in Part," Patterson introduces the litany of evidence by stating that, due to the effects of residential segregation, including barred access to health care and discrimination in employment, "more than 30,000 Negroes die each year in the United States that would not have died if they had been white" (CRC [1951] 2020, 125). This is a devastating statement suggesting that premature death by preventable causes, and a lifespan more than eight years shorter than the national average, is a direct consequence of racism, imposed residential separation, and its limit manifestation, genocide. Indeed, this statement anticipates prison abolitionist and geographer Ruth Gilmore's (2002, 261) incisive definition of racism: "the state-sanctioned and/or extra-legal production and exploitation of group-differentiated vulnerabilities to premature death, in distinct yet densely interconnected political geographies."

Because the CRC petition strictly follows the order in which the UN genocide criteria are presented, some of its most powerful arguments only appear halfway through the document. For example, on page 126, Patterson and his collaborators zero in on "the imposition of genocidal conditions"—that is, "inferior living and health conditions"—whose deadly consequences eclipse the number of Black people killed each year by legal and extralegal means. Just when readers are perhaps coming to terms with the ubiquity and undeniability of physical and psychological terror against Black people, they learn that such facts are mere details of a much broader, deeper, and determining context in which "genocidal factors begin with conception" (CRC [1951] 2020, 126). Prefiguring research and theoretical developments on the myriad forms of "killing the Black body" (Roberts 1997; see also Washington 2006), Patterson shows how perinatal death and infant and maternal mortality are consistently and uniquely more frequent among Black people. For example, according to several government sources of data, such as the Office of Vital Statistics, there were, in 1948 alone, 7,808 "non-white children under one year of age . . . and 959 non-white mothers . . . killed by the genocidal conditions." Compounding the case for a context in which "genocidal racism" continuously generates early death by preventable causes, the petition exposes the toll of several diseases on the Black population. Tuberculosis, pneumonia, influenza, nephritis and nephrosis, syphilis, gastritis, enteritis, colitis: all are shown to disproportionately cut short the lives of those living in hypersegregated Black environments (CRC [1951] 2020, 126–27). As well, fatal work-related accidents indicate not only discrimination against Black workers but also a highly segregated health care system that mostly refuses to serve Black people and/or admit Black doctors. Regarding the discrimination against Black workers, the CRC states that it does not always take place overtly, and indeed is more effective when, for example, insurance companies refuse to insure or charge higher premiums to those occupations in which Black people are overrepresented.

As a paradigmatic expression of the normative authorization of violence, sexual terror reveals the limits of the concept of racism; it demands a more precise conceptualization. *We Charge Genocide* recognizes the centrality of rape as constitutive of the climate of terror formatted by racism and genocide: false accusations of rape of white women by Black men and unpunished rape of Black women by white men. Such a climate of terror is highly effective politically: it discourages collective mobilization, protest, registration, and voting. Yet the petition's narrative vacillates conceptually because, while it recognizes the deeply ingrained false accusations and inconsequential actualizations of rape against Black people, it demands that such deeply ingrained imposed abjection and brutality be acknowledged and redressed.

We Charge Genocide presents sexual terror as a technology of social and ontological border enforcement. Articulated with imposed residential segregation, constantly reinforced by symbolic and actual physical violence, containment, and hypersurveillance (Sugrue 1996; Vargas 2018), sexual terror grounds fundamental aspects of social organization, including imputed degrees of humanity. Drawing on a rich tradition of Black research, as indicated above, and anticipating studies conducted decades later (e.g., Davis 1978, 1983; Baldus, Pulaski, and Woodworth 1983; Marquart, Ekland-Olson, and Sorensen 1998), the petition's Appendix Document B presents a detailed analysis by Dr. Oakley Johnson that draws on prison records from the state of Louisiana. Johnson shows how the death sentence for accusations of rape is applied almost exclusively to Black defendants. Concluding the thorough investigation, Johnson affirms that "the Negro press is right in seeing a connection between segregation and white supremacy on the one hand, and police brutality on the other, and right to see a connection between both and those rape trials in which the death sentence is reserved for Negroes" (CRC [1951] 2020, 226).

Following this line of reasoning, we argue that the systematic rape of Black people—as well as the cultural climate and juridical apparatus that legitimize it—is a bond that connects, expands, and in turn is energized by the various molecular aspects of what the petition presents as genocide. Put in another way, the rape of Black people—and, paradigmatically, rape of Black women and trans Black people (McGuire 2010; Rosen 2009; Snorton 2017; Vargas and Jung 2021) and its constellation of accusations, fears, and impunity—constitutes the very fabric of the US polis. Rape is ubiquitous and formative. Yet rape does not need to be always and already actualized for its symbolic power of terror to be activated. The threat and accusation of rape are sufficient to configure a transhistorical context of sexual terror. They bring together the symbolic (dehumanization of Black people), the pragmatic (geographies as actualized in patterns of residential segregation), constitutional and customary law (prohibition of interracial marriage and its reverberations), and law enforcement (Black brutalization/criminalization and/or incapacity to claim harm and non-Black culpability), including constant scrutiny deployed via the afterlives of the plantation (Hartman 1997, 2006).[5] The ubiquity of rape as it impacts primarily and fundamentally Black people unveils a social and ontological structure in which the Afro-descended, in multiple and effective manners, are simultaneously rendered permanent *flesh* (Spillers 2003, 206) and subjected to a terrorist panoptical surveillance apparatus.

The UN's and thereby the CRC's definition of genocide is the most widely cited among genocide scholars, according to Claudia Card. Nonetheless, she notes, "every clause in the UN definition is controversial." With regard to the first clause on killing, for instance, what would be the qualifying number? Shifting the focus away from "body counts" and toward conceptual clarity, Card identifies *social death* as the defining quality: "genocide is social death." The converse is not necessarily true, as social death is not unique to genocide and "has many sources—slavery, banishment, disfigurement, illness, even self-chosen isolation." Still, among them, genocide, like slavery, is "an extreme of social death"—an evil (Card 2010, 237). Card argues further that "social death is utterly central to the evil of genocide, not just when a genocide is primarily cultural but even when it is homicidal on a massive scale . . . distinguish[ing] the peculiar evil of genocide from the evils of other mass murders" (2003, 63).[6]

Although Card adopts *social death* from Orlando Patterson's (1982) classic *Slavery and Social Death*, her conceptualization is distinct from his. In his formulation, slavery is social death, and this death has three "constituent elements." It is directly violent through and through. As Patterson notes, "There is no known slaveholding society where the whip was not considered an indispensable instrument." Slavery also natally alienates, rendering the enslaved a "genealogical isolate." With "no socially recognized existence outside of [their] master," the enslaved has no legitimate familial claims and obligations—past, present, or future. Finally, slavery entails general dishonor: "The slave could have no honor because of the origin of [their] status, the indignity and all-pervasiveness of [their] indebtedness, [their] absence of any independent social existence, but most of all because [they were] without power except through another." In sum, "slavery is the permanent, violent domination of natally alienated and generally dishonored persons." Consequently, the enslaved is a "socially dead person" or a "social nonperson" (Patterson 1982, 4–5, 10, 13).

Card does not claim that genocide and slavery have in common the same constituent elements. In her theorization of genocide, social death denotes a "major loss of social vitality" that "exists through relationships, contemporary and intergenerational, that create contexts and identities that give meaning and shape to our lives" (Card 2003, 63). She continues, "Some of those relationships are with kin, friends, and coworkers. Others are less personal and mediated by basic social institutions—economic, political, religious, educational, and so on. Loss of social vitality comes with the loss of such connections" (Card 2010, 237).

Genocide is inflicted upon and suffered by a *people*. It is a collective loss. Reminding us of the term's etymology—Lemkin's (1944, 79) portmanteau of the Greek *genos*, for race or tribe, and the Latin *cide*, for killing—Card conceives of genocide as "the murder of a people" (2010, 243, 246). In fact, "harm to a people does not necessarily harm an individual member" (Card 2010, 247). In this way, it differs from slavery, which does destroy each and every enslaved person. The social death of genocide begets a *social nonpeople*, whereas the social death of slavery produces *social nonpersons*—an all-important distinction that neither Card nor Patterson makes clear. Genocide can involve the social death of each and every person in the most extreme cases, such as Nazi death camps, but such instances are not paradigmatic of genocide in general.

What is the nature of the *social* in the social death of a people? As Card explains, it refers to the collective life of interpersonal as well as institutional relationships internal to and constitutive of a people. Undiscussed by Card, the social death of genocide, a condition imposed from without, also entails a second, external sense of the social—that of the dominant society or state: it is the loss of legitimate standing or recognition of a people qua a people because of and relative to a dominant power. Again, this loss does not necessarily mean a likewise loss for individual persons. For example, forced assimilation—as infamously captured in the late nineteenth-century utterance of US Army captain Richard Pratt, "Kill the Indian in him and save the man," and in the unilateral extension of US citizenship to all American Indians in 1924—aims to eliminate Indigenous peoples even as it confers legitimate standing on individual Indigenous persons in relation to the dominant social, which is to say the US empire-state.

For Card, genocide is relative, not absolute. At odds with a sense of categorical finality or qualitative break with life we associate with death, genocide is the *major* but *not necessarily complete* loss of social vitality, and it can have phases of varying intensity (Card 2003, 63). Even the Nazi genocide of Jews "was not only a program of mass murder but an assault on Jewish social vitality" that "had stages": "The Nazi genocide was not simply the final slaughter. It was the whole process." For example, "converts to Christianity and descendants of converts were stripped of social relationships that shaped and animated their daily lives and so suffered a *degree* of social death" (Card 2010, 239, 248; emphasis added). By contrast, according to Patterson (1982), even the most seemingly privileged, palatine enslaved are no less enslaved: despite outward appearances, they are still subject to total domination.

As implied in the central term of loss, genocide is suffered by a people—whether a sovereign external polity or a recognized internal minority—that enjoyed a certain coherent social existence, standing, and vitality, which are then forcibly lost. It is the coerced downfall of a people. It is a process of dispossession, not a mere absence. In other words, there is historical movement—with the possibility of countermovement: "In genocides, survivors experience a social death, to a degree and for a time. Some later become revitalized in new ways; others do not." Cautioning us that physical death is not necessarily worse or more extreme than social death, Card (2010, 262) writes, "Whether it is may depend on the degree of social death in question and the possibilities for revitalization."

At first glance, Card's retheorization of genocide only confirms the correctness of the CRC's analysis. Shifting our attention away from physical death and keying in on social death as the sine qua non make clear that Black people during the Jim Crow era were undergoing a genocidal regime of terror: of course, the social vitality of Black communities was systematically and brutally imperiled at every turn, as the CRC petition and recent historical scholarship amply document (Blackmon 2008; Chafe et al. 2001; Haley 2016; Litwack 1998; Muhammad 2011; Williams 2012). As the CRC was at pains to point out, "The genocide of which we complain is as much a fact as gravity" ([1951] 2020, 4). The original authority on social death, Orlando Patterson (2018, xix), writes, "Jim Crow was neoslavery, pure and simple, a system of terror that partly inspired German Nazism, enforced by a police state and collectively reinforced by lynch mobs"—words that would not be out of place in the CRC petition. Under Jim Crow, as under slavery, Black people were denied "any recognition as legitimate members of the community" (Patterson 2020)—community here indexing the second sense of the social discussed above.

Surely, the analyses of Lemkin, Power, and many other genocide experts are misguided to dismiss *We Charge Genocide* as hyperbole. They underestimate and thereby reproduce antiblackness.[7] Nevertheless, we ultimately arrive at the same conclusion—that *genocide* is indeed inapt—but for the opposite reason. As Card points out, genocide is a loss, a major loss of a people. There is a necessary narrative arc of descent—from a condition of peoplehood toward its obliteration, from collective social life toward collective social death. As the CRC and many others have documented, Black people of the United States under Jim Crow (and since) have indeed suffered conditions indicative of the social death of genocide. However, what preceded this social death? It was not a condition of social life, legitimacy, and standing. Rather, it was the social death of slavery. The narrative arc of antiblack genocide that the CRC plotted was not one of descent but one of continuity: "In one form or another [genocide] has been practiced for more than three hundred years. . . . Its very familiarity disguises its horror" (CRC [1951] 2020, 4).

Black people became Black people through the social death of slavery. They did not preexist it. This is "the peculiar experience of Africans under Western modernity, which originally turned them into 'negroes' (lowercase), creating a race where previously none had existed," according to philosopher Charles Mills (2013, 35). Put simply, no racial slavery, no Black people. For Black people, "peoplehood" and "social life" were forged in this *extreme antisocial situation* marked by *radical ontological insecurity* and therefore do not mean the same things as for non-Black peoples.[8] Such "social" categories were always already "thrown in crisis" (Spillers 2003, 221). Black "peoplehood" and "social life" under racial slavery were supreme achievements *in spite of* and *against* the social that refused the enslaved all legitimate recognition and standing: "Black life is not social life in the universe formed by the codes of state and civil society. . . . Black life is not lived in the world that the world lives in" (Sexton 2011, 24). If genocide is the murder of a people, it is, for Black people, the murder of an already murdered "people"—or, more precisely, the murder of a *nonpeople of nonpersons*. If there is no loss of social vitality because there was always already social death, is it still genocide? Antiblackness, part and parcel of racial slavery and its ongoing afterlife, is genocide beyond genocide.

Crowded out of the CRC's progressive and radical perspective, which embraces salvation history, are the propositions that (a) the systematic injuries imposed on Black people are not an accidental defect that can be repaired, or a disease that can be cured, and thus that (b) what it conceptualizes as genocide, rather than a repairable defect, is constitutive of US democracy and, more generally, of the Human.[9] Suggesting an unshakable belief and optimism in how organized collectives can pressure democratic institutions and bring about much-needed change and the reconstitution of the country, in the 1970 foreword to the second edition of *We Charge Genocide*, William Patterson affirms, "History dictates the cure: a people united in struggle for the peace of the world and their own security. This is written with the hope that it will help affect this unity. . . . History calls for an end to genocidal relations at home and abroad. This Petition is called for by history and the people are its bearers" (CRC [1951] 2020, xxi).

It takes prodigious confidence in democracy's self-correcting abilities to move beyond the overwhelming historical and contemporary evidence of democracy's own enabling of Black social and physical death, and project an improved future. For us, the petition's copious evidence signals the contents and contours of an immovable and overdetermining algorithm of the empire-state, including its democratic institutions and so-called civil society. If the culturally sanctioned manifestations of what Patterson defines as genocide determine and express the "nation's fabric"—and, indeed, the world's embracing of the Human as an ontological, juridical, and political categorical rubric—then there is no end to this regime of terror unless there is an end of the empire-state's own primordial substance, which means an end to the empire-state. Yet the CRC presents genocide as a composite deadly phenomenon, an illness, that, like the particular US democratic experiment, can be remedied. We propose that antiblackness, not genocide, accounts for the foundational, ubiquitous, permanent, and unique structural fact of the physical, social, and spiritual death of Black people. To identify and oppose antiblackness requires a unique set of analytical and political tools that the concepts of genocide, racism, and antiracism, in their embracing of democracy's perfectibility, legality, salvation history, and analogy between Black and non-Black experiences (Vargas 2021), are unable to provide. Pessimistic an analysis rooted in antiblackness is not. Quite the opposite. By increasing the analytic granularity—by attending to the hieroglyphs of the flesh (Spillers 2003)—a perspective on antiblackness provides a more accurate and detailed report of what's out there. Instead of discarded, or subsumed under a teleology of perfectibility, or analogized to non-Black experiences, the unruly phenomena that the concepts of racism and genocide cannot account for become that which abolitionist political imagination must contend with. Without recourse to sanctuary (in the empire-state) and normative linear hope (of modernity), antiblackness establishes that the current and future conditions of existence are untenable—not only for Black people but also for all non-Black people because they depend on a concept of the Human that is parasitic on Black lives and makes the Black Human a foundational and perpetual oxymoron. To embrace the inventions that arise in and must come after, against, despite modernity's constitutive antiblackness is to abolish this world.

NOTES

1. On the history of lynching in North Carolina, see Newkirk 2009.
2. "Nature of Genocide," *New York Times*, June 14, 1953, E10.
3. On *antiblackness*, see Vargas and Jung 2021; Jung and Vargas 2022.
4. On the United States as an *empire-state*, see Jung 2015.
5. Hartman (1997) suggests that Jeremy Bentham's reflections on the panopticon were likely influenced by his travels to the US South, in which plantations dependent on the labor of the enslaved relied on constant surveillance and its corresponding employment of terror.
6. For a discussion of Card's conceptualization of genocide as social death, see Snow 2016.
7. For recent reappraisals of *We Charge Genocide* and its critics, foremost Lemkin, see Docker 2010; Frankowski 2019; Frankowski and Skitolsky 2018; Guenther 2020; Hinton 2021; Meiches 2019; Samudzi 2020–21; Skitolsky 2021; Solomon 2019; Weiss-Wendt 2017, 2019.
8. On *extreme antisocial situation* and *radical ontological insecurity*, see Steinmetz 2016 and Giddens 1984, respectively. With regard to racial slavery, see Jung 2019.
9. We capitalize *Human* to specify its modernity. See Vargas and Jung 2021.

WORKS CITED

Alves, Jaime, and João H. Costa Vargas. 2019. "The Specter of Haiti: Structural Antiblackness, the Far-Right Backlash and the Fear of a Black Majority in Brazil." *Third World Quarterly* 41 (4): 645–62.

Anderson, Carol. 2003. *Eyes Off the Prize: The United Nations and the African American Struggle for Human Rights*. New York: Cambridge University Press.

Baldus, D. C., C. Pulaski, and G. Woodworth. 1983. "Comparative Review of Death Sentences: An Empirical Study of the Georgia Experience." *Journal of Criminal Law and Criminology* 74 (3): 661–753.

Blackmon, Douglas A. 2008. *Slavery by Another Name: The Re-Enslavement of Black Americans from the Civil War to World War II*. New York: Anchor.
Card, Claudia. 2003. "Genocide and Social Death." *Hypatia* 18 (1): 65–79.
Card, Claudia. 2010. *Confronting Evils: Terrorism, Torture, Genocide*. New York: Cambridge University Press.
Chafe, William H., Raymond Gavins, Robert Korstad, and the Staff of the Behind the Veil Project, eds. 2001. *Remembering Jim Crow: African Americans Tell About Life in the Segregated South*. New York: New Press.
CRC [Civil Rights Congress]. (1951) 2020. *We Charge Genocide: The Crime of Government Against the Negro People*. 3rd ed. Edited by William L. Patterson. New York: International Publishers.
Davis, A. 1978. "Rape, Racism, and the Capitalist Setting." *Black Scholar* 9 (7): 24–30.
Davis, A. 1983. *Women, Race, and Class*. New York: Vintage.
Docker, John. 2010. "Raphaël Lemkin, Creator of the Concept of Genocide: A World History Perspective." *Humanities Research* 16 (2): 49–74.
Frankowski, Alfred. 2019. "Spectacle Terror Lynching, Public Sovereignty, and Antiblack Genocide." *Journal of Speculative Philosophy* 33 (2): 268–81.
Frankowski, Alfred, and Lissa Skitolsky. 2018. "Lang's Defense and the Morbid Sensibility of Genocide Studies." *Journal of Genocide Research* 20 (3): 423–28.
Giddens, Anthony. 1984. *The Constitution of Society*. Berkeley: University of California Press.
Gilmore, Ruth Wilson. 2002. "Race and Globalization." In *Geographies of Global Change: Remapping the World*, edited by Ron Johnston, Peter J. Taylor, and Michael Watts, 261–74. New York: Wiley-Blackwell.
Guenther, Lisa. 2020. "'We Charge Genocide': Anti-Black Racism in the United States as Genocidal Structural Violence." In *Logics of Genocide: The Structures of Violence and the Contemporary World*, edited by Anne O'Byrne and Martin Shuster, 134–51. New York: Routledge.
Haley, Sarah. 2016. *No Mercy Here: Gender, Punishment, and the Making of Jim Crow Modernity*. Chapel Hill: University of North Carolina Press.
Hartman, Saidiya. 1997. *Scenes of Subjection: Terror, Slavery, and Self-Making in Nineteenth-Century America*. New York: Oxford University Press.
Hartman, Saidiya. 2006. *Lose Your Mother*. New York: Farrar, Straus, and Giroux.
Hinton, Alex. 2021. "70 Years Ago Black Activists Accused the U.S. of Genocide. They Should Have Been Taken Seriously." *Politico*, December 26, 2021. https://www.politico.com/news/magazine/2021/12/26/black-activists-charge-genocide-united-states-systemic-racism-526045.
Horne, Gerald. 2013. *Black Revolutionary: William Patterson and the Globalization of the African American Freedom Struggle*. Urbana: University of Illinois Press.
Jung, Moon-Kie. 2015. *Beneath the Surface of White Supremacy: Denaturalizing U.S. Racisms Past and Present*. Stanford, CA: Stanford University Press.

Jung, Moon-Kie. 2019. "The Enslaved, the Worker, and Du Bois's *Black Reconstruction*: Toward an Underdiscipline of Antisociology." *Sociology of Race and Ethnicity* 5 (2): 157–68.

Jung, Moon-Kie, and João H. Costa Vargas. 2022. "More than and Beyond Racism: Theoretical and Political Meditations on Antiblackness." *Souls* 23 (3–4): 235–53.

Lemkin, Raphaël. 1944. *Axis Rule in Occupied Europe*. Washington, DC: Carnegie Endowment for International Peace.

Lemkin, Raphaël. 2013. *Totally Unofficial: The Autobiography of Raphael Lemkin*. Edited by Donna-Lee Frieze. New Haven, CT: Yale University Press.

Litwack, Leon F. 1998. *Trouble in Mind: Black Southerners in the Age of Jim Crow*. New York: Vintage.

Marquart, J., S. Ekland-Olson, and J. R. Sorensen. 1998. *The Rope, the Chair, and the Needle: Capital Punishment in Texas, 1923–1990*. Austin: University of Texas Press.

McGuire, Danielle L. 2010. *At the Dark End of the Street: Black Women, Rape, and Resistance*. New York: Vintage.

Meiches, Benjamin. 2019. "The Charge of Genocide: Racial Hierarchy, Political Discourse, and the Evolution of International Institutions." *International Political Sociology* 13:20–36.

Mills, Charles. 2013. "An Illuminating Blackness." *Black Scholar* 43 (4): 32–37.

Muhammad, Khalil. 2010. *The Condemnation of Blackness: Race, Crime, and the Making of Modern Urban America*. Cambridge, MA: Harvard University Press.

Newkirk, Vann R. 2009. *Lynching in North Carolina: A History, 1865–1941*. Jefferson, NC: McFarland.

Patterson, Orlando. 1982. *Slavery and Social Death: A Comparative Study*. Cambridge, MA: Harvard University Press.

Patterson, Orlando. 2018. "Preface, 2018." In *Slavery and Social Death*, vii–xxvi. Cambridge, MA: Harvard University Press.

Patterson, Orlando. 2020. "The Long Reach of Racism in the US." *Wall Street Journal*, June 5, 2020. https://www.wsj.com/articles/the-long-reach-of-racism-in-the-u-s-11591372542.

Patterson, William. 1971. *The Man Who Cried Genocide: An Autobiography*. New York: International Publishers.

Power, Samantha. (2002) 2013. *"A Problem from Hell": America and the Age of Genocide*. New York: Basic Books.

Roberts, Dorothy. 1997. *Killing the Black Body: Race, Reproduction, and the Meaning of Liberty*. New York: Pantheon.

Rosen, Hannah. 2009. *Terror in the Heart of Freedom: Citizenship, Sexual Violence, and the Meaning of Race in the Postemancipation South*. Chapel Hill: University of North Carolina Press.

Samudzi, Zoé. 2020–21. "Paradox of Recognition: Genocide and Colonialism." *Postmodern Culture* 31 (1–2).

Sexton, Jared. 2011. "The Social Life of Social Death: On Afro-Pessimism and Black Optimism." *InTensions* 5 (November).

Skitolsky, Lissa. 2021. "American Slavery, the New Jim Crow, and Genocide." In *Critical Perspectives on African Genocide: Memory, Silence, and Anti-Black Political Violence*, edited by Alfred Frankowski, Jeanine Ntihirageza, and Chielozona Eze, 39–54. Lanham, MD: Rowman and Littlefield.

Snorton, C. Riley. 2017. *Black on Both Sides: A Racial History of Trans Identity*. Minneapolis: University of Minnesota Press.

Snow, James. 2016. "Claudia Card's Concept of Social Death: A New Way of Looking at Genocide." *Metaphilosophy* 47 (4–5): 607–26.

Solomon, Daniel. 2019. "The Black Freedom Movement and the Politics of the Anti-Genocide Norm in the United States, 1951–1967." *Genocide Studies and Prevention* 13 (1): 130–43.

Spillers, Hortense. 2003. *Black, White, and in Color: Essays on American Literature and Culture*. Chicago: University of Chicago Press.

Steinmetz, George. 2016. "Social Fields, Subfields and Social Spaces at the Scale of Empires: Explaining the Colonial State and Colonial Sociology." *Sociological Review Monographs* 64 (2): 98–123.

Sugrue, Thomas. 1996. *The Origins of the Urban Crisis: Race and Inequality in Postwar Detroit*. Princeton, NJ: Princeton University Press.

Vargas, João H. Costa. 2006. *Catching Hell in the City of Angels: Life and Meanings of Blackness in South Central Los Angeles*. Minneapolis: University of Minnesota Press.

Vargas, João H. Costa. 2018. *The Denial of Antiblackness: Multiracial Redemption and Black Suffering*. Minneapolis: University of Minnesota Press.

Vargas, João H. Costa. 2021. "Terror sexual é genocídio: o estupro da mulher negra como elemento estrutural e estruturante da diáspora—por uma análise quilombista da antinegritude." *Revista Latino-Americana de Criminologia* 1 (2): 35–67.

Vargas, João H. Costa, and Moon-Kie Jung. 2021. "Antiblackness of the Social and the Human." In *Antiblackness*, edited by Moon-Kie Jung and João H. Costa Vargas, 1–14. Durham, NC: Duke University Press.

Washington, Harriet. 2006. *Medical Apartheid: The Dark History of Medical Experimentation on Black Americans from Colonial Times to the Present*. New York: Doubleday.

Weiss-Wendt, Anton. 2017. *The Soviet Union and the Gutting of the Genocide Convention*. Madison: University of Wisconsin Press.

Weiss-Wendt, Anton. 2019. "When the End Justifies the Means: Raphaël Lemkin and the Shaping of a Popular Discourse on Genocide." *Genocide Studies and Prevention* 13 (1): 173–88.

Williams, Kidada E. 2012. *They Left Great Marks on Me: African American Testimonies of Racial Violence from Emancipation to World War I*. New York: New York University Press.

4

From Minneapolis to Dessau, from Moria to Tripoli

Breathing, Resistance, and International Pathways of Abolition

Vanessa E. Thompson

Suez steals his water. Société Générale steals his money and finances the pollution of Africa with coal-fired power plants. Thales builds the weapons with which they wage war. The same people who destroy our lives over there are waging war here!

Gilets Noirs, France

What happens in the prison cells in Dessau or the *Lager* in Ellwangen, the detention centers in Libya, the torture of Sudanese activists, or the mass murder in the Mediterranean is connected, our resistance must be connected too.

Ibrahim S., refugee activist from Ellwangen, Germany

The Dying in the Mediterranean Sea is directly linked to our work because we believe in humanity and will keep being loud and clear. Because we cannot watch people perish in the sea while the E.U. walls get higher to protect a fortress Europe.

Women in Exile, Germany

- Black revolts in 2020 had a global impact as millions hit the streets, rebelled against state and border violence, and many organized for abolition, not only in the United States but also in various other contexts. These uprisings not only exposed policing and its connections to bordering and the prison system as methods of capitalism to contain and control mobile (and increasingly rendered surplus) working-class and working-poor masses (disproportionately but not exclusively black and brown).[1] They furthermore mirrored what abolitionists have long argued: that abolition is a global project of liberation that not only attends to policing, prisons, or borders (or, historically, plantations or colonies) but also dismantles the societal and economic conditions and modes of production that breed these methods of global capitalism in the first place (Gilmore 2017). This includes dismantling the refashioning of these conditions and their ideologies, such as liberal reforms and humanism.

Abolitionist collectives and organizations are making international abolition geography (Gilmore 2017) on an everyday basis and in this very moment are encountering pitfalls, obstacles, and possibilities. This chapter engages articulations of abolitionist struggle and how they currently unfold in transnational and transcontinental dimensions beyond a comparative framework. Thinking with Ruth Wilson Gilmore's call that abolition must be international by definition (in relation to it being "red" and "green") (Gilmore 2020), and drawing on transnational and transcontinental formations of abolitionist practice, this piece engages abolition with regard to its possibility as a form of contemporary internationalism "from below" (Heatherton 2022). Focusing on struggles against policing and bordering regimes in and beyond Europe, and in engagement with the abolitionist work and theorizing of abolitionist movements across the Black Atlantic (Gilroy 1993) and the Black Mediterranean (Black Mediterranean Collective 2021; Di Maio 2012; Smythe 2018), as well as building on previous work on breathing and policing, and activist engagements (Thompson 2020, 2021), this chapter attends to the transnational dimensions of abolition, which are often constrained within approaches that focus on one context only and thereby risk reproducing methodological nationalisms and continentalisms. Mobilizing struggles for breath in and beyond Europe as method, and thereby tracing how abolitionist solidarity unfolds internationally, I discuss abolition as a reactualized form of internationalism.

Struggles of the dispossessed, displaced, and controlled, such as people rendered refugees and migrants, superexploited workers, criminalized groups as well as those rendered surplus (Davis 2005) play a central role in the formation of international abolition, especially in this current conjuncture of the capitalist crises of mass displacement (Walia 2021) and the policing and incarceration of the poly-crisis (Hall et al. 1978; Gilmore 2007; Robinson 2020). Against this background, this form of abolitionist internationalism, which also exposes the liberal framework of humanitarianism as reform, attends as much to struggles of labor as it does to surplus people's struggles against state, extralegal, and pervasive violence (Thompson 2024), abandonment and their building of different worlds.

The first part of this chapter discusses struggles for breath as transcontinental struggles for abolition. In the second part, I discuss three engagements of transnational abolition in practice by drawing on the work of black and anti-racist movements in and beyond Europe. I conclude with a note on the multi-racial potential of these struggles as surplus people's struggles toward abolitionist internationalism.

From the Land to the Shores and the Sea: Struggles for Breath

By implicitly as well as explicitly referring to breathing, the global black rebellions in 2020 articulated a shared condition of the racialized working class, working poor, and those rendered surplus (Thompson 2021). Mobilizing George Floyd's last words, "I can't breathe," in slogans and on leaflets, on murals and in tags, as well as on large demonstration banners, the condition of un-breathing produced through policing as an ongoing albeit changing method of racial capitalism (Alexander 2008; Robinson 1983; Gilmore 2022) is addressed as universal while simultaneously contextual. Slogans like "We Also Can't Breathe" or "Black Lives Matter! In the Mediterranean Sea Too!" already indicate that many radical black and anti-racist abolitionist movements are engaging in organizing that not only goes beyond the US/North American context but, further, have their own (connected) histories and present formation of abolitionist struggles. Tracing the articulations of un-breathing is helpful as a heuristic as well as a political device (instead of just a description or metaphor) to understand the transnational dimensions of policing *as well as* the transnational connections of abolitionist struggles.

The condition of un-breathing as a political device for struggle has, in fact, a long history in anti-colonial critique. Frantz Fanon famously conceptualized breathing with regard to colonial violence (Gibson 2020, 2024; Thompson 2019, 2022). Policing, as a social relation and mode of governance, mediates the process of differential violence within the mode of capitalist production. Fanon delivers a powerful account of this relation:

> In the colonies it is the policeman and the soldier who are the official, instituted go-betweens, the spokesmen of the settler and his rule of oppression. In capitalist societies the educational system, whether lay

or clerical, the structure of moral reflexes handed down from father to son . . . all these aesthetic expressions of respect for the established order serve to create around the exploited person an atmosphere of submission and of inhibition which lightens the task of policing considerably. In the capitalist countries a multitude of moral teachers, counselors and "bewilderers" separate the exploited from those in power. In the colonial countries, on the contrary, the policeman and the soldier, by their immediate presence and their frequent and direct action maintain contact with the native and advise him by means of rifle butts and napalm not to budge. (Fanon 1963, 38)

Recognizing the "lightened task" of policing when it comes to the control of labor implies understanding the difference with regard to the everyday notion of brute violence to control less-free labor and enslaved labor (see also Singh 2016; Hudis 2021). Fanon turns to combat breathing or un-breathing as a condition produced by superexploitation and colonial domination. First mentioning the notion in *Black Skin, White Masks* (1967), where he also engages with the black condition and workings of colonial racism in France as well as challenges to culturalist and identity essentialisms, Fanon refers to the Indo-Chinese resistance with regard to breathing and argues that it "is not because the Indo-Chinese discovered a culture of their own that they revolted. Quite simply this was because it became impossible for them to breathe, in more than one sense of the word" (Fanon 1967, 21).

The impossibility of breath is thus more than a metaphor. It is an effect of colonial violence, dispossession, and expropriation, and describes the constant reality of (slow and fast) coercive force, a breathing that is characterized by living under the conditions of occupation and war. Fanon picks up breathing again in his *A Dying Colonialism* (1965):

> There is no occupation of territory, on the one hand, and independence of persons on the other. It is the country as a whole, its history, its daily pulsation that are contested, disfigured, in the hope of a final destruction. Under these conditions, the individual breathing is an observed breathing. It is a combat breathing. (Fanon 1965, 50)

Fanon analyzed colonial violence in a specific historic and conjunctural context that can't simply be transferred to our current moment as neither articulations of colonial violence nor of racism are simply transhistorical (Balibar and Wallerstein 1991; Gilmore 2007, 2022; Hall 1980). However, breathing is still at stake in the workings of race as the modality through which class relations are lived (Hall et al. 1978, 394), albeit within changing conjunctures when it comes to policing as a method of capitalism. As abolitionist and critical scholars have argued, policing itself has changed its function and role against the background of neoliberal restructuring, globalization, and the state response to capitalist crisis (Gilmore 2007, 2020; Johnson 2023; Robinson 2020) as well as against the background of previous resistances and struggles against state control and policing (Camp and Heatherton 2016; Elliott-Cooper 2021). To put it succinctly, (differential) policing, historically crucial for forming the class of wage laborers and the protection of the capitalist social order (Neocleous 2000) as well as other outcomes such as unfree or less-free labor, has increasingly migrated to the function of concentrating, punishing, and warehousing surplus populations, the dispossessed, and the ghettoized (Gilmore 2007; Johnson 2023). This does not mean that the policing of waged or less-free labor—with the residual function of a flexible reserve army—has become irrelevant (Shaw and Waterstone 2021). However, against the background of the massive production of relative surplus populations (Davis 2005) often racialized, and "rendered 'structurally irrelevant' to capital accumulation" (Hallsworth and Lea 2011, 142), policing is increasingly about controlling and containing poor (often but not exclusively racialized) people as surplus (Gilmore 2007).

Thus, with the advent of neoliberal capitalism, the function and basis of policing changes as well. The prisons and the detention centers, the migrant boats, borderscapes, and the urban concentrations of houseless people and working-poor classes increasingly become the spaces of humanity rendered surplus. As Gilmore has argued, labor exploitation of the incarcerated populations is not the central or only category when it comes to the analysis of the political economy of the carceral condition (Gilmore 2007; Gilmore, Toscano, and Bhandar 2022). It is, rather, surplus in its relational configuration as well as the stealing of time of those rendered redundant (Gilmore, Toscano, and Bhandar 2022; Khosravi 2018).[2]

Un-breathing is the modality through which this relation of surplusification, racism, and capitalism is expressed and endured beyond and across specific locations and contexts. Breathing is a form of being in relation in and with the world. It is the precondition for sociality and for being in contact with the human and non-human world (Thompson 2021). Breathing in "more than one sense of the word" (Fanon 1967) refers to this physical, social, and ecological process of exchange and relationality. As I have argued elsewhere, combat breathing is embodied in and through the pant for breath, the gasp of air, the compression of air supply, the chokehold, and the panic attack (Thompson 2021).

Police stops and searches impact breathing, just like running away from police, as happened to Zyed Benna and Bouna Traoré in a racialized working-class suburb of Paris France, in 2005. Being humiliated by police speeds up breath as well as blood pressure. Policing also ends breath, as the murders of George Floyd, Eric Garner, Breonna Taylor, Tina Ezekwe, João Pedro Mattos Pinto, Adama Traoré, William Tonou-Mbobda, Roger Nzoy Wilhelm, Mike Ben Peter, Sean Rigg, Samuel Dolphyne, João Alberto Silveira Freitas, A.P., Vitali N., and so many others show. Policing as un-breathing is thus not an individual expression, nor does it articulate only through the explicit plea "I can't breathe," though breathing finally stopped nevertheless. The murders of Christy Schwundeck in Frankfurt am Main, of N'deye Mareame Sarr in Aschaffenburg, Germany, of Sista Mimi in Berlin (who taught us how police repression against refugee activists is all-pervasive), of Breonna Taylor, and of Ifeoma Abugu point to this. Combat breathing also refers to the inhalation of water, as in drowning (through letting die or active pushbacks, both forms of mass murder), as a result of the policing of the oceans, especially the Black Mediterranean—an articulation of the control of the border regime as a labor regime but also increasingly a regime of the production of premature death of those that no longer present value for racial capital. Un-breathing also speaks to the lack of air in the detention centers and prisons, the carceration of breath as a relational process of movement and life. The mass protests of hundreds of refugees in Libya against detention, against border externalization and control, and for safe passage referred to breathing, just as did the mass protests in Nigeria waged against the Special Anti-Robbery Squad (SARS), a special police unit responsible for the deaths of Kolade Johnson and hundreds more. Un-breathing, as the condition of surplus populations, often black but in no way exclusively so, travels from the domestic to the welfare and urban space, from the borderscape to the prison concentration, from the shores to the land and the sea (Thompson 2022). The resistance of surplus populations, however, not merely responds to but also generates internationalist dimensions.

Three Accounts Beyond National Confines

The history of revolutionary internationalism is multifold and characterized by the entangled geographies of socialist, communist, and tricontinental as well as anti-colonial national politics of liberation that were articulated in the colonial metropoles as well as the Tricont (Anderson 2022; Getachew 2019; Gopal 2019; Kipfer 2021; Prashad 2007; Rodney 2022). These revolutionary internationalist networks, also shaped by points of tensions such as around the national question, were organized as networks that brought together parties and organizations such as the Second or Third International. They coordinated their trajectories and struggles via congresses and conferences, such as the First Solidarity Conference of the Peoples of Africa, Asia and Latin America in Havana in 1966. Among other things, internationalisms "from below" are characterized by their multiplicity, immanent critique of various centralisms, and avant-garde conceptions. Radical internationalist politics also expand the conventional understanding of class politics, as they engage various forms of labor exploitation as well as questions of occupation, dispossession and expropriation (Fanon 1963). Further, instead of focusing on single leaders, they attend to the perspectives and resistances of ordinary people who build and sustain movements and build history from below (Davis 1981; Heatherton 2022; Linebaugh and Rediker 2004; Sinha 2016).

Many contemporary radical abolitionist collectives stand in this tradition. They struggle on the many fronts against organized abandonment, oppression, and exploitation as well as against the methods of capitalism such as policing, *Lagers* (camps), borders, and prisons as well as for alternative modes of production and relations. They thus form an abolitionist multitude that attends to the multiplicities and expansion of class struggles as in terms of disrupting the processes of valorization (Gilmore 2024), also through organizing blockades and occupations as well as strikes and struggles for safe passage. These formations also challenge methodological nationalisms and continentalisms as they move beyond national contexts in their analysis and practice—when, for instance, organizing no-border camps and campaigns in various parts of Europe and West Africa.

In the following, I want to draw on three accounts of abolition geography (Gilmore 2017) that are struggling toward internationalism. As an activist-scholar who has been engaged in abolitionist organizing in Germany and Europe more broadly for two decades, I have collaborated with many of the movements and initiatives discussed here. In the following, I draw on accounts of events in which I either participated myself or am engaged through collaborations and/or the public interventions of movements.

Self-Organization Against Policing

In October 2019, the Initiative in Remembrance of Oury Jalloh organized a conference in Berlin, Germany, where groups and collectives of families and friends and anti-police activists and initiatives from all over Europe were invited to join and discuss the current conjuncture of state racism in and beyond Europe, policing, and possible resistance strategies. Oury Jalloh was a migrant from Guinea who was murdered in a German police holding cell in Dessau on January 1, 2005. While his hands and feet were tied to a fireproof mattress, police and public prosecutors claimed that he burned himself. Yet the lighter was only added to the stock of evidence three days later and does not contain traces of Jalloh's DNA. The narrative of suicide is, of course, a common one to cover state murders. At the same time, it is important to understand suicides in camps and prisons and detention centers as forms of state murder, too, as these cannot be separated from the structural conditions that render disposable (people turned into) migrants, refugees, and people behind bars of any form.

The Initiative in Remembrance of Oury Jalloh was founded by friends of Jalloh shortly after his murder, many of them refugees and asylum seekers who were deported after founding the initiative and forming resistance. Since then, the initiative has been supporting the family, has mobilized media and protest, and has commissioned several independent reports that prove that the fire was set with an accelerant and that Jalloh's nose, ribs, and skull were severely injured before his death. They further continue to support families who have lost their loved ones through state violence and to support activists. Over these twenty years, they have also struggled for complete resolution of the case, realizing after several years that they would need to take fact-finding into their own hands. This realization, for many, came after the criminalization of their justice work. Many members of the initiative are facing criminal charges, are severely criminalized, including losing shop permits, etc. The initiative draws on legal strategies as a mode of organizing rather than affirming liberal law. This means that they do not believe that justice will be served through the liberal justice framework, as the justice system is itself part of a carceral apparatus and class justice system. However, they draw on legal cases as a strategy to mobilize critical publics. In their work, they further dismantle the inherent connections between the police apparatus and extralegal fascist formations that have a long and context-specific history in Germany and elsewhere.

The case of Oury Jalloh has become one of the most well-known cases of police murder in Germany, the result of the struggle of this initiative. The case has sensitized many Left movements and civil society initiatives about the reality of policing in Germany, where the routine deployment of brute violence with impunity is not new to the racialized and migrant sections of the working class and working poor. Though the initiative is in contact with several other initiatives of families and friends and abolitionist "copwatch" collectives within Germany as well as in other European countries, they realized that these collectives are often only loosely connected, and that collective space and time are needed to discuss the contextual similarities as well as differences when it comes to policing in Germany and in Europe more broadly. Further, while cases of people dying at the hands of police in the United States are often known in Germany, France, and the United Kingdom, the initiative realized that many activists in Germany are not aware of cases and struggles in neighboring countries, and that this is related to the conjuncture of carceral racism in capitalist Europe (Thompson, forthcoming 2025).

Since the counterrevolution of the 1970s and the processes of neoliberal restructuring, the expansion of carceral modes of control, police violence and state violence have increased in Europe. This becomes evident when considering mass resistances in impoverished, often migrant and racialized, working-class and working-poor neighborhoods—resistances that are often responses to the state killing of migrant working-class youth. The increasing criminalization of labor migration since the 1970s, the strengthening of deportation regimes, and the fortification of external(ized) border control in the 2000s are further expressions of the current crisis conjuncture of capitalism (Georgi 2019). While these processes and carceral responses are increasingly transnationalized, activist movements remain rather bound to their national and even local contexts. If carceral racism expressed through policing is thematized beyond one European context, it is mainly discussed with regard to the United States.

In Germany, an activist meeting took place in October 2019 to start to challenge this national focus within struggles against policing. It was particularly instructive because it entailed a move beyond national frontiers and shaped more transnational conversations about policing in Europe. This activist conference brought anti-police movements, relatives, and activist-scholars in and beyond Germany together beyond one local or national context. It was thus one of the first of its kind, as it pulled together families' and friends' initiatives and collectives, within as well as beyond Germany, that struggle against policing, against state racism, and for the abolition of the murderous and exploitative system at its center. The conference also enabled discussion about the EU security complex, its relation to border imperialism and war (Walia 2021), the genocidal policing of the deserts and oceans, and the increasing production of surplus populations that are contained in border camps and by frontiers. The conference further brought together multiracial collectives. Their focus was not on a specific form of racism, such as anti-black racism, but on an understanding of racism as a conjunctural social relation that produces and exploits "group-differentiated vulnerability to premature death" (Gilmore 2007, 28). They also engaged with the structural state violence that white poor groups such as houseless people or drug users experience, and developed the understanding that, though policing as a method of capitalism affects racialized poor masses disproportionately, it by no means affects them exclusively. Against this background, the collectives and initiatives pushed for multiracial solidarity. Collectives and initiatives from all over Germany joined the conference, such as the Initiative Amad Ahmad (Kleve) and the Initiative in Memory of Laye Condé (Bremen). The conference approached the nexus of policing and right-wing terrorism not only by linking the role of police during the terrorist attacks and murders in Duisburg (1984) and Mölln (1992) to the murders of (post-)migrants by the so-called National Socialist Underground (NSU) but also by discussing the inherent and functional relation between state racism and right-wing extremism.

Anti-fascist and anti-racist initiatives that work on these cases, such as the Initiative Keupstraße Ist Überall (Initiative Keupstraße is Everywhere) and the action committee Unraveling the NSU Complex, were present as well. Anti-fascist collectives and anti-police collectives have identified these connections in the abstract, and the conference centered the analysis of the connections between fascism and carceral capitalism. Collectives and family members discussed how state policing is itself a fascist method, especially when considering the fascist history of policing. They also discussed the relation to internal as well as external colonialism. In Germany, for instance, as in many other parts of Europe, the policing of Roma people as well as poor masses, often racialized, dates back to the early formation of the police in the sixteenth century. Policing had an internal as well as external colonial function. During National Socialism, policing played a crucial and genocidal role, and much of the police knowledge and archives created during that time were also in place after 1945.[3] So-called scandals of "discovering" rightwing extremists within the policing apparatus thus have to be understood in relation to this history. Further, the role that police plays when neo-Nazi networks attack/kill/execute migrant and racialized folks was pointed out. Usually the police not only are inactive when this happens but also actively criminalize victims and cover up neo-Nazi structures, if they are not themselves connected to these. The case of the murder of Halit Yozgat, the ninth and last victim of the NSU murder series, and the role of Andreas Temme, a former member of the German Federal Office for the Protection of the Constitution who had deep connections to the neo-Nazi scene and who was present when Halit Yozgat was murdered, demonstrates this connection.[4]

Several collectives from France, the United Kingdom, and Turkey also joined, emphasizing the transnational dimension of policing as well as of anti-police and anti-border struggles. During the conference, contextual differences as well as similarities were discussed, and various strategies shared and explained. A special space was held for the affected families, who met with other families and therefore connected the dots beyond nation-states. As Marcia Rigg, the sister of Sean Rigg, who was killed by police in 2008 in Brixton, said at the press conference after the activist gathering, she realized that other families in other countries are "going through exactly the same pain and suffering." The gathering was also a space for families and loved ones to connect and to share experiences as well as reflections. For the initiatives, often run by family members, exchange of strategies—for example, about campaigning, legal struggles, independent reports, media literacy, and connections between movements—was crucial as well. At the conference, it again became obvious that abolition is a feminist project. In many discussions, the role of working class women and non-binary people was underscored because women and queer folks, in particular, are on the front lines of organizing resistance against policing in all contexts involved. They are also providing the emotional support for families and friends of victims. Often they themselves are family members of people who died at the hands of the state. While this was considered as a feminist care practice, it is important also to consider the gendered division of labor within abolitionist organizing, so that this work may be collectivized instead of romanticized. Abolition is a feminist project not only because carcerality unfolds alongside patriarchal relations, reproduces gender orders, and affects multiply marginalized groups disproportionally (Stanley and Smith 2011; Sudbury 2005) but also because abolition projects are projects of radical transformation of our relations as well. They seek to radically transform the modes of production, re-production as well as how we relate to and interact with each other or engage in interdependency.

Abolish Frontex

Abolish Frontex is a campaign of an international network of groups and collectives that was born to struggle against the expanding militarization of migration control and violence of the EU border regime and industrial complex, crystallized in but not limited to the Border and Coast Guard Agency of the European Union (Frontex). Since the agency's formation in 2005, the budget of Frontex has increased by 7,000 percent. By 2027, Frontex plans to expand its army of border and coast guard officers by ten thousand officers. Inspired by the struggles against policing in the summer of 2020, and linking these to the conditions in the Moria camp in Greece (the fire in the camp as well as ongoing resistance in the camp and other camps at the outer borders of Europe) as well as the continuing mass premature death produced by Europe's border regime, more than seventy migrant justice and self-organized groups and collectives active within as well as beyond Europe decided to push for a more internationally coordinated response and created the network in June 2020. The aim was to go beyond the locally grounded framing and context and to join forces in the struggle for the abolition of Frontex and the dismantling of the border-industrial complex instead of the liberal mobilizations for human rights and reform which conceal the essence and function of borders and border control as racialized labor and death regimes (Sharma 2022; Walia 2021). They organize toward the abolition of borders and Frontex and lay bare the functions of borders and their inherent violence.

The campaign was inaugurated with actions in eight countries and an open letter expressing the refusal of "fortified borders to protect the wealth of the rich from the desperation and righteous anger of the poor and oppressed."[5] Since then, more than one hundred collectives have joined together to act in decentralized concert. The claims and organizing of Abolish Frontex focus on the abolition of Frontex and encompass a broad spectrum of goals: regularization of migration; stopping deportations; an end to detention and the militarization of borders as well as the surveillance of migrants; highlighting the EU's role in forcing people to move based on wars, neo-imperialism, global inequalities, and climate destruction; supporting freedom of movement; and putting an end to the EU border regime. At the same time, they struggle and organize toward solidarity infrastructures such as public housing, health care and education, community centers, childcare, a clean environment for everyone, decent wages, support services, and an end to privatization, exploitation, and austerity as well as an end to the financialization of urban landscapes and housing. Attending to the abolitionist politics of dismantling systems of exploitation and criminalization as well as building people's infrastructures from the ground up, Abolish Frontex presents a network that is transnational in scope and multidirectional in form as the network connects struggles for housing, healthcare, freedom of movement, and a redistribution of wealth. The network organizes sit-ins, blockades, demonstrations, information tours, commemorations, and campaigns. The decentralized yet concerted workings of the network make for a nonhierarchical structure and process.

Internationalism, however, is not truly international when not engaging struggles beyond Europe and the so-called Global North. Abolish Frontex responds to the call of Refugees in Libya, a collective that was born out of the mass protests and rebellion of mainly black workers rendered refugees in October 2021. Thousands of refugees were protesting against their detention and for freedom of movement and for their evacuation. As Refugees in Libya states on its website: "The main focus of the organization is in Libya, but the movement has been growing across other northern African countries, namely Tunisia, Morocco, Egypt, and Sudan where similar problems are faced by refugees, and across Europe where demonstrations and presentations have taken place in France, Germany, Italy, Netherlands, Spain, Sweden, Switzerland and the United Kingdom."[6] The group organizes mutual aid, campaigns, and strikes as well, building a movement with self-organized refugee groups as well as solidarity formations within Europe and on the African continent. Several Alarm Phone collectives, such as Alarm Phone Sahara, working with groups in Niger, Mali, Burkina Faso, Togo, and Morocco and several collectives in European countries, are part of the Abolish Frontex network as well, organizing toward infrastructures of life and freedom of movement.

Au Foyer, Au Travail, Dans Les Gares: Resistons

In July 2019, seven hundred so-called undocumented migrant workers stormed and occupied the Pantheon in Paris in their struggle for regularization, labor rights, and the abolition of the migration regime. This gathering presented the public formation of what is currently the largest movement of illegalized and irregularized migrant workers in France: the Gilets Noirs (Black Vests). Inspired by the Gilets Jaunes (Yellow Vests) movement while critiquing their lack of attention to the question of superexploitation and the migration regime, the Black Vests put a focus on the conditions of undocumented racialized workers that occupy the lower strata of the workforce and bear the primary brunt of the expansion of the French carceral anti-state state (Gilmore 2022) and its deportation regime. The occupation of the Pantheon, at which the Black Vests demanded their regularization and better working and housing conditions, was not their first intervention. Since winter 2017, their many protests and strikes include mass public insurgences such as the May 2019 occupation of a terminal of the Charles de Gaulle airport in protest of deportations of illegalized and undocumented migrants, as well as protests against camps and detention centers, against horrific working conditions, and for labor rights, permanent contracts, an end to subcontracts, and decent wages for all. On leaflets distributed at their occupation of the Pantheon they stated: "We don't just want papers, we want to break the system that also creates undocumented migrants. We must organize actions, occupations, demonstrations, strikes, blockades."

The Black Vests are fighting not only against the logics of differentiality in terms of legalization but also against a system that puts profit over people, is based on various forms of exploitation, and functions through the production and exploitation of difference. They link struggles that belong together. They organize around housing issues, mainly from the *foyers* (overcrowded and overpriced hostels for migrants through which companies such as Adoma—formerly Sonacotra—gain profit), though many have to live in tents due to a severe housing crisis in larger French cities and urban financialization (which hits undocumented migrant workers hardest). These are connected to their struggles against labor exploitation (especially subcontracting) and for fair wages for all as well as their struggles against the deportation regime. The Black Vests thus engage in a multidirectional abolitionist class struggle that mobilizes against racial capital, its methods of policing, and borders, as well as increasing surplusification.

The Black Vests also join strikes and actions by regularized precarious workers—for instance, joining striking hotel maids in their struggle for a living wage, for job security, for respect of work hours, and against wage theft. The target of their opposition, the multinational hotel group Accor (Ibis, Novotel, Pullmann, etc.) and the subcontractor company STN-TEFI, met their demands after a twenty-two-month strike. They continue to struggle alongside white French workers against labor exploitation and the increasing carceral violence of the state. Here we can see a move that already characterized many radical migrant worker activisms in Europe, as they struggle not only for regularization and wages that match those of French workers but also for better conditions for all. They further organize with movements against neoimperial Françafrique, against what they call "the heart" of French imperialism and its "plundering of Africa," Paris's business district: "Suez steals his water. Société Générale steals his money and finances the pollution of Africa with coal-fired power plants. Thales builds the weapons with which they wage war. The same people who destroy our lives over there are waging war here."

The Black Vests are in direct engagement with movements against neocolonialism in Françafrique, and organize against border regimes as well as the imperial formations that these border regimes are part of. Like the other collectives discussed here, these networks engage the possibility of an abolitionist international.

Windy Abolitionist International

Capital no longer needs living labour as before, not in the same numbers, in the same place, at the same time; Labour can no longer organise on that basis, it has lost its economic clout and, with it, whatever political clout it had, whatever determinacy it could exercise in the political realm. What is crucial here is not that the productive forces have altered the balance of dependency between Capital and Labour, but that they have altered it so radically as to allow Capital to free itself of Labour and yet hold Labour captive.

Ambalavaner Sivanandan, "All That Melts into Air Is Solid"

The three accounts discussed above—the transnational political gathering on police violence, the organizing of Abolish Frontex and Refugees in Libya, and the organizing of the Black Vests—are all forms of abolitionist struggles, and all, despite their differences, have an internationalist dimension. They further employ political blackness as communities of abolitionist struggle within the context of Europe and thus vis-à-vis the circuits of empire. They connect groups of people who are exploited and abandoned, and thereby build power. What we see in motion here are struggles of the dispossessed and exploited. And, in their interconnectedness, they build a field antagonistic to the geographies of capitalism and abandonment, crystallized in the camp, the police, the border. This, of course, includes the multiplicity of strategies of resistance of working-class, working-poor, stateless, and surplus folks. As the Black Vests, with their focus on the connection between superexploitation, surplusification, state violence, and abandonment teach us (Gilmore 2017), this includes strikes, blockades, disturbances of capital infrastructures and flows, campaigns, protests, and rebellions. Abolitionist formations are not centralized or one-dimensional; they unfold as radical multitudes. The central field of struggle against capitalism is not singular, and actually never really was.

Drawing on examples of movement organizing in Europe, the accounts here point to the possibilities of abolitionist internationalism and multitude formations as they consider the multiplicity of surplus struggles and go beyond the bounds of the nation-state in analysis and practice. At the same time, and as seen with the Black Vests, abolitionist struggles truly come to fruition when they also engage in the expansion of class struggle, and thus connect struggles against exploitation, surplusification, state violence, and abandonment.

There is, however, the need to build more than spontaneous abolitionist infrastructures for the possibility of composing international relationships and multitudes between the local and the global, between domestic and global articulations of struggle and transformation. "Global and international connections have to be regarded as an essential basis not merely an add-on when there is extra time and energy" (Hardt and Mezzadra 2016). Archives of the long histories of radical internationalisms can be helpful as long as we also confront some of their pitfalls, centralistic failures, and ongoing problematic nostalgias. The neoliberal counterrevolution of the 1970s as well as the collapse of anti-colonial international infrastructures had a severe impact on the possibilities of radical internationalism. Reimagining and building international abolitionist infrastructures in which these multitudes can appear, in conversation with the radical movements of the last decades, is what brings life to the abolitionist international that is already breathing in many parts of this world.

NOTES

I want to thank Ananya Roy and Veronika Zablotsky for compiling the inspiring Sanctuary Shorts conversations, and for their hard work on putting these conversations in a relational form. I am also grateful to my comrade, and fellow author in this edition, SA Smythe for ongoing conversations about black liberation and abolition. As always, I am grateful to, inspired by, and humble to be in connection and relation with the abolitionist collectives and movements (many of which appear in this chapter) I continue to learn from.

1. Following various black scholars, I write *black* in lowercase as part of a politics of black liberation. I do this for two main reasons. The first is that I find

it crucial to challenge the subjectivizing dimension that is transported with a capital *B*, as radical blackness subverts and challenges the modes of liberal subjectivity, subjecthood, and recognition and also attempts to "ironize and de-transcendentalize the whole concept of race" (Delany 2018, 86). The second, related one is that I understand blackness as a genuine political concept of liberation that speaks to structural locations of superexploitation and surplus, and thereby to global struggles and radical transformation, rather than simply to an identity. There are of course different ways that black scholars attend to this question, and I think there are good reasons for both versions as well. I prefer lowercase, though.

2 From this materialist abolitionist perspective, prisons and policing are not a simple continuation of the plantation (Gilmore 2007). Rather, the reason working-class and working-poor groups racialized as black and brown are disproportionately affected by the securitization of the capitalist crisis is that they represent a large segment of the lower strata of the working class and working poor. This is mainly due to their structural and historical disadvantage as "competitors" in the capitalist labor market, which is historically linked to the history of slavery as well as regimes of colonial labor migration and its modes of under-stratification. With regard to post-/neocolonial migration regimes, national-racist policies continue to structure modes of exploitation.

3 "Die Polizei hat sich schuldig gemacht," Romani Phen, n.d., https://www.romnja-power.de/die-polizei-hat-sich-schuldig-gemacht (accessed October 9, 2024).

4 Forensic Architecture, "The Murder of Halit Yozgat," June 8, 2017, https://forensic-architecture.org/investigation/the-murder-of-halit-yozgat.

5 Abolish Frontex, "Abolish Frontex, End the EU Border Regime," June 9, 2021, https://abolishfrontex.org/blog/2021/06/09/abolish-frontex-open-letter/.

6 "About Us," Refugees in Libya, n.d., https://www.refugeesinlibya.org/about-us (accessed October 8, 2024).

WORKS CITED

Alexander, Neville. 2008. "An Illuminating Moment: Background to the Azanian Manifesto." In *Biko Lives!: Contesting the Legacies of Steve Biko*, edited by Andile Mngxitama, Amanda Alexander, and Nigel C. Gibson, 157–70. New York: Palgrave Macmillan.

Anderson, Paul. 2002. "Internationalism: A Breviary." *New Left Review* 14:5–25.

Balibar, Etienne, and Immanuel Wallerstein. 1991. *Race, Nation, Class: Ambiguous Identities*. London: Verso.

Black Mediterranean Collective. 2021. *The Black Mediterranean: Bodies, Borders and Citizenship*. London: Palgrave.

Camp, Jordan T., and Christina Heatherton. 2016. *Policing the Planet: Why the Policing Crisis Led to Black Lives Matter*. London: Verso.

Cossé, Eva. 2023. "New Frontex Director for Reform." Human Rights Watch, March 1, 2023. https://www.hrw.org/news/2023/03/01/new-frontex-director-offers-chance-reform.

Davis, Angela Y. 1981. *Women, Race and Class*. New York: Vintage.

Davis, Mike. 2005. *Planet of Slums*. London: Verso.

Delany, Samuel R. 2018. *The Atheist in the Attic*. Oakland, CA: PM.

Di Maio, Alessandra. 2012. "The Black Mediterranean: Migration and Revolution in the Global Millennium." Public lecture presented at the University of Palermo, May 7, 2012.

Du Bois, W. E. B. 1999. *Black Reconstruction in America 1860–1880*. New York: Free Press.

Elliott-Cooper, Adam. 2021. *Black Resistance to British Policing*. Manchester: Manchester University Press.

Fanon, Frantz. 1963. *The Wretched of the Earth*. New York: Grove.

Fanon, Frantz. 1965. *A Dying Colonialism*. New York: Grove.

Fanon, Frantz. 1967. *Black Skin, White Masks*. New York: Grove.

Getachew, Adom. 2019. *Worldmaking After Empire: The Rise and Fall of Self-Determination*. Princeton, NJ: Princeton University Press.

Gilmore, Ruth W. 2007. *Golden Gulag: Prisons, Surplus, Crisis, and Opposition in Globalizing California*. Berkeley: University of California Press.

Gilmore, Ruth W. 2017. "Abolition Geography and the Problem of Innocence." In *Futures of Black Radicalism*, edited by Gayle T. Johnson and Alex Lubin, 225–40. London: Verso.

Gilmore, Ruth W. 2020. *Abolition on Stolen Land with Ruth Wilson Gilmore*. Sanctuary Shorts, UCLA Luskin Institute on Inequality and Democracy. https://challengeinequality.luskin.ucla.edu/abolition-on-stolen-land.

Gilmore, Ruth W. 2022. *Abolition Geographies: Essays Towards Liberation*. Edited by Brenna Bhandar and Alberto Toscano. London: Verso.

Gilmore, Ruth W., Alberto Toscano, and Brenna Bhandar. 2022. "The Prison-Industrial Complex Goes Beyond Cops and Jails. It's All Around Us." *Jacobin*, February 8, 2022. https://jacobin.com/2022/08/prison-industrial-complex-race-capitalism-abolitionism.

Gilroy, Paul. 1993. *The Black Atlantic: Modernity and Double-Consciousness*. London: Verso.

Gopal, Priyamvada. 2019. *Insurgent Empire: Anticolonial Resistance and British Dissent*. London: Verso.

Hall, Stuart. 1980. "Race, Articulation, and Societies Structured in Dominance." In *Essential Essays*. Vol. 1 of *Foundations of Cultural Studies*, edited by David Morley, 172–221. Durham, NC: Duke University Press.

Hall, Stuart, Chas Crichter, Tony Jefferson, John Clarke, and Brian Roberts. 1978. *Policing the Crisis: Mugging, the State, and Law and Order*. London: Palgrave.

Hallsworth, Simon, and Jon Lea. 2011. "Reconstructing Leviathan: Emerging Contours of the Security State." *Theoretical Criminology* 15 (2): 141–57.

Hardt, Michael, and Sandro Mezzadra. 2016. "The Power of the Movements Facing Trump." *Roar*, November 16, 2016. https://roarmag.org/essays/trump-power-movements-protest.

Heatherton, Christina. 2022. *Arise! Global Radicalism in the Era of the Mexican Revolution*. Oakland: University of California Press.

James, Selma. 1975. *Sex, Race and Class*. Oakland, CA: PM.

Johnson, Cedric. 2023. *After Black Lives Matter: Policing and Anti-Capitalist Struggle*. London: Verso.

Khosravi, Sharam. 2018. "Stolen Time." *Radical Philosophy* 203:38–41.

Kipfer, Stefan. 2021 "Comparison and Political Strategy: Internationalism, Colonial Rule and Urban Research After Fanon." *Urban Studies* 59 (8): 1636–54.

Linebaugh, Peter, and Marcus Rediker. 2004. *The Many-Headed Hydra: Sailors, Slaves, Commoners, and the Hidden History of the Revolutionary Atlantic*. Boston: Beacon.

Neocleous, Mark. 2000. *The Fabrication of Social Order: A Critical Theory of Police Power*. London: Pluto.

Prashad, Vijay. 2007. *The Darker Nations: A People's History of the World*. New York: New Press.

Robinson, Cedric J. 1983. *Black Marxism: The Making of the Black Radical Tradition*. Chapel Hill: University of North Carolina Press.

Rodney, Walter. 2022. *Decolonial Marxism*. London: Verso.

Sharma, Nandita. 2022. *Home Rule: National Sovereignty and the Separation of Natives and Migrants*. Durham, NC: Duke University Press.

Shaw, Ian G. R., and Marv Waterstone. 2021. "A Planet of Surplus Life: Building Worlds Beyond Capitalism." *Antipode* 53:1787–806.

Singh, Nikhil P. 2016. "On Race, Violence, and So-Called Primitive Accumulation." *Social Text* 34 (3) (128): 27–50.

Sinha, M., 2016. *The Slave's Cause: A History of Abolition*. New Haven, CT: Yale University Press.

Sivanandan, Ambalavaner. 1990. "All That Melts into Air Is Solid: The Hokum of New Times." *Race and Class* 31 (3): 1–30.

Smythe, SA. 2018. "The Black Mediterranean and the Politics of Imagination." *Middle East Report* 286:3–9.

Stanley, Eric, and Nat Smith. 2011. *Captive Genders: Trans Embodiment and the Prison Industrial Complex*. Edinburgh: AK.

Sudbury, Julia. 2005. *Global Lockdown: Race, Gender, and the Prison-Industrial Complex*. London: Routledge.

Thompson, Vanessa E. 2020. Contribution to *Anti-Blackness: Transatlantic Worlds of Abolition: A Conversation with Eddie Bruce-Jones, Lorgia García Peña, Shana L. Redmond, Vanessa E. Thompson, João H. Costa Vargas, and Françoise Vergès*. Sanctuary Shorts, UCLA Luskin Institute on Inequality and Democracy. https://challengeinequality.luskin.ucla.edu/abolition-on-stolen-land.

Thompson, Vanessa E. 2021. "Beyond Policing, for a Politics of Breathing." In *Abolishing the Police*, edited by Koshka Duff, 179–91. London: Dog Section.

Thompson, Vanessa E. 2022. "From Minneapolis to Dessau, from Moria to Tripoli, from the Shores to the Land and the Sea: Global Geographies of Abolition." Disembodied Territories Project. https://disembodiedterritories.com/From-Minneapolis-to-Dessau-from-Moria-to-Tripoli-from-the-shores-to.

Thompson, Vanessa E. 2024. "Surplus people of the world unite! On borders, policing, and abolition." In *Border Abolition Now*, edited by Sara Riva, Simon Campbell, Brian Whitener, Kathryn Medien, 36–53. London: Pluto Press.

Thompson, Vanessa E. Forthcoming, 2025. *Black Socialities: Urban Resistance and the Struggle beyond Recognition in Paris*. Manchester: Manchester University Press.

Walia, Harsha. 2021. *Border and Rule: Global Migration, Capitalism, and the Rise of Racist Nationalism*. Chicago: Haymarket.

5

Abolition Is My Sanctuary

A Love Letter to Freedom

Lorgia García Peña

A love ethic presupposes that everyone has
the right to be free, to live fully and well.

bell hooks, *All About Love*

Over the past decade we have witnessed a slew of disgraces related to the university: the Varsity Blues scandal in 2019 that shed light on the corruption of elite college admissions of wealthy students; the series of sexual misconduct cases involving prestigious faculty; the graduate student strikes at places like Columbia, Berkeley, and the New School; the denial of tenure to accomplished faculty of color all over the country. The list can go on and on. Pair that with growing student debt; the ongoing crisis in the studies of humanistic subjects that no longer seem to serve the purpose of the neoliberal structures of the university and our society (why do we need art or literature when we have Tesla?); the continuously growing unfair labor practices that limit the number of secured long-term full-time employment for faculty; the rise of a managerial, customer-service like approach to teaching and research; the recent attacks on affirmative action that threaten the possibility of more scholars like myself—a product of affirmative action—to exist; the legal actions in states like Florida,

Texas, and Georgia making the work we do as scholars of critical race and ethnic studies illegal; ending the tenure system that protects our free speech and ability to criticize the systems of oppression. Given all that, it might be fair to say that the university is doomed. If so, what is next for our society?

I became a scholar at the sunset of the "diversity and inclusion" frenzy and at a moment in which the university functioned *only* as a neoliberal machine and not for the sake of knowledge-making. Yet I was also fortunate enough to become a scholar at a moment in which "politics" had entered the university, years after the 1960s worldwide university movements had flung open the campus gates to political movements and actions that made college campuses from Paris to Mexico City to San Francisco into battlegrounds for asserting freedoms and rights for all peoples, as well as becoming sanctuaries for learning beyond the colonial regime of the neoliberal university. The 1960s was also a decade of deep critical questioning of the role of education, and in particular higher education, in shaping social movements and changing the direction of society for the better. We have Paolo Freire publishing his *Pedagogy of the Oppressed*; we have people rediscovering, reprinting, and translating the work of Antonio Gramsci and thinking deeply about hegemony and the need for public scholarship; and we have students reading Marxist and feminist theory together, thinking about and through Black feminists, and organizing in unprecedented ways in places such as France, Italy, Mexico, and the United States.

That first wave started, roughly, with Freire and lasted until the mid-1980s with the work of Black and queer scholars of color (I am thinking here about the Combahee River Collective as well as the publication of *This Bridge Called My Back*). Now, once again we are seeing an unprecedented number of scholars who are public-facing. We have scholars of critical race and ethnic studies as regular contributors to news outlets, with important public platforms through their private social media accounts, and who are creating new media, as seen in Keeanga-Yamahtta Taylor's *Hammer and Hope*. Such public scholarship is threatening to many, though. There is so much fear of what can be possible and so much fear of losing the privilege that is inherited through whiteness, that our fields, what we do, our knowledge, and also especially who we are in the world—as scholars and thinkers forcing people to think about systemic racism all the time—are threatening to the systems that have been sustained precisely on said inequities. So, as in other historical moments, our work and our personas are under attack. Literally, they are trying to make us illegal, make our work and our methods illegal. Still worse, we are being asked by our own institutions to decide between what is ethical and what is legal when it comes to students' safety, to truth and peace (as seen recently in universities' decisions to attack peaceful students protesting the genocide in Palestine, the firing of dissident scholars, and the attacks on academic freedom and faculty governance). What is the role scholars have in this moment of impossibility? I would like to suggest that radical hope has always emerged from such impossibility—or, as one of my favorite Mexican slogans of this century states: "They tried to bury us, but they did not know that we were seeds." One example is Freedom University.

In January 2022, I was invited to give a lecture, "Teaching in Freedom," to reflect on the ways the classroom can be a site for social change. During the question-and-answer period, one of the attendees, a young scholar of Latinx studies, asked if I would share a little bit about my experience as the co-creator of and a teacher for Freedom University Georgia. They wanted to know what drove me to do my activism in support of undocumented students and what lessons I learned from the experience. I have been asked similar questions over the years, and I am always surprised at how emotional the question makes me feel, despite the passage of time and the fact that I have moved geographically and psychically further from Georgia and Freedom U and into other spaces of freedom-making. This time, however, was different. We had lost bell hooks only a month before. I was still grieving. I was trying to figure out how to live in a world that did not have her. As I answered, my eyes welled up, and I just let it happen: I let her *montarme*.[1] She possessed my words, and I heard myself say, "I was driven by love." And then the tears came. I didn't get to answer the second half of their question.

I cannot think of a more radical action as a scholar than to write and speak about love (bell hooks was such a badass). In academia, love is the ultimate taboo—particularly for women, more so for women of color. We are primed to write about death, dispossession, violence, oppression, domination, patriarchy, capitalism. In other words, we are expected to produce work about, and think about, the antithesis of love: the unloving. And for many of us, particularly those of us from colonized and oppressed communities, not only are these topics our research agendas, but they are also familiar as our life experiences, they are how we have been socialized as beings; they are, as Christina Sharpe (2016, 7) reminds us, "the ground we walk on." The unloving world in which we racialized, colonized, otherized peoples have come to exist is the norm, even as we seek to fight for change and attempt to redress the harm. As a society, we understand love as a feeling—as something we happen upon rather than something we practice.

We fall in love. We are, if we are lucky, loved by our families, and love them in turn simply because they are our blood, our original community, or sometimes our imposed community. The passivity through which love is written into our consciousness clouds our understanding of it as a radical act. Love is also, though, transformation, justice, freedom, the fabric that can and should sustain not just our individual relationships (romantic and platonic) but also our communities, our institutions, our nations, and our world. Love is a praxis and an ethics against the threat of spiritual, social, civic, and physical death. Abolition as love.

We understand praxis as the application of theory. Understanding love as a praxis means we recognize we need to learn to love; it also means we know love is not a static object, as hooks reminds us, but rather an action, a doing. Like all practices, loving perfects itself in its doing. hooks (2000) talked about six dimensions of love: care, commitment, trust, responsibility, respect, and knowledge. We tend to recognize the first three as central to our loving relationships. Yet for those of us in academia, knowledge is central to how we practice love. Following hooks's very defiant and rebellious definition of love as a practice of knowing and doing, I want to reflect in these pages on the meaning of love as praxis and ethics in my attempt to answer the second part of the question that young Latinx scholar asked during my talk in January 2022 that I could not answer then: "What are the lessons you learned from Freedom University?"

In *Abolition. Feminism. Now*, Angela Y. Davis, Gina Dent, Erica R. Meiners, and Beth Richie remind us that abolition is always a both/and project. It is about "moving beyond the binary either/or logic and the shallowness of reforms" to both attend to the emergency at hand (whether it's caring for migrant children and refugees at the border or providing healthcare and housing to those in need or educating the incarcerated) *and* to dismantle the racial capitalist structures (police, prisons, borders) that create the state of emergency and the violence that produce harm every day (Davis et al. 2022, 3). As we—Pam Voekel, Bethany Moreton, Betina Kaplan, and the undocumented students and activists who came together to create it in Athens, Georgia, in 2011—conceived of it, Freedom University (FU) Georgia was an abolitionist project, grounded in radical love that sought to fight injustice through civil disobedience and defiance and provide a sanctuary for undocumented students under attack in the state of Georgia.[2] Since its creation in 2011, FU Georgia has done exactly that. It has become a national model for abolition education in the face of state disavowal, persecution, and hate. Through a both/and philosophy, those of us who have been part of

FU Georgia co-created a sanctuary for learning in freedom while also fighting against the "civil murder" of human beings the state deems "unlawful."[3]

In the wake of 2020, as universities and other neoliberal institutions were forced to confront their colonial and antiblack structures, we witnessed a growth in public dialogues about the need to "decolonize" the university and to create antiracist structures that lead to justice and equity (de Sousa Santos 2019; Gum and Saliari 2022). We have also witnessed a set of practices become the norm in most universities: reading land acknowledgments, adopting gender-neutral pronouns, providing trigger warnings, and holding lecture series and creating postdoctoral cohorts that focus on Black knowledge and decolonial thought. While all these practices are helpful and meaningful to students and faculty, they often do not go beyond the symbolic or "reformative" to truly address what causes harm. This is because what is needed in the university is not inclusion nor reform but abolition: a "both/and" strategy that *both* fights the structures that produce harm *and* creates learning sanctuaries that can help us attend to the state of emergency that our educational system is now in by practicing love as bell hooks invited us to do.

It has taken me over a decade to grasp the profundity and immensity of the lessons I learned from the co-creation of FU Georgia: how to believe in the dream and how to trust that something that seems utopian is worth working for, even when—especially when—the moment presents us with nothing but despair. "What are the lessons?" This question, which I hope to never answer to the fullest, is a reminder of the importance of Freedom University Georgia not only for the students it served and continues to serve in its new iteration in Atlanta under the leadership of fierce scholar-activist Emiko Soltis but also for the impact it had on me as a teacher, scholar, and activist committed to abolition feminism as love.[4]

Both: In Defiance of Injustice, Toward an Ethics of Love

If a dream comes from a divine source and it tells us that our way of life will come to an end and it tells us how to survive the destruction of our traditional way of life, we should expect that there is much about the message and much about the future that we do not yet understand.

Jonathan Lear, *Radical Hope*

On October 14, 2010, as I began my first year as assistant professor of Latino/a studies at the University of Georgia, the university's board of regents voted 14–2 to prohibit public universities from enrolling students without papers in "any school that has rejected other qualified applicants for the past two years because of lack of space" (University System of Georgia 2010). The policy, which keeps academically qualified students from attending the top five public research universities in Georgia, was based on the belief that the presence of undocumented students was preventing citizens from enrolling in the public university system. This logic was based solely on anti-immigrant bias and xenophobia that had escalated over the decade that followed September 11, 2001, rather than actual facts (Jamal and Naber 2008). A study conducted by the very board of regents enacting this policy found that undocumented students constituted less than 0.2 percent of all public university students; most of these students were enrolled in technical and community colleges rather than the "top public universities" that were deemed too good for undocumented people (University System of Georgia 2010).

Georgia's 2010–11 iteration of xenophobic anti-immigrant legislation, which came on the heels of the 2010 Arizona State Bill 1070, commonly referred to as the "show me your papers law," followed a public controversy surrounding an undocumented college senior, Jessica Colotl, who faced deportation in the spring of 2010.[5] Colotl, a student in political science at Kennesaw State University, had been arrested on campus while waiting for a parking spot due to failure to present a driver's license (Muñoz and Espino 2017, 533). Cobb County deputies transferred Colotl to US Immigration and Customs Enforcement agents, who planned to deport the college senior to Mexico, her country of birth. After Kennesaw State president Daniel Papp appealed for Colotl's release, she was permitted to stay in the country for her senior year and graduate. Colotl's arrest augmented an ongoing public discussion about whether undocumented students "deserved" to access public college education in Georgia, leading to the passing of multiple state policies, including House Bill 87 in April 2011, which, similarly to Arizona SB 1070, required law enforcement officers to inquire about immigration status during routine stops for minor traffic violations and to hand over any undocumented suspects to federal authorities. The bill also required employers to check immigration status through the federal E-Verify database, and stipulated prison sentences for those convicted of "knowingly harboring or transporting undocumented residents." While the "show me your papers" provisions of Georgia's HB 87 and similar laws in other states prompted civil liberties lawsuits and preliminary injunctions by federal judges, ending in the eventual dismissal of the provisions, insufficient attention was given to the move by the board of regents to deny undocumented students access to state universities and colleges. The unintended result was, however, the emergence of a new movement that, as Nicole Guidotti-Hernandez (2011) argues, employed tactics similar to those used during the civil rights struggles of the 1960s.

Faculty and students began to mobilize immediately after the ban was announced. We circulated petitions, wrote letters, organized teach-ins, and looked for ways to create dialogue, bring attention to the issue, and, most importantly, pressure the administration to reverse the ban. It soon became evident, however, that the actions we could take within the system were not enough to address the state of emergency we were living in or to offer consolation, support, and refuge to the people under attack. Within days of the introduction of HB 87, I began to notice in my own neighborhood that immigrants were simply disappearing. When talking to my friends and activists in my community, I heard distress in their voices about the intimidation they felt from the local law enforcement officers who had begun to patrol immigrant neighborhoods and communities. They were living in a climate of fear. One morning in May 2011, at the end of my Introduction to Latino/a Literature class, one of my students told me that he would not be coming back to school the following year. His family was moving "up north" because they were afraid of what was coming. He was the only documented person in his family. He needed to go with them. That very afternoon, I bumped into my friend and colleague Betina Kaplan, who was as distressed as I was. We looked at each other and shook our heads in tacit knowledge, and then she asked me in very simple words a very complicated question: "What are we going to do about this situation?" A handful of other faculty members were asking themselves similar questions. Bethany Moreton and Pamela Voekel soon approached us with the impulse and energy to act. They brought with them years of organizing experience in community activism. I was new to Athens, but Pam, Betina, and Bethany had connections to various community organizations in the Atlanta and Athens areas. I was honored to follow their lead. The four of us would become the founding faculty members of Freedom University Georgia.

FU Georgia was first and foremost an act of defiance against unloving practices. As a faculty member of the University of Georgia, the flagship school banning undocumented students in Georgia, I found myself living in contradiction: I was working for a state and an institution that was actively harming the people I came from, study, and sought to serve—the people I love. When Betina, Bethany, Pam, and I first began to organize for FU Georgia, we did not think much about the potential risks this project represented to our individual persons and lives—facing legal action because we were "harboring undocumented immigrants," risking retaliation from our employer, and, in my case, risking tenure (joke's on UGA). Family and friends would reach out in concern, particularly after the project became public and we became the faces associated with it. It is not a coincidence that we were queer women, immigrant women, women from colonized countries and countries that survived dictatorships and war. People often called us brave. We were, and are, but mostly we were feminist organizers who came from communities that experienced risk and pain. We recognized as a collective the urgency to act immediately and to face the public head-on, particularly when the population we were supporting was already doing so while quite tangibly risking their freedom, facing incarceration and deportation. We came together because we knew the need for both/and: the importance of organizing for the future while taking care of the now. In the process we also found ourselves part of a historical tradition of defiance.

I have written and spoken many times about the incredible experience of co-creating Freedom University alongside these amazing feminist warriors and brave undocumented people, about the simplicity of the mandate to teach that brought us together, and about the radical abolitionist ethos that sustained our work and guided our praxis of love (García Peña 2012, 2022a). Recently, I also wrote about the centrality of Black politics and Black freedom struggles in our theory and our practices (García Peña 2022b). Freedom University would have been an impossible dream had it not been for the community of Black activists in Athens that supported it. Organizations like the Economic Justice Coalition and its leader, Linda Lloyd, who recognized in the state-mandated civil murder of undocumented youth the ghost of segregation that still lingers in places like Georgia. Or people like Congressman John Lewis, who spoke at one of our rallies and bailed out some of the FU activists who were arrested during an act of civil disobedience. They, too, recognized that anti-immigrant legislation in Georgia, and especially the ban against undocumented students, stemmed from the same colonial legacy that engendered slavery and segregation and continues to sustain antiblackness in the United States and beyond. Likewise, FU Georgia recognized, as Angela Davis reminds us, that the legacy of Black politics and Black struggles for freedom are central to all anticolonial and liberation struggles—particularly in the US South—and that our project was part of a much longer legacy: "Black struggles in the United States serve as an emblem of the struggle for freedom." Davis goes on to note that the Black radical tradition is relevant not simply to Black people in the United

States but to "all people who are struggling for freedom, including Latinxs, LGBTQ people, immigrants, Palestinians, Native Americans, and incarcerated people." She adds, "So within the sphere of Black politics, I would also have to include gender struggles, struggles against homophobia, and I would also have to include struggles against repressive immigration policies" (Davis 2016, 39). We were not alone or unloved, despite the despair. That gave us comfort.

Anti-immigrant racism emerges out of the same colonial capitalist structures that engendered slavery and that continue to sustain the existence of immigrant subjects in the afterlife of slavery. Our coalitional work through FU Georgia allowed us to extend the historical line that holds struggles for freedom and democracy in Georgia, showing how the past is not gone; it just changes names and form. As we organized protests and staged acts of civil disobedience and defiance, we also reminded the public of the presence of the past—of the specter of segregation and slavery in its multiple present-day manifestations, from the attacks against the undocumented to the economic inequality that kept Black people under the poverty line in Athens for generations. In so doing, FU Georgia's existence was not only in defiance of the university but also in defiance of systemic racial capitalism and antiblackness. Our demands, then, were not only about access to education but also about abolition of the systems that continue to keep us living in the afterlife of slavery.

And: A Sanctuary to Learn in Freedom

Born in the 1960s during the civil rights movement, Freedom Schools centered the lives of Black Americans and the sociopolitical issues affecting their communities. Students were invited to theorize based on their lived experiences. As FU Georgia co-creators reimagined the university we wanted—outside of the institution we worked for and that deeply harmed us—we dared to dream about the utopian. As we did, we leaned on the educational traditions that have come from defiance, including freedom schools, ethnic studies methodologies, and participatory pedagogies, to create a learning sanctuary where undocumented students in Georgia could learn in freedom. In spiritual terms, sanctuary is a place of respite, renewal, and even bliss. In its political iteration, sanctuary is always in contradistinction to war, devastation, and struggle. In bell hooks's terminology, a sanctuary is a place of love, and the result of a praxis of love *in* devastation, rather than against it. Freedom University Georgia was a living sanctuary, one created with and by the lived experiences of being with each other, being seen by others in our totality, and feeling safe to learn and live despite devastation.

For undocumented communities, particularly for undocumented students in the United States, the word *sanctuary* summons palimpsestic political movements of resistance: the early 1980s religious and political campaign to provide safety for Central American refugees fleeing civil war that was a response to federal immigration policies that made obtaining asylum difficult for Central Americans, and the demands for and movements in favor of creating sanctuary spaces in cities and institutions across the United States following the 2016 election of Donald Trump and the anti-immigrant xenophobic policies of his administration. In both moments the term *sanctuary* signified both defiance and love.

In the fall of 2016, as the election unfolded, I was teaching a Latinx studies lecture course for a predominantly Latinx student group, many of whom came from mixed-status families or had been or were themselves undocumented/DACAmented. The day after the election I witnessed my students' distress as they waited for the devastation they expected would come in January. I also saw their resolve to figure out solutions to contrast with it. They organized quickly, staged public protests, and drafted a list of demands that began with first declaring their campus a sanctuary for undocumented people and followed with a list of concrete requests for supporting students day to day. These included mental health, legal, and financial support; peer counseling; meeting spaces; and more. Their both/and project was grounded in a desire to fight back *before* the war came; it was forcing power structures to institutionalize their choices through public announcements and statements. In the weeks that followed the election, we saw universities, institutions, and even cities throughout the United States declare themselves sanctuaries for the undocumented. In the years that followed we saw legislation, violence, microaggressions, and exclusion continue to materialize in those very spaces declared sanctuaries—in the treatment of workers, the continuous exploitative practices, and the blatant disregard for Black, Indigenous, and undocumented lives. In 2020 we saw a similar display, this time in support of Black lives. As we moved away from the state of emergency brought forth by the COVID-19 pandemic and as protests decreased, we have seen broken promises and "business as usual" continue at the expense of Black, Indigenous, immigrant, and Global South peoples. Those places never were sanctuaries.

When those of us who are safe think about sanctuary, we often think about respite. We imagine sanctuary in contradistinction to what we are running away from. But for people who suffer, respite cannot be disentangled from risk. Rather, as my experience with Freedom University taught me, for communities at risk, respite can only be found in the common acknowledgment of the threat. It was in seeing themselves as part of a community of students who were undocumented in Georgia in 2011 who faced the overlapping threats of deportation, incarceration, and exclusion that Freedom University students found their sanctuary. Their sanctuary was not the space we created for them, nor the political mandate of a moment, but rather the praxis of love we developed together.

When asked to reflect about Freedom University through the framework of sanctuaries for this edited volume, I struggled with my own discomfort with the contemporary political meaning of the term *sanctuary* and its subsequent co-optation by neoliberal institutions such as the university. I wrestled with honoring the political legacies of two waves of the sanctuary movements—the one that emerged during the Central American wars and the one that followed Trump's election—and my own longing for and commitment to sanctuary as a love praxis toward the creation of sustainable communities of care that prioritize safety because of the devastation that has been and continues to be the world for Black, Indigenous, undocumented, and colonized peoples. In my previous writing I called for the classroom to be a space for freedom-making. I still believe it can be. And yet, as I sat to reflect once more on the creation of Freedom University Georgia, now over a decade ago, and its impact on how I imagine the classroom, I also call for teachers to think about their teaching in relation to a loving praxis and to think of the classroom as a space in which everyone can and should feel free and safe. This is particularly urgent for those of us teaching in Black and ethnic studies, prison studies, Palestinian studies, and anticolonial and Global South studies, as our areas of study face violence and attacks by our institutions and as the people who come from the communities we center in our studies confront civil, social, and corporeal death. It is not enough to read and study about the harm; we must undo it in our teaching.

How do we practice love in our teaching? How do we, as scholars and teachers, teach and write in and through love? I would like to offer some suggestions following the teachings of bell hooks.

First, recognize what is *not* of love. For example, hooks (2000, 139) reminds us that "love and abuse cannot coexist." Working in institutions that are still grounded on heteropatriarchy, colonialism, and white supremacy, as universities are, means we are essentially not loved by our institutions. It also means that our presence in them is a disruption of the unloving fabric that sustains them. Recognizing this fact can allow us to protect ourselves from harm, seek refuge in sanctuaries, and find and make alternative, radical communities of love within our classrooms and outside the institution. Working within structures that are unloving does not mean we must be unloved; it means we must create pockets of love where our whole beings can be sustained.

Second, understand love as a choice. We get to have agency in our loving. We get to decide whom to love. When we make this choice, we also make the choice to release that which does not sustain our commitment to loving. As scholars of color, we are often pulled in many directions; our lives are filled with the expectations of others. We pay the service tax, and we are supposed to do so with gratitude. Our students expect us to be more for them; the administration expects us to solve their unloving structures of inequality and exclusion with our magic BIPOC wands. As soon as we are hired the demands start pouring in, and we become tired and overwhelmed. An ethics of love can guide us to decide what to invest our bodies, energies, and souls in—which projects are worth our love and which must be released so that we may continue to grow and thrive. A loving ethics brings us closer to a life of radical, shameless joy in which we only make room for that which is of love.

Third, and perhaps most important in building our loving praxis, we must recognize ourselves beyond the performative or the expected. To practice love is to let ourselves be vulnerable to our own shortcomings, to see our mistakes reflecting to us as they are, without judgment—something my favorite poet and guide, Josefina Báez, calls the "as is." We must meet life right where we are, not where we aspire to be. In this world of social media avatars in which we are primed to perform a better, braver, smarter, thinner, prettier version of ourselves for the world to see and admire, hooks and Báez invite us to do the opposite: to embrace our failures and shortcomings and recognize them as part of a whole and as legacy. Growth comes from that awareness. Growth is always of love.

Fourth, forgive. hooks (2000, 202) invites us to let go of that which hurts us, to detach from its pain and death in loving ways. That is perhaps the most challenging act, but also the most necessary to live and practice in love. Forgiving does not mean we do not hold others accountable for harm they cause. It does not mean we allow ourselves to be used and exploited. It means we detach; we protect our hearts; we invest in healing from trauma; we practice care with ourselves and our communities. We take ourselves out of situations that are hurtful and speak up to protect the most vulnerable in our communities and our classrooms. Forgiveness is an act of self-preservation. We forgive to release that which hurts us and blocks our loving praxis.

The last step hooks outlines is very dear to me: communion—the creation of connections and bonds with other human beings grounded in the praxis of love. Now, this is no easy task. Building community is almost the antithesis of academia. As scholars, we are trained to believe that we "find" documents in the archive and that makes us owners of history. We are rewarded for individual success from very early on, from the proverbial A all our students seek in our courses to the holy grail of tenure and full professorship that rewards our individual achievements. In a culture of protectiveness of one's individuality and success, building communities of love is challenging. It is painful and, at times, demoralizing. How many of us have tried, to no avail, to find or build those spaces? How many of us have felt betrayed, ostracized, hurt, and broken in the process? hooks reminds us that building communities of love does not mean that we live happily ever after, nor does it mean that there are no conflicts and betrayals; it simply means that we are equipped to confront them, make people accountable for their mistakes, and find a path forward. Building a loving community requires all the elements of love: trust, commitment, care, respect, responsibility, and knowledge (hooks 2000, 94). To be in communities of love, against the death that surrounds us, is the ultimate revolutionary act. It is our revenge against the unloving isms that try to destroy us. Loving community is our salvation.

What lessons did I learn from the co-creation of Freedom U? I am still learning.

NOTES

1 In Afro-Caribbean religions, *montarse* refers to the act of the dead taking possession of a living person's body to share truth.
2 For more on the creation of Freedom University, read Muñoz and Espino 2017; Smith 2013; Soltis 2015; Voekel 2016.
3 Writing about denationalized Dominicans of Haitian descent, Amarilys Estrella (2020) theorizes the exclusion of undocumented immigrants as "civil death." I use the word *murder* to signal the intention of the state.
4 In 2014, Emiko Soltis was selected as director of Freedom University and has since led with the support of the board and volunteers. She talks about her experiences in Soltis 2015.

5 The Support Our Law Enforcement and Safe Neighborhoods Act (introduced as Arizona Senate Bill 1070 and commonly referred to as Arizona SB 1070) is a 2010 legislative act in the US state of Arizona that was the strictest anti-illegal-immigration law in the United States when passed. It required immigrants to carry documentation at all times and empowered police to enforce immigration checks. In practice, it legalized racial profiling of Latinx people. Jessica's arrest happened in the context of a larger national controversy around illegal immigration. See Simmons 2013.

WORKS CITED

Davis, Angela Y. 2016. *Freedom Is a Constant Struggle: Ferguson, Palestine, and the Foundations of a Movement*. Chicago: Haymarket.
Davis, Angela Y., Gina Dent, Erica R. Meiners, and Beth Richie. 2022. *Abolition. Feminism. Now*. Chicago: Haymarket.
de Sousa Santos, Boaventura. 2019. "Decolonizing the University." In *Knowledges Born in the Struggle: Constructing the Epistemologies of the Global South*, edited by Boaventura de Sousa Santos and Maria Paula Meneses, 298–311. New York: Routledge.
Estrella, Amarilys. 2020. "Muertos Civiles: Mourning the Casualties of Racism in the Dominican Republic." *Transforming Anthropology* 28 (1): 41–57.
Freire, Paulo. 1968. *Pedagogy of the Oppressed*. New York: Continuum.
Garcia Peña, Lorgia. 2012. "New Freedom Fights: The Creation of Freedom University Georgia." *Latino Studies* 10:246–50.
García Peña, Lorgia. 2022a. *Community as Rebellion: A Syllabus for Surviving Academia as a Woman of Color*. Chicago: Haymarket.
García Peña, Lorgia. 2022b. *Translating Blackness: Latinx Colonialities in Global Perspective*. Durham, NC: Duke University Press.
Guidotti-Hernandez, Nicole. 2011. "Old Tactics, New South." *Ms. Magazine Blog*, November 16, 2011. http://msmagazine.com/blog/blog/2011/11/16/old-tactics-new-south/.
Gum, Bethany, and Stella Saliari. 2022. "Rethinking Decolonizing the University: A More Nuanced Approach Toward Decolonization." *Junctions: Graduate Journal of the Humanities* 6 (1): 14–20.
hooks, bell. 2000. *All About Love: New Visions*. New York: HarperCollins.
Jamal, Amaney, and Nadine Naber, eds. 2008. *Race and Arab Americans Before and After 9/11: From Invisible Citizens to Visible Subjects*. Syracuse, NY: Syracuse University Press.
Lear, Jonathan. *Radical Hope: Ethics in the Face of Cultural Devastation*. Cambridge, MA: Harvard University Press, 2006.
Moraga, Cherríe, and Gloria Anzaldúa, eds. 1981. *This Bridge Called My Back: Writings by Radical Women of Color*. Albany: SUNY Press.

Muñoz, Susana M., and Michelle M. Espino. 2017. "The Freedom to Learn: Experiences of Students Without Legal Status Attending Freedom University." *Review of Higher Education* 40 (4): 533–55.

Sharpe, Christina. 2016. *In the Wake: On Blackness and Being*. Durham, NC: Duke University Press.

Simmons, Andria. 2013. "Charges Against KSU Graduate Jessica Colotl Dismissed." *Atlanta Journal-Constitution*, January 10, 2013. https://www.ajc.com/news/local/charges-against-ksu-graduate-jessica-colotl-dismissed/y3QNa8a7HK2E1ifCP65WtJ.

Smith, Emily J. 2013. "Out of the Shadows and into the Spotlight: Undocumented Students in Pursuit of Higher Education and the Case of Freedom University, Georgia." PhD diss., Florida Atlantic University.

Soltis, Laura Emiko. 2015. "From Freedom Schools to Freedom University: Liberatory Education, Interracial and Intergenerational Dialogue, and the Undocumented Student Movement in the US South." *Souls* 17 (1–2): 20–53.

University System of Georgia. 2010. "Regents Adopt New Policies on Undocumented Students." https://www.usg.edu/news/release/regents_adopt_new_policies_on_undocumented_students.

Voekel, Pamela. 2016. "Organizing for Freedom." *NACLA Report on the Americas* 48 (1): 68–78.

INTERLUDE

Abolitionist Praxis

Bringing Our
Imagination to Life

Veronika Zablotsky

In the wake of the police murders of Breonna Taylor and George Floyd in 2020, the Black Lives Matter movement inspired a global uprising for Black lives and put demands for the abolition of police and prisons on the agenda of many mainstream institutional spaces. As defunding strategies were being debated in the United States and elsewhere, the Miami-based queer-feminist collective (F)empower, while in virtual residency with the Sanctuary Spaces Sawyer Seminar, convened the online conversation "Abolitionist Praxis: Bringing Our Imagination to Life," to insist on investment in community-based alternatives.[1]

Moderated by Niki Franco, (F)empower's co-founder and political education director, this event exemplifies deep thinking across interconnected geographies of struggle for abolition on stolen land. Tune in to the recording to learn about abolition feminist organizing for reproductive justice, community care, decolonization, and economic transformation from Ruth Jeannoel, Haitian-born founder and director of Fanm Saj, Inc.; Shariana Ferrer-Núñez, Afro–Puerto Rican co-founder of La Colectiva Feminista en Construcción; and Francisco Pérez, executive director of the Center for Popular Economics. As abolitionist practitioners, the speakers commune with Franco on repair and redress through life-affirming institutions that build collective capacities for self-determination in the here and now—"'til we free us" (Kaba 2021)—toward large-scale structural change.

Community resources for Black, Brown, and Indigenous liberation (Hassan 2022) "calibrate power differentials anew," Ruth Wilson Gilmore (2022, 486) argues and help us "recognize that the negation of the negation [of racial capitalism] is always abundantly possible." We are reminded by (F)empower that abolition geographies are constituted by abolitionist praxis, including artistic performance and political education, to give life to radical imaginings of a new world that support and care for all, not just a few.

NOTE

1 The convening "Abolitionist Praxis: Bringing Our Imagination to Life" can be viewed at https://challengeinequality.luskin.ucla.edu/abolitionist-praxis.

WORKS CITED

Gilmore, Ruth Wilson. 2022. *Abolition Geography: Essays Towards Liberation*. Chicago: Haymarket.

Hassan, Shira. 2022. *Saving Our Own Lives: A Liberatory Practice of Harm Reduction*. Chicago: Haymarket.

Kaba, Mariame. 2021. *We Do This 'Til We Free Us*. Chicago: Haymarket.

UCLA Luskin Institute on Inequality and Democracy. 2020. *Abolitionist Praxis: Bringing Our Imaginations to Life*. Featuring Niki Franco, Sharianna Ferrer-Núñez, Ruth Jeannoel, and Francisco Pérez. https://challengeinequality.luskin.ucla.edu/abolitionist-praxis.

PART II

The End of Humanitarianism

6

"Mujer Migrante Memorial (MMM)" and Necro-Art

Maite Zubiaurre

"Mujer Migrante Memorial (MMM)" (Adamo 2021; Diaz 2021; Zubiaurre 2023a) is a virtual and "real" urban collective art installation in Venice Beach, California, that honors the lives and deaths of female migrants who have died in the desert of Arizona since the 1990s. "MMM" is a guerrilla-style memorializing effort that happened on June 19, 2021, as part of yet another ongoing intervention, "The Wall That Gives / El Muro Que Da," created by Filomena Cruz, my alter ego as an artist, in 2015 (Camp 2018; Zubiaurre 2023b). In this case, "The Wall That Gives / El Muro Que Da," a wall that gives away art for free, gifted its surface to a migrant memorial that calls attention to the close to four hundred female migrants whose bodies have been recovered from the Sonoran Desert. "MMM" is meant to raise awareness about migrant death, "wasted lives" (Bauman 2004), and necropolitics (Mbembe 2019) at the US-Mexico border. An urban street art installation conceived as a traveling exhibit, it "transports" migrant death to the city, or, rather, highlights the fact that the Arizona desert is part of the urban imaginary: the Latinx communities in Los Angeles know the desert full well, since so many have crossed it during their harrowing journey into the United States, and many have family members and friends who have perished in it. It is important to note that "MMM" does not happen in a void: as this chapter shows, it partakes in the ethical implications of necro-art and the representation of extreme suffering (Butler 2004; Sontag 2013) and should be read in the context of the various artistic practices that dare to give expression to migrant death in the US-Mexico borderlands.

Let me clarify. If you look up "necro-art," the internet will tell you, "It looks like there aren't many great matches for your search." And if you look up "border necro-art," digital wisdom has even less of a clue. And yet, border necro-art—art that dares to face, and gives expression to, migrant death—exists, though it is not as prevalent as it should be (we offer some examples in this chapter), and clearly not acknowledged enough. The postcolonial depredatory capitalism of the West is cynical enough to blame nature (the desert kills) for the thousands of displaced subjects who have perished and who keep dying in the US-Mexico borderlands. Necro-art, however, debunks cynicism. It identifies and artistically represents the desert as a paradigmatic necropolitical space purposely turned into a lethal weapon by the American and global necropolitics of migration. The aim thus of "MMM" (and of necro-art at large) is threefold. It seeks to (1) raise awareness about migrant death as the tragic consequence of forced mobility and mass displacement, (2) point the finger at the necropolitical machinery and systemic violence of the West that willfully exterminates, and (3) exert its healing powers through repairing acts and rituals of remembrance and memorialization. Lastly, "MMM" is a reflection about how abstraction dialogues (or not) with concreteness and the representation of the specific and singular in the context of migrant death. Abstract forensic data and death maps shed necessary light onto the necropolitical reality of the US-Mexico border. But at the same time, art identifies the need to return to the very concrete and palpable, for it is that, not the abstract and intangible, that will appeal to our emotions. Ultimately, it is through the heart, through the body, and through the senses that we will be able to grasp the unthinkable, and thus find the determination to passionately rebel and resist.

"Mujer Migrante Memorial (MMM)": A Real and Virtual Installation

In 1994, during the Clinton administration, the United States Border Patrol formally implemented the immigration enforcement strategy known as "prevention through deterrence," which militarizes urban border crossing points and forces migrants into remote and dangerous natural terrain. "Prevention through deterrence" is still the primary border enforcement strategy being used at the US-Mexico border today. This set of policies fails to deter border crossers; instead, the number of migrants who die during their harrowing border crossing experience is increasing. The US Border Patrol records that the remains of more than seven thousand migrants were recovered between 1998 and 2020, but humanitarian groups and forensic experts overwhelmingly agree that the real numbers of those who died are much higher (NNiRR n.d.). In fact, it is estimated that for each body found, there are another five that the desert will never give back.

Forensic work and data gathering on migrant death on the US side of the border vary widely. In my book *Talking Trash: Cultural Uses of Waste* (Zubiaurre 2019), I take up what anti-immigrant groups, disguised as (pseudo) environmentalists, to this day call "migrant trash"—namely, the personal belongings migrants leave behind while crossing the arid borderlands. I ask what role these artifacts play in the process of identifying deceased migrants and how these personal belongings are stored and cataloged. Thus when I approached Dr. Gregory Hess, the chief medical examiner at the Pima County Office of the Medical Examiner (PCOME), in Tucson, Arizona, back in 2016 for the first time, I did so with what was (in hindsight) a scandalously naïve question: "I imagine, Dr. Hess," I contended, "that the archival methods for forensic identification purposes of the personal belongings found on deceased migrants are standardized all along the US-Mexico border." Dr. Hess looked at me musingly and responded with a sentence that I will never forget: "In the matter of death, nothing is standardized."

Time and research have shown that Dr. Hess's dictum could not have been more faithful to the truth: the US-Mexico border is intricately chaotic, and the state laws pertaining to unidentified human remains are either nonexistent, as is the case in Arizona, or are "not systematically followed by many counties," as in the case of Texas (Spradley et al. 2019). In other words, systemic structural violence and chronic invisibilization are exerted not only against the bodies of living migrants but also against their lifeless remains. In August 2016, there was a very important convening where the main players dealing with migration at the southwestern border (policymakers, Border Patrol authorities, forensic personnel, and humanitarian organizations) met to gather knowledge on migrant death. Called "Responding to Migrant Deaths Along the Southwest Border: Lessons from the Field" (Police Executive Research Forum 2016), it starts by establishing a clear distinction between Arizona and Texas. Texas is the state where damaging chaos reigns more rampantly. While in Arizona 57 percent of land along the border is public, in Texas 96 percent of the state's borderlands are expansive private cattle ranches where access is not permitted and where migrant bodies rot and disappear; worse still, in Texas the matter of migrant death overwhelmingly rests in the hands of justices of the peace who are charged with determining cause of death and with signing death certificates even though they are not required to have any medical knowledge. In Arizona, this is the responsibility of medical examiners. In other words, each state (and, in Texas, each county along the border) has its own protocols regarding migrant death. Some chief examiners' offices report the cases of migrant death to the National Missing and Unidentified Persons System (NAMUS), while others don't. Some carefully archive and classify personal belongings found on the bodies of migrants for identification purposes; others disregard them and stuff them into a dusty jumble of file cabinet drawers. Some bend over backward to do anything they can to identify the bodies of migrants, while others carelessly and criminally throw the unidentified bodies into unmarked mass graves.

As an example, in 2013 and 2014, forensic anthropologists and students from Baylor University, Texas State University, and the University of Indianapolis exhumed a total of 162 remains of migrants from mass graves at a cemetery in Falfurrias, Brooks County, Texas. "The bodies are believed to have been buried by a local funeral home since 2005 in the Sacred Heart Burial Park in [Falfurrias,] Brooks County," says *Borderzine: Reporting Across Fronteras* (Collette 2014). There is no "method"—or basic decency, for that matter—when it comes to burying migrant bodies: there were multiple remains found in just one body bag, buried with no container at all, or jammed into shopping bags and trash bags.

In stark opposition to that reality, the PCOME in Arizona is well known for its ethically infused scientific rigor and the exemplary thoroughness it applies toward the identification of migrant remains. The PCOME carefully registers and publishes statistical information in its annual reports, separating out homicide deaths, accident deaths, suicide deaths, natural deaths, cases of undetermined manner of death, overdose deaths, and motor-vehicle-related fatalities, but it stands out prominently for devoting an increasingly detailed section to "Undocumented Border Crosser (UBC) Remains." As the 2021 annual report explains,

> The term "Undocumented Border Crosser" (UBC) refers to foreign nationals who die attempting to cross the southern Arizona desert without permission from the United States government. Since January 1, 2000, the PCOME has received 3,483 recovered remains

of suspected UBCs. To date, the highest number of UBC recoveries recorded at the PCOME in a given calendar year (CY) was in 2010 (222). The past two calendar years, CY2020 and CY2021, recorded the next highest UBC recoveries to date, 215 each year. In terms of Federal fiscal years (FY), FY2021 (Oct 1, 2020—Sept 30, 2021) saw the highest number of UBC recoveries in a given FY (226). The number of UBC recoveries per year are adjusted annually to account for the association of remains found months or years apart, which are later discovered to be remains of the same individual. (PCOME 2021, 31)

The section "Undocumented Border Crosser (UBC) Remains," with its detailed statistics and graphics, not only provides information on the bodies retrieved from the Arizonan desert in the year of the report but also includes comparative statistics that shed light on the number of remains found between 2000 and 2021. The statistics register UBC recoveries by identification status (between 2000 and 2021, of the total of 3,483 recovered, 2,239 bodies have been identified, but 1,244 remain unidentified; the numbers for 2021 specifically are 104 identified and 111 unidentified); by age group (the overwhelming majority of recovered and identified bodies between 2000 and 2021 belong to individuals in the 20–29 age group, with 811; 721 were between 30 and 39 years old; and 237 died very young, between 13 and 19 years old); by nationality (of the recovered identified remains, 1,768 were Mexican, 284 Guatemalan, 69 Honduran, 68 Salvadoran, and 17 Ecuadorian; Peruvians, Brazilians, Colombians, Costa Ricans, Indians, Venezuelans, Dominicans, Chileans, and Jamaicans have also died in the desert of Arizona); and by cause of death (in 2021, the report states, "the most common cause of death . . . has been undetermined, followed by environmental exposure. An undetermined cause is primarily due to limitations of the examination of the decomposed and skeletal remains. Environmental exposure includes death related to extreme heat, cold or dehydration" [PCOME 2021, 36]). The statistical data above attest to the grim reality of migrants dying of hypothermia, hyperthermia, and dehydration, and of their bodies decomposing on the desert soil. The "prevention through deterrence" policies that were implemented along the US-Mexico border in 1994 have turned the Sonoran Desert into "a land of open graves, as the tragically fitting title of Jason de León's book reads" (De León 2015).

The PCOME also presents statistics for the category of gender. Between 2000 and 2021, 513 bodies retrieved from the Arizona desert were identified as female. In 2021, the remains of 30 female migrants arrived at the Tucson morgue. "Only" 15 percent of the recovered bodies from 2000 to 2021 were female. In 2021 the percentage was slightly lower, 14 percent. It is precisely this 15 or 14 percent that "Mujer Migrante Memorial (MMM)" wishes to honor. "MMM" is an homage to the invisible among the invisible, to the migrant women who more often than not come from Indigenous communities in Mexico and Guatemala and lose their lives on the hardened sands of the Sonoran Desert. It is no secret that for women, migration holds even more dangers than it does for men. It is no secret that sexual abuse and rape are their faithful companions along the migrant trail, and that gender violence is one of the main causes that compels them to leave their homes and communities behind. A migrant woman in a shelter in Nogales only needed to utter the following about her excruciating migration journey to make me understand: "Para las mujeres es peor," she said, lowering her eyes. For women, it is worse.

"Mujer Migrante Memorial (MMM)" is a three-pronged endeavor seeking to promote action and reaction against female migrant death and necropolitical violence: it is art, it is activism, it is pedagogy. Or rather, it is activism, pedagogy, art. It aims at raising awareness in and out of the classroom, on the streets, and in the virtual realm, via art. "MMM" was born out of a UCLA Mellon Foundation–sponsored Urban Humanities Initiative graduate capstone seminar with a very specific goal: to design an awareness-raising urban and digital art installation that honors the lives of female migrants whose bodies were recovered from the southern Arizona desert. From its inception—and this is very important—the guiding principle of "MMM" was not aesthetics but "aesth-*ethics*": Fundamental questions about the ethical responsibility of making (forensic) art or necro-art remained at the center of our reflections throughout the whole process (Butler 2004; Sontag 2013). More importantly, the five members of our "MMM" team—master's of architecture students Maha Benhadmi and Miranda Hirujo-Rincón, master's of urban planning student Eliza Franklin-Edmondson, and PhD student in the humanities Cristina Vázquez and I as the leading Professor and instructor—had one obsessive goal in mind: to create a memorial that respects and honors the deceased migrants and does not retraumatize their families and loved ones. It is important to stress that state violence keeps exerting its destructive power on the bodies of deceased migrants. As mentioned above, state laws regulating the forensic procedures around unidentified remains along the US-Mexico border are grossly insufficient, even nonexistent. Migrant remains are cremated, buried in paupers' cemeteries, even thrown into mass graves unregistered and unidentified. Migrants are forcefully erased, their lives and deaths unaccounted for; hence our fixation with memorializing the invisibilized and with seeking repair through rituals of collective remembrance and mourning. Guided by this obsessive purpose, "Mujer Migrante Memorial (MMM)" was installed on June 19, 2021, at "The Wall That Gives / El Muro Que Da" in Venice Beach.

"The Wall That Gives / El Muro Que Da" is an ongoing urban intervention created by Filomena Cruz, my alter ego as an artist, in 2015. In response to rampant state violence and anti-migrant sentiment, Filomena Cruz conceived a wall that, unlike border walls, is not hostile but welcoming: every day since 2015, Filomena Cruz has left a four-by-four-inch tile with one of her collages in a seven-by-seven-inch niche on the wall as an anonymous gift, and very often the community gives back, not only taking the tile but also leaving a small present or trinket in return (Camp 2018; Zubiaurre 2023b).

"The Wall That Gives / El Muro Que Da" is a ninety-five-foot-long wall, and on June 19, 2021, it became a memorial. A vinyl banner that reproduces the desert landscape of southern Arizona was turned into the background for 389 crosses that honor the life and death of the 389 migrants whose bodies were recovered from the southern Arizona desert between January 2001 and May 2021 (figures 6.1 and 6.2).

Four laser-engraved wooden panels screwed onto the wall offer the necessary explanation and background to the installation in both English and Spanish. The English version reads as follows:

> In 1994, the U.S. Government instituted a set of policies known as "Prevention Through Deterrence" that made it more difficult for undocumented migrants to cross near the urban points of entry at the U.S.-Mexico border. Forced to traverse remote rural areas and harsh terrain, many migrants have perished in the attempt. Since January of 2001 and as of May of 2021, 2733 migrant remains have been recovered from the Southern Arizona desert (Pima County) alone. It is estimated that for each body found, there are five more the desert will never give back. This is a memorial in honor of the female migrants who have lost their lives during their harrowing journey across the Sonoran desert. Each of the 389 crosses bears the topographical imprint of the site where the remains were found. It registers the first name of the female migrant, and, if unknown, crosses read "unidentified" or "sin identificar," in Spanish. The desert topographies on the crosses are tinted in different hues of pink and purple, the

FIGURE 6.1 "Mujer Migrante Memorial (MMM)," urban artistic installation by Maha Benhachmi, Eliza Franklin-Edmondson, Miranda Hirujo-Rincón, Xiuwen Qi, Cristina Vázquez, and Maite Zubiaurre / Filomena Cruz, Venice Beach, 2021. Credit: Maite Zubiaurre / Filomena Cruz.

FIGURE 6.2 "Mujer Migrante Memorial (MMM)," urban artistic installation by Maha Benhachmi, Eliza Franklin-Edmondson, Miranda Hirujo-Rincón, Xiuwen Qi, Cristina Vázquez, and Maite Zubiaurre / Filomena Cruz, Venice Beach, 2021. Credit: Maite Zubiaurre / Filomena Cruz.

colors of feminism fighting gender violence. The QR Code will take you to the virtual "Mujer Migrante Memorial (MMM)." It includes a searchable map, an extensive illustrated narrative, and a multilingual poem originally composed in English and then translated into Spanish and a number of Indigenous languages from Mexico and Central America, in homage of female migrants who leave their countries and indigenous communities behind.

As described above, "MMM" has both a "real" component and a virtual component. The digital component of MMM is of crucial importance, since it makes sure that efforts at memorialization and repair are perpetuated in time and expand in space. A public urban intervention has a shorter life span and a limited audience; hence the need to fight oblivion and to warrant permanence to healing rituals of mourning and remembrance. Moreover, MMM's virtual expansion offers additional context, and also painstakingly documents the artistic thought process.

The "real" urban "MMM" installation that took place on "The Wall That Gives / El Muro Que Da" in Venice Beach, California, is not as "exportable" as its digital component, needless to say, but has been conceived as a traveling exhibit that nonetheless can be detached from the wall that first housed it. The traveling installation thus includes (1) the aforementioned vinyl banner that reproduces the desert landscape of southern Arizona, to be attached to a wall or other type of supporting structure; (2) the laser-engraved wooden panels, also mentioned earlier; and (3) the 389 death-site-specific crosses that honor and mourn the female migrants whose remains were recovered as of May 2021.

On the day of the initial installation, between eighty and one hundred participants, including activists from California and Arizona, members of the Venice Beach and Los Angeles communities, and academics from different institutions, gathered to put up the crosses. The somber performance was accompanied by the recitation, amplified with the help of loudspeakers, of the first and last names of the 389 victims when they were known. The recitation went on and on so that we would hear the names repeatedly. Repetition is a memorializing device, an awareness-raising strategy, and a powerful tool that fights individual and collective oblivion. Thus, repetition is crucial to "MMM" at various levels: "The Wall That Gives / El Muro Que Da" is a ninety-five-foot-long "repetition" of crosses and death sites, enforced by equally iterative mantra-like recitation. Moreover, at the same time the 389 crosses were being put up against the wall and the backdrop

FIGURE 6.3 "Mujer Migrante Memorial (MMM)," urban artistic installation by Maha Benhachmi, Eliza Franklin-Edmondson, Miranda Hirujo-Rincón, Xiuwen Qi, Cristina Vázquez, and Maite Zubiaurre / Filomena Cruz, Venice Beach, 2021. Credit: Maite Zubiaurre / Filomena Cruz.

of the vast Sonoran Desert landscape, another group of participants, led by Colombian-born artist Álvaro Enciso, were writing the first names of the 389 female migrants with chalk on the sidewalk along the wall.[1] The names of the victims are so many that the sidewalk was not long enough: the seemingly endless list of names continued on a long pedestrian alley that leads to the beach, and almost reached the ocean (figure 6.3).

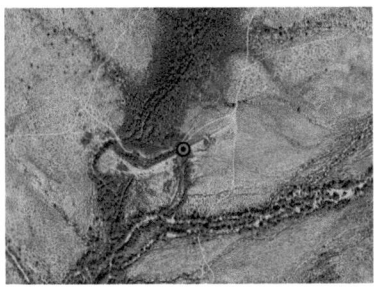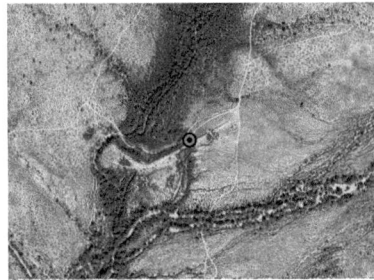

Case ML 01-01076

FIGURE 6.4 "Mujer Migrante Memorial (MMM)," urban artistic installation (digital component) by Maha Benhachmi, Eliza Franklin-Edmondson, Miranda Hirujo-Rincón, Xiuwen Qi, Cristina Vázquez, and Maite Zubiaurre / Filomena Cruz, https://storymaps.arcgis.com/stories/5a0f3d3b42634812b33ae64b1924cd9a. Credit: Maha Benhachmi, Miranda Hirujo-Rincón, and Xiuwen Qi.

The vinyl banner reproducing the vast Arizona desert landscape was designed and made in Tijuana, Mexico, and our team crossed the border into Mexico to pick it up and transport it to LA. As for the crosses, our shared task was to (1) geolocate the 389 death sites on Google Maps; (2) take a screenshot of each of them; (3) tint each of them in purple and pink tones, the colors of the global fight against gender violence, and the colors as well of the somberly emblematic crosses that denounce the Cuidad Juárez femicides (figure 6.4); (4) design 389 vinyl cross patterns with the tinted screen shots (for the sake of perspectival effect when placed on the vinyl landscape, the crosses come in four different sizes; the same graphic designer from Tijuana that created the banner made the customized and tinted covers); (5) cut out 389 wood crosses; and, finally, (6) paste the self-adhesive vinyl covers onto the crosses.

The reason behind photographically portraying and "personalizing" each of the sites where the remains of female migrants were found and to then paste them on the crosses was the following: We know barely anything of the lives of migrants who die. It would be unethical to presume we know and try to represent artistically what we clearly ignore. But what we do know, tragically, because of the data provided by the PCOME and the "Map of Migrant Mortality" created by the nonprofit organization Humane Borders / Fronteras Compasivas (figure 6.5), is the exact geospatial location where each of the female migrants lost her life.[2] Thus "MMM" honors the lives of the deceased by acknowledging the otherwise invisible and ignored—

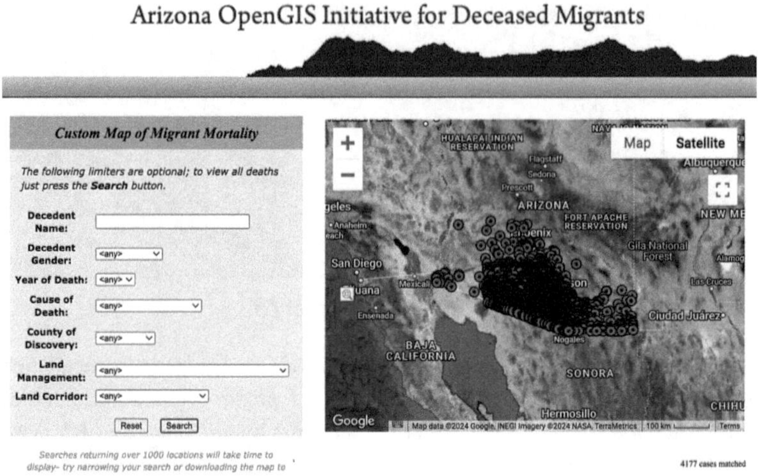

FIGURE 6.5 Arizona Open GIS Initiative for Deceased Migrants, https://humaneborders.info/app/map.asp. Credit: Humane Borders / Fronteras Compasivas.

namely, the distinctive, sacred site where life left the body, the last landscape that the female migrant saw before dying. "Personalization" through the photographic depiction of the specific death sites of each of the deceased female migrants restores memory and dignity to the women whose bodies were found in the desert. But it is also a tool to denounce and counteract the necropolitical apparatus at the US-Mexico border and its efforts at systematically erasing migrant existence and personhood.

The "Map of Migrant Mortality" is of fundamental importance to "MMM" and has been an indispensable source for the project's real and virtual components. Part of an unavoidably sinister and increasingly frequent cartographic subgenre meant to locate and represent widespread violence and death—such as Spain's "Mapa de las Fosas Comunes de la Guerra Civil y el Franquismo," the "Mapa de Fosas Clandestinas en México," the "Mapa de Femicidios de Argentina," the "Mapa de Feminicidios en México," and "Ellas Tienen Nombre," an interactive map that registers femicides in Ciudad Juárez—the "Map of Migrant Mortality" is a cartographic and interactive tool meant to help families and communities looking for their loved ones left behind in the southern Arizona desert. The "Map of Migrant Mortality" mirrors the visual language of the Ciudad Juárez femicides mortuary map "Ellas Tienen Nombre" mentioned above. Like in the case of "Ellas Tienen Nombre," in the "Map of Migrant Mortality" the relatively simple spatial representation adheres to the two-dimensional Euclidean plane implemented by the world's largest GIS provider, Google. The "Map of Migrant Mortality" thus is a GIS-based tool kit "that use[s] publicly available information to grant access to high quality downloadable spatial data regarding migrant deaths. Data are updated monthly, and the search tools allow any user to a) query data concerning migrant deaths; b) view the data using online maps and tables; and c) download the data for further use" (PCOME and Humane Borders 2024). The location at which a deceased migrant was found is punctuated by a simple red dot. As of November 2024, the map shows 4,308 red dots geolocating the sites where migrant bodies were recovered from the Sonoran Desert in Arizona since the 1990s. The simple red dots sinisterly blend into what appears to be an ever-expanding sea of blood.

The "Map of Migrant Mortality" inspired "MMM" to move away precisely from the abstraction that is inherent to any cartographic exercise and to return to the concrete site and reality from which the map derived its abstractions. For its "real" installation, "MMM" went "back" to the Arizona desert, reproduced its landscape on a vinyl canvas, hung it on an urban wall, and through death-site-specific crosses made the desert landscape where female migrants had lost their lives concrete, almost palpable.

But the "Map of Migrant Mortality" is equally crucial to the virtual installation. The latter, which can be accessed via the QR code laser-engraved on the explanatory panels attached to the "MMM" memorial, includes (1) an extensive narrative on female migrant death in the US-Mexico borderlands; (2) an interactive digital map created by Xiuwen Qi that topographically locates the death sites of the 389 female migrants whose remains were recovered from Pima County, Arizona, between January 2001 and May 2021 (figure 6.6), and, arguably even more important, (3) a poem in homage of the deceased female migrants composed in English by Eliza Franklin-Edmonson, and translated into Spanish and into Tzotzil, Zapotec, Nahuatl, Purépecha, and Mixtec, some of the Indigenous languages more frequently spoken in the communities and countries of origin of the great majority of female migrants that die in the desert. (Soon it will also include a short documentary of the "real" installation and memorializing wall.)

We know that "at the U.S.-Mexico border . . . a significant number of the individuals now being detained are people of Indigenous origin" (Riley and Carpenter 2021, 38). Moreover, according to the forensic anthropological findings of the PCOME, more than 90 percent of the bodily remains retrieved from the Southern Arizona desert belong to Indigenous migrants. Not unlike the Mediterranean, the desert along the US-Mexico border is

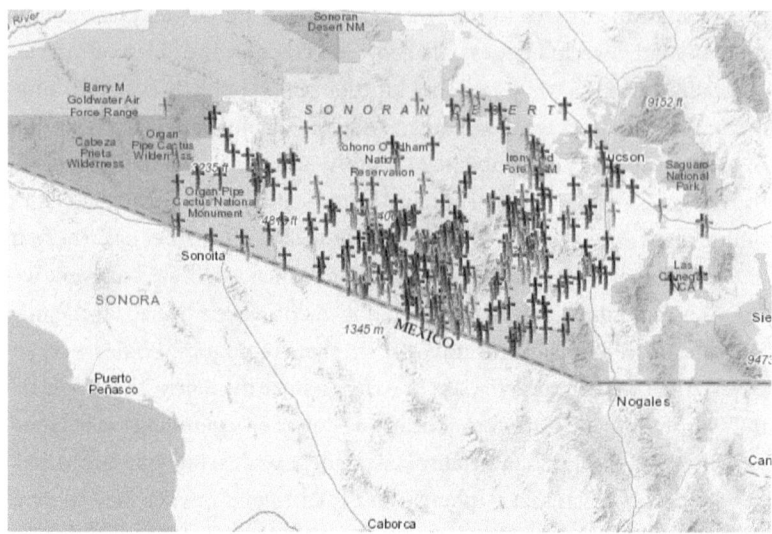

FIGURE 6.6 "Mujer Migrante Memorial (MMM)," artistic installation (digital component and interactive map) by Maha Benhachmi, Eliza Franklin-Edmondson, Miranda Hirujo-Rincón, Xiuwen Qi, Cristina Vázquez, and Maite Zubiaurre / Filomena Cruz. Credit: Xiuwen Qi.

an ever-growing cemetery to Black and Brown bodies. Many Indigenous migrants do not speak Spanish, or speak it only as their second language. It was very important to us that "MMM" acknowledge this fact and honor not only the lives and deaths of migrants but also their often silenced mother tongues as inextricably tied to their identities, equally subjected to systemic discrimination and repression. It is relevant to stress that whereas the poem has been deliberately "thickened" with its various versions in Indigenous languages, the map has been subjected to an inverse operation and purposely "thinned" and trimmed of certain information.

The "MMM" map resorts to the "Map of Migrant Mortality" as its base map but, driven by the ethical imperative not to further retraumatize families and loved ones, it avoids forensic descriptions of the cause of death and the state of the body when found. It only reveals the case number, the migrant's age and name when known, the day the body was recovered from the desert, and the county and state (Pima County, Arizona). In our map, icons in the form of crosses replace the red dots of the "Map of Migrant Mortality." Gray crosses stand for the female migrants whose bodies remain unidentified, whereas the different shades of pink and purple of the crosses of identified migrants refer to different age groups. Also, it was important for us to use the same color palette for the "personalized" crosses on the "real" "MMM" wall and the crosses on the digital map in the virtual installation: we wanted to make sure that the dialogue with the pink crosses of the Ciudad Juárez femicides and the fight against gender violence expand from the real into the virtual realm, and vice versa.

In sum, pasted on the crosses, the tinted screenshots of the Google map become not only concrete and tangible (vinyl on wood attached to a wall) but also affect-laden: "Mujer Migrante Memorial" uses empathy to first "thin" a virtual map, and then turns cartographic abstraction into a personalized landscape drenched in emotion. The elimination of potentially (re)traumatizing forensic information has the power to bring us closer to the deceased migrant, to evoke her presence through her name, to think about her and *not* about the circumstances of her death. Our hearts open up, and empathy and emotion take the upper hand.

"MMM" in the Context of Necro-Art at the Arizona-Sonora Border

"MMM" happens not in a void but in the accompanying context of necro-art at the US-Mexico border. The "Map of Migrant Mortality" and the PCOME forensic data and archives not only have been of invaluable help to "MMM" but are also a fundamental tool and even a constant source of inspiration to artists portraying the reality of migrant death in southern Arizona. One of these artists is Colombian-born and Tucson-based Álvaro Enciso, mentioned before. When Enciso first saw the "Map of Migrant Mortality," his life took a radical turn: he decided to retire from a well-paying job as cultural anthropologist in New Mexico and since 2013 has made it his mission to place crosses at the exact geospatial locations where migrant remains were found. Called "Donde Mueren los Sueños / Where Dreams Die," his land art installation uses the abstraction of the map to restore the concreteness that made abstraction possible: the red dot on the map suddenly shows up on the desert and becomes a cross made of recycled wood, with a red dot (a deliberate reference to the red dots on the "Map of Migrant Mortality") cut out of the rusty frijoles and tuna cans migrants leave behind at its very center. Note that Alvaro's cross is an agnostic, even atheistic one: according to the Colombian artist, who believes not necessarily in God but in humanity and the ultimate power of empathy and solidarity, the vertical bar of the cross represents the verticality of life, the horizontal bar represents the horizontality of death, and the center of the cross with its red dot represents precisely the point where life and death converge.

So far, Enciso has been able to place close to twelve hundred crosses. However, he knows full well that, ultimately, "Donde Mueren los Sueños / Where Dreams Die" will be "mission unaccomplished": his crosses honor only one-fourth of the total number of migrant remains found, and migrants keep dying in the Sonoran Desert and all along the US-Mexico border. But there are other examples, such as Alyssa Quintanilla's digital intervention "Vistas de la Frontera."[3] Inspired by Enciso's long-standing practice of land art that memorializes, Quintanilla films the sites where a migrant died and where now one of Alvaro's crosses stand. The approximately two-minute-long videos, seventy-six so far, are heart-wrenching: they quietly and hauntingly film the death sites and record the sounds of the desert: the wind, the distant rumbling of highway traffic, the song of birds, or just the silence. Quintanilla's videos are embedded in an interactive digital map, and so the move from the concrete to the abstract, and vice versa, continues. A similar strategy underlies the latest artistic intervention put forward by Jason De León's Undocumented Migrant Project, called "Hostile Terrain 94."[4] Here, migrant death maps of the southern Arizona border pop up at multiple sites (museums, community centers, universities, etc.) and are covered in toe tags with the names of and information about migrants who perished during their border crossing ordeal. On the abstract surface of a map, an artifact as somberly concrete as an identifying tag hanging from the toe of a cadaver suddenly materializes.

"La Casa de los Puntos Rojos / The Red-Dotted House" is yet another collaborative artistic intervention in which the "MMM" team participated. Enciso, who was an active participant at the "MMM" installation on June 19, 2021, and, as mentioned, had put forward the initiative of writing the first names of the 389 migrants with chalk on the pavement, invited us to travel to the Arizona desert in August. He had spotted a dilapidated adobe construction at the end of a migrant trail, very close to the *levantón* site (pickup point) where migrants are hastily pushed into cars and driven to their final destinations. On August 5, 2021, under a merciless sun that raised the temperature to 110 degrees Fahrenheit, Enciso and the "MMM" team stenciled the four sides of the abandoned house with big red dots (figures 6.7 and 6.8). Once again, we move from cartographic abstraction to palpable concreteness, for here the red dots of the virtual "Map of Migrant Mortality"

FIGURE 6.7 "La Casa de los Puntos Rojos / The Red-Dotted House," artistic installation by Álvaro Enciso, in collaboration with Maha Benhachmi, Eliza Franklin-Edmondson, Miranda Hirujo-Rincón, Xiuwen Qi, and Maite Zubiaurre / Filomena Cruz, southern Arizona desert, 2021. Credit: Maite Zubiaurre / Filomena Cruz.

FIGURE 6.8 "La Casa de los Puntos Rojos / The Red-Dotted House," artistic installation by Álvaro Enciso, in collaboration with Maha Benhachmi, Eliza Franklin-Edmondson, Miranda Hirujo-Rincón, Xiuwen Qi, and Maite Zubiaurre / Filomena Cruz, southern Arizona desert, 2021. Credit: Maite Zubiaurre / Filomena Cruz.

suddenly show up on "real" adobe walls that offer refuge to migrants. It is part of Enciso's project "Las Que No Llegaron / The Women Who Did Not Arrive"; the artist says, "The house of the red dots is a visual metaphor for the broken dreams, violence, and suffering that is experienced daily here at the borderlands."

The "Map of Migrant Mortality" takes center stage and is the primary trigger of artistic reflection in all the aforementioned artistic interventions: "Mujer Migrante Memorial"; Alvaro Enciso's two installations, "Donde Mueren los Sueños / Where Dreams Die" and "La Casa de los Puntos Rojos / The Red-Dotted House"; Jason De León's "Hostile Terrain 94"; and Alyssa Quintanilla's "Vistas de la Frontera." But at the same time, and despite their very different nature and style, all five installations are quick to escape cartographic abstraction and to confront head-on the tragic concreteness of migrant death as the direct and deliberate consequence of border necropolitics. Empathy drives all of them back into a morgue that has become the permanent ghastly home to the remains of close to thirteen hundred unidentified migrants, back into a desert turned into a lethal weapon by state violence, back into a "natural" scenery where, perversely, to stumble upon migrant bodies in different stages of decomposition is now "normal" and normalized. Importantly, when empathy-driven art "moves back" and decidedly encounters and even embraces the concrete instead of seeking refuge in the "safety" of the abstract, the only choice is to move forward. For once art has forcefully revealed the ethico-political stakes of migrant death, once we have seen necropolitics rearing its ugly head, we have reached the point of no return: the desert will never be the desert again.

NOTES

1 Information about Álvaro Enciso's work is at https://ecologiesofmigrantcare.org/alvaro-enciso.
2 Also known as the "Arizona OpenGIS Initiative for Deceased Migrants," and created by the nonprofit organization Humane Borders / Fronteras Compasivas in collaboration with the PCOME, whose forensic experts and medical examiners provide all the statistical data, the "Map of Migrant Mortality" is at https://humaneborders.info/app/map.asp.
3 Quintilla's work can be seen at https://www.vistasdelafrontera.com.
4 De León's work can be seen at https://www.undocumentedmigrationprojectfcfc.org/hostileterrain94.

WORKS CITED

Adamo, Madeline. 2021. "Mural Pays Respect to Remains of Women Found Near the U.S.-Mexico Border." UCLA Newsroom, July 18, 2021. https://newsroom.ucla.edu/stories/maite-zubiaurre-mujer-migrante-memorial.

Bauman, Zygmunt. 2004. *Wasted Lives: Modernity and Its Outcasts.* Cambridge: Polity Press.

Butler, Judith. 2004. *Precarious Life: The Powers of Mourning and Violence.* London: Verso.

Camp, Melanie. 2018. "El Muro Que Da and the Gang That Took Over." *Beautiful Hollywood*, August 19, 2018. https://beautifulhollywood.com/2018/08/19/el-muro-que-da-and-the-gang-that-took-over.

Collette, Mark. 2014. "Mass Graves of Immigrants Found in Falfurrias." *Borderzine: Reporting Across Fronteras*, June 26, 2014. https://borderzine.com/2014/06/mass-graves-of-immigrants-found-in-falfurrias.

De León, Jason. 2015. *The Land of Open Graves: Living and Dying on the Migrant Trail.* Oakland: University of California Press.

Diaz, Breanna. 2021. "UCLA Professor, Students Create Project to Honor Deaths of Migrant Women." *Daily Bruin*, September 18, 2021. https://dailybruin.com/2021/09/18/ucla-professor-students-create-project-to-honor-deaths-of-migrant-women.

Mbembe, Achille. *Necropolitics.* Durham, NC: Duke University Press.

NNiRR. n.d. "Stopping Migrant Death at the Border." National Network for Immigrant and Refugee Rights. https://nnirr.org/programs/seeking-border-justice/stopping-migrant-deaths (accessed October 9, 2024).

PCOME. 2021. "Annual Report 2021." Pima County Office of the Medical Examiner. https://content.civicplus.com/api/assets/271d4f4a-2e86-4214-b2c3-837e4275b54d.

PCOME and Humane Borders. 2024. "Arizona OpenGIS Initiative for Deceased Migrants." Last updated November 26, 2024. https://missingpersons.icrc.org/index.php/library/arizona-opengis-initiative-deceased-migrants.

Police Executive Research Forum. 2016. "Responding to Migrant Deaths Along the Southwest Border: Lessons from the Field." https://www.policeforum.org/assets/respondingmigrantdeaths.pdf.

Riley, Angela R., and Kristen A. Carpenter. 2021. "Decolonizing Indigenous Migration." *California Law Review* 109:64–139. https://www.californialawreview.org/print/decolonizing-indigenous-migration.

Sontag, Susan. 2013. *Regarding the Pain of Others.* New York: Farrar, Straus and Giroux.

Spradley, Katherine, Nicholas P. Herrmann, Courtney B. Siegert, and Chloe P. McDaniel. 2019. "Identifying Migrant Remains in South Texas: Policy and Practice." *Forensic Sciences Research* 4 (1): 60–68. https://doi.org/10.1080/20961790.2018.1497437.

Zubiaurre, Maite. 2019. *Talking Trash: Cultural Uses of Waste*. Cambridge, MA: MIT Press.

Zubiaurre, Maite. 2023a. "*Mujer Migrante Memorial (Memorial de la Mujer Migrante*—MMM): La Muerte Que No Cesa." Colección conmemorativa de los 30 años del PUEG-CIEG, UNAM, Mexico City.

Zubiaurre, Maite. 2023b. "The Wall That Gives / El Muro Que Da: Trash in a Box." In *Archaeology Outside the Box*, edited by Hans Barnard, 513–42. Los Angeles: UCLA Cotsen Institute of Archaeology.

7

From Camp to Commons

Infrastructures of Decolonial
Solidarity in Europe

Charalampos Tsavdaroglou and Maria Kaika

Introduction

This chapter unveils housing solidarity practices that both confront and challenge the colonial aspects of state-run camps. Focusing on newcomers' self-organized housing projects in Greece, we argue that these practices constitute decolonial solidarity infrastructures against the European Union's and the Greek state's racialized migration housing practices and policies.[1]

Since the Syrian refugee crisis of 2014–15, the image of long rows of white containers lined up in the midst of rudimentary infrastructures in periurban areas in Greece has become the symbol of Europe's housing policies for newcomers (see figure 7.1). In the past seven years, more than 2.3 million newcomers from the Middle East, Central Asia, and Africa entered the EU (UNHCR n.d. b). More than 1.3 million entered via Greece, and many among them remained "trapped" in Greece for long periods, unable to move onward to their final destinations in northern Europe (UNHCR n.d. a). In line with state and EU policies, they have been offered accommodation in camps run by the Greek state, most of which are located in abandoned factories or on military bases in the periphery of the country's two main cities, Athens and Thessaloniki. Most of the camps'

FIGURE 7.1 Containers in Skaramagas refugee camp in Athens. Credit: Charalampos Tsavdaroglou and Maria Kaika.

residents dwell in white containers under living arrangements that provide newly arrived populations with only the bare necessities to stay alive. The life expected to be lived there is a standardized, anonymous life that cannot accommodate cultural, ethnic, religious, or other social needs. The current European institutional arrangements allow for a kind of living that is close to bare life, stripped of meaning other than the struggle for survival.

However, despite living under these conditions, newcomers build relations and interactions with each other and with local support groups; these relations and interactions often shape the conditions for forming new material and social infrastructures of decolonial solidarity in the form of self-organized community centers and often even lead to alternative housing projects. Many of these alternative social and material infrastructures are self-managed as forms of urban commons where locals and newcomers make decisions together and engage with and learn from each other's culturally informed practices. We argue that these solidarity practices can provide inspiration and form the basis for revising migrant housing policies and practices. Based on extensive ethnographic fieldwork conducted between 2017 and 2022 in state-run camps and migrant squats in Athens and

Thessaloniki, this chapter juxtaposes the colonial aspects of official European Union institutional arrangements to migrant housing with the decolonizing and commoning practices of grassroots newcomers' housing projects. The fieldwork involved sixty semistructured interviews (thirty interviews per city) and informal discussions. Some of the interviews were conducted with the help of interpreters, and all names of research participants are anonymized. The newcomers who participated in the research are from Syria, Algeria, Morocco, Iraq, Afghanistan, and Iran.

Colonial Aspects of Refugee Camps and Decolonial Solidarity of Common Spaces

Several scholars depict refugee camps as regimes of control and as a state of exception, marginality, and invisibilization of displaced people (Agier 2011; Turner 2016; Wacquant 2007). For Petti (2013), a refugee camp is an "anti-city"; for Sharma (2009), it is a "non-place"; and for Bauman (2000), the twentieth century was "the century of camps." In 2021, six million people were living in camps, a number that is expected to increase further in the coming years (UNHCR 2021). In "camp studies," several scholars (Diken and Laustsen 2004; Edkins 2000; Pasquetti 2015), inspired by Foucault's "panopticon" theory and by Agamben's notion of "bare life," conceptualize camps as biopolitical structures of confinement, securitization, and control over newcomers. However, in recent years, a conceptual shift emerged, as many scholars (Christidis 2023; Katz 2017; Martin, Minca, and Katz 2020; Sanyal 2010; Sigona 2015; Tsavdaroglou and Kaika 2022a; Turner and Whyte 2022) focused on and highlighted the potentialities for agency-building and subjectification of newcomers inside the camps. In light of this turn, many scholars propose that the camps constitute "hybrid," "contested," and "ambiguous" spaces (Kreichauf 2018; Maestri 2017; Oesch 2017; Ramadan 2013).

However, with very few exceptions (Davies and Isakjee 2019; Gilroy 2004; Minca 2015), scholars fall short of examining state-run camps as a (neo)colonial apparatus. This is somewhat surprising, given that the very origins of the camps can be found in colonial practices enacted by the Spaniards at the end of the nineteenth century in Cuba, followed by the British in South Africa, the US Army in the Philippines, and the Germans in South-West Africa (now Namibia) in the early twentieth century, in the concentration camps of the First World War, and later in the Soviet gulag and the Nazi death camps (Diken and Laustsen 2004; Pitzer 2017). Embedding the contemporary practices of camps in Europe within the Western colonial legacy of running camps is particularly important for understanding some of the practices that are normalized in contemporary state-run camps across Europe. According to Minca (2015, 78), "In the colonies, the future Nazis learned a great deal about not only how to exploit people and resources, but also about race division and the breaking down of the human species into a biological hierarchy that was applied by all colonial powers to the subjugated populations."

Although we certainly do not suggest any parallel between Nazi concentration camps and contemporary state-run camps, we argue here that it is worth exploring the extent to which the colonial legacies of camps are deeply embedded in cultural, political, and material architectural and planning practices. Our main argument is that these legacies of the camp, as a product of colonial history, account to a great extent for the fact that today's camps function primarily as mechanisms of producing totalitarian environments for controlling the "other" (of whatever origin). The fact that the vast majority of residents in camps across Europe do come from former European colonies adds gravity to the need to explore these connections (Mayblin 2017). To put it succinctly, the camp reflects "how the historical reality of colonialism continues to pattern the present" (Danewid 2017, 1680). In general, many contemporary state-run camps across Europe share features of the European colonial camp legacy.

For Athens and Thessaloniki in particular, the cases we examine here, we can document the following characteristics that are shared with Europe's longer colonial legacy of camp-building. First, it is well documented that most camps in Greece are located in nonresidential periurban areas, and often in areas characterized as industrial or military zones (Gemenetzi and Papageorgiou 2017; Pechlidou, Frangopoulos, and Hatziprokopiou 2020; Tsavdaroglou and Lalenis 2020). Second, they are often characterized by low standards of living, lack of democratic processes in decision-making, top-down management policies, technocratic and expert-centric governmentalities, the racial division of newcomers into living sectors according to their ethnicity, and a failure to adhere to urban planning guidelines. Moreover, in most camps the basic housing unit is the container: a product of modernity, once purpose-built to transport cargo, and now used also for the containment of newcomers, as "objects" that are transported from one place to another.

However, if we take seriously Lefebvre (1991), who highlighted that space is not a static container but a social process, and Massey (2005), who proposed that space is always under construction and open to the possibilities of multiplicity and heterogeneity, then the crucial question that arises is whether there is the potentiality for newcomers to challenge and contest the camps' confinement, and the colonial relations embedded within that legacy. Indeed, our research shows that newcomers in the camps in Athens and Thessaloniki often develop practices of commoning while living in containers; in some cases they even flee the camps to create self-managed housing commons outside (Tsavdaroglou and Kaika 2022b). We argue that these attempts to turn spaces conceived for cargo transport into lived spaces for human communities could be seen as a kind of anticolonial project, a project that can potentially decolonize the "military humanitarianism" (Tazzioli and Garelli 2020) of "custody and care" (Minca 2015) enacted by state policies and NGOs.

At this point, it is worth mentioning that spaces serving as commons usually involve projects of social groups that are homogeneous in terms of ethnicity, citizenship, language, and cultural and political motives. However, our research on newcomers' housing commons demonstrates the potential to create forms of decolonial commons that go beyond those fault lines; these include real, existing places where people from different countries of origin and with a multitude of cultural and social identities coexist. Thus, the newcomers' commons raise the question of "decolonial otherwise" (Mignolo and Walsh 2018) and open new conceptual avenues to extend the Lefebvrian concept of "the right to the city" (Lefebvre 1996) to rethinking the newcomers' right to the city.

Camp-Based State Accommodation Policies in Athens and Thessaloniki

After the declaration-agreement between the European Union and Turkey in March 2016 (European Council 2016) and the closure of the borders in the Balkan corridor, the Greek state was faced with the necessity of accommodating an ever-increasing number of newcomers who crossed the country's borders looking for a way to move toward the European North. To manage the situation, the Greek state organized thirteen accommodation centers (camps) in the periphery of Athens and another thirteen in the periphery of Thessaloniki (see map 7.1). These campsites were abandoned former military training camps, abandoned factories and other industrial sites, shipyard piers, and abandoned former airport facilities. The number of people who stayed in these accommodation centers (camps) in the summer

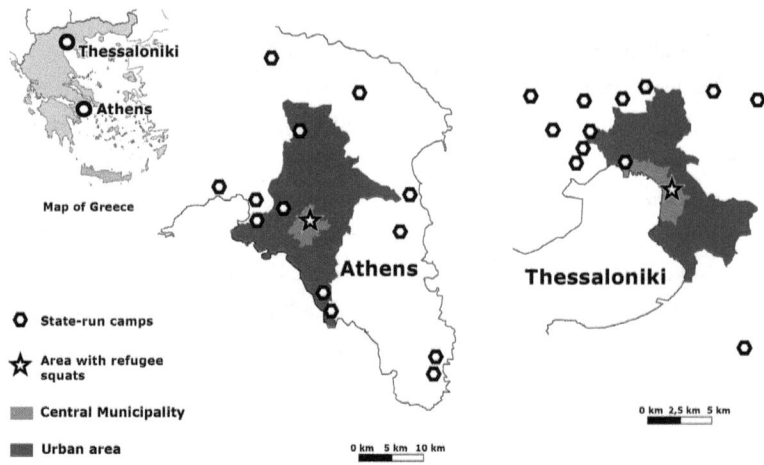

MAP 7.1 Locations of state-run camps and housing squats in Athens and Thessaloniki. Credit: Charalampos Tsavdaroglou and Maria Kaika.

of 2016 in the metropolitan region of Athens was 15,192; those who stayed in Thessaloniki numbered 19,859 (Coordination Centre for the Management of Refugee Crisis in Greece n.d.). In the following years, several of the state-run camps were closed down, while those remaining operational after the summer of 2021 were walled in and fenced off with three-meter-high concrete walls, thus preventing any visual contact with the areas outside the camps, and reinforcing the feeling of isolation for residents. Although materially people were free to move in and out of the camps, symbolically these spatial interventions turned camps from open-type accommodation structures into closed-type camps.

According to several scholars (Gemenetzi and Papageorgiou 2017; Papatzani et al. 2022; Pechlidou, Frangopoulos, and Hatziprokopiou 2020; Tsavdaroglou and Lalenis 2020) who have examined the social-spatial features of state-run camps and the living conditions of newcomers there, these camps violate Greek spatial planning regulations. They are located in areas that according to local urban planning guidelines do not allow residential uses, they are places of exclusion (as there is significant difficulty in accessing places of education, healthcare, and employment), and there are few possibilities of interaction with local communities. Also, the administration and management of the camps follow a top-down and expert-centric model in which the Ministry of Migration, the army, and police authorities, alongside international NGOs (such as the Office of the United Nations High Commissioner for Refugees [UNHCR] and the International Organization for Migration [IOM]), exert control and make decisions. As a consequence, there is a significant lack of participatory processes involving camp residents in decision-making and an absence of democratic processes such as freedom of speech, voting, or assembly. Finally, newcomers are very often confronted with xenophobic reactions from local communities that demand the removal of the camps.

At the same time, around the end of 2015, accommodation programs were set up within the urban fabric. Under the management of the UNHCR in collaboration with NGOs and municipalities, and in the form of the ESTIA program (Emergency Support Program for Integration and Housing), private apartments were rented and assigned first to asylum seekers eligible for family reunification and then to vulnerable asylum seekers. However, the ESTIA program ended in 2022, and several thousand asylum seekers were evicted and became homeless. According to several scholars, living conditions in the rented apartments prolong precariousness because the rental contracts are temporary (Kourachanis 2019a; Papatzani et al. 2022) and because these kinds of policies are limited to "residual type interventions with philanthropic features" (Kourachanis 2019b, 70). These arrangements favor welfare dependency for asylum seekers, as they are not coupled with labor training or opportunities for work. Asylum seekers are referred to as "beneficiaries" and reduced to depending on relationships of charity while at the same time their livelihoods become auxiliaries for the expansion of "philanthrocapitalism," which offers revenues to housing companies and landlords (Chuang 2015; Mitchell and Sparke 2016; Webber, Leitner, and Sheppard 2020).

Still, the ESTIA rental programs offered the opportunity for newcomers to live outside camps, to claim their right to the city, and to produce new relationships and commoning practices within and beyond their own communities. However, the Greek state's decision, without any sufficient justification (Refugee Support Aegean 2022), to end the accommodation program in rental apartments inside the urban fabric and to maintain only the state-run camps outside the cities cut off these possibilities abruptly. Most newcomers were left with limited options. Only a few among them had the choice to even return to camps. The changes in Greek policies correspond to the broader European Union restrictive migration policies, which carry explicit colonial legacies (Spijkerboer et al. 2021). In reality, in Greece, due to its geographical position on the perimeter of the European Union, the externalization of the EU immigration policy is applied (Bousiou 2020; Cobarrubias et al. 2023). For instance, the Dublin Regulation III (European Union 2013), which permits newcomers to apply for asylum only in the first arrival country, like Greece and other southern European countries, aims to prevent the movement of newcomers to countries in central and northern Europe. Thus, newcomers remain in the category of the unwanted foreigner, for whom a kind of "military humanitarianism" is foreseen (Tazzioli and Garelli 2020), which in the case of Greece manifests itself through marginalization, deprivation, and invisibility of newcomers in the precarious conditions of state-run camps and living in cargo containers.

Turning White Containers into Living Space

In the words of Fatima, a woman from Syria who lived in the state-run camp Diavata, outside of Thessaloniki: "People who leave the camps have psychological problems and traumas because they spent most of the time inside the container looking out through the little windows, like prisoners, desperate, disappointed, without having anything to do to keep themselves busy and distracted" (interview, September 5, 2020).

As we noted in the beginning, the white container has become a distinctive feature of state-run camps in Europe. The container was standardized by the US Army Transportation Corps in the late 1940s and was used during the Korean War and later on in the Vietnam War (Levinson 2016) for freight transport on ships, by rail, or on trucks. Today, in the format of the so-called isobox, it is widely used to accommodate newcomers in state-run camps. The initial idea behind the container was to move "goods from anywhere, to anywhere, with a minimum of cost and complication on the way" (Levinson 2016, 2). In a similar way, to achieve minimum cost—and at the same time reflecting the colonial legacies of camps—the isobox is a white container and, regardless of the cultural and social background of the newcomers, is used to house all newcomers.

Living in containers, newcomers are treated as a homogenized group, and the uniqueness, culture, customs, and desires of each individual mobile subject are erased and silenced. According to Dalal (2017, 1), these arrangements "generate an assumption that all refugees are the same." Thus, the newcomer is dehumanized and objectified; just like an object in transfer, she is placed in a container in so-called accommodation centers (camps).

According to Peck et al. (2023, 60), "The notion of accommodation, as opposed to dwelling or housing, is highly problematic as it denies any active designing of one's everyday life by reducing it to the container space where one sleeps, eats and stores his or her things." Moreover, the characteristic white color of the containers, as well as of the famous white tents of the UNHCR, reflects the whiteness of the Western perception of humanity. Critical race theory on whiteness shows that practices and policies of whiteness reproduce racial oppression and colonize every aspect of the social world, including the reception of migrants (Bhambra 2017; De Genova 2017; Owen 2007). In the case of camps, the white color symbolically and visually reflects Western ideas about purity and therefore also expresses the process of purification of the other, the racialized stranger from the East or the South, who is usually perceived with "stereotypes ... and well-worn cliché[s]" (Roy 2011, 225) as filthy, dirty, and uncivilized. Here, through the containerization of newcomers, the colonial aspect of Western humanitarian policies becomes more evident than ever.

Nevertheless, it is worth noting several counterpractices, which transform the containers according to the needs of their occupants. For example, in many camps in Athens and Thessaloniki, due to the lack of refrigerators, newcomers have hung cages holding fruit right outside the window of the containers to remain cool in the winter. Also, the camps' residents often reuse pieces of tents to create storage spaces outside the container. Many create small gardens in front of the containers to grow vegetables or flowers (see figure 7.2). In addition to these imaginative micromodifications of containers, newcomers often create hidden spaces in the gaps between the containers (see figure 7.3). For instance, during our visit to the Diavata camp, outside of Thessaloniki, newcomers kindly offered us tea and falafel and showed us around the camp. It was precisely 5:00 p.m., when the manager of the camp left, after which the camp changed radically. Until 5:00 there was absolute silence, with most of the residents inside the containers. But after 5:00 the camp came to life, with everyone hanging out outside the containers and with several small shops appearing out of nowhere in between spaces. Newcomers showed us around all the hidden shops. In the gaps between the containers, they created spaces partitioned with pieces of fabric—barbershops, mini markets, and small falafel kitchens. These secret small practices of necessity and contestation that remain hidden during daytime working hours are crucial for the daily life and reproduction of the newcomers in camps. After all, practices of camouflage are a typical

FIGURE 7.2 Garden in front of a container in Schisto refugee camp in Athens. Credit: Charalampos Tsavdaroglou and Maria Kaika.

decolonial subversive technique, which unveils subaltern resistance activities (Bhabha 1994). However, we should be particularly careful not to romanticize these practices, as they can by no means overthrow the very essence of the camp as an oppressive structure of marginalization. The more radical practices of challenging the camps' regime can be observed in the newcomers' efforts to create housing commons within the urban fabric of Athens and Thessaloniki, which we shall turn to in the next section.

Inventing Housing Commons

Against the aforementioned state accommodation policies, alternative arrival infrastructures (Meeus, Arnaut, and van Heur 2019), such as housing projects, were created in Athens and Thessaloniki, seeking on the one hand

FIGURE 7.3 Informal market in Vasilika camp in Thessaloniki. Credit: Charalampos Tsavdaroglou and Maria Kaika.

to respond to the immediate needs of newly arrived populations and on the other hand to experiment with forms of coexistence and symbiosis within the urban fabric. These are forms of self-housing that are defined by practices of reciprocity, inventiveness, and solidarity (Agustín and Jørgensen 2019; Lafazani 2018; Tsavdaroglou 2018; Tsavdaroglou and Kaika 2022b). Specifically, in Athens and Thessaloniki, since the fall of 2015 multiple abandoned public and private buildings within the urban fabric have been squatted by groups in solidarity with newcomers and have been transformed into housing commons for the newcomers (see figure 7.4).

At this point it is worth noting that the concept of commons and specifically urban commons has in recent years been linked to the practices of mobile populations. The literature describes a wide variety of self-managed urban commons projects, including urban gardens, housing projects, cooperatives, and self-organized healthcare, education, and work structures (Dellenbaugh et al. 2015; Newton and Rocco 2022; Stavrides 2016). Regarding the commoning practices of mobile populations, Trimikliniotis, Parsanoglou, and Tsianos (2015, 19) have introduced the term "mobile commons," which refers to "the shared knowledge, affective cooperation, mutual support and

FIGURE 7.4 Housing squat for refugees and immigrants, Notara 26, five-year anniversary, 2020. Credit: Charalampos Tsavdaroglou and Maria Kaika.

care between migrants, when they are on the move, when they arrive and/or settle." Those features are unmistakably noticeable in the cases of self-managed housing projects in Athens and Thessaloniki.

The sharp contrast between the camps and the self-organized housing commons is clear in the words of Salim, a newcomer from Afghanistan who stayed in the City Plaza migrants' squat in the center of Athens, an abandoned hotel that was turned into a migrants' housing project hosting about four hundred people.

> There is no life in the camp; to be precise, I have absolutely nothing to do in the camp, just chat with the other migrants about the unpleasant things that happen inside the camp. The camp is like a strange prison, cut off from the outside world. It is a boring and miserable place, like a cemetery. The security guards and the camp manager want us to be silent, as if we are dying. You have nothing to do in the camp. You talk about the ugly things, you get sad, you go to your container, like you go to your grave, you play on your mobile phone and sleep. This is the life in the camp. An absolute nothing. (Interview, February 12, 2018)

In contrast, he described his experience of the City Plaza migrants' squat, which is located in the very center of Athens:

> Joy, care, and creativity prevail in City Plaza. It's like a big hug that welcomes everyone regardless of ethnicity, religion, and language. Many times, I talk about the life in City Plaza to the migrants in the Skaramangas camp and many of them have asked me if there is a room available in the City Plaza in order to leave the camp. Everyone wants to leave the camp. They see me every time I go from City Plaza to the camp, they see how I am changing. . . . They [are] always asking me if there will be a party at City Plaza, so they can leave the camp and come to the city. (Interview, February 12, 2018)

In addition, Karima, a refugee woman from Syria who stayed in the occupied Orphanage in Thessaloniki, describes her experience as follows: "It was an important project because it covered the immediate housing needs of many people who had no place to stay, people who had no papers, people who were homeless, who could not find a house in the city to stay. It was a safe place, a safe haven for refugees" (interview, April 29, 2019).

Fatima, an Iraqi woman, describes the daily functions of the Orphanage squat by emphasizing the processes of coexistence and sharing:

> In the shifts, we made sure they were mixed—for example, every day there was a cooking group, and we made sure people from different countries participated in it. This was done both for practical reasons, so that food could be eaten by all the inhabitants of the squat, but also to create bridges of communication between the inhabitants—i.e., to break down social and cultural boundaries in practice. There are big differences in how rice is cooked in India and Pakistan compared to how it is cooked in Africa, so there had to be a variety of flavors every day so that everyone felt familiar and of course to avoid complaints. (Interview, June 18, 2021)

Here, the hybrid and mixed character of the newcomers' housing commons comes into view, framing them as cross-cultural and hybrid spaces (Bhabha 1994) where different cultures do not demarcate borders but bridge diverse subjectivities, create new spaces of in-betweenness, and produce correlations and interconnections in the process of everyday homemaking.

In practice, the residents of housing commons demonstrate that they exceed the Western categorizations of immigrants as either victims or criminals, which is how they have been depicted by humanitarian organizations and state policies. Beyond those dichotomies, newcomers demonstrate agency, as they claim social and political rights and tangibly practice the right to the city. Ahmed, a newcomer from Algeria who lived in the Orphanage housing squat in Thessaloniki, emphasizes that the occupation is more than a housing project; it is also a political process of making claims.

> In addition to the daily functions of the squat, we also organized political actions, such as protests in the city center. The Orphanage squat was not just a home in the narrow sense of the term; it was a political project, and perhaps that made it more complete as a home. I left my home, my country, for political reasons, because I felt political oppression, and at the Orphanage I participated in the creation of a political home, where I could express myself freely. I could say my opinion and along with other migrants. We built a political house that spoke, demonstrated, claimed in the center of the city for the rights of refugees. For me the Orphanage was the door or the window to enter the city. (Interview, May 10, 2019)

The above narratives show that the self-organized housing commons have been innovative and inventive thresholds for the entry of newcomers to the city. The residents of housing commons experiment with forms of equality, participation, coexistence, and negotiation of various identities and social borders. It is worth mentioning here that newcomers' housing commons are not utopian locations, as they are constantly faced with a multitude of challenges and difficulties, and several times they have failed to constitute permanent and safe places of residence for the newcomers (Fisher and Jørgensen 2021; Lafazani 2018; Tsavdaroglou and Lalenis 2020). The most important challenge is the confrontation with state policies, such as the violent evictions of dozens of newcomers' squats that took place in the years 2016–21. The newcomers' housing squats were blamed for "degrading" the localities within which they were embedded. The localities were stigmatized as run-down areas by both the central and local governments, and there were arguments that these areas lost their "Greekness." The central government and mayors were in unison when they decided on the eviction of the occupied buildings (Tsavdaroglou and Kaika 2022b). The violent police evacuation operations of the self-organized housing projects in the centers of Athens and Thessaloniki and the relocation of their residents to the state-run camps outside of the cities confirm the colonial aspect of state migration policies that aim to recolonize newcomers' homes and neighborhoods and to ostracize them, forcing them to the outskirts of the cities.

Concluding Remarks: Asserting the Newcomers' Right to the City as a Decolonizing Process

Migration is treated by most European states, including Greece, primarily as a matter of security and humanitarian interventions (Darling 2014). In fact, migration policies increasingly take the form of "military humanitarianism" (Tazzioli and Garelli 2018). Newcomers are perceived as passive and helpless beings in need of humanitarian aid. At the same time, they are treated as unwanted foreigners who can only be offered hospitality under military rule—that is, through technologies and mechanisms of control, identification, and discipline—and are placed in state-run camps, which often deviate from official urban planning regulations. These policies for migrants draw on and extend the colonial legacies of camps, which form the basis of today's socio-spatial configurations of European state-run camps as places of exclusion and suspension of the "other," the unwanted stranger who is perceived as a threat to European sovereignty (Davies and Isakjee 2019).

It seems that in the cases of Athens and Thessaloniki, in particular, institutional migration policies are defined by racist practices with little effort at inclusion. Numerous policies marginalize and stigmatize newcomers, while in recent years any acts of solidarity are increasingly demonized and criminalized. Consequently, the management of the so-called refugee crisis is based on the logic of "the further away the better" or at least "out of here" (Papataxiarchis 2020, 22), adopting punitive and xenophobic practices of invisibilization and seclusion of newcomers in state-run camps outside the cities.

Against the policies of exclusion and marginalization and the enclosure of state-run camps, but also beyond the humanitarian actions of compassion and philanthrocapitalism, the self-organized commoning practices of newcomers in self-managed housing projects opened a new decolonial horizon of inventions in coexistence and solidarity. The inhabitants of housing commons undermine the colonial management of state-run camps and explore new transnational modalities and transformative spatialities within the urban fabric. These are socio-spatial inventions of personal and collective empowerment, cohabitation, and claiming the right to the city. Yet it is also clear that newcomers' housing commons are not utopian locations.

They are better understood as an open dialogue to discover passages of communication between different cultures and identities.

Therefore, the examples of Athens and Thessaloniki highlight the limits of institutional policies when it comes to dealing with newly arrived people. If state migration policies are given meaning in terms of national purity aided by colonial supremacy and xenophobia, then newcomers' urban commons welcome new alterities; modify, decolonize, and disturb that context; and welcome difference by encouraging considerations and active practices of horizontal inclusion, symbiosis, transnational coexistence, and living-in-common. Newcomers' housing commons therefore cast light upon the limits and weaknesses of state policies, serve as a decolonial counterexample, and call for a reorientation of thinking and acting toward a reinvention of the newcomers' right to the city.

NOTE

1   We use the term *newcomers* to avoid institutional taxonomies and categorizations of refugees, migrants, asylum seekers, and displaced persons.

WORKS CITED

Agier, Michel. 2011. *Managing the Undesirables: Refugee Camps and Humanitarian Government*. Cambridge: Polity.

Agustín, Óscar García, and Martin Bak Jørgensen. 2019. *Solidarity and the "Refugee Crisis" in Europe*. Cham, Switzerland: Palgrave Macmillan.

Bauman, Zygmunt. 2000. "The Century of Camps." In *The Bauman Reader*, edited by Peter Beilharz, 266–81. Oxford: Blackwell.

Bhabha, Homi. 1994. *The Location of Culture*. London: Routledge.

Bhambra, Gurminder. 2017. "Brexit, Trump, and 'Methodological Whiteness': On the Misrecognition of Race and Class." *British Journal of Sociology* 68 (1): 214–32. www.doi.org/10.1111/1468-446.12317.

Bousiou, Alexandra. 2020. "From Humanitarian Crisis Management to Prison Island: Implementing the European Asylum Regime at the Border Island of Lesvos 2015–2017." *Journal of Balkan and Near Eastern Studies* 22 (3): 431–47. www.doi.org/10.1080/19448953.2020.1752560.

Chuang, Janie A. 2015. "Giving as Governance? Philanthrocapitalism and Modern-Day Slavery Abolitionism." UCLA *Law Review* 62:1516–56.

Christidis, Ioannis. 2023. "Singing and Dancing for Freedom of Movement: Enacting Citizenship and Resisting Forced Confinement in 'Hotspot' Refugee Camps in Thessaloniki, Greece 2016." In *Internment Refugee Camps: Historical and Contemporary Perspectives*, edited by Gabriele Anderl, Linda Erker, and Christoph Reinprecht, 177–91. Bielefeld: Transcript Verlag.

Cobarrubias, Sebastian, Paolo Cuttitta, Maribel Casas-Cortés, Martin Lemberg-Pedersen, Nora El Qadim, Beste İşleyen, Shoshana Fine, Caterina Giusa, and Charles Heller. 2023. "Interventions on the Concept of Externalisation in Migration and Border Studies." *Political Geography* 105:102911. www.doi.org/10.1016/j.polgeo.2023.102911.

Coordination Centre for the Management of Refugee Crisis in Greece. n.d. "Summary Statement of Refugee Flows at 12.07.2016." http://www.media.gov.gr (accessed November 30, 2022).

Dalal, Ayham. 2017. "Uncovering Culture and Identity in Refugee Camps." *Humanities* 6 (3): 61. www.doi.org/10.3390/h6030061.

Danewid, Ida. 2017. "White Innocence in the Black Mediterranean: Hospitality and the Erasure of History." *Third World Quarterly* 38 (7): 1674–89. www.doi.org/10.1080/01436597.2017.1331123.

Darling, Jonathan. 2014. "Asylum and the Post-Political: Domopolitics, Depoliticisation and Acts of Citizenship." *Antipode* 46 (1): 72–91. https://doi.org/10.1111/anti.12026.

Davies, Thom, and Arshad Isakjee. 2019. "Ruins of Empire: Refugees, Race and the Postcolonial Geographies of European Migrant Camps." *Geoforum* 102:214–17. www.doi.org/10.1016/j.geoforum.2018.09.031.

De Genova, Nicholas. 2017. "The 'Migrant Crisis' as Racial Crisis: Do Black Lives Matter in Europe?" *Ethnic and Racial Studies* 41 (10): 1765–82. www.doi.org/10.1080/01419870.2017.1361543.

Dellenbaugh, Mary, Markus Kip, Majken Bieniok, Agnes Katharina Muller, and Martin Schwegmann. 2015. *Urban Commons: Moving Beyond State and Market*. Basel: Birkhäuser Verlag.

Diken, Bulent, and Carsten Laustsen. 2004. *The Culture of Exception: Sociology Facing the Camp*. London: Routledge.

Edkins, Jenny. 2000. "Sovereign Power, Zones of Indistinction, and the Camp." *Alternatives: Global, Local, Political* 25 (1): 3–25.

European Council. 2016. "EU-Turkey Statement, 18 March 2016." Press release. https://www.consilium.europa.eu/en/press/press-releases/2016/03/18/eu-turkey-statement.

Fisher, Leandros, and Martin Bak Jørgensen. 2021. "'We Are Here to Stay' vs. 'Europe's Best Hotel': Hamburg and Athens as Geographies of Solidarity." *Antipode* 53 (4): 1062–82. www.doi.org/10.1177/0896920520980053.

Gemenetzi, Georgia, and Marilena Papageorgiou. 2017. "Spatial and Social Aspects of the Housing Policies for Refugees and Immigrants in Greece: A Critical Overview." *Greek Review of Social Research* 148(A):39–74. www.doi.org/10.12681/grsr.14709.

Gilroy, Paul. 2004. *Between Camps: Nations, Cultures and the Allure of Race*. London: Routledge.

Katz, Irit. 2017. "Between Bare Life and Everyday Life: Spatializing Europe's Migrant Camps." *Architecture_MPS* 12 (2): 1–21. www.doi.org/10.14324/111.444.amps.2017v12i2.001.

Kourachanis, Nikos. 2019a. "From Camps to Social Integration? Social Housing Interventions for Asylum Seekers in Greece." *International Journal of Sociology and Social Policy* 39 (3–4): 221–34. www.doi.org/10.1108/IJSSP-08-2018-0130.

Kourachanis, Nikos. 2019b. Πολιτικές στέγασης προσφύγων : προς την κοινωνικήή ενσωμάτωση ή την προνοιακή εξάρτηση [Refugee housing policies: toward social integration or welfare dependence]. Athens: Topos.

Kreichauf, René. 2018. "From Forced Migration to Forced Arrival: The Campization of Refugee Accommodation in European Cities." *Comparative Migration Studies* 6, art. 7. www.doi.org/10.1186/s40878-017-0069-8.

Lafazani, Olga. 2018. "Homeplace Plaza: Challenging the Border Between Host and Hosted." *South Atlantic Quarterly* 117 (4): 896–904. www.doi.org/10.1215/00382876-7166043.

Lefebvre, Henri. 1991. *The Production of Space*. Oxford: Blackwell.

Lefebvre, Henri. 1996. *Writings on Cities*. Oxford: Blackwell.

Levinson, Mark. 2016. *The Box: How the Shipping Container Made the World Smaller and the World Economy Bigger*. Princeton, NJ: Princeton University Press.

Maestri, Gaja. 2017. "The Contentious Sovereignties of the Camp: Political Contention Among State and Non-State Actors in Italian Roma Camps." *Political Geography* 60:213–22. www.doi.org/10.1016/j.polgeo.2017.08.002.

Martin, Diana, Claudio Minca, and Irit Katz. 2020. "Rethinking the Camp: On Spatial Technologies of Power and Resistance." *Progress in Human Geography* 44 (4): 743–68. www.doi.org/10.1177/0309132519856702.

Massey, Doreen. 2005. *For Space*. London: Sage.

Mayblin, Lucy. 2017. *Asylum After Empire: Colonial Legacies in the Politics of Asylum Seeking*. London: Rowman and Littlefield.

Meeus, Bruno, Karel Arnaut, and Bas van Heur. 2019. *Arrival Infrastructures: Migration and Urban Social Mobilities*. Cham, Switzerland: Palgrave Macmillan.

Mignolo, Walter, and Catherine E. Walsh. 2018. *On Decoloniality: Concepts, Analytics, Praxis*. Durham, NC: Duke University Press.

Minca, Claudio. 2015. "Geographies of the Camp." *Political Geography* 49:74–83. www.doi.org/10.1016/j.polgeo.2014.12.005.

Mitchell, Katheryne, and Matthew Sparke. 2016. "The New Washington Consensus: Millennial Philanthropy and the Making of Global Market Subjects." *Antipode* 48 (3): 724–49. www.doi.org/10.1111/anti.12203.

Newton, Caroline, and Roberto Rocco. 2022. "Actually Existing Commons: Using the Commons to Reclaim the City." *Social Inclusion* 10 (1): 91–102. www.doi.org/10.17645/si.v10i1.4838.

Oesch, Lucas. 2017. "The Refugee Camp as a Space of Multiple Ambiguities and Subjectivities." *Political Geography* 60:110–20. www.doi.org/10.1016/j.polgeo.2017.05.004.

Owen, David. 2007. "Towards a Critical Theory of Whiteness." *Philosophy and Social Criticism* 33 (2): 203–22. www.doi.org/10.1177/0191453707074139.

Papataxiarchis, E. 2020. "*Η νέα γεωγραφία του προσφυγικού: Βία και πολλαπλασιασμός των συνόρων στο Αιγαίο*" [The new geography of the refugee issue: violence and the multiplication of borders in the Aegean]. *Σύγχρονα Θέματα* [Synchrona Themata] 147:21–25.

Papatzani, Eva (Evangelia), Panos Hatziprokopiou, Filyra Vlastou-Dimopoulou, and Alexandra Siotou. 2022. "On Not Staying Put Where They Have Put You: Mobilities Disrupting the Socio-Spatial Figurations of Displacement in Greece." *Journal of Ethnic and Migration Studies* 48 (18): 4383–401. www.doi.org/10.1080/1369183X.2022.2090158.

Papatzani, Eva (Evangelia), Timokleia Psallidaki, George Kandylis, and Irini Micha. 2022. "Multiple Geographies of Precarity: Accommodation Policies for Asylum Seekers in Metropolitan Athens, Greece." *European Urban and Regional Studies* 29 (2): 189–203. www.doi.org/10.1177/09697764211040742.

Pasquetti, Silvia. 2015. "Negotiating Control: Camps, Cities and Political Life." *City* 19 (5): 702–13. www.doi.org/10.1080/13604813.2015.1071121.

Pechlidou, Efrosyni, Yannis Frangopoulos, and Panos Hatziprokopiou. 2020. "The Spatial Management of the 'Migration Crisis' and Local Opposition: Public Discourse, Actors and Reactions Against Refugee Accommodation in Thessaloniki." In *Post-Urbanities, Cultural Reconsiderations and Tourism in the Balkans*, edited by Aikaterini S. Markou and Meglena Zlatkova, 137–60. Athens: Éditions Hêrodotos.

Peck, Dominique, Anna Richter, Christopher Dell, and Bernd Kniess. 2023. "Unsettling Planning Practices: From Accommodation to Dwelling in Hamburg." In *Unsettled Urban Space Routines, Temporalities and Contestations*, edited by Tihomir Viderman, Sabine Knierbein, Elina Kränzle, Sybille Frank, Nikolai Roskamm, and Ed Wall, 52–66. New York: Routledge.

Petti, Alessandro. 2013. "Architecture of Exile." Campus in Camps, June 11, 2013. http://www.campusincamps.ps/about.

Pitzer, Andea. 2017. "Concentration Camps Existed Long Before Auschwitz." *Smithsonian Magazine*, November 2, 2017. https://www.smithsonianmag.com/history/concentration-camps-existed-long-before-Auschwitz-180967049.

Ramadan, Adam. 2013. "Spatialising the Refugee Camp." *Transactions of the Institute of British Geographers* 38 (1): 65–77. www.doi.org/10.1111/j.1475-5661.2012.00509.x.

Refugee Support Aegean 2022. "A Step Backwards for Protection and Integration: On the Termination of the ESTIA II Housing Programme for Asylum Applicants." December 22, 2022. https://rsaegean.org/en/termination-of-the-estia-ii-for-asylum-applicants.

Roy, Ananya. 2011. "Slumdog Cities: Rethinking Subaltern Urbanism." *International Journal of Urban and Regional Research* 35 (2): 223–38. www.doi.org/10.1111/j.1468-2427.2011.01051.x.

Sanyal, Romola. 2010. "Squatting in Camps: Building and Insurgency in Spaces of Refuge." *Urban Studies* 48 (5): 877–90. www.doi.org/10.1177/0042098010363494.

Sharma, Sarah. 2009. "Baring Life and Lifestyle in the Non-Place." *Cultural Studies* 23 (1): 129–48. www.doi.org/10.1080/09502380802016246.

Sigona, Nando. 2015. "Campzenship: Reimagining the Camp as a Social and Political Space." *Citizenship Studies* 19 (1): 1–15. www.doi.org/10.1080/13621025.2014.937643.

Spijkerboer, Thomas, Lea Espinoza Garrido, Sylvia Mieszkowski, Birgit Spengler, and Julia Wewior. 2021. "Migration Emergencies in the European Postcolony: An Interview with Thomas Spijkerboer." *Parallax* 27 (2): 223–39. www.doi.org/10.1080/13534645.2021.1995953.

Stavrides, Stavros. 2016. *Common Space. The City as Commons*. London: Zed.

Tazzioli, Martina, and Glenda Garelli. 2020. "Containment Beyond Detention: The Hotspot System and Disrupted Migration Movements Across Europe." *Environment and Planning D: Society and Space* 38 (6): 1009–27. www.doi.org/10.1177/0263775818759335.

Trimikliniotis, Nicos, Dimitris Parsanoglou, and Vassilis Tsianos. 2015. *Mobile Commons, Migrant Digitalities and the Right to the City*. Cham, Switzerland: Palgrave Macmillan.

Tsavdaroglou, Charalampos. 2018. "The Newcomers' Right to the Common Space: The Case of Athens During the Migrant Crisis." *ACME: An International Journal for Critical Geographies* 17 (2): 376–401.

Tsavdaroglou, Charalampos, and Maria Kaika. 2022a. "Refugees' Caring and Commoning Practices Against Marginalisation Under COVID-19 in Greece." *Geographical Research* 60 (2): 232–40. www.doi.org/10.1111/1745-5871.12522.

Tsavdaroglou, Charalampos, and Maria Kaika. 2022b. "The Refugees' Right to the Centre of the City: City Branding Versus City Commoning in Athens." *Urban Studies* 59 (6): 1130–47. www.doi.org/10.1177/0042098021997009.

Turner, Simon. 2016. "What Is a Refugee Camp? Explorations of the Limits and Effects of the Camp." *Journal of Refugee Studies* 29 (2): 139–48. www.doi.org/10.1093/jrs/fev024.

Turner, Simon, and Zachary Whyte. 2022. "Introduction: Refugee Camps as Carceral Junctions." *Incarceration* 3 (1): 1–9. www.doi.org/10.1177/26326663221084591.

UNHCR. 2021. "Refugee Camps Explained." Office of the United Nations High Commissioner for Refugees, April 21, 2021. https://www.unrefugees.org/news/refugee-camps-explained/#How%20many%20refugees%20live%20in%20refugee%20camps.

UNHCR. n.d. a. "Greece, Mediterranean Situation." Operation Data Portal, Office of the United Nations High Commissioner for Refugees. https://data.unhcr.org/en/situations/mediterranean/location/5179 (accessed September 11, 2024).

UNHCR. n.d. b. "Mediterranean Situation." Operation Data Portal, Office of the United Nations High Commissioner for Refugees. https://data.unhcr.org/en/situations/mediterranean (accessed September 11, 2024).

Wacquant, Loïc. 2007. "Territorial Stigmatization in the Age of Advanced Marginality." *Thesis Eleven* 91 (1): 66–77. www.doi.org/10.1177/0725513607082003.

Webber, Sophie, Helga Leitner, and Eric Sheppard. 2020. "Wheeling Out Urban Resilience: Philanthrocapitalism, Marketization, and Local Practice." *Annals of the American Association of Geographers* 111 (2): 343–63. www.doi.org/10.1080/24694452.2020.1774349.

8

Humanitarian Racism

Saree Makdisi

"An extraordinary gathering took place in Israel's Mount Herzl Cemetery in Jerusalem on September 30, 2016," we hear in the instantly familiar dulcet tones of George Clooney through the opening frames of a recent film now streaming on Netflix. "An event unlike any other since the Jewish state's founding in 1948," Clooney continues, "it included presidents and prime ministers, kings and queens, religious leaders and international dignitaries. They had all come to attend the funeral of Shimon Peres, Israel's ninth president, a three-time prime minister, a Nobel Peace Prize laureate, and one of the most respected and beloved elder statesmen in the world." The film in question, *Never Stop Dreaming: The Life and Legacy of Shimon Peres*, was produced in 2022 by Moriah Films, the propaganda arm of the Simon Wiesenthal Center in Los Angeles, home of the so-called Museum of Tolerance. This is an outfit that has earned notoriety around the world for having opened a clone of itself over the deliberately desecrated ruins of the Mamilla Cemetery, the largest and most important Muslim cemetery in Jerusalem: a monument supposedly dedicated to the value of "tolerance" erected over an ethnically cleansed graveyard from which human remains had been hastily removed and disposed of in order for its construction to take place (Makdisi 2022).

The question I would like to investigate in this chapter is quite simple: what does it mean that an actor such as Clooney—well known for his professed progressive politics and defense of human rights around the world—would knowingly collaborate with a Zionist organization staunchly committed to the cause of an apartheid regime (Amnesty International 2022; Falk and Tilley 2017), and, in this particular instance, narrate the life of a man accused of war crimes who, in his earlier years, had played a key role in procuring the weapons that had helped make possible the 1948 Zionist ethnic cleansing of Palestine? In the 1970s or 1980s, given the general absence or suppression of Palestinian narratives in English in the United States, it might have been possible for someone in Clooney's position to have claimed (or feigned) ignorance; indeed, Jane Fonda occupied a very closely analogous position on the spectrum of entertainment politics and is a case in point from that period as a prominent advocate of progressive politics and women's rights who was nevertheless also supportive of the 1982 Israeli invasion of Lebanon (Freeman 1982). Today, however, any potential claims of ignorance or lack of knowledge of Israeli violations of Palestinian human and political rights are simply no longer credible. On the very same streaming platform hosting the new hagiography of Peres, after all, there are more than three dozen Palestinian films, some of which are specifically devoted to the Nakba, the catastrophe that took place in Palestine in 1948 as a result of the Zionist ethnic cleansing of most of the indigenous Palestinian population from their land. Only hardened Zionists continue to deny that the ethnic cleansing of Palestine took place— and even some of them have found themselves forced to admit it (Simon Schama's 2013 BBC series *The Story of the Jews* presents an unapologetically Zionist narrative, for instance, but even an unreconstructed Zionist like him has to confess that the Nakba took place, however much he also tries to equivocate his way around it).

Clooney here exemplifies a broader cultural and political position that I will identify as humanitarian racism: a position that expresses racism—and in this instance a system of apartheid—in the language of contemporary liberal and progressive politics, as I will elaborate in the pages to follow. The other chapters in this volume—and the collection as a whole—take up the critical reimagination of the concept of sanctuary and the humanitarian discourses in which it has been framed and from which it is inextricable. What we see in the case of Clooney's collaboration with the organization behind the Museum of Tolerance is the extent to which the language of humanitarianism can be mobilized for the purposes of one of the most violent undertakings of inhumanity in the contemporary world. In this instance, we can see how a professed sanctuary space—claiming to be dedicated to tolerance—is something more than merely cover for racial violence: it is the very expression of racial violence itself. The museum expresses in that sense a metonymical relationship to the state project to which Clooney addresses himself in the Peres hagiography: the alleged site of sanctuary for one people marks the violent usurpation of the home of another. After all, how many times have we heard Joe Biden say, "Without Israel as a freestanding state, not a Jew in the world is safe"? (Biden 2023).

That Biden repeated that statement several times in the fall of 2023 as Israel was undertaking its campaign of genocidal violence against the Palestinian people in Gaza speaks to the nature of the apparent contradiction that I aim to explore in this chapter: the putative sanctuary space has now become the agent of full-blown genocide.

Needless to say, the Peres documentary narrated by Clooney makes no mention of the Nakba; it is, if anything, an exercise in Nakba denial. Saturated with the smarmy self-congratulation characteristic of anything so much as brushed by the Museum of Tolerance, the film elides the Palestinian presence in Palestine altogether. There is a clip of Peres recalling receiving Jaffa oranges "from Israel" in the 1930s—in other words, long before the ethnic cleansing and the foundation of the Zionist state. When he arrived in Palestine himself, he recalls, "everything was Hebrew" in and around the port of Jaffa—which it certainly was not. The closest the film comes to mentioning the Palestinians is when Peres recalls living in a Zionist settlement "surrounded on all sides by Arab [i.e., Palestinian] villages." At night, he adds, "the Arabs [i.e., Palestinians] used to shoot at our village." Quite why these natives were so restless remains clouded in obscurity, but in any case, in Clooney's narrative the real enemies of the Zionists in Palestine were not these generic and deracinated "Arabs" but rather the British occupiers. "Some Jews joined the Haganah," Clooney says, "and its elite fighting division, the Palmach, to continue resisting the British mandatory authority." (There was, in fact, nothing "elite" about either the Haganah or the Palmach: they were among the Zionist militias who drove Palestinians from their homes through massacre, bombing, rape, and racial terror [Khalidi 2020; Masalha 2012; Pappe 2006].) The perfidious British, the narrative continues, had issued a policy "restricting Jewish immigration to Palestine, making it impossible for Jews to flee Nazi-occupied Europe."

Note the framing: according to the film, stopping the Zionist colonization of Palestine meant condemning European Jews to death, as though they had nowhere to escape to during the period of Nazi ascendancy in Europe other than Palestine. No mention is made of the possibility of their flight to, for instance, Britain or the United States—countries that, even short of undertaking an active rescue, could certainly have worked harder to make room for Jewish refugees fleeing Nazi brutality in Germany, but which, as David Wyman, among others, has shown, systematically failed to do so (Wyman 2007). And this narrative necessarily excludes those European Jews who refused the path of Zionism whether they had the means to find somewhere else to turn to (like Albert Einstein) or not (like Walter Benjamin), as well as Jewish thinkers who proposed a binational state instead of Zionism (like Martin Buber and Judah Magnes), not to mention prominent Jews who refused Zionism altogether, whether before the establishment of the state (like Hans Kohn) or after it (like Moshe Machover). Finally, of course, the narrative spoken by Clooney but actually scripted by his handlers at the Wiesenthal Center makes no mention of the vibrant multiconfessional and ecumenical culture in Palestine—in which Palestinian Jews enjoyed a sense of shared rather than exclusive belonging, alongside equally Palestinian Muslims and Christians—that Zionism would ultimately supplant and destroy (Glass 1975; Makdisi 2019). This teleological and actively, even violently simplifying narrative of Zionism recurs in the presentations of the Museum of Tolerance itself, to which we will shortly return.

There's nothing particularly interesting, creative, or surprising about *Never Stop Dreaming* other than the fact that this tedious hagiography of an advocate of ethnic cleansing, occupation, and apartheid is narrated by someone who's supposed to be a human rights activist. Clooney was, after all, designated a UN "Messenger of Peace" by UN secretary-general Ban Ki-Moon in 2008. That same year, with fellow Hollywood luminaries Matt Damon, Brad Pitt, and Don Cheadle, among others, Clooney launched Not on Our Watch, a project "committed to robust advocacy and research in support of global human rights," as its website proclaimed in 2019. In 2010, he co-launched, with John Prendergast, the Satellite Sentinel Project, which aimed "to focus global attention on mass atrocities in Sudan" and "was the first sustained public effort to systematically monitor and report on potential hotspots and threats to human security in real time," as the related Enough Project (which Prendergast had launched on his own in 2007) claims on its website. In 2016, Clooney co-founded yet another human rights organization, The Sentry, an "investigative and policy organization that seeks to disable multinational predatory networks that benefit from violent conflict, repression, and kleptocracy," and in 2019 the two Clooney-funded outfits merged under the Sentry name. The Sentry has published reports on the Democratic Republic of the Congo, Zimbabwe, the Central African Republic, and Sudan, with an especially heavy emphasis on the last. The supporters and financial backers of Enough, Not on Our Watch, Satellite Sentinel, and now The Sentry include Clooney himself (a constant presence across all these initiatives), Don Cheadle, Javier Bardem, Kristen Bell, Sheryl Crow, Mia Farrow, Ryan Gosling, Ashley Judd, Matt Damon, Brad Pitt, and Hans Zimmer, among others from across the progressive spectrum of Hollywood and the entertainment industry writ large. Such initiatives enabled Clooney to transform himself (or so we are told) from "just another Hollywood liberal with a pet cause to a genuine expert and campaigner on Sudan" (Harris 2012). In 2016, Clooney launched yet another organization, this time with his wife, the prominent human rights lawyer Amal Clooney, called the Clooney Foundation for Justice.

The Clooney Foundation today sponsors projects in three dozen countries around the world, from Mexico to Indonesia and from Zimbabwe to Russia. Although Amal Clooney is Lebanese, it's notable that the foundation steers well clear of the question of Palestine. When Amal Clooney refused an appointment by the United Nations to serve on a commission to investigate Israeli war crimes committed during the Israeli bombardment of Gaza in 2014, the refusal was issued by Stan Rosenfeld, Clooney's Hollywood agent, even though they were not yet married at the time (Carroll 2014). And even after five months of the Israeli siege and bombardment of Gaza in 2023–24—which, as of the time of writing, had killed or injured more than 100,000 Palestinian civilians—neither Clooney has had anything to say about Gaza. Like most of Clooney's initiatives, the Clooney Foundation's center of gravity remains squarely in Africa, notably Sudan and the Darfur region, where Clooney first became involved in what Alex de Waal refers to as the humanitarian carnival (de Waal 2008). Of course, in Africa Clooney had joined an already crowded field of white European and American celebrities espousing humanitarian causes, going back to Bob Geldof and U2's Bono in the 1980s (and there is a much longer heritage for such forms of humanitarian intervention connected to liberal imperial projects, if not outright white supremacism, running through, for instance, European programs to assist Armenian orphans in the interwar period and indeed going all the way back to the campaign to abolish the slave trade in the name of free-market imperialism in the nineteenth century [Williams 2021; Zablotsky 2023]).

Regardless of how genuine such humanitarian interventions actually are (or, indeed, whether they are at all sincere in the first place, which is impossible to judge), several factors stand out in such celebrity involvements in Africa. First of all, as Patricia Daley points out, they are readily mappable onto a preexisting template established over more than a century of Western narratives of progress, enlightenment, and so on, dating to the first colonial and missionary involvements in the continent (Daley 2013). According to this narrative, European or American celebrities can cast themselves in the well-known role—all too easily transposed from screen roles they may also have played—of white saviors coming to rescue Africans from their various problems (which, needless to say, are never portrayed in political and historical context, let alone in connection to the history of European colonialism in the region). Moreover, "since the celebrities do not seek their legitimacy from Africans," Daley argues, "they present humanitarian crises not as political but as moral problems" (Daley 2013, 388). The celebrities in question can lend their images and names to various human rights causes—and benefit from that identification in their own branding as well. These crises, as de Waal observes, end up seeming as much about "us," the "faraway, affluent, anguished of America and Europe," as they do about the people on the ground in Africa (de Waal 2008, 43).

Celebrity humanitarian interventions in Africa have other benefits as well. First of all, partly because of their decontextualization and their mapping onto older colonial narratives, they seem to offer a sense of moral simplicity. "There are many other crises killing and displacing comparable numbers," de Waal points out with reference to the African cause attracting the most celebrity attention, "but Darfur has the attraction of a moral narrative that, at first glance, features only black hats and white horses (and silent victims)" (de Waal 2008, 46). There's an attractive simplicity to this cause, in other words (from a Western point of view): it seems to operate along an (apparently) simple binary register, making it (apparently) so easy to distinguish right from wrong, perpetrators from victims, that calling for violent outside military intervention seems, paradoxically, to be positively humanitarian. Thus, for instance, not only could Clooney call for armed intervention in Darfur, but Mia Farrow could arrange a meeting with the notorious for-profit Blackwater mercenary organization—still mired in bad press at the time from its involvement in a massacre in Iraq (Singer 2007)—to inquire as to its availability to "save" Darfur (de Waal 2008, 44).

This brings up the second benefit to this set of narratives: there no immediately obvious sense of American or European complicity, involvement, or benefit to be gained from an intervention in Darfur, unlike, say, Iraq, Libya, Afghanistan, and so on, where the presence of oil or clear geopolitical imperatives make Western claims of humanitarian interest (e.g., the professed interest in saving Afghan women and girls from the Taliban) seem much more obviously like a veneer or excuse for neocolonial intervention. Moreover, there is also no US presence (in the media, in entertainment, or in popular culture more broadly) speaking for "the other side" of a conflict like that in, say, Darfur. There is, in other words, no equivalent of the array of well-funded institutions ready to spring to the public defense of Israeli apartheid, for instance, so that one can espouse support for intervention in Darfur without worrying about being hassled in the Western media: no one is going to speak up on CNN to defend the cause of those accused of human rights abuses in the Darfur region. For celebrities, in other words, being seen to intervene in a situation like that in Darfur offers only upside and no downside: Western entertainers can add to their moral capital, boost their sense of humanitarian prestige, and enhance the visibility and resonance of their personal brands, with little cost and even less adverse consequence. This would not be the case if they were to call for outside military intervention to protect innocent civilians from indiscriminate bombardment or siege warfare in, say, Gaza.

Moreover, there are other factors at play in Western representations of the Darfur crisis specifically, in which Clooney made his name as a humanitarian. Not only were the dynamics of the conflict in Darfur and the subtleties and ramifications of its causes (including the role played by drought and desertification rather than outright "genocide") either simplified or elided altogether, but it was, for American audiences, the right issue at the right time. "For Americans tired of Iraq," as Mahmood Mamdani explains, "Darfur is a place of refuge. It is a surrogate shelter. It is a cause about which they can feel good" (Mamdani 2009, 64). This was partly enabled, as Mamdani argues, by the reduction of the conflict into simple decontextualized and ahistorical binary terms, seeming to pit good against evil without (apparently) any of the complexity of, say, America's invasion of Iraq and indeed US imperialism in the Arab world more generally. Even more importantly, it stems from the fact that the "bad guys" in Darfur were (and are) consistently represented, in the forms of humanitarian discourse connected to Hollywood, as "Arabs" oppressing "Africans," a binary opposition that is so utterly nonsensical in the Sudanese context that its insistent expression in an American setting exposes the motivations behind it. For Americans, Mamdani points out, "Darfur is a place without history and without politics—simply a place where perpetrators clearly identifiable as 'Arabs' confront victims clearly identifiable as 'Africans'" (Mamdani 2009,

60). The overall conflict is, in other words, stripped of any context and reduced to a caricature-like simplicity premised on a supposedly racial opposition between "outsider," "invading," "light-skinned," "settler" "Arabs" and "dark-skinned," "indigenous" "Africans." Such a racial binary breaks down altogether in Sudan, where it's impossible to delimit the African from the Arab given the country's racial and cultural hybridity (who can forget the line in al-Tayyib Salih's *Season of Migration to the North* in which Isabella Seymour asks the Sudanese Mustafa Said, "Are you African or Asian?" to which he replies, "I am like Othello, Arab-African") (Salih 1969, 46).

For liberal Americans weary of guilt from their own country's disastrous imperial adventures in the Arab world, then, Darfur in the 2000s offered the opportunity to cast "Arabs" in the role of marauding villains rather than victims for a change. But more was at stake. This casting of "Arab" "settlers" in a negative light also provided the perfect occasion for those American institutions heavily invested in the defense and justification of Zionist occupation and apartheid policies to draw attention away from Jewish settlers in the West Bank and toward evil "Arab" "settlers" in Darfur, and the greater the number of Hollywood personalities who could be persuaded to join the effort—and hence the more visible and mainstream it could become—the better. For it is unlikely to be merely a coincidence that the efforts to raise distorted "awareness" of Darfur in the United States were initiated and sustained above all by Jewish and/or Zionist organizations in the United States, including the Simon Wiesenthal Center and its Museum of Tolerance in LA. The Save Darfur Coalition—the first effort to draw attention to the issue in the United States—was launched by the US Holocaust Memorial Museum and American Jewish World Service, the latter a human rights organization that (like the Museum of Tolerance) claims to be concerned with human rights all around the world except in the one place where its intervention could actually make the biggest difference: Palestine. "Because the crimes in Darfur were perpetrated by 'Arabs,' they could be demonized as genocide," Mamdani points out. "For the Christian Right and secular Zionist groups in particular, Darfur is the site of a contemporary holocaust with the 'Arabs' cast in the role of contemporary Nazis" (Mamdani 2009, 64–65).

All this background helps to explain the convergence that brought together George Clooney with the Simon Wiesenthal Center and the Museum of Tolerance and eventually to his narration of the 2022 Shimon Peres hagiography. As far as Clooney is concerned, there's no way for me to know his motivations, though, for the record, I did reach out to him to see if he wanted to discuss his relationship to the museum given its record of supporting apartheid and its desecration of the Mamilla cemetery in Jerusalem; I received no response. Maybe he has been led on by his PR people; maybe he is naïve; maybe he somehow really does not know what the Museum of Tolerance is up to in Jerusalem; maybe he really does think that a man who played a pivotal role in Israel's racist suppression of Palestinian rights actually was a "respected" and "beloved" elder statesman; maybe (despite his Lebanese human rights lawyer wife) he does not know about Peres's orders for Israeli forces to indiscriminately bombard Lebanon in 1996, which led to, among other calamities, the Israeli artillery massacre of civilians sheltering at a UN compound near Qana, killing over a hundred people, including children (United Nations 1996). Maybe. Or maybe his portfolio of human rights campaigns is merely a cynical ploy to build his own brand—"performative activism," as someone familiar with Hollywood politics put it to me. I'm not in a position to know.

Clooney's motivations, however, are ultimately not nearly as interesting as those of the Wiesenthal Center and the Museum of Tolerance, which honored George and Amal Clooney at its gala in 2020 (Wiesenthal Center 2020). In collaborating with Clooney, the Museum of Tolerance simultaneously immeasurably boosted both its own claim to be interested in human rights and, just as important, its affiliations with the most liberal sector of Hollywood, with which it has assiduously worked to connect itself. Apart from Clooney himself, the institution has persuaded Barbra Streisand, Ben Kingsley, Michael Douglas, Christoph Waltz, Sandra Bullock, Leonard Nimoy, and Morgan Freeman, among others, to appear in or narrate its films. These cultural and political affiliations have helped the institution to add to its moral capital and to enhance its claim to liberal values such as progress, equality, and, obviously, tolerance.

Which brings us to the Museum of Tolerance in Jerusalem. I have written about this project extensively in other places, so, in this context, I will just summarize the nature of this project and bring things up to date (Makdisi 2010a, 2010b, 2022). In February 2004, it was announced that the municipality of Jerusalem had approved a site for the construction of a local branch of the Los Angeles Museum of Tolerance. Frank Gehry was to be the project architect, and he drew up elaborate plans for a titanium-clad citadel costing nearly a quarter of a billion dollars. It turned out, of course, that the site chosen for this shrine to "tolerance" was on the Mamilla cemetery, the oldest and most important Muslim burial ground in all of Palestine, dating back to the time of the Crusades and in active use until the Nakba of 1948. Palestinians and Muslims protested, to no avail—until excavations began in

2006 and quickly (and unsurprisingly) turned up human remains, at which point the project was suspended for further legal contestations. "Israel Plans to Build 'Museum of Tolerance' on Muslim Graves," read a headline in the British newspaper *The Independent* in its succinct summary of the situation (Macintyre 2006).

In the fall of 2008, after several years of legal prevarication, the Israeli High Court gave its final approval to the construction. "Moderation and tolerance have prevailed," announced the director of the Museum of Tolerance in Los Angeles; "from this half-century[-old] parking lot in the center of west Jerusalem will rise an institution that offers hope and reason to all the people of Israel and the world" (Makdisi 2022, 109). And so construction resumed, despite the ongoing protests by the Muslim community of Jerusalem and Palestinians around the world. In 2010, I published a piece about the project in the *Los Angeles Times* and an article about it in the journal *Critical Inquiry*, which led to an unpleasant debate in the pages of that journal among myself, Gehry, the museum directors, and a few other people invited by the journal to express their opinion on the matter. The end result of that episode is that Frank Gehry withdrew from the project. The years dragged on, and the directors of the museum doggedly persevered with their mission to desecrate the cemetery and build their monument to "tolerance." Eventually they found another architect, and then, when they had a falling out with *that* one, yet another one. Almost two decades after the initial groundbreaking ceremony, the museum opened in 2023. Florida governor Ron DeSantis was one of the speakers at the first public event there, celebrating the destruction of Palestine and the dispersal of the Palestinians in 1948.

The website of the Museum of Tolerance in Jerusalem has come and gone as the project mutated over the years after Gehry withdrew from it. A new version of the website was launched as the site was preparing to open in 2022–23. "A museum like no other in the heart of Jerusalem," the home page promises, over a video loop offering a series of clips of the museum site in which the discerning viewer can still make out Muslim tombstones (the site covers only part of the cemetery, leaving much of the ruined remainder in view). It promises "a museum for visitors of all ages, religions and cultural backgrounds from throughout the region and the world that will encourage democracy, combat the roots of anti-Semitism and extremism, and promote regional stability, global harmony, human dignity and a love of Israel" (Museum of Tolerance 2023). In another video, speaking over a musical theme presumably selected to signify "stirring and uplifting" (which sounds as though it was borrowed from the soundtrack to the

Peres hagiography narrated by George Clooney because it plays the same role there), Rabbi Marvin Hier, the director of the museum, explains the nature of the new Jerusalem museum to us. "The vision for the Museum of Tolerance, Jerusalem, is in five million square miles, around the whole of the Middle East," he says. "The state of Israel is the only democracy, and it should say to the world, 'What is a democracy? Come into this building and you'll find out.' A democracy is a place where we don't muzzle people, where people who are, let's say, right wing in their politics, left wing in their politics, Christian, Arabs, Jews, are all welcome here, to learn the magnificent story of the Jewish people, and to commit themselves to the principles of tolerance and human dignity." Following a biblical recitation in badly American-accented Hebrew involving a message about the Torah going out from Jerusalem and something about the word of God, he then goes on to say, "What is the word of God? That we should respect each other, that we should not hate each other. That is what this institution is all about. The Museum of Tolerance, Jerusalem, is a gift to tomorrow's generation. It'll attempt to say to them, 'Do the right thing, as your ancestors have done, to make sure that the great legacy of the Jewish people and the world continues around the principles of tolerance and human dignity.'"

It's difficult to know where to begin in attempting to read this inarticulate farrago of disconnected sentence fragments. The obvious temptation is to dismiss the self-congratulatory talk of "tolerance and human dignity" as either an elaborate hoax or grotesque hypocrisy. This is, after all, an edifice implanted by force over the shattered remains of another people's graveyard—how could it stand for anything other than the exact opposite of the values the rabbi claims to espouse? But it's not mere hypocrisy. What, then, is this museum all about? Is it a project about democracy? Is it about tolerance and human dignity? Is it about the Jewish people? Is it about the Zionist state? Or is it about the whole world? If this building is meant to represent the Zionist state telling "the world" what democracy is, well, what is democracy? None of the values that Hier enumerates has anything to do with democracy as such. The coexistence of right-wing and left-wing people or Christians and Jews is neither unique to nor an essential feature of democracy.

More interesting is the repeated expression of positive values ("tolerance," "human dignity," "harmony," etc.) inextricably combined with expressions of devotion to and even love of the Zionist state. It's clear from the descriptions of the exhibitions and galleries (about which more in a moment) that this is not actually a museum about the state. It is, rather, a museum dedicated to expressing these values and merging them with the state as though by metonymy: a museum that conflates and merges together the positive values already mentioned with "love of Israel." The Zionist state here becomes, in other words, the living metonymical embodiment of these values. "Global harmony," "human dignity," "the magnificent story of the Jewish people," "a love of Israel": these are all, interchangeably, versions of the same thing. To cherish these values is to cherish the state, and vice versa. And, just as importantly, to criticize the state is to criticize these values, and hence to engage in divisiveness, "extremism," and (of course) antisemitism. This is the only possible way to derive meaning from the mishmash of slogans on the museum website. Thus, the Zionist state (and hence Zionism itself) is not to be equated with ethnic cleansing, racial violence, home demolition, torture, checkpoints, indiscriminate bombardment, and apartheid—its minutely documented material legacy over the decades of its existence—but rather with democracy, tolerance, human dignity, "the magnificent story of the Jewish people," and so on.

What's happening here is not simply the blunt denial of the amply documented actual history and legacy of the Zionist state, but more specifically the transaction of that denial by and through the affirmation of the positive values of tolerance, human dignity, and so on. The history of racial violence and dispossession endured by the Palestinian people is not merely denied—it's denied specifically by being repackaged as what the museum refers to as "democracy" and "tolerance." And hence it can no longer be registered as denial at all. In other contexts, I have referred to this mode of expression as the denial of denial (Makdisi 2022). Here, Palestinian experience, Palestinian history, Palestinian reality, Palestinian rights, Palestinian demands, and even the very presence of Palestinians (in a Palestinian Muslim cemetery, for instance) are subject to a form of denial that rewrites itself—even as it is being expressed—as an affirmation of various disconnected bits and pieces of positive liberal value. Not only is the person transacting the affirmation unable to recognize the denial taking place at the same time (hence the smarmy smile): he is also exhorting others to participate in the denial as well by relentlessly drawing their attention to the positive values being affirmed. In the process, the shattered remains of the desecrated cemetery are occluded, as it were, in plain sight (including on that clip on the museum website).

We can think of this as a form of humanitarian racism: a discourse that conveys racist politics not in the older and outmoded language of, say, nineteenth-century colonialism (including nineteenth-century liberalism), with its civilizational hierarchies and claims of moral tutelage, benign intervention, civilizing missions, the white man's burden, and so on, but, on the contrary, in the language of contemporary progressive politics: democracy, equity, diversity, inclusion, tolerance. Here, the language of contemporary liberalism expresses, enables, and sustains a project of racial violence. It's important, however, not to think of this as either hypocrisy or mere cynical cloaking or masking of racial violence. Rather, as we see in the case of the denial of denial, the affirmation of racial violence seamlessly colonizes the language of liberalism. That is why it is unable to recognize itself for what it is: the racism is occluded by the liberal discourse. This helps us make sense of the otherwise incoherent mélange of slogans on the museum website, Rabbi Hier's disordered and rambling stream-of-consciousness narrative, and the discordant jumble of half-sentences and incomplete phrases in both that seem to slide from one into another without any sense of logical progression.

And there's one more piece to this puzzle: at the end of his little video, Hier exhorts us to "do the right thing, as your ancestors have done, to make sure that the great legacy of the Jewish people *and* the world continues." What does it mean to say that "our" ancestors did "the right thing"? Were no wrongs committed in the past, either by Jews or by anyone else? Or by "the right thing" are we to understand "the great legacy of the Jewish people and the world"? But, again, is there no difference between the legacy of "the Jewish people" and that of "the world"? The repeated slippage between "the Jewish people" and "the world" (which recurs throughout the museum's documentation) is striking. On the one hand, the "you" being interpellated here must logically mean "you, the Jewish people," because it's clearly *your* ancestors whose values the museum claims to represent in its representation of "the magnificent story of the Jewish people." On the other hand (and I have suffered through that video enough times to make absolutely sure of this), Hier clearly says "and the world." This is most certainly not a museum devoted to "the world's" values or "the world's" legacy, however. What's happening here, then, is that "the Jewish people" and "the world" have become the same. There is no sense of an other; there is only a (Jewish) self. The other has been purged from these incoherent phrases—as purged as the other has also been *materially* purged from the ground in which the museum's display spaces have been implanted, in what the post-Gehry project architects refer to as a "black box," an underground display space literally interred in and now occupying a site formerly devoted to the remains of dead Muslims.

But what, then, does the word *tolerance* mean in this context? The concept of tolerance implies, by definition, some sort of self, power, authority, or force being (or at least claiming to be) tolerant of some "other." The concept of tolerance requires some kind of otherness to be tolerated, in other words, whether as an act of grace, mercy, or, ultimately, power. "Tolerance" devoid of otherness is quite literally meaningless: it becomes an empty shell of a word. And that's what makes it perfect for the Museum of Tolerance: a project that has no interest in any kind of other, but only in a self—and, at that, a self violently occupying a space from which the last traces of otherness have been remorselessly purged. The violence of dispossession is transacted in and through the empty claim of "tolerance" itself. In this sense, the museum offers a synecdoche for the Zionist state itself.

This helps us make sense of the museum's exhibition spaces. For all the slogans about "democracy," "human dignity," "harmony," and so on, which make it sound as though this is a museum about the global value of inclusivity and multicultural integration, this is clearly a museum purportedly devoted to what it claims are Jewish values, and specifically to renarrating "the magnificent story of the Jewish people" from the teleological standpoint of Zionism. The website's overview of the main exhibition in the museum, "A People's Journey," thus conflates what it calls Jewish values with the Zionist colonization of Palestine: "How did the Jewish people survive? What was it that kept them alive for more than 2,000 years when they had no state, no army to protect them, were scattered far and wide around the world and were often persecuted or unable to live freely as Jews?" it asks. "It was their values. These values inspired and nurtured the Jewish people and have also influenced other religions and cultures throughout the ages and they continue to do so today." The exhibition space begins "as visitors board the legendary ship, Exodus 1947." The ship, notorious rather than legendary, was acquired and renamed by Zionist organizations after the Second World War and used to transport would-be Jewish colonists to Palestine, where it was barred from docking by British forces then in control. The ship and its passengers were returned to Europe, where, we are informed, the passengers went on an ultimately unsuccessful hunger strike. "The ensuing public embarrassment for Britain played a significant role in the diplomatic swing of sympathy toward the Jews and the eventual recognition of a Jewish state in 1948," according to the (rather more polished and professional) website of the US Holocaust Memorial Museum.

In the Museum of Tolerance exhibition, then, visitors "will 'meet' Holocaust survivors, many of them orphans, and Jewish volunteers from the US, the UK, and North Africa. At key points throughout the 7 pavilions in The People's Journey, visitors return to the story of the Exodus [i.e., the ship *Exodus 1947*] to see how the values which kept the Jewish people alive for thousands of years also sustained the desperate passengers during their difficult voyage." The history of Jewish people is thus conflated with the Zionist colonization of Palestine: the Jewish "people's journey" through history is the journey of the passengers of *Exodus 1947*. Missing here, ironically, is the fact that the ship did not make it to Palestine after all (that the people paid to write these scripts failed to notice this is striking). Jewish "values" are thus reduced to Zionism itself rather than, say, specific Jewish cultural or religious values, about which no mention is ever made. Judaism and Zionism are thoroughly conflated and mixed with other random positive values—so that to endorse the Zionist project is to endorse "tolerance," "human dignity," and so on, and to criticize the Zionist project for its racism and violence is, by definition, to engage in the opposite values.

And that's not all. A bit deeper into the description of the seven exhibition spaces devoted to "A People's Journey" is the promise that "some of the best-known names from the world of film and television will narrate the films and interactives in each of the 7 pavilions." Given the Museum of Tolerance's affiliations with those liberal Hollywood personalities mentioned above, it should come as no surprise if Barbra Streisand, Morgan Freeman, Sandra Bullock, and George Clooney turn out to be among those narrating these obsessively self-regarding little vignettes in a space violently purged of otherness.

Violence, ethnic cleansing, and racism are thus being repackaged before our eyes as cultural objects produced by (or in relation to) Hollywood for consumption by liberal audiences. This is why, to return to George Clooney, he is the perfect narrator of that hagiographic documentary about Shimon Peres, and why he would make the perfect narrator for one of these films to be shown in the "black box" embedded in the Jerusalem soil from which Muslim graves were so violently exhumed during the construction of the museum. The human rights crusader would be transacting the denial of ethnic cleansing and settler colonialism in his seductive baritone. Humanitarian racism has found the perfect spokesman in the context of the twenty-first-century culture industry.

All this is taking place in the broader context of a recent and ongoing attempt by Zionist writers and institutions to claim the moral high ground of human rights. In their recent book *The Human Right to Dominate*, Nicola Perugini and Neve Gordon argue that the discourse of human rights can easily be reconciled with and even put to the service of projects of domination. They draw on recent Zionist discourse for one of their prime examples (Perugini and Gordon 2015). Not only does the Israeli army claim to reconcile its bombardments of Palestinian civilian targets with the discourse of human rights, they point out, but a range of Zionist NGOs have sprung up recently in all parts of occupied Palestine, laying claim to a discourse of indigeneity and human rights to sanctify and protect their project of settler colonialism. The early Zionists, of course, from Theodor Herzl and Vladimir Jabotinsky onward, recognized that their project was one of colonial settlement.

Today, however, as Perugini and Gordon point out, a strand of Zionism has emerged that, in keeping with other principles of humanitarian racism as I have outlined them here, claims to represent an indigenous movement of return to a native land. What had been launched in the age of Theodor Herzl and Vladimir Jabotinsky (and endorsed by the British Empire) as a settler-colonial project bent on coercing indigenous people's land from them for the purposes of settlement is now (or so we are told) born anew as an indigenous movement itself, claiming to be set upon by marauding outsiders—the Palestinians. "Settler human rights NGOs portray, for instance, the indigenous Palestinians as the invaders and thus perpetrators of human rights violations, while Jewish settlers are conceived of as natives and depicted as victims of abuse," Perugini and Gordon point out. "For these settler NGOs the Israeli Jew is the subject of human rights, while the Palestinian is not. In fact, once human rights are identified with the Jew, they serve to bolster the Zionist project of sustaining Israel's Jewish character" (Perugini and Gordon 2015, 22). This is, clearly, part of what is at stake in the Museum of Tolerance in Jerusalem: having eliminated the other, the Jewish self is left alone in a space of self-contemplation. This is how it can make sense (from this point of view) that tolerance, human dignity, the Jewish people and "love of Israel" are all versions of the same thing: there is no sense of a humanity beyond the (conflated) Jewish-Zionist self. The language of indigeneity—which, as J. Kēhaulani Kauanui has warned, is all too open to appropriation (Kauanui 2007)—is here deployed in order for the agents of a project of apartheid and ethnic cleansing to claim affiliation with the language of rights and humanitarianism with which we (naïvely, it turns out) thought they ought to be irreconcilable.

More significantly, perhaps, this also allows us to recognize the claim to "return" that the Museum of Tolerance also articulates in its vision of rights and tolerance. If the Jewish people and the Zionist state are coextensive, as the museum seeks to claim, the "return" to what in Zionist parlance is referred to as Eretz Israel ("the land of Israel") makes perfect sense. Hence, in the museum's exhibition spaces, the conflation of "Jewish values" with the colonial vessel *Exodus 1947*. This positions the museum perfectly in line with recent Zionist claims that Zionism is a form of "national liberation" or even represents the return of an "indigenous people" to their ancestral land—as we see, for instance, in the publications of the Israeli settler NGO Regavim, according to which Jewish settlers are natives and indigenous Palestinians are rapacious settlers seeking to usurp Jewish human rights (Perugini and Gordon 2015, 101–2). At first glance, such a formulation may seem laughable, but it must be taken seriously.

The best way to address such a position is to historicize it. After all, a self-identification with Western colonialism is evident across the board in early Zionist writing about the project in Palestine. The early Zionists, from Herzl onward, knew exactly who was the settler and who the native, because they wrote explicitly about it. "Any native people—it's all the same whether they are civilized or savage—views their country as their national home, of which they will always be the complete masters," writes Jabotinsky in his prophetic 1923 piece "The Iron Wall." "Compromisers in our midst attempt to convince us that the Arabs are some kind of fools who can be tricked by a softened formulation of our goals, or a tribe of money grubbers who will abandon their birth right to Palestine for cultural and economic gains," Jabotinsky argues. "I flatly reject this assessment of the Palestinian Arabs. Culturally they are 500 years behind us, spiritually they do not have our endurance or our strength of will, but this exhausts all of the internal differences. We can talk as much as we want about our good intentions; but they understand as well as we what is not good for them. They look upon Palestine with the same instinctive love and true fervor that any Aztec looked upon his Mexico or any Sioux looked upon his prairie." Jabotinsky's point was quite simple. If, he argues, "every indigenous people will resist alien settlers as long as they see any hope of ridding themselves of the danger of foreign settlement," the point is not that the Zionists should abandon their colonial project to transform Palestine into a Jewish state; the point is that that project can only be instituted and maintained by the uncompromising subjugation of the will of the Palestinians. "Zionist colonization, even the most restricted, must either be terminated or carried out in defiance of the will of the native population," he insists. "This colonization can, therefore, continue and develop only under the protection of a force independent of the local population—an iron wall which the native population cannot break through. This is, *in toto*, our policy towards the Arabs. To formulate it any other way would only be hypocrisy" (Brenner 1984, 147–48).

Rereading this text by Jabotinsky (or, for that matter, the writing of other early Zionists, including Theodor Herzl and Chaim Weizmann, who also unabashedly present themselves in the language of Western settler colonialism) makes it possible to see the recent wave of Zionist attempts to claim the moral high ground of human rights, national liberation, and indigenous rights for what it is. But I want to insist, again, that we would be mistaken to think of this set of discourses as mere hypocrisy. The Museum of Tolerance, with its deep and long-standing affiliations with the most liberal components of Hollywood—Clooney is surely the paradigmatic example—is engaged above all in a project of denial. The language of rights, dignity, tolerance, and so on with which the museum invests itself is not merely an attempt to repackage a violent project of racial settler colonialism in the language of liberal virtue but a way to transact denial in and through the affirmation of these positive values. And, everywhere in attendance, an obverse narrative has been set in place: if Zionism represents "tolerance," then, clearly, anti-Zionism represents intolerance.

Thus, humanitarian racism not only packages and transmits the logic of racial violence and ethnic cleansing in the progressive discourse of liberal values, but it also attempts to negate any form of critique by reflexively identifying it with the opposite of all those values. Irrespective of his own personal beliefs (to which we have no access), George Clooney is the perfect vehicle for this humanitarian racism. The good looks, the sense of ease and style, the profession of liberal political sentiments, and the portfolio of human rights campaigns—in a word, Clooney's political *brand*—lend themselves directly to the Museum of Tolerance project. It is no coincidence, then, that he is the one narrating that unbearably hagiographic documentary on Shimon Peres with which this chapter opened. Humanitarian racism in the hands of someone like Clooney may seem irresistible, but it may already have run its course, at least as far as Israel is concerned. The campaign of genocidal violence that Israel inflicted on the Palestinians of Gaza in 2023–24 has surely dealt a severe and hopefully irrecoverable blow to at least this manifestation of humanitarian racism. In the face—and in the wake—of Gaza, international acts of solidarity have never been more necessary, as we work together toward a common liberation.

WORKS CITED

Amnesty International. 2022. "Israel's Apartheid Against Palestinians." February 1, 2022. https://www.amnesty.org/en/latest/campaigns/2022/02/israels-system-of-apartheid.

Biden, Joe. 2023. "Remarks at a Campaign Reception." December 12, 2023. https://www.whitehouse.gov/briefing-room/speeches-remarks/2023/12/12/remarks-by-president-biden-at-a-campaign-reception-5.

Brenner, Lenni. 1984. *The Iron Wall: Zionist Revisionism from Jabotinsky to Shamir*. London: Zed.

Carroll, Rory. 2014. "Amal Alamuddin Refuses UN Offer to Investigate Possible War Crimes in Gaza." *The Guardian*, August 11, 2014.

Daley, Patricia. 2013. "Rescuing African Bodies: Celebrities, Consumerism and Neoliberal Humanitarianism." *Review of African Political Economy* 40 (137): 375–93.

De Waal, Alex. 2008. "The Humanitarian Carnival: A Celebrity Vogue." *World Affairs* 171 (2): 43–55.

Falk, Richard, and Virginia Tilley. 2017. "Israeli Practices Towards the Palestinian People and the Question of Apartheid." United Nations Economic and Social Commission for Western Asia.

Freeman, Kevin. 1982. "Fonda Condemns Double Standard Which Has Been Applied to Israel over War in Lebanon." Jewish Telegraphic Agency, December 6.

Glass, Charles. 1975. "Jews Against Zion: Israeli Jewish Anti-Zionism." *Journal of Palestine Studies* 5 (1–2): 56–81.

Harris, Paul. 2012. "George Clooney's Satellite Spies Reveal Secrets of Sudan's Bloody Army." *Guardian*, March 24, 2012.

Jabotinsky, Vladimir. 1923. "The Iron Wall." Jabotinsky Institute in Israel. https://en.jabotinsky.org/media/9747/the-iron-wall.pdf.

Kauanui, J. Kēhaulani. 2007. "Indigeneity." In *Keywords for American Cultural Studies*, edited by Bruce Burgett and Glenn Hendler, 133–37. New York: NYU Press.

Khalidi, Rashid. 2020. *The Hundred Years' War on Palestine*. London: Profile.

Macintyre, Donald. 2006. "Israel Plans to Build 'Museum of Tolerance' on Muslim Graves." *Independent*, February 9, 2006.

Makdisi, Saree. 2010a. "The Architecture of Erasure." *Critical Inquiry* 36 (3): 519–59.

Makdisi, Saree. 2010b. "A Museum of Tolerance We Don't Need." *Los Angeles Times*, February 12, 2010.

Makdisi, Saree. 2022. *Tolerance Is a Wasteland: Palestine and the Culture of Denial*. Oakland: University of California Press.

Makdisi, Ussama. 2019. *Age of Coexistence: The Ecumenical Frame and the Making of the Modern Arab World*. Oakland: University of California Press.

Mamdani, Mahmood. 2009. *Saviors and Survivors: Darfur, Politics and the War on Terror*. New York: Doubleday.

Masalha, Nur. 2012. *The Palestine Nakba*. London: Zed.

Museum of Tolerance. 2023. "Overview." https://www.museumoftolerance.com/motj/experience.

Pappe, Ilan. 2006. *The Ethnic Cleansing of Palestine*. Oxford: Oneworld.

Perugini, Nicola, and Neve Gordon. 2015. *The Human Right to Dominate*. Oxford: Oxford University Press.

Salih, al-Tayyib. 1969. *Season of Migration to the North*. Translated by Denys Johnson-Davies. London: Heineman.

Singer, Peter. 2007. "The Dark Truth About Blackwater." Brookings Institution, October 2, 2007. https://www.brookings.edu/articles/the-dark-truth-about-blackwater.

United Nations. 1996. "Letter Dated 7 May 1996 from the Secretary-General Addressed to the President of the Security Council." https://www.un.org/unispal/document/auto-insert-187312.

Wiesenthal Center. 2020. "George and Amal Clooney Honored at Wiesenthal Center Gala." October 29, 2020. https://www.wiesenthal.com/about/news/clooney.html.

Williams, Eric. 2021. *Capitalism and Slavery*. Chapel Hill: University of North Carolina Press.

Wyman, David. 2007. *The Abandonment of the Jews: America and the Holocaust, 1941–1945*. New York: New Press.

Zablotsky, Veronika. 2023. "Armenian Refugee Narratives in the Archives of Early Humanitarian Discourse." In *The Routledge Handbook of Refugee Narrative*, edited by Evyn Lê Espiritu Gandhi and Vinh Nguyen, 305–16. New York: Routledge.

9

trans/BORDER/*ing*

(an un-play 4 accompaniment)

*Amy Sara Carroll
and Ricardo Dominguez*

Under the imperfect sun, in Kumeyaay/Kumiai, no word corresponds to borders in English.

FIGURE 9.1 Baseball cap. Credit: Amy Sara Carroll and Ricardo Dominguez.

Line drawings ————
Pastoral, picaresque, panoramic. As nature is to culture, no place is neutral ground. As far as the eye can see—from sea to shining sea—we are called upon to witness the categorical intimacies of labor, capital, and territory. Settler colonialisms, integral to US racial capitalism, linked resource and population management to seizure, detention, and displacement, reconfigured a national project of dispossession predicated on the hetero-patriarchal tenets of possessive individualism. The United States thereafter has been ghosted by the "foundational fictions" (national romances) of the cowboy-Indian and the deracinated (white) immigrant's transformation into propertied citizen.

The Mexico-US border cannot be disentangled from this history of "unspeakable violence" (Guidotti-Hernández 2011). Following the Mexican-American War and the US acquisition of significant territory, Mexico's 1965 passage of the Border Industrialization Program (BIP), first designed to absorb Bracero laborers' regress, synced to the development of the US Sunbelt, remapped the Americas as a "state of permanent displaceability" (see introduction). The BIP as homecoming produced the border industrial park city on the Mexican side of the Mexico-US

Prelude
The End/s of Humanism

The scene opens onto the desert's solar excess. A human voice—after Américo Paredes (2008)—bounces off walls:

O, New York Declaration on Refugees and
    Migrants!¹
Protocols that guard suppliant hands
Look down benign on we who crave
Thine aid, whom winds and waters drove
From where, through drifting shifting sands,
Last sustenance disposed and left behind
    with the unconfessed.
From whence the north land, angry law
    dispossessed,
Closes all fronts in fearful and constant haste,
We arrive as exiles to reach evermore and
    higher walls
Sentenced to death by the stutter of global
    clause-cause.

Scene 1
Ghostthymics (more than the spirit of borderization)

Chords discord exorcisms, emanating from the ruins of Anza Borrego State Park's entrance checkpoints:

Sovereignty: Manifest Destiny's divine right to determine market-states of exception.

Ghostthymics.

Ghostthymics.

border. On the US side, Mexican border industrial park cities were twinned by fortified ports of entry, designed to re/move and process parts, products, disposable labor. Cities fused into points dotting the two-thousand-mile length of the backslash separating and uniting the Mexico-US borderlands.

Conquest-era spatialization extends to the Americas' detention center of the twenty-first century. The planet's first acknowledged immigrant detention centers on Ellis Island (New Jersey) and Angel Island (California) opened in the 1920s. They were preceded in the United States by the violent containment, relocation, and hypervisualization/erasure of Indigenous communities; practices of policing honed in the post–Civil War era of Reconstruction; and legislative precedent like the late nineteenth-century Chinese Exclusion Act—to selectively recount the machinations of US exceptionalism.

Despite the twinned isles' 1960s shuttering, the migrant detention center in the late twentieth century experienced a dramatic renaissance, paralleled by a sharp uptick in US incarceration rates. The Nixon administration's "War on Drugs," initially touting rehabilitation over incarceration, soon flipped the script to target Brown and Black bodies. Tough-on-crimes laws turned prisons into profit-making engines from the 1980s onward. Concomitantly, as the Reagan administration and a bipartisan Congress reconfigured the "War on Drugs" as a hemispheric initiative, US detention rates spiked in response to Cuban, Haitian, and Central American immigration.

*trans/*BORDER/*ing*   197

Ectoplasmic overflows exceed the boundaries that would box us in.

Where everything's the nowhere of the extractive value of expulsions—what confines, cuts out, circulates beyond borders is transformed into missives from the "New World Border."

Ghost borders, spectral borders capture the living, the dead, and the undead.

Ghost borders medium the messenger—those who cross, those who are crossed over, those who are crossed out.

Hystorical Male Line_De-Tourism

The simple fact is that we must not and we will not surrender our borders to those who wish to exploit our history of compassion and justice.

President Bill Clinton, July 27, 1993
(*Congressional Quarterly* 1994)

The U.S. Border Patrol will control the borders of the United States between the ports of entry, restoring of Nation's confidence in the integrity of the border. A well-managed border will enhance national security and safeguard our immigration heritage.

Border Patrol Strategic Plan 1994 and Beyond, vision statement (Nevins 2002, 1–4)

Scene 1.∅. 1.∅. 1.∅. 1.∅. 1.∅. 1.∅. 1.∅. 1.∅.
How to See Like a Market-State in the Twenty-First Century

A drone is a nobody. *Nada, nadie.* The animal that lends its name to these machines was

The Drug Enforcement Administration (DEA) redirected hemispheric narcotics routes through the Greater Mexican corridor. Timed to coincide with the North American Free Trade Agreement's passage, the US federal government's "Prevention Through Deterrence" philosophy undergirded, coordinated a series of Operations from Hold the Line to Gatekeeper, Safeguard, and Rio Grande, that simultaneously rerouted migration away from densely populated urban areas like the Tijuana–San Diego corridor to the remote and treacherous desert biome traversing Sonora and Arizona.

> Another Prelude, Recalculating the "Things They Left Behind"
> A toddler's orphaned shoe.
> A pink hairbrush.
> Lines of scripture in Mandarin.
> Size 6 Batman underwear.
> *Entregas.*
> May's popped, empty foil of birth control.
> A smuggler's creed.
> Let's call it code.

born from unfertilized eggs—parthenogenic as the anomaly of a Costa Rican crocodile's clutch. A drone is a pixel become object—a floater—the bloated tick or tock of insistence. Originally used for target practice. Catch the buzz: demons or daemons, drones mediate physical and virtual reality; becomes state departments in transit or cartel carrier pigeons.

ACTIVATION INSTRUCTIONS (vii)

FLIP   the page   like a script

Waters / \ / \ choppy / \ / \ / \ / \ / \as / \ / \ / \ dashed lines - - - - - - - - - - - - CUT

Borders-fortified-as-continuous-lines——————————————————————FOLD

ASSEMBLE   Lesbos   Greece   as in "woody"   Hittite borrowing   as in regional unit of the North Aegean Sea   as in geopark   "we cannot see   the petrified forest   through the trees"   as in birthplace of lyric   poetry   Sappho   as in LGBTQ   tourist destination ("chasing the rainbow")   as in 2015 "migrant crisis"   at least 450,000 displaced persons   as in the Syrian Civil War   overcrowded boats   makeshift rafts   unseaworthy vessels & craft   flooding shores as in international NGOs   as in 2016 European-Turkish agreement   as in waves & tides   at their metaphoric limits   as in Ai Weiwei's 2016 eyes-wide-shut restaging   of a viral photograph   drowned toddler   face down   on the beach   as in   Moria Refugee Camp   operating at six times   its maximum capacity   as in 2020 rising   anti-immigrant sentiment   (Golden Dawn   at its own meteoric   metaphoric   limit)   as in

TAPE or GLUE   the very shape of this   triangular   island

FIGURE 9.2 Activation instructions (vii) for 3D poem "Lesbos," 2020. Credit: Amy Sara Carroll.

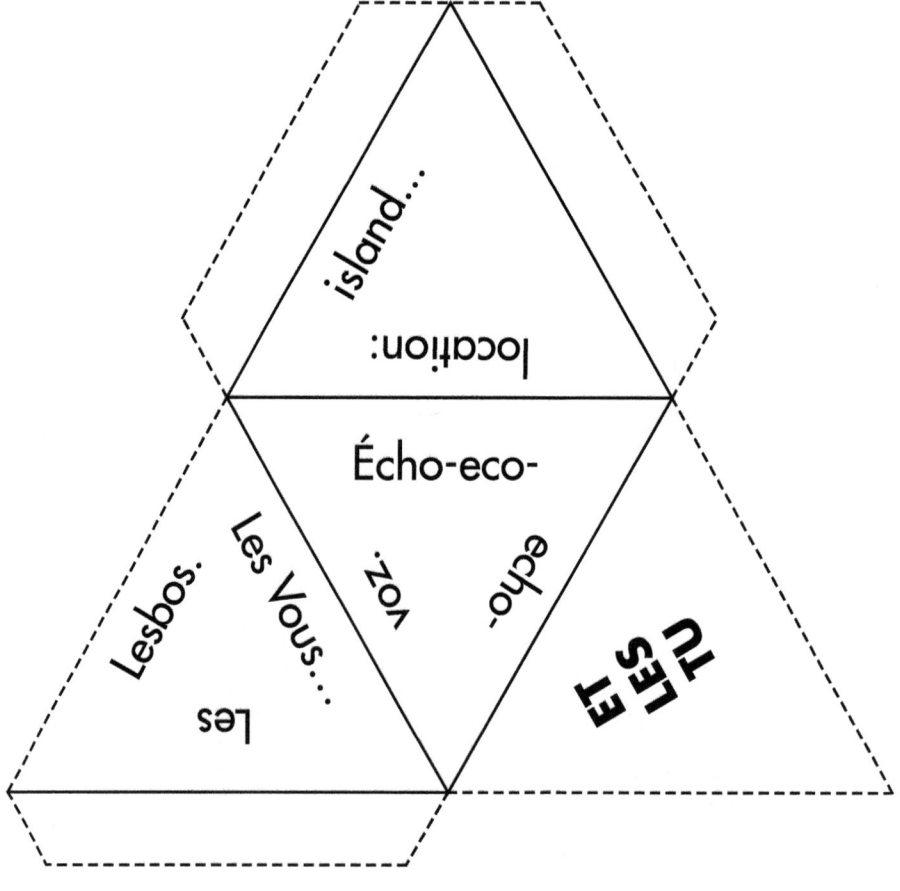

FIGURE 9.3 3D poem "Lesbos," 2020.
Credit: Amy Sara Carroll.

Prevention Through *Virtual* Deterrence

The digitization of the border with autonomous technology is a multinational project supported by players spanning the political spectrum. Decades in the making, the virtual wall runs parallel to physical border wall/s. The Tijuana–San Diego border has always been a fertile staging ground for virtual "border games" (Andreas 2000). In a crowded field of gamers, one program stands out, however: from 1968 until 1973, the US military spent close to $1 billion a year on Operation Igloo White.

Historically without precedent, Igloo White was funded by ARPA (now DARPA), the Defense Department's edge technology research unit. In the revolutionary summer of '68, forty-five scientists from US tier 1 research universities, self-christened the JASON group (after Jason and the Argonauts), gathered at the University of California, San Diego (UCSD) to begin their quest for the golden fleece—a computerized border field of networked sensors. While their virtual fence quest failed to deliver the technology necessary to augment and maintain an omniscient fence to detect North Vietnamese movements crossing into South Vietnam—the so-called McNamara Line—Operation Igloo White lived on in 1970s San Diego's actions related to the US "War on Drugs." In this critical decade, smugglers, immigrants, refugees crossing the MX-US border were transformed into perpetual "persons of interest," archetypes of dangerous penetration. Meanwhile, San Diego's early experiments with virtual walls met with the same fate as the McNamara

As US deindustrialization ramped up in the late 1980s, crippling debt accelerated the United States' dismantling of its social safety net. Meanwhile, in Mexico, border maquilization proved directly proportional to the state's denationalization of industry and dismantling of social services. Both nation-states in turn dictated the terms of a hemispheric reconfiguration of racial capitalism. The Mexican and Central American working poor, frequently Indigenous peoples, shouldering the consequences of US socioeconomic and military intervention and domestic corruption and mismanagement of public resources, risked crossing the Mexico-US border in unprecedented numbers. The dispossessed and displaced were met with rising binational anti-immigration sentiment, further border militarization, and industrialization.

The US 1986 Immigration Reform and Control Act granted amnesty to most undocumented workers who arrived in the United States before January 1, 1982, but penalized employers who hired them. Backlash and cultures of mis- and disinformation were magnified. In 1996 the US Congress ratified legislation, the Antiterrorism and Effective Death Penalty Act (AEDPA) and the Illegal Immigrant Reform and Immigrant Responsibility Act (IIRIRA), that expanded immigrant detention. The week of September 2, 2001, Presidents George W. Bush and Vicente Fox met to hash out, draw up the terms of a guest worker program for Mexican nationals in the United States. The guest worker program swiftly dematerialized after the hemisphere's second 9/11.

Line; proved to be no match for the ingenuity and low-tech hacks of seasoned transborder subjects.

Undeterred, the dream of "Prevention Through *Virtual* Deterrence" powered on. In 1993 Sandia National Labs, a military research facility commissioned to assess enforcement efforts, officially recommended a new necropolitical strategy of "Prevention Through Deterrence." Formally developed with the launch of Operations Blockade and Gatekeeper in 1993 and 1994, the strategy becoming a policy and philosophy hinged on

Post-9/11 (2001), the Bush administration moved the Immigration and Naturalization Service (INS) from the Department of Justice to the newly created Department of Homeland Security (DHS) where it was divided into three parts: US Citizenship and Immigration Service (USCIS), Immigration and Customs Enforcement (ICE), and Customs and Border Protection (CBP). Incarceration and detention became not only a mainstay of US Reconstruction and immigration policies, but also the United States' go-to responses to so-called enemy combatants.

the surveillance and mobilization of geographic space via the deployment of advanced technologies or the perceived deterrent power of the southwestern landscape. State officials invested billions of dollars in new surveillance equipment, including night-vision goggles, seismic sensors, low-light CCTVs, and high-tech aircraft for nocturnal detection to monitor highly trafficked binational corridors.

In 1995, San Diego's Border Research and Technology Center (BRTC) opened. Operated by Sandia National Laboratories, BRTC worked with the US Customs Service and Border Patrol and later with Homeland Security, the US Attorney's office, and law enforcement agencies to strengthen technology border capabilities. BRTC has been involved in joint ventures to identify technology to stop the flow of undocumented people crossing the Mexico-US border. In 2004, for example, it participated in a project to detect the heartbeats of people concealed in vehicles or other containers. Identical technology reappears in an artwork by Rafael Lozano-Hemmer, featured in Washington's National Gallery, delighting countless museum-goers. Sync your heart with another's, marking time on both sides of the Border's arrhythmic techno-futures, no longer "New World," but in perpetuum capital's capitalized Conceptual ism.

Scene/ry (Take 2)
". . . between fear and there . . ."

When the Berlin Wall fell, records indicated that ninety-eight people in total had perished trying to scale the wall between East and West Germany.[2] In contrast, local and transnational NGOs estimate that thousands have died in remote areas of the MX-US borderlands following the US government's 1994 adoption of a "Prevention Through Deterrence" philosophy, a calculated weaponization of environment. The US Customs and Border Protection Agency's fiscal report for the 2010s tallies 3,858 border-crossing-related deaths on the US side of the border.

Each year another record is broken. Pre-pandemic, the United Nations migration agency called 2019 the deadliest year on record for migrants across the Americas. Nearly two-thirds of reported deaths occurred on the Mexico-US subcontinent. The *Guardian* declared 2020 the deadliest year on record for migrants in the Sonoran Desert. In July 2020 the remains of two undocumented entrants were found in the southwest corner of Arizona. One body lay next to an arrow drawn in the sand, pointing north with the word HELP (in English) written beneath it (Gilbert 2021). Two men perished attempting to walk into the US interior in search of work and vaccinations. A third man who survived told US federal agents that the men's *coyote* had abandoned them in the remote wilderness area. In reality, human traffickers in the MX-US corridor routinely look the other way as the weakest walkers in a group of undocumented entrants fall behind. The *Wall Street Journal* reports that US authorities in fiscal year 2022 recovered a record number of bodies: more than 890 migrants perished along the border, a 58 percent increase over 2021. By March 2023, the year's count had already exceeded the fiscal 2021 year total of 566, and was on track to be deadlier than 2022 for migrants (Pérez and Caldwell 2023). Dehydrated, disoriented, baked by the sun. Drowned, bobbing in reeds or washed up on the banks of a river. Crossing the Mexico-US international boundary—a wall or wire, a line in the dirt or the water—remains the easiest leg of any migrant's gerrymandered journey south to north.

The Obama administration's expansion of deportation landed thousands of migrants, sometimes whole families, in migrant detention centers. The aughts accelerated the divvying up of Mexico's national and regional economies into parallel universes—the formal and the informal. Mexican narco-violence skyrocketed. The Mexican government embarked on its own string of Operations from Michoacán to Baja California and the joint Operation Nuevo León–Tamaulipas, only matched in sound and fury by US border and drug enforcement efforts. Fast-forward through the Obama "Greater Deporter" era: from 2016 onward, the first Trump administration significantly expanded the United States' "Prevention through Deterrence" philosophy, implementing draconian travel bans, stepping up migrant detention and deportation (per a range of expanding planetary carceral logics), sometimes in the guise of "migrant protections protocols" (also known as the Remain in Mexico program, whereby asylum seekers are forced to wait in Mexico while seeking asylum in the United States).

"It's like a graveyard out there," emote El Paso officials, who keep a refrigerated truck for casualties of the Rio Grande. In Piedras Negras, Mexico, families picnicking along the waterfront routinely encounter floating corpses. Migrants, on the other hand, utilize applications like WhatsApp to communicate with contacts on the other side of the river in order to keep track of crossing conditions, from law enforcement presence to the river's currents, attuned to "routes of forced mobility."

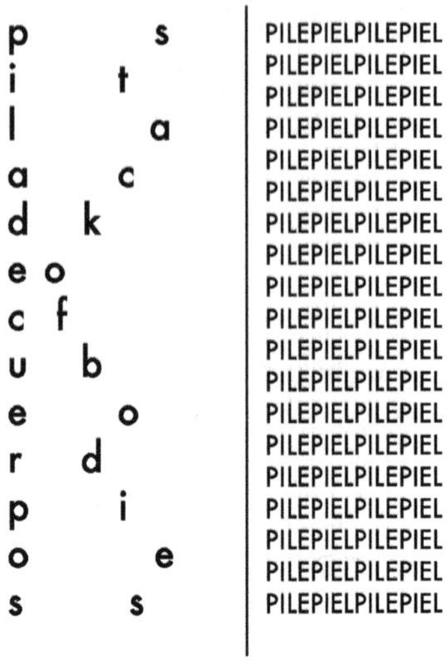

Intertitle 42

On March 20, 2020, the Department of Health and Human Services issued an emergency regulation to implement Section 265 of Title 42 of the US Code, which permits the director of the Centers for Disease Control and Prevention (CDC) to expel migrants, refugees, and asylum seekers believed to pose a serious danger of introducing disease into the United States. Despite CDC scientists' objections to the invocation of Section 265 and public health experts' observations that there was no need to turn away refugees while international borders remain open to other travelers, CDC director Robert F. Redfield cited Title 42 when he ordered the suspension of the introduction of any persons into the country who had been in "coronavirus impacted areas." Redfield's junk science detailed particular concerns about those who had entered into a "congregate setting" at a port of entry or in a Border Patrol station—namely, individuals arriving at the Mexico-US border.

Redfield's opportunistic invocation of Section 265, grounded only in then senior adviser to the president Stephen Miller's weaponization of arcane legislation, continued under the Biden administration. From March to November 2020, CBP not only turned away adults requesting humanitarian aid (echo "the problem of sanctuary—its unfulfillable promise") but also refused entry to more than thirteen thousand unaccompanied children despite the Trafficking Victims Protection Act's mandate that the US government protect children who arrive at the border without a parent or legal guardian.[3] On November 18, 2020, a federal judge halted all expulsions of unaccompanied children. In January 2021, after a

FIGURE 9.4 Visual poem "PILEPIEL," 2024.
Credit: Amy Sara Carroll.

federal court upheld that decision, the Biden administration amended the CDC's previous Title 42 order to exempt unaccompanied children, but did not abolish it altogether.

In late January 2022, US Department of Justice lawyer Sharon Swingle successfully argued in federal appeals court for Title 42's restrictions to prevail. Public health experts weighing in on the situation noted that the administration's continued reliance on Title 42 was not based in science, that migrants could be safely processed at the border. Even Dr. Anthony Fauci, widely regarded as the top infectious disease expert in the United States, weighed in, stating forcefully that "expelling [migrants] . . . is not the solution to an outbreak" (Narea 2022).

> The invocation of public health relative to US immigration policy is old hat—think Zyklon B and gasoline-delousing of Mexican workers and asylum seekers at early twentieth-century Texas-Tamaulipas and Chihuahua checkpoints (what historians have identified as prototypes for Nazi Germany's gas chambers [e.g., Molina, 2006; Stern 1999]). To be clear and cognizant of present implications, what the invocation of Title 42 ensures is not only a reduction in current migration but also an expansion and outsourcing of the US policy of "Prevention Through Deterrence." On February 4, 2021, DHS secretary Alejandro Mayorkas announced the administration's decision to expand the CBP's use of Title 42 to ramp up deportations of migrants from nation-states Cuba, Nicaragua, and Venezuela to third-party off-sites like Colombia, this being in addition to asylum seekers typically being turned back overland to Mexico. Setting aside the intricacies of various nation-states' willingness to participate in the United States' expansion of its border control, in the Mexican case it's worth noting that then left-leaning president André Manuel López Obrador (AMLO), who early on in the pandemic laughed off COVID-19, in March 2021, after his first COVID-19 infection, video-conferenced with Biden and Mayorkas. A deal was struck, amounting to another trafficking of drugs: in exchange for US AstraZeneca COVID-19 vaccine stockpiles, AMLO pledged that Mexico would double down on Central America's exodus, guaranteeing his administration's continued participation in the United States' Remain in Mexico program.

Karla Marisol Vargas, senior attorney at the Texas Civil Rights Project, framed the counterargument concisely: "Scapegoating Black, [I]ndigenous, and other migrants of color as vectors of disease [reflects] the ongoing racism entrenched in our immigration system." Notwithstanding repeated calls to lift Title 42 restrictions, the CBP between January 2021 and May 2023 expelled more than 2.3 million migrants.[4] On the ground a contagion of doublespeak prevails. In March 2021, Mayorkas counseled each suppliant to wait their turn: "We are not saying don't come; we are saying don't come now."[5]

> In the lead-up to the lifting of Title 42, Operation Lone Star went into warp drive. All over the state, Lone Rangers saddled up, wishing one another "good hunting." Texas governor Greg Abbott commended these Terminators' patriot actions, even as he mourned the loss of innocent life in Allen's and Brownsville's mass shootings. In West Texas, Kinney County sheriffs enshrined in their offices cut-outs of Donald Trump (for inspiration) and Kamala Harris (for social media foil). Like their Texas compatriots, they continue to guard local backyards, have taken on the job of border patrol, detaining migrants. The *Washington Times* reports that county arrest records reveal that state trooper Orlando Rivera first pulled a vehicle on a county road over for its tinted windows. When the trooper determined that the tint was legal, a scent raised his heckles. Rivera annotated: "I identified the smell as an odor that is associated with human smuggling. Undocumented aliens emit a distinct odor due to sweat and being exposed to the environment" (Hernández 2023). As if Operation Lone Star's mandate wasn't enough, Rivera's admission of his heightened olfactory policing tactics recalls the rotten-to-the-core stench of the US crimmigation system's strategic mobilization of Brown-on-Brown "driving while Mexican" racial profiling. To paraphrase and decontextualize one of the most memorable lines of cinematic history, uttered in an otherwise unforgivable flight of fantasy of (meta-, read Good Neighborly) North-South extractivism, "We don't need [your] stinkin' badges!" (Huston 1948).

The hype surrounding the May 11, 2023, end of Title 42's enforcement ultimately reinforces Vargas's declaration. Media outlets across the political spectrum predicted border surges that never materialized. What happened instead reflects the United States' increasing recourse to the border's technological mediation: since May 11, 2023, encampments on the Mexican side of the border have grown in size exponentially, evidencing the geofencing inherent in the United States' glitch-ridden rollout of its CBP One App to Rule Them All, denounced by the left and right respectively as dysfunctional and a "concierge service." Required until recently to apply for asylum with the app alone before presenting at a port of entry, asylum seekers clustered in areas devoid of infrastructure, amplifying the already "fractal geography of camps and crossings" (see the introduction to this volume). CBP One regenerated the cognitive map, barriers, and queues, forcing migrants into waypointed hostile terrain quadrants without running water, secure housing, food, or other basic human necessities. *The newest border wall, to expand its functionality for a wider public, was an app to download, before Trump 2.0 suspended its use.*

Scene 3
When Does a Desert Look Like a Sea?

The International Organization for Migration (IOM) has recorded more than 25,000 deaths since 2014 in the infamous Africa-to-Italy crossing, deeming it to be the deadliest migratory passage on the planet. Smugglers crowd boats, often establishing hierarchies of personhood, locking the least "worthy" in the ships' holds. The circumstances of the second deadliest Mediterranean maritime disaster on record remain unclear. On June 10, 2023, roughly a month after Title 42 was lifted, the *Andrianna* left Tobruk, Libya, with hundreds of migrants onboard. On June 14, 2023, the fishing trawler sank in international waters off the coast of Pylos, Greece. In official statements, Greek authorities insist that migrants onboard the ship's crowded upper and lower decks refused assistance. Alarm Phone, a European based rescue support network, testifies otherwise, claiming it received distress calls from the *Andrianna* and notice of the ship's status as a "left-to-die boat." What's certain is that on June 13, the Italian coast guard alerted the Greek coast guard and Frontex, the European Union's border protection agency, of a vessel's irregular movements. The Greek coast guard, Frontex aircraft, and merchant ships tried to establish contact with the *Andrianna*. Passengers maintained the ship was not in distress, asking only for food and water, which were supplied. At 1:40 a.m., the Greek coast

**footfootfootfootfoot
footfootfootfootfoot
footfootfootfootfoot
footfootfootfootfoot
footfootfootfootfoot
footfootfootfootfoot
foot |l|a|d|d|e|r|**

FIGURE 9.5 Visual poem "31 Foot Ladder" (after Andrew Sturm), 2023. Credit: Amy Sara Carroll.

Another Prelude Is Due Too Late, or, How to Build an Echo Chamber

Hyperenclosure: San Diego's triple fence becomes more than overcompensation or protection.

Border Patrol agents kettle migrants between the walls for days without food or blankets.

The *San Diego Union-Tribune* reports, "Obaidullah found himself trapped with more than 100 other asylum seekers in what has become an open-air holding cell between the two layers of border wall. He said US Border Patrol agents required them to wait there in custody with no shelter, no food and minimal water, the latest in what has become a pattern for the San Diego sector" (Morrissey 2023).

A human voice ricochets between walls.

guard was told that the *Andrianna*'s engine had broken down. As officers tried to approach the ship, they reported that the vessel jagged sharply right and left, then capsized. Within fifteen minutes, it was completely submerged in an area 4,000 to 5,200 meters deep. Migrants struggled to stay afloat; no one was wearing a lifejacket. The BBC (like Alarm Phone) contradicts the coast guard's account, saying the boat was stationary for at least seven hours before sinking. The Greek coast guard and military coordinated a massive search-and-rescue operation. The 104 male survivors report that women and children were locked in the *Andrianna*'s hold. Nine Egyptian smugglers were initially charged by the Greek government with human smuggling, mass murder, and thirty-eight other crimes. The charges against them were dismissed by Kalamata judges in May 2024 on the grounds that the *Andrianna* sank in international waters outside the jurisdiction of Greek courts. The Greek government, the EU, and Frontex in contrast never faced charges. Greek opposition leader Alexis Tsipras spoke with survivors; all claimed to have cried out for help repeatedly. Responding to the weaponization of the Mediterranean—Europe's own "Prevention Through Deterrence" philosophy—Tsipras queried, "What sort of protocol does not call for the rescue . . . of an overloaded boat about to sink?" (Smith and Henley 2023).

Scene IV
Dronology@Un/Homely

Now the old dronology dream returns with a vengeance. Anduril Industries offers another layer of "Prevention Through *Virtual* Deterrence" that echoes the glitches of the past with the force of a techno-dystopian future-now (think autonomous drones, autonomous sentry towers, and autonomous ghost robotic dogs). Arriving on the scene in 2017, Anduril from the get-go had the blessing of Palantir executives. Palantir Technologies, a big data-filtering engine or intelligence fusion system founded by Peter Thiel, the CEO of PayPal and staunch financial backer of Vice President J. D. Vance's political aspirations, in 2003 to protect and pacify the homeland, morphed into a pro-Trump Cloud First company. Palantir and Anduril form part of a global network underwritten by Whitepower coding, driven by Cloud First US policies. Amazon, Salesforce, Microsoft, Dell, Hewlett-Packard number among the couple's Silicon Valley digital hookups. In 2021, Anduril tested their virtual wall all "along the watchtowers" of the MX-US border, utilizing fusion software to link a network of surveillance towers, SkyGuardian, the Border Patrol, and the San Diego Police. In 2022, Anduril won a flexible contract, capped at $950 million, to contribute elements of technology to the US military's Advanced Battle Management System. The sweet deal generates only a portion of Bajalta California's growing Drone Valley windfall profits. Anduril's #AutonomyForBorderSecurity has received contracts worth almost a billion-plus with CBP since 2018.

New border wide-area sensing networks like Anduril's Lattice System consolidate long-term aerial surveillance, long-range border tracking, and big data aggregation in the San Diego–Tijuana corridor. The Lattice fence will be plugged into a data fusion network connected to Gorgon unmanned aerial systems like the Sky Guardian, a General Atomics hypersurveillance drone force focused on deep and durational "pattern-of-life" analysis. Palantir's big data analytics are correlated and shared with DHS and local police via smartphone applications like Patternizr, used in Los Angeles and San Diego. Such systems have been sold to city councils like San Diego's under the sign of the "Smart City." The Lattice system was constructed not only to secure the border but also as a general platform for "geographic omniscience." Municipalities find out only later that it is part of an inter-intelligence fusion and mass supervision network envisioned as an expanded algorithmic caging system to capture the real bodies and data bodies of immigrants, refugees, and the undocumented crossing the border and moving and living within the United States. To date, in the San Diego area, CBP agents have deployed thirty-five new surveillance towers at Friendship Park, Del Mar Dog Beach, and Fashion Valley Mall; on private property in Hillcrest, Imperial Beach, El Cajon, Chula Vista, Otay Mesa, along the Gaslight District Downtown, and along the new metro Blue Line connecting the San Ysidro port of entry to UCSD. Each autonomous sentry tower stands between thirty-three and eighty feet tall and is embedded in an intricate network of streetlights. Meanwhile, Chula Vista's police drone program is singled out as a model for cities inside and outside the United States.

Inspired by what it's seen north of the border, Tijuana has launched its own drone force. Both Tijuana and San Diego use the drones to assist with emergency calls. The Tijuana Ministry of Citizen Safety and Protection Center for Unmanned Aerial Vehicles proactively flies its drones to monitor public space in select neighborhoods. The expansion of the border under the signs of Trumpism's "force multiplier" 1.0 and 2.0 and Biden's "smart security" spreads across Mexico and Central America, flying drones deeper into Mexico's interior, pushing migrants into ever more hostile terrain like the Darién Gap.

Parallel Universes Masquerading as Critical Fabulation

> Walrus, walls are [not] us, lean into the *khôra*:
> "*I am he as you are he*
> [*as you are she as you are they*]
> *as you are me*
> *And we are all together . . .*"

Accompaniment 4 an un-play: Hold up a Mylar blanket to site yourself. Borders open after Title 42 lifts like techno-cloud cover. Migrants are transported across deserts, rivers, seas. Buckets of de-thorned roses are strewn across bridges, landing strips, and docks. Walkways became pathways

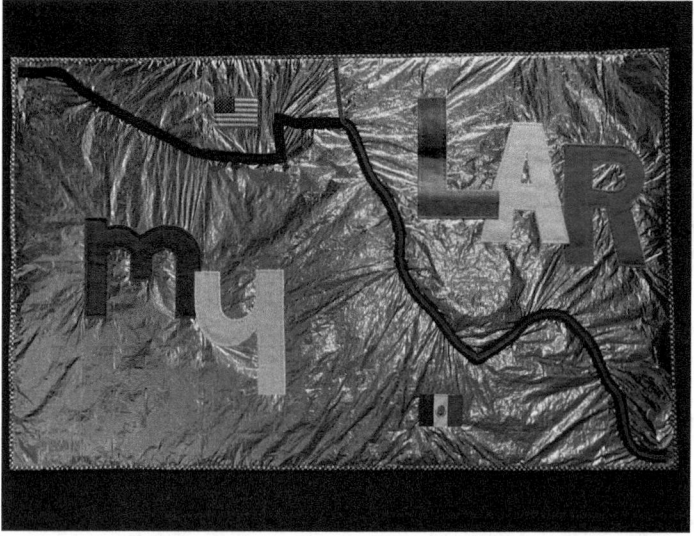

FIGURE 9.6 "My Lar" poem-quilt, 2020. Credit: Amy Sara Carroll and Donna Senf Carroll.

> The ubiquitous Mylar blanket of the detention center, repurposed as a poem-quilt, maps Gloria Anzaldúa's "third country"; separates syllables, not families. In the break: my "Lar," a Roman spirit of the home, proxies a continental higher law doctrine for the 2020s, undocumenting histories of the vanishing present.

to citizenship, *mejor dicho*, to the abolishment of the category of citizenship altogether. ICE and Frontex agents, alongside you and me, flank the streets to welcome migrants. Drones and helicopters, repurposed, shower asylum seekers with lilacs. Homeland security vehicles, repainted as mobile murals, transport the weary to hotel rooms, medical attention, and hot meals. Or, the actions of multiple nations lead to the redistribution of wealth and resources; the obsolescence of the categories of Man, the refugee, undocumented, unauthorized, migrant, even the "problem of sanctuary." We understand that we are stewards, not owners, of place—"No Ban on Stolen Land." We meet one another in the air we breathe. We recognize water as always-already recycling itself—for better or worse.

Postlude
Synesthesia sans *paredes*

The scene folds into the desert's solar excess.
But ye, kept outside, with your cause true,
Pass hence with trust into the fenced town,
Ringed with a wide confine of guarding towers.
Therein are many dwellings for such immigrant guests
As the State honors you all; there we are housed
Within neither greedy nor ungiving.
There dwell ye, if ye will to lodge at ease
In streets well-thronged: yet, if your soul prefer,
Tarry secluded in a separate homes.
Choose ye and cull, from these our proffered gifts,
Whiche'er is best and sweetest to your needs be:
And I and all these citizens whose vote
Stands thus decreed, will your rights be.
Look not to find elsewhere more loyal care.

NOTES

1 Providing protection to people fleeing in search of refuge is one of humanity's most long-standing traditions—a shared value embedded in many religious and cultural traditions, now partially enshrined in international law, most recently articulated by all 193 United Nations member states in the New York Declaration on Refugees and Migrants, adopted in September 2016.

2   The apt line "between fear and there" belongs to and is borrowed from Cog•nate Collective (2021).

3   For a chilling parallel, consider the weaponization of quarantine regulations by European Union countries that declared their ports "unsafe" and closed them to asylum seekers at the height of the COVID-19 pandemic (Tazzioli and Stierl 2021). Many thanks to Veronika Zablotsky and Ananya Roy here and throughout this volume for reminding us to scan for structural violences half-rhyming across continents and oceans.

4   For more information on Title 42, including its suspension, see American Immigration Council 2022; National Immigrant Justice Center 2023.

5   Is it possible not to hear in Mayorkas's "humanitarian reason" liberal injunctions to civil-rights-era organizers to bide their time? In this continental theater of operations, we were never a'Biden players, much less true believers in a two-party system of government.

WORKS CITED

American Immigration Council. 2022. "A Guide to Title 42 Expulsions at the Border." Last modified May 25, 2022. https://www.americanimmigrationcouncil.org/research/guide-title-42-expulsions-border.

Andreas, Peter. 2000. *Border Games: Policing the U.S.-Mexico Divide.* Ithaca, NY: Cornell University Press.

Carroll, Amy Sara. 2020. "My Lar," "Activation Instructions (vii)," and "Lesbos," *Michigan Quarterly Review* 59 (4): 652–54 and cover. https://sites.lsa.umich.edu/mqr/2020/09/mqr-issue-594-fall-2020/.

Congressional Quarterly. 1994. "Presidential News Conference: Clinton Announces Policy on Illegal Immigration." In *CQ Almanac 1993*, 49th ed., 40-D–41-D. Washington, DC. http://library.cqpress.com/cqalmanac/cqal93-844-25162-1104265.

Cog•nate Collective (Amy Sánchez Arteaga and Misael Díaz). "Circumlocution: Border/Circunlocución: Frontera." 2021. 4 mins., 59 sec. https://www.cognatecollective.com/intergalactix-en.html.

Gilbert, Samuel. 2021. "2020 Was Deadliest Year for Migrants Crossing Unlawfully into US via Arizona." *Guardian.* January 30, 2021. https://www.theguardian.com/us-news/2021/jan/30/us-mexico-border-crossings-arizona-2020-deadliest-year.

Grandin, Greg. 2020. *The End of the Myth: From the Frontier to the Border Wall in the Mind of America.* New York: Metropolitan.

Guidotti-Hernández, Nicole M. 2011. *Unspeakable Violence: Remapping US and Mexican Imaginaries.* Durham, NC: Duke University Press.

Hernández, Arelis R. 2023. "Texas Uses Aggressive Tactics as Title 42 Ends." *Washington Post*, May 10, 2023. https://www.washingtonpost.com/nation/interactive/2023/texas-title-42-end.

Huston, John, dir. 1948. *The Treasure of the Sierra Madre*. Los Angeles: Warner Bros. 2 hrs., 6 mins.

Molina, Natalia. 2006. *Fit to Be Citizens? Public Health and Race in Los Angeles, 1879–1939*. Berkeley: University of California Press.

Morrissey, Kate. 2023. "Migrants Say Border Patrol Is Keeping Them Between the Border Walls for Days Without Food or Shelter." *San Diego Union Tribune*, April 13, 2023. https://www.sandiegouniontribune.com/news/immigration/story/2023-04-13/migrants-say-border-patrol-is-keeping-them-between-the-border-walls-for-days-without-food-or-shelter.

Narea, Nicole. 2022. "Biden Is Defending Key Trump Immigration Policies in Court." *Vox*, January 25, 2022. https://www.vox.com/22893065/biden-family-separations-title-42-border-court.

National Immigrant Justice Center. 2023. "FAQ: The End of Title 42 Expulsions." May 10, 2023. https://immigrantjustice.org/staff/blog/faq-end-title-42-expulsions.

Nevins, Joseph. 2002. *Operation Gatekeeper: The Rise of the "Illegal Alien" and the Making of the U.S.-Mexico Boundary*. New York: Routledge.

Paredes, Américo. 2008. *With His Pistol in His Hand: A Border Ballad and Its Hero*. Austin: University of Texas Press.

Pérez, Santiago, and Alicia P. Caldwell. 2023. "'It's Like a Graveyard': Record Number of Migrants are Dying at the U.S. Border." *Wall Street Journal*. Last modified March 17. https://www.wsj.com/articles/illegal-immigration-mexico-us-border-deaths-c35cf892.

Smith, Helena, and Jon Henley. 2023. "Greece Shipwreck: Up to 100 Children Were Below Deck, Survivors Say." *Guardian*, June 15, 2023. https://www.theguardian.com/world/2023/jun/15/greece-refugee-shipwreck-rescuers-scour-sea-for-survivors.

Stern, Alexandra Minna. 1999. "Buildings, Boundaries, and Blood: Medicalization and Nation-Building on the U.S.-Mexico Border, 1910–1930." *Hispanic American Historical Review* 79 (1): 41–81.

Tazzioli, Martina, and Maurice Stierl. 2021. "Europe's Unsafe Environment: Migrant Confinement Under Covid-19." *Critical Studies on Security* 9 (1): 76–80.

10

Postcoloniality, Race, and the Ruse of Asylum

An Interview with Nicholas De Genova

Ananya Roy and Veronika Zablotsky

In this interview with Nicholas De Genova conducted in 2021, parts of which are featured in the Sanctuary Short ~~Asylum~~: *At the Borders of Humanitarianism*, Ananya Roy and Veronika Zablotsky explore the interconnections of asylum seeking and labor migration, the rejection of refugees and the illegalization of migrants, and the postcolonial and racial underpinnings of contemporary border regimes.[1] With a special emphasis on Europe but also a comparative interest in the United States, the interview highlights the global coordinates that make the historical and contemporary linkages between European colonialism and US empire a necessary analytical framework for understanding sanctuary spaces. De Genova emphasizes how migration and refugee movements provoke critical questions about counter-cartographies that problematize the methodological nationalism that customarily infuses the humanitarian conceits of the wealthiest and most powerful states confronting the incorrigibility of the autonomy of human mobility.

> *We want to explore how the terms of protection through which liberal democracies in the West constitute themselves are turned around and used to produce racial others, in order to constitute the West as a space of sanctuary and refuge to so-called strangers, and how such constitution rests on the inscription of border crossers (migrants, refugees, asylum seekers) as less than, or barely, human. Please tell us how you think about these issues.*

One of the important things to reckon with in any discussion about refugees and asylum is that we see a major historical transformation take place over the course of the twentieth century. The institutionalization of the question of asylum and asylum seeking is something that occurs as a result of World War II and the Holocaust but very quickly gets subsumed by the politics of the Cold War. And so for an extended period, the figure of the refugee is a relatively celebrated figure, a de facto heroic figure, and that serves political purposes. The numbers of people who are seeking asylum are relatively small but nonetheless very politically useful from the point of view of appearing to verify or validate certain kinds of Cold War narratives about people fleeing from persecution and tyranny.

Then there's a major transformation whereby, with the foreclosure of other forms of migration, the foreclosure of the opportunity for various kinds of migratory movement, increasingly asylum becomes the only channel available for various people who want to migrate. Indeed, people who've already been migrating as workers, as labor, find themselves with no other options. With the bringing to an end of guestworker programs in Europe, you have a new regime for asylum that is simultaneously a regime of migration, and asylum seeking becomes very deeply associated with the migration of many people who are presumed to not be "legitimate" refugees. Those programs and their historical contexts sustain a deep interconnection between the places from which migrants originate and the places to which they migrate. By the time the rules change, migration infrastructures are well established. And in that sense, asylum seeking becomes riddled with a politics of suspicion, and the governance of asylum becomes predicated upon suspicion. Hence, the idea of "fake" refugees is always there to haunt anyone who is seeking asylum, as indeed the numbers of people seeking asylum also grow remarkably. Furthermore, the larger working of that system, very predictably, becomes a machinery for the rejection of asylum seekers and their rejection, of course, tends to be part of a larger process of their illegalization.

You argue that the European asylum system is not a system for granting asylum to refugees. Could you please explain this?

What on its surface appears to be about a humanitarian commitment on the part of European countries and the larger European Union, a humanitarian commitment to protecting and welcoming and receiving refugees—that asylum regime has as its very predictable and durable material outcome the production of *rejected* asylum seekers. Overwhelmingly, in practice, it's a machinery for their rejection and conversion from the once-hallowed figure of "the refugee" to the more derisive figure of "the migrant." This is the other key point: there is a discursive economy that unequally and unevenly distributes certain connotations and meanings among different categories of human mobility.

The "migrant" is fashioned as a figure that is inherently opportunistic, inherently driven by self-interest. The "refugee" has a more rarefied status as someone who is presumed to be a pure victim. The humanitarian logic and rationale of asylum is one whereby wealthy countries can congratulate themselves for their humanitarian commitments. They can demonstrate, or presume to demonstrate, that they are committed to the protection of people in need, people fleeing persecution and violence. Yet, nonetheless, that becomes a part of the larger working of this machinery that rejects the vast majority of those same people. That large-scale rejection, in material and practical terms, is the real result of that system.

One of the many instructive aspects of your work is the way in which you think across the US and European contexts and beyond. In that sense, could you expand on the production of migrant illegality as you just began to discuss?

In the larger trajectory of my work as a scholar, there was always a focus on the United States—in particular, the United States' relationship to Mexico—and in my earlier work, a central focus on Mexican migration to the United States became the basis for an argument about what I call "the legal production of migrant 'illegality.'" In short, I contend that there is a spectacle produced at the US-Mexico border that appears to verify the presumptive reality that people are somehow really "illegal," that there are migrants who somehow by crossing the border are engaged in some sort of presumptive violation of the law, some sort of transgression, and thus, that their "illegality" is something of their own doing as the result of their own actions. What I argue, however, is that if we look at the history of lawmaking with respect to immigration in the United States, then it's possible to see that some migrations and some categories of migrants historically are produced as "illegal," that there are certain categories of human mobility that are actively illegalized by various kinds of interventions that take place very far removed from the border—in other words, through lawmaking. Thus, that legal production of migrant "illegality" becomes a central feature for understanding the historical specificity of the construction and ultimately the criminalization of particular categories of migrants as "illegal aliens."

As the focus of my work shifted into the European context—partly in concert with my own relocation to Europe, as I was living and working in Europe, and increasingly interested in these questions there—I began to try to think about the significant and substantial differences between the regimes for the governance of human mobility between the US and the European contexts. I was seeing an increasing prominence in the European context of this larger-scale process of the illegalization of migration and migrants. For the great majority of people who would migrate to Europe, particularly those who were poor, the only opportunities available would be to come as asylum seekers. But again, that meant that the workings of that system became saturated with the idea that the mere act of seeking asylum is always already a certain kind of chasing after opportunities, and thus that asylum seeking is understood to be somehow illegitimate, or manipulative.

So, for example, in the British context, the tabloid press has been very active for decades in associating asylum, asylum seeking, and asylum seekers with every conceivable abuse. They use phrases like "benefits shopping," referring to social welfare benefits as something for which asylum seekers are actively shopping around, looking for the place with the most generous social welfare system, in order to take advantage of the opportunity to go someplace to simply collect a welfare check from the government without having to work and so forth.

Consequently, asylum seekers' opportunities are pervasively and increasingly foreclosed, and we can observe their conversion, in other words, into a marginalized and subordinate labor force within the European context. That process is inseparable from these larger processes of governing various kinds of human migratory movement and ultimately the rejection of the great majority of people who cross borders as asylum seekers, as refugees, converting them into illegalized migrants and social formations that are overwhelmingly impoverished. Rather than receiving asylum seekers with hospitality and welcome, Europe has increasingly met them with suspicion, hostility, and rejection.

What brought you to this work? Please tell us about the key lineages of thought and struggle that you draw upon.

The intersection of my personal biography with my research and my intellectual interests begins with the fact that my interest in Mexican migration to the United States really grew out of my own immediate life experience, which operates at two levels. I was born and raised in Chicago during an era when Mexican migration transformed the city and its racial politics. The transformation of the politics of labor and class in this context coincided with what was a larger-scale process whereby a city that historically had been predominantly white and Black was becoming one in which there was a more and more prominent third term, so to speak, in that dominant racial order. And that was overwhelmingly associated with Mexican migration. Those social transformations were very relevant in a different sense to me personally, because of my political activism in that city, Chicago, when I was young. Many of the people with whom I was working closely in my political activism as a teen were themselves Mexican migrants. Thus, what it meant for me to think about the politics of race and class came to be challenged in new and interesting ways by their experiences. Eventually, that activism and the questions it provoked are what drove me in this direction, intellectually and in terms of an eventual doctoral research project. My research interests grew out of fundamentally political concerns and questions that arose from a certain personal experience, a certain intersection of my personal biography with larger social transformations that were underway. That was initially an interest in the politics of migration, but specifically a migration that was overwhelmingly illegalized and associated with labor.

What does it mean to do this scholarship with a commitment to analyzing and dismantling empire within the global imperial university?

I came into academic life with a very deep and intense activist background that began relatively early, and which preceded my applying to graduate school, and I continued to be active in various ways. For me, the questions that motivated me and inspired me about migration were, on the one hand, located in a very important way in a US context, in a conversation about race and class and the lived experience, the everyday life, and the everyday struggles and conflicts and antagonisms that were evident in working-class life in the United States. On the other hand, migration in particular, because it involved the whole question of national identity and the crossing of borders, was always for me also a question of internationalism, and it was related to a politics of class that was necessarily global in its outlook. There's simply no way to think about questions of social justice or inequality in the United States without situating them in a global context and an internationalist framework of analysis, as an effect of the larger weight of what William Appleman Williams, the US historian, famously called "empire as a way of life." In an important sense, then, the migrations that I was interested in, in the US context, must be understood to be a "harvest of empire," to borrow a phrase from Juan Gonzalez—a larger-scale gathering of the human consequences of a global regime in which the United States is deeply implicated.

I like to say that the first half of my life can be understood in very consequential ways under the heading of one word, and that word is *Vietnam*. And the second half of my life can be understood, very consequentially, to have been determined under the heading of another word, and that word is *Iraq*. That means that my politics have always been deeply informed by a very fundamental critique of US imperialism. It also means that I have always approached the lived experience of people who migrated in terms of the evidence in those experiences of the consequences of US empire. To come at the question more directly in relationship to asylum, and even to resituate that question in the European context, you have European countries where the largest numbers of migrants—which is to say, disproportionately, people who have been granted asylum and recognized as refugees—are people from Iraq, people from Afghanistan, or Palestinians. There is not any one-to-one correspondence between the matter of who has to flee a situation of war or conflict or persecution and where they arrive. In other words, the whole question of asylum seeking in Europe is deeply impacted by the weight of US power on a global scale. That is to say, the "colonial present," so to speak, is one in which the ramifications and repercussions of US empire are global in their distribution.

We are very interested in your argument that Europe has managed to convert the precarious lives and bodies of migrants and refugees— disproportionately racialized as not white, and in fact often racialized as Black—into overtly deracialized "migrant" lives. Can you talk about the way in which you conceive the relationship between systems of migration and systems of extraction?

Every discourse of migration, asylum seeking, and refugees in the European context is always a discourse of race. Those terms serve as proxies to talk about race while evading a more frank confrontation. Part of the peculiarity, historically, of the post-Holocaust cultural politics of race in Europe is aversion and evasion with respect to questions of race. People want to say that they're against racism and identify as antiracist, but they don't have the analytical category of race available. You have this peculiar situation of an antiracism without race, and such a stubborn institutionalized resistance to a conversation about race as such that people don't have the most elementary tools with which to think about it and talk about it. Indeed, what that serves to do is reanimate a very backward, anachronistic notion of race as biology. For lack of the capacity to have a serious interrogation of race as something social and political—as something consequential and meaningful, precisely because it's a social fact, because it's a political fact—you then have a completely anachronistic and mistaken notion that race names some basic biological truth about human differences. You remain in this trap where somehow in the European context it's illegitimate to talk about race.

As a result, migration is always burdened with doing the work of giving people the means to talk about race. So then you have these peculiar neologisms: people are described as being "of immigrant background," which is the way to say they are not white, the way to say that they are not really Europeans, which is to say, even though they were born and raised in Europe in whichever European country, that we recognize them immediately, transparently, to be somehow not really admissible to the category of "European"-ness, where, again, Europeanness is itself a racial formation of whiteness.

All of that begs a deeper question, which is about the postcoloniality of Europe, the legacy of European colonialism, and its impact on our modern world. For centuries, the implicatedness of Europe in various forms of, to use your phrase, extraction—which is to say colonial conquest, pillage, and exploitation—was part and parcel of the historical production of race as we know it. That long legacy of the colonial relationship between Europe and the rest of the world was central to the historical production of race in its modern sense. And that was about enforcing a global regime of colonial capitalism that was inherently always already a racial regime, a colonial regime of white supremacy on a global scale. That is indeed the "harvest of empire" in the European context. Migration becomes one of the key sites in the world today for really trying to understand and grapple with the enduring unresolved conflicts of our postcolonial condition on a global scale.

In your writings, you have also noted that the figure of the Muslim/ migrant, in both the US context and the European context, is especially subject to suspicion. And you have used the phrase "racial instability" to explain how that figure is constructed and understood. Tell us a bit more about this.

This question is inseparable from the so-called War on Terror and the larger extended historical moment that comes to be defined by securitization. The simple fact is that terrorism provided a very convenient surrogate in the post–Cold War era for a nefarious enemy, which allowed it to serve as an organizing conceptual framework for a renewed global politics of empire. And it was convenient in a variety of ways.

What was at stake in the machinations of various competing formations of imperial or quasi-colonial power on a global scale was the central importance of petroleum, and therefore the Middle East region. A demonized figure of Muslim menace could be located in that region. It was also convenient in another sense, which is that the figure of terrorism supplies a kind of enemy that was unlike another state. It was not identifiable as an enemy that had its own military, that abided by the conventions of a customary grid of geopolitical intelligibility. It does not correspond to the Cold War sensibility. Instead, you could create an elusive enemy, global in scope and extent, both everywhere and nowhere, including, of course, next door. This serves to blur the distinction between inside and outside—of the nation-state, as defined by state borders—and thus between the domestic and the international.

In addition to the global geopolitical competition between the United States and the Soviet Union, or between the so-called free world and the so-called Communist bloc, the Cold War always included a domestic feature: the notion of subversives at home, who could be targeted by McCarthyite sorts of witch hunts against communists in the United States. But it was configured differently with the War on Terror. Suddenly you have the racialization of that nefarious and elusive figure of this new terrorist threat "at home" and abroad:

one that is predominantly associated with Arabs, Muslims, and the Middle East but one that also takes a more amorphous form that is, most importantly, not always instantaneously recognizable according to the conventional logics of race. The racialization of the figure of "the Muslim" that comes with the War on Terror is part of a larger-scale transformation of the politics of race to a formation of racial difference and antagonism that is increasingly culturalized. Complex constellations of markers of racial difference associated with the body and presumed differences among imagined types of humans—bodily and biological features—come now to be conjoined with all sorts of other associations of cultural or religious difference.

Consequently, the Muslim as a racialized figure is a particularly productive one, precisely because of its ambiguities, precisely because of its capacious way of encompassing all kinds of different people who look all kinds of different ways, and who nonetheless are distributed on an effectively global scale. Therefore, again, you can find the enemy anywhere and everywhere. Nonetheless, you can also target particular populations as inherently suspect. This culturalized figure of the enemy is thoroughly racialized and inseparable from a politics of race that, particularly in the European context, becomes inseparable also from various kinds of expressions of generalized anti-immigrant hostility. As a result, more and more, in the European context, the debate around migration inevitably comes up against a notion of the incommensurability, the inherent incompatibility, of certain kinds of culturalized differences. Thus, you inevitably convert every conversation in the European context about migration into one that's about so-called integration, and whether or not certain kinds of cultural difference and certain kinds of religious or even "civilizational" differences become apprehensible as inimical, impossible to integrate or assimilate.

Your work emphasizes the spatiotemporality that migrants have to endure, such as the forced mobility of deportation, the enforced waiting and immobilization that come with illegalization and the constant threat of detention and expulsion. In particular, you have developed the concept of deportability. Please tell us more about this spatiotemporality and what it reveals about state power.

Part of the argument that I develop about deportability is that, almost always, many people who are vulnerable to deportation are in fact not deported. The state needs only to deport some in order to be able to discipline the rest, who must live under the prospective horizon of the possibility of being deported, who will be made to feel palpably their own vulnerability to deportation. Deportation, of course, is in a fundamental sense a spatial tactic or technology of power that is about removing people physically from one space to another, expelling them. Deportation is most productive in actually creating and sustaining a lived condition of deportability that serves to discipline those who are illegalized but not deported, who remain as illegalized migrants, as illegalized workers, as labor. That is also a temporal condition in the sense that they must continue to exist under those conditions. The uncertainties and the unknowability of that question of whether or not that particular deportation power will be brought to bear upon you means that your life is disciplined and conditioned in both spatial and temporal ways. Indeed, people might live out the rest of their lives in this indefinite condition of illegality—migrant illegality—but also deportability. Similarly, if people are susceptible to being arrested and detained, then there's a fundamentally similar dynamic at play.

Notably, one of the remarkable things about detention is that some people might be detained but for a variety of reasons not deported, and even ultimately released from detention. We could examine a whole variety of particulars in a whole variety of specific places with respect to different detention regimes, but there is a fundamentally comparable and analogous way that it becomes operative in migrants' lives as an extended *temporal* disciplinary power. Waiting under an indefinite horizon of not knowing whether or not you will be ultimately subjected to that particular form of punishment involves uncertainty. Whether you end up being punished with detention or not, you are nonetheless subjected to that particular disciplinary power of detainability.

We can't only see those direct acts of power upon the bodies of migrants, those specific occasions where someone is apprehended and detained or deported. We have to see the productivity of the working of that power by producing the social and ultimately political condition that disciplines them, renders them particular kinds of subjects, and that, without assurances, requires people to live to a certain degree in fear. Thereby, this indefinite condition of deportability and detainability contributes to people accepting conditions of life that are highly exploitative, marginalized, et cetera. So it's very productive, and in that sense it's always biopolitical, it's not only necropolitical. This touches on the bigger question about border regimes and border violence that produce death for migrants in transit across borders.

The same can be argued for the ways in which border regimes produce death and other kinds of violence to which people are subjected in the course of crossing borders, such as incredibly heightened risks of not only outright death but also injury, mutilation, torture, rape—all of which is inevitably a deeply traumatizing experience. But for all those who don't die, which is ordinarily the majority, what's the consequence of that trauma? The actual crossing of the border under illegalized circumstances becomes an endurance test that is like an apprenticeship because it's a preparation for a lifelong career as illegalized labor, which entails extraordinary exploitation and exceptional vulnerability. And so, again, without belittling or trivializing the horrific violence to which people are subjected, and the reality of mass death and increasing escalating death in various border zones—such as the US-Mexico border, such as the Mediterranean in the European context—it nonetheless remains the fact that many more people survive. Those border violences then contribute to conditioning them for a certain way of life—because to ever go through that again becomes increasingly unthinkable. As a result, increasingly militarized and physically fortified borders and their manifold forms of violence function as a strategy of capture: once people have made their way across the border, and have found their way into a new way of life as illegalized migrants, the very thought of risking being expelled and deported, and thus of having to cross again and be subjected anew to all of those forms of violence, contributes in a very productive way to their subjection and subordination as labor in the context where they are illegalized migrants.

What are some of the counter-cartographies through which the hegemonic formations that produce the idea of a refugee crisis, or a border crisis, can be challenged?

The first point is to say that there is a customary and conventional cartographic imagination that lends itself to various kinds of anti-immigrant politics and policies. It is predicated on the simplistic notion that, somehow, we are here and they are there, this is our country and they're coming in, such that there's a basic antagonism between "us" and "them," which I describe in terms of nativism.

The term *nativism* has much more currency in the US context, where it originated. It doesn't have the same currency in many other contexts, but the term *nativism*, if we use it as an analytical category, is more precise, I think, than other terms for anti-immigrant hostility, such as *xenophobia*. Ordinarily if you call somebody a nativist, it's understood to be inherently derogatory. Even people who espouse nativism have often been shy to endorse it and promote it as their position. A term like *xenophobia*, for example, seems too narrowly construed around the idea that the rejection of migrants is driven by an irrational fear or an aversion to their foreignness. I think those are all analytical limitations of the concept of xenophobia, whereas nativism tells us that it's actually about the promotion of the priorities and the prerogatives of the so-called natives on no other grounds than that they are "natives." It is native-ism that says, "This is 'our' thing and we're entitled to it simply because we are who we are." So nativism is a classic example of identity politics.

The point is that the nativist conceit defies the real history of the world, which is about interconnection and interdependency. The real history of the world involves long legacies of colonialism, the pillage and exploitation of people in places elsewhere. And yet the predominant politics of immigration—certainly the predominant logic of immigrant or refugee exclusion or restriction—is to uphold the notion that "they're coming from elsewhere. It's somebody else's problem; we can't be asked to solve all the problems of the world; our country is full, we don't have room for them; we don't have the resources to provide for them." As a result, immigration debates frequently devolve to fiscally conservative arguments about costs: we simply can't afford it. Hence, much of such immigration discourses operates within the realm of what is understood to be the legitimate debate that citizens can have about their own democratic self-government. It doesn't necessarily articulate itself as xenophobic in the sense of hostile racist antagonism toward foreigners. Yet it's predicated in a deep and fundamental way on a nativist conceit, a nativist politics of identity that says, "We're entitled to decide what happens here. This is our space, and our wealth belongs to us. We will draw up the borders and then police them as we choose."

Consequently, a counter-cartography related to migration and refugee movements would have to be, first of all, one that could identify and expose the deep complicities, the deep legacies and historical interconnections, that tie these seemingly remote and disparate places and phenomena that are happening in other parts of the world to the places that otherwise want to insulate and partition and bunker themselves with borders and say, "We'd love to help you, but you're not our problem." That points to a different conception of our world as a whole—our social and political world, the world economy, centuries of colonial capitalism—that confirms that these apparently disparate and remote places are in fact inseparable from each other, and that contributes to recognizing the inevitability that these migratory and refugee movements will inevitably deliver more and more people to the wealthiest and most powerful countries in the world. And not only those—of course, we see these phenomena across the world, and even relatively marginal differentials of wealth between countries can make the difference. This means that many countries are increasingly seeing new influxes of migration and refugee movements, and many countries now are both sending and receiving countries at the same time.

Tell us a bit more about what you mean by the "incorrigible subject," especially in the ways in which you have argued that it's genuinely productive to note the affinity between this radically open-ended politics of migrant presence with the similarly abject and profoundly destabilizing politics of queer presence.

The deeper conversation here is really about the capital-labor relation. Marxists have long had the habit of referring to labor—or perhaps the working class—as "the subject of history." That is instructive for the purposes of this conversation in the sense that part of my analytical framework is inspired by a deep interest in the subjectivity of labor and therefore of migrants and migration. What do I mean by that? In my view, the capital-labor relation is one in which human creative capacities and productive powers—which is to say human subjectivity, human subjective power—are the real motor, the real force, that creates our world. Their conversion into capital is something that happens after the fact. It's human ingenuity and human creativity and human productive power in all its manifestations as human work and labor that produces all the wealth of the world. And that gets converted into things, objects, the products of labor that can be turned into commodities and sold in the marketplace, and thus converted into money. That, indeed, is the basis of capital. Human beings and human life come first, and this creative capacity and productive power is only something we would call "labor" once it's subjected to certain kinds of social relations of domination and exploitation. With that as a backdrop, it seems to me that that migration presents us with another occasion to understand that elementary subjective way that human beings are involved in the production of our world, that we are implicated in the creation of everything we know, of everything about the world—all wealth. All the things we see are the products of human effort, human energies.

Thus, thinking about migration, confronting the realities of migration, theorizing migration, is about asking the question of whether a different world is possible. Fundamentally, it's about the question of whether we can envision a different way of life. But it works its way through that site where we encounter the human freedom of movement in particular, which for me is not a right granted by some constituted power but is rather an exercise, a practice, something we could say is existential to the human condition. If we start there, that power and that subjectivity are indeed incorrigible from the point of view of the forces that would seek to discipline, subject, dominate, and exploit them. There's an incorrigibility inherent in that relationship. There's an antagonism inherent in that relationship. We could say that that's true of labor, from the point of view of capital: there's this incorrigible subjective force. I'm interested in the manifestations of that in the context of migration, specifically.

What are the consequences of this argument, which maybe I'm expressing in an overly theoretical way? Well, it means that every border regime, all border policing, all immigration law—they're all reaction formations. What came first? The primacy of human mobility, the actual exercise in practice of a human freedom of movement, the appropriation of mobility by human beings who've decided to put their needs first in disregard of any state, in defiance of any law, including the subversion of any border, and against any forms of border and immigration policing—all of which are reaction formations meant to interrupt and discipline, in one form or another, that basic expression of this human freedom. There's something monumental and profound at stake in understanding the struggles over migration because what's at stake finally is what is the relationship of the human species to the space of the planet and whether another world is possible.

That brings us back to this counter-cartography question. There's something completely fabricated and artificial—and, historically speaking, quite recent—about a global political order of territorially defined states that are understood to be "national." There's something fundamentally fabricated and artificial about a world crisscrossed by borders that are increasingly militarized and increasingly violent. The consequences of those things are profound and real, and yet this fundamental human incorrigible subjective power, this human appropriation of mobility, this human determination to actually move across space to make life, to put human needs first—it can never be suppressed, and there's no formation of border violence, no border regime, no system of immigration lawmaking that is ever sufficient to actually completely contain and suppress that incorrigible force of the human freedom of movement and its active material and practical expression.

Consequently, the other dimension of this politics of incorrigibility is that it's not only a politics of mobility but also a politics of presence. Even under conditions of incredible material constraints and vulnerability, once people make it across the border, they are still trying to make a new life for themselves. That becomes inseparable from their presence and their indispensability as labor, the necessity of their labor and their subjection to capital within the capital-labor relation. Even despite a grand spectacle of nativist politics—the xenophobic and racist politics of rejecting and excluding and keeping them out—in fact there's a fundamental way that employers are always implicated in enthusiastically recruiting migrant workers, indeed importing them, in order to exploit their labor. So, again, there's this fundamental affinity between the subjective force and creative power of labor and the way that I'm repurposing it in the context of migration. It manifests itself as an incorrigible politics also in the sense that it says it doesn't matter how completely illegalized migrant labor may be, it doesn't matter how thoroughly criminalized and persecuted and marginalized, there's a politics of presence that makes that labor indispensable because it plays a productive and crucial role. Moreover, it manifests itself politically in various expressions when migrants do mobilize and do engage in overt, organized, articulate struggles.

This recalls the events of 2006 when migrants in the United States mobilized on a mass scale in an utterly unprecedented social movement of many millions of people across the country, which is where this argument of mine comes from. It was in thinking about a particular chant or slogan that ran through that movement. People everywhere were chanting (in Spanish): "Here we are, and we're not leaving! And if you throw us out, we'll come right back!" In that sense, it was a very overt reference to the fact that they were susceptible to deportation. That was remarkable, and this is why I characterize it as a "queer" politics of migration—because of how consonant it was with the proposition "We're here, we're queer, get used to it!" They were effectively saying: "We're here, we're illegal, get used to it. You can never get rid of us." They were illegalized, they were vulnerable to the recriminations of the law. They were susceptible to deportation. And yet in their millions, ultimately people were saying, "You can never get rid of us, and if you throw us out, we'll come right back." It was a defiant politics, and one that wasn't asking for clemency, wasn't begging for mercy, wasn't petitioning for legal status. It wasn't asking for anything. It was saying, "We're here and there's nothing you can do about it." In part, it was the recognition "We're here because you need us, you depend upon us." That is what I would characterize as an anti-assimilationist politics. It's not asking to be included. It's not asking to be given any permission, but actually saying: "Where do we go from here? Let's deal with reality."

NOTE

1   The Sanctuary Short can be viewed at https://challengeinequality.luskin.ucla.edu/the-end-of-humanitarianism.

INTERLUDE

Sanctuary and Solidarity

Resisting the US War
on Refugees and Migrants

Veronika Zablotsky

In response to the first Trump administration's war on refugees and migrants, amid the first year of the COVID-19 pandemic, the virtual convening "Sanctuary and Solidarity: Resisting the US War on Refugees and Migrants" brought together legal scholars and activist attorneys, Indigenous leaders, and anti-detention organizers to discuss abolitionist strategies of resistance and solidarity.[1] The conversation foregrounds Indigenous and migrant-led mobilizations against border imperialism on stolen land, the ethics of accompaniment, pro bono assistance, and sanctuary practices grounded in Indigenous sovereignty.

Listen to Jennifer M. Chacón, professor of law at Stanford University, elaborate on the colonial continuities of human rights violations at the US-Mexico border. Building on her work on the "hypercriminalization" (2019, 1336) of racialized migrants, she connects federal immigration enforcement to "deep histories" of antiblackness in the United States, a "settler colonial nation whose boundaries *still* dissect the nations of peoples here before us." Nicole Elizabeth Ramos, director of Al Otro Lado's Border Rights Project, argues that the US immigration system produces "deportation and death" by design (Cavise 2019) and makes the case for strategic impact litigation in US federal courts. As a core member of the abolitionist collective Detention Resistance, Brendan Cassidy talks about the importance of nonreformist relief work and organizing with detained migrants to #AbolishICE and #FreeThemAll. The intersectionality of struggles for migrant justice and Indigenous liberation is highlighted by the Red Nation Tiwa Territory (ABQ) Freedom Council chair and co-chair for the Beyond Borders Caucus, Hope Angelique Alvarado (Diné and Mescalero Apache). Concluding the convening with a powerful call to action, Juan B. Mancias, chairman of the Carrizo/Comecrudo Nation of Texas, explains that providing sanctuary to migrants and resisting the construction of a physical US border wall is an integral part of the ongoing land and water defense of the Carrizo/Comecrudo people (Tuhus 2020).

NOTE

1   The convening "Sanctuary and Solidarity: The U.S. War on Refugees and Migrants" can be viewed at https://challengeinequality.luskin.ucla.edu/sanctuary-solidarity-resisting-the-us-war-on-refugees-and-migrants.

WORKS CITED

Cavise, Leonard. 2019. "Manufactured Misery at the Tijuana Border Crossing." *Truthout*, September 28, 2019. https://truthout.org/articles/manufactured-misery-at-the-tijuana-border-crossing.

Chacón, Jennifer M. 2019. "Immigration Federalism in the Weeds." *UCLA Law Review* 66 (6): 1330–93.

Tuhus, Melinda. 2020. "The Carrizo Comecrudo Tribe of South Texas Struggles for Sovereignty and Environmental Justice." *Between the Lines*, June 24, 2020. https://btlonline.org/the-carrizo-comecrudo-tribe-of-south-texas-struggles-for-sovereignty-and-environmental-justice.

UCLA Luskin Institute on Inequality and Democracy. 2020. *Sanctuary and Solidarity: The U.S. War on Refugees and Migrants*. Featuring Hope Angelique Alvarado, Brendan Cassidy, Jennifer M. Chácon, Juan B. Mancias, Nicole Elizabeth Ramos, and Veronika Zablotsky. August 28, 2020. https://challengeinequality.luskin.ucla.edu/sanctuary-solidarity-resisting-the-us-war-on-refugees-and-migrants.

PART III

Freedom and Fugitivity

11

Fugitive Relation and Errant Social Reproduction

A Note

Sarah Haley

Esther Shawboose Mays never met Mattie Jackson, never found Jackson's pens and stationery or the letters she wrote describing prison life and planning rebellion. Between the two purportedly fiery women there are, certainly, geographies of relation, paradoxes of possession and dispossession, decades of violation, vicissitudes of rebellion, and gulfs of experience and belonging. Between them there were nearly seven hundred miles of territory and overlapping histories of war, urban transformation, dispossession, relation, and estrangement. Their creative practices and their relationships to place and upheaval were dramatically different. Between them and us, there is more territory and time; there are more questions of Black practice, sociality, gender, place, and history; more relatives and more strangers to consider.

Mattie Jackson and Esther Mays open this essay because both women's histories anchored the conversation upon which it focuses. What follows is an annotation of a June 2021 online public conversation, titled "Freedom and Fugitivity," among Saidiya V. Hartman, Kali Tambreé, Kyle Mays, Aisha Finch, and Tiffany Lethabo King.[1] "Freedom and Fugitivity," organized by Ananya Roy and Kali Tambreé, was part of Roy's UCLA Sanctuary Spaces Seminar Series. Kyle Mays (Saginaw Chippewa) opened the conversation with the story of his great-grandmother Esther Shawboose Mays and her search for Black and Indigenous freedom, or what he called co-liberation. Shawboose Mays was sixteen when she left her Saginaw Chippewa reservation and moved to Detroit, perhaps seeking autonomy over her sexual and romantic life; there she married a Black man, Robert Isiah Mays. This migration and reconstitution of family was, in Kyle Mays's words, her first act of refusal.[2] In Detroit her home became a sanctuary for Indigenous children vulnerable to kidnapping by the state. Kyle Mays's aunt Judy Mays founded one of the first Indigenous-led schools for Native and Black students in the United States. Esther Shawboose Mays's migration is not a representative story in Native women's history, but it is a provocative one, one that raises questions about the nexus of political and intimate sanctuary, about reinvention born from gendered modes of refusal, and about the tensions between familial love and forms of autonomy that sometimes require familial abdication and reinvention among strangers. Less is known about Mattie Jackson, but her history will be a referent as the conversation continues.

The UCLA Sanctuary Spaces Series and this subsequent volume seek to destabilize what Roy gracefully described during the event as the "universal grammar of Western humanism, its frames of liberal recognition and settler assimilation." The histories under study here operate, of course, *without sanctuary*, in the afterlife of slavery, the time of institutionalized rape, lynching, and imprisonment.[3] This annotation will end up in the world that Saidiya Hartman has made; this world, I would argue, contests the violence of normative humanism produced by the historical archive through a practice of creative social reproduction that entails inhabitation, confrontation, elusion, and intuition.

Although there is no sanctuary on the page, Black creative life undermines the terror of Western humanism and charts possibility in its beyond. While it has not been possible to bring about the demise of white supremacist normativity, such encounters have the capacity to make prospects for elsewhere, excess, and errancy beyond racial and gendered dominion in the time and tense of the speculative and the subjunctive. The central concern of this chapter is the domain of Black feminist making, or practice, which is also the domain of reproduction (Brown 2015; Hartman 2016, 2019; Hunter 1997; Kaplan 2021; Morgan 2007; Sharpe 2010);[4] the dominion of Black feminism *is* life even as it is life without sanctuary, which means in proximity to eradication. The absence of sanctuary and the proliferation of its ruse has been a defining feature of Black women's history (Davis 1971); safe harbor has been, and continues to be, ephemeral. Instead, slender sanctuary has been conceived in the realm of political strategies such as dissemblance and respectability, projects designed to evade white supremacist violence that could not be quelled. Thus, this chapter asks if we might look to strange intimacies, transitory as they may be, and insurgent composition, mediated as it may be, not as sanctuaries in themselves but as critical fugitive terrain where sanctuary fails.

What follows is an event annotation that traces the contours of the "Fugitivity and Freedom" conversation, a dialogue that contributes to the unsettling of Western humanism by exploring questions of Black life, practice, and dissidence that antagonize normative humanity and operate under regimes of gendered racial terror and settler colonialism. I will linger with Saidiya Hartman's proposition that the stranger, a minor subject of history, is a pivotal pathway for thinking otherwise about relation and the organization of living.

Following Kyle Mays's opening remarks about Esther Mays and Black and Indigenous co-liberation, the "Fugitivity and Freedom" event proceeded with a question from Kali Tambreé about archival encounter and ways of knowing. She asked if we, as interlocutors and audience, might spend a few moments with Saidiya Hartman in the archive. Was there an example of an archival encounter that was particularly elucidating? Could Hartman reflect upon the epistemological capacity of critical fabulation? In responding to this succession of important questions, Hartman described her encounter with the case file of Mattie Jackson in terms of what is known and what is knowable. She described the process of unfurling state-produced knowledge about Mattie, a criminalized young Black woman sent to the New York State Reformatory for Women at Bedford Hills for three years in 1919. Hartman described the process of extricating knowledge from imprints, suggestions, fragments, and context; this is the process of history-making with minor figures, historical subjects made strange by slavery, people whose predicaments of familiarization, legibility, selective recognition, opacity, and transparency are all topics for Hartman's cultural history, historical poetics, and theory of history. Variously diminished, disappeared, and extinguished by the state and its records, the minor figure holds little claim to permanence beyond captivity; rather, her experience is one of furtive or harried movement, erratic and evasive, but in ephemera nevertheless eminently productive of intimacy, insurgency, and intellectual life.

Tambreé and Hartman's portion of the event moved toward a close with a turn to how the study of minor figures generates a productive disordering of historical categories, Black scholarly form, and the stakes of audience.

Centrally, Hartman's work grapples with the political economy of Black subjection; she argues that Black women's thorough relegation to wage work as domestic laborers throughout much of US history vexes prevailing ways of thinking about industrial capitalism, capitalist terms of order, and subject positions under gendered racial capitalism. For her, grasping the relationship between interiority and the economic perils facing Black women and girls requires an original form, creative thinking, and prodigious historical scrutiny. And while Hartman offers many descriptions of the work produced by her writerly and research practice in her most recent (2019) book *Wayward Lives* (a serial biography of a generation, a portrait of the chorus, a moving picture of the wayward, an archive of the exorbitant, a dream book for existing otherwise), I suggest that the questions of family, fugitivity, territory, and belonging that she raises also may lead us toward thinking of this work as archival social reproduction: the work of social reproduction of Black aliveness amid death. This requires intense archival exhumation, antagonism, and experimentation. Rather than social reproduction of the worker or capitalist subject (categories themselves under pressure in Hartman's theorization), this is social reproduction of Black queer subjectivities enclosed by and exceeding territory, captivity, respectability, heteronormativity, erasure, archive, violence, and stasis.

Making Strange

A "narrative written from nowhere" (Hartman 2019, xiii), *Wayward Lives* clearly extends Hartman's previous work in *Lose Your Mother* (2007) in thinking about the subjectivity of the stranger produced by both the specificities of place and an enormity of abyss and as structured by captivity and always impending annihilation. As a space of specificity and consumption, the family emerges as a site in which relation is made and from which Black queer subjects are fugitive. In her 2018 article "Black 'Feminisms' and Pessimism: Abolishing Moynihan's Negro Family," Tiffany Lethabo King asks us to consider disavowing forms of affinity that reify world-destroying categories of the human. While noting the family's primacy in Black cultural and political life, she raises the possibility of an abolitionist orientation toward family as a life structure that often "crowds out the dynamic and emerging ways that Black people reimagine and invent new modes of relation" (King 2018, 70). Drawing from the canon of Black feminist criticism of "The Moynihan Report" and from Hortense Spillers's classic theorization of the flesh as both the site of extreme violation and as a productively deviant Black subject position, Lethabo King asserts the necessity to both recognize strange relationality *as* Black relationality and further make relation strange—to denaturalize the family and defamiliarize social congregation and connection in order to build novel and peculiar modes of being with one another.

King extends Hartman's analysis in *Lose Your Mother*, noting with respect to the final chapter's rendering of fugitive intimacies between girls in Gwolu, Ghana, that it is rift, ephemerality, dislocation, precariousness, breach (scurried temporalities of relation), rather than lineage, kinship, genealogy (temporalities of long durée, permanence, immemorial time) that define recaptured Black relation. Gwolu was a place in which those fleeing apprehension by slave traders assembled to create sanctuary and became lovers or friends or conspirators, making new lives for a time in a place they sought, ultimately unsuccessfully, to defend from encroaching colonialist raids. This process of becoming fugitive intimates is, for King, an intramural horizon; relatedly but secondarily, it is an alternative to Western genres of the familial and a rejoinder to the tropes of Black familial pathology and structures of Black familial annihilation that mark Western modernity, a rejoinder that is at once an intense relation and discarding of respectability. Those who fled to Gwolu were strangers, and they were also fugitive from the category of stranger, since, as Hartman (2007, 5) explains, "the most universal definition of the slave is stranger." And while the violence of the production of the stranger is what necessitates new narrative form, new scholarly intimacies, the position of the Black subject as stranger also might demand a degree of deference. That which made Black subjects outsiders also catalyzed Black radical forms of relation, Black relation on the go, intimacies that variously contain, tolerate, promote, and exalt provisionality, nonpossession, impermanence, transience, and transgression. King's writing helps elucidate the political stakes and directions of "Fugitivity and Freedom"; perhaps most crucially for the conversation, a reverence for Black stranger subjectivity helps envision geographies of living that unsettle settler colonialism, but which may also challenge lineage and other temporalities of permanence as criteria for emplacement. A conundrum animates the inquiry: that of breached sociality as the founding violence of the slave trade, colonialism, and racial capitalism, and the breach as a foundation for sociality in which affection, care, provision, and harm are more richly apprehended as a basis for intimate living. Together, King and Hartman ask us to consider relation as aperture: a chasm that creates an opening for intimacy and creation.

A stranger subjectivity that haunts "Fugitivity and Freedom" is that of the Black domestic. Black women and girls have, for most of US history, been confined to the labor of domestic servitude—that is, the work of reproducing the materials and conditions of life for others under conditions of relative unfreedom, coercion, extraction, emotional and cultural violation, and austerity; this work consists of both drudgery and creativity and is also a form of affective labor. What's more, their historical lives, the subjects of dazzling Black feminist histories (see especially Hunter 1997), are relegated to objects of history, acted upon, void of intellectual, artistic, strategic, political, and emotional material in dominant historiographies of the United States. The minor figure, prototypically Black working-class, domestic, criminalized, and queer, has been, to the political and scholarly establishment, "catalysts of nothing" (Hartman 2019, 260). Given this, the work of writing and archival crate-digging to produce new ways of seeing Black women is itself another layer of life work; another order of creativity; another form of intellectual, expressive, emotional, and material reproduction of life by expanding what it is possible to think about its capacity and meaning. The new formal reading and writing practices that Hartman and others have developed and employed insist on reinventing life's rendering and in so doing reproduce the capacity for making lives beyond capitalist domesticity. This is work of significance, not triumph. If, according to Tithi Bhattacharya, "the best way to define social reproduction is the activities and institutions that are required for making life, maintaining life, and generationally replacing life" (Jaffe 2020), close narration as a Black feminist archival reinvention provides an expanded way of seeing how racial capitalist life is made, maintained, and undone in various often elusive and ephemeral modalities, and in so doing expands the possibility for the creation of anticapitalist work.[5] And while this dynamic may be said to apply to many forms of scholarly and intellectual work, it is the nexus of form (archival excavation, pressure, evasion, disruption, interrogation, and inhabitation) and subject (the minor figure shrouded in domestic and reproductive labor) that makes critical fabulation, close narration, and other related innovative interpretive and imaginative modes of Black feminist archival engagement the work of errant social reproduction itself.

Hartman's history of subjectivity and meaning represents a mode of life-making, rather than mere historical witnessing or documentation. In this way, errant and fugitive forms of social reproduction of the sort that Mattie performs and King advocates and Hartman writes are practices of theorizing and creating meaningful life in the face of gendered racial capitalism. This practice is beyond respectability, necessarily in motion, usually inchoate, bound by affection, criminalized, and smashed up. The framing of errant social reproduction, while its vast potential for representing and fueling subjects antagonistic to capitalist subordination is acknowledged, is not meant to romanticize the practices of critical fabulation or intimate narration as a means of producing or sustaining life; social reproduction, after all, is often conducted under conditions of deep exploitation, reproduces the worker and capitalism, consists of interpersonal violation, is colored by quotidian and extraordinary mess and misstep. Social reproduction is often captured under the auspices of the familial enclosures that Tiffany Lethabo King and family abolitionists identify.[6] To propose this social reproduction as errant cannot remediate its complexity; so, this line of thinking is meant to raise questions about the stakes of the affective intellectual work of Black liberatory life-making, incomplete as it is, and to emphasize its ingenuity, creativity, and skill and its production under conditions of extraction and constriction. This line of thinking is meant to emphasize the magnitude of form's significance for Black and queer living. We might think about this as Assata Shakur's "life exploding green" (Shakur 1987, 271) or Sula's "experimental life" (Morrison 1974, 118).[7] Close narration and critical fabulation expand possibilities for understanding Black life through unabashed care in narrating it, while also deeply attending to and excavating the pervasiveness of violation, extraction, and premature death for Black people. It is also important to note that critical fabulation is a living method in that it is an evolving and contested way of reading and writing the past, rather than an authoritative or static mode of scholarly production. One of the things that close narration and critical fabulation allow is an evasion of the enclosures of respectability, as respectable historical figures are usually the ones represented in their own words in the archive. Critically, these practices can bring into view subjects of history who had a range of postures toward the family: anti, ambivalent, queer, conflicted, mercurial, deserting. Critical fabulation is able to bring into view subjects of history who lived transversal lives. As C. Riley Snorton (2017, 57) explains, "Fugitive narratives featuring 'cross-dressed' and cross-gender modes of wander and escape, most often described in terms of 'passing,' function as a kind of map for a neglected dimension of what Spillers defined as the semiotic terrain of black bodies under captivity, wherein gender refers not to a binary system of classification but to a 'territory of cultural and political maneuver,'" not at all gender-related, gender-specific.

Black queer histories in which neither family nor gender is presumed, and in which the stranger is both a historical subject position in the afterlife of slavery and a category of experience, provide new sensorial terrain, and new permutations of affinity and intimacy under enclosure. Snorton (2017) explains that transversal history is at once about submerged thought, disciplinary transgression, and interstitial life. To "recover the insurgent ground" of Black lives in the face of archival structures of violence and annihilation, Hartman (2019, xii) famously "recreate[s] the voices and use[s] the words of these young women when possible and inhabit[s] the intimate dimensions of their lives." This historical *poēsis* positions accountability as part of the practice of inhabitation. As she explained in dialogue with Kali Tambreé, after writing a chapter of *Wayward Lives* on the relationship between domestic work and feudalism she wondered, "Who is that for? I mean, certainly Mattie and all of these young women conscripted to that labor . . . that's what they know, so who am I trying to convince? And at that moment I discarded that chapter, and I wrote 'Manual for General Housework,' which is a kind of prose experiment, manifesto."

> Manual: as opposed to mental, as in not an exercise of rational faculties. As opposed to the formation of critical reflections as opposed to contemplation of the self or the world. A method of operating or working. A function. Short for manual exercise. Short for manual tool.
>
> Manual: as opposed to automatic, as opposed to starting or functioning by itself and for itself, as opposed to deliberation and judgment, as in the need for direction, as in the imposition of a mistress or master.
>
> Manual: As of pertaining to the hand or hands. The hands to be outmoded or made obsolete by the machine. Of or pertaining to the mule more than the machine. Worked with the hands, finished with the hands. No more than a pair of hands. Hands cracked and swollen from harsh soap and ammonia. Hands burnt taking the pies out of the oven. Hands stiff and disfigured from wringing cold sheets and towels outside in the winter before hanging to dry on the line. Hands, no longer yours, contracted, owned, and directed by another, like a tool or object. The hands that handle you.
>
> . . .
>
> Manual: as opposed to contemplation, or theory. As opposed to the use of the intellect. As opposed to looking, viewing, contemplat-

ing. As opposed to thinking, reflecting, scheming, plotting, planning, weighting, brooding . . . (Hartman 2019, 77–78)

In describing the genesis of the prose experiment/manifesto, Mattie Jackson and the other subjects of *Wayward Lives* emerge as collaborators, conspirators, and audience. "Manual for General Housework" describes their subjection and objectification both in history and as objects of history, imagines entries of a handbook to which they might have contributed or which they might have ripped to shreds in anger; she elicits their contemplation as readers. This kind of unrelenting focus on the historical subject facilitates their entry into a complex temporality of the living even as their place in history is meticulously examined.

This complex relationship to the subject that merges past and present is a form of attachment. Black attachment expands belonging beyond knowable history, which in turn situates Black place-making in tension with constructions of sovereignty defined by lines of descent and historical kinship. It therefore raises questions about how Black aspirations for sanctuary and the commons might be mobilized toward the end of destroying settler colonialism and toward Black and Native co-liberation and yet under the auspices of fragmentary history, through a politics of autonomy and transversality rather than historical linearity and lineage.

Domain of the Inchoate

The fragment has been Black feminist history's unit of analysis for generations. As Aisha Finch argued during "Freedom and Fugitivity," and as her own influential work reveals, Black feminist reading practice is a form of refusal, in her words a way of taking "historical material that was never intended to be put to productive use," or even "intended to be waste," and using that archival resource toward other means. Hartman explained, "Maybe there are Mattie's three statements, but then those statements are in relationship to hundreds of others . . . even if it's just one line of direct testimony in each case file . . . together we produce the ensemble. Right? We produce the kind of, the conversation, the intimacy, the relation that only ever comes into view in the archival account as a site of punishment, right? It comes into view as a form of sociality to be negated, stopped, and punished." Crucially, Finch noted that this means "sort of producing, effectively, or allowing Black life where it was never meant to be." Finch is a historian of slave rebellion, and her work models Black feminist reading practices; for example, her pathbreaking (2015) excavation of enslaved women's rebellion in Cuba traces women like Rita Carabalí, whose attendance with her husband at a meeting of enslaved rebels was mentioned in passing reference, but whose life reflects a broader prevalence of women in organized slave rebellion in Cuba and whose presence reinforces the need for a gendered analysis of revolt. As Finch's work reveals, archival silence often reflects the extreme violence that eradicated minor figures from the world and, by extension, the official record as anything other than objects of violence, if that. If the organized revolt has been cast in some corners of Black history as a kind of family affair, in which structures of power and leadership prevail toward the goal of Black futurities of independence, Finch's analysis and archival practice are in line with King's thinking about the family, demanding that the political unit of the family, the collective rebellion, be complicated and radically refigured. Hartman's staggering insights in conversation with King and Finch elucidated the stakes of archival encounter:

> We live in the context of enormous violence, that racialized enclosure, defines our situation, it defines our life. And yet in the context of that . . . we, you know, try to live; we envision, plan, dream about ways to live in radically different terms. We imagine our lives not being confined by the stranglehold of antiblackness or managed depletion. And so I think that for me the violence actually only serves to intensify the brilliance then that is required to try to live in a context in which one was not intended to live. What does it mean to try to make a beautiful space for yourself and those you love when you're not doing enough to literally reproduce the terms of everyday life? Or what is it that would make you believe that *anything else* is possible when *every, when every empirical sign* seems to confirm the given and offer the lie that, as things are they will always be? . . . I think that what I appreciate about those moments is that, you know, one can enter the space of daydreaming, one can enter that domain of the inchoate where, oh, anything might happen or unfold in a moment.

What might unfold in the moment, King suggested later in "Freedom and Fugitivity," is a different relationship to the earth, crafted by people who have been made to move. Prompted by a set of quandaries posed by Hartman about the role of the outsider and those natally alienated from place and belonging under frameworks of indigeneity, King's commentary on the centrality of fugitivity to relation gestured back to the fugitive sociality and "relations on the run" that she delineated in her aforementioned work on the family. Joining King's work are important analyses by scholars including Iyko Day (2021) and Justin Leroy (2016) that productively complicate understandings about the nexus of genocide and antiblackness, Black and Indigenous positionalities, Black radical critique, and analyses of settler colonialism. Wrestling with questions of ontology, sovereignty, and historicity, such analyses ask us to rethink relation on the scale of both the political claim and everyday refusal. That the family represents a primary unit of political recognition and claim, and a source of state annihilation and intramural harm, does not necessarily provide evidence for its obsolescence, but it does put pressure on the necessity of its interrogation and of elaborating other modalities of relation, modalities that are deeply embedded in the practices of the fugitive, stateless, deviant, delinquent, and wayward. Black feminist social reproduction places pressure on the character of claims to place and place-making that constitute intimate sociality, otherwise relation, affinity, and bondedness.

Errant social reproduction—disobedience, affection, mutual aid, provision of need, amelioration of want, assembly, oneness, treason against discipline, study—as a project of flux presents one possibility of cheap socialist relation.[8] Borrowing from Hartman and Esther Brown, by cheap socialism I mean to suggest forms of collectivity that are provisional, made possible in the context of the long not-forever present of racial capitalism and yet nevertheless rich and robust and evocative of whimsical and intrepid forms of living and sharing that might characterize a not-immanent future beyond gendered racial capitalism, forms in which improvisation, caprice, and incipience are elements of social life that might exist valuably and productively alongside the temporalities of safety, duration, and ancestry. If questions of both archival practice and relationality hinge on what it means to be known, how one comes to be known, and whether becoming known is an ideal or a requisite for social bondedness, fugitive practices of life-making become crucially important; the Black queer fugitive, fleeing recognition and seeking relation, reconfigures sanctuary and community.

NOTES

1 I am using annotation to describe this chapter's form, which blends event review, essay, and annotated bibliography entry. This essay is a reflection upon a conversation with multiple participants and therefore conveys the ideas of

multiple interlocutors and collective insight; misinterpretations are my own. Aisha Finch is associate professor of women's, gender, and sexuality studies at Emory University and author of *Rethinking Slave Rebellion in Cuba: La Escalera and the Insurgencies of 1841–1844* (2015). Saidiya Hartman is University Professor at Columbia University and author of three books, *Scenes of Subjection: Terror, Slavery, and Self-Making in Nineteenth-Century America* (1997); *Lose Your Mother: A Journey Along the Atlantic Slave Route* (2007); and *Wayward Lives, Beautiful Experiments: Intimate Histories of Social Upheaval* (2019). Tiffany Lethabo King is associate professor of women, gender, and sexuality at the University of Virginia and author of *Black Shoals: Offshore Formations of Black and Native Studies* (2019). Kyle Mays is associate professor of African American studies, American Indian studies, and history at the University of California, Los Angeles, and author of *Hip Hop Beats, Indigenous Rhymes: Modernity and Hip Hop in Indigenous North America* (2018), *An Afro-Indigenous History of the United States* (2021), and *City of Dispossessions: Indigenous Peoples, African Americans, and the Creation of Modern Detroit* (2022). Kali Tambreé is a doctoral candidate in gender studies at UCLA and is completing her dissertation, "Grammars of Death, Revisited."

2   On refusal as it is invoked in this essay, see Damman 2020, as well as the broader work of the Practicing Refusal Collective and Tina Campt's *Listening to Images* (2017) and her many essays on the subject.

3   James Allen's (2000) landmark collection of lynching photographs, *Without Sanctuary*, must be considered among the critical works on sanctuary and its utter illusiveness. On "the afterlife of slavery," see Hartman (2007).

4   The question of Black women's reproduction is too complex to engage here, but it is important to note that in this essay reproduction encompasses Black women's biological and social reproduction, which is and has been altogether queer, vexed, severed, economically extracted, anti-anatomical, propertied, violated, sensual, and intimate.

5   In *Wayward Lives* (2019), Hartman employs a "mode of close narration, a style which places the voice of narrator and character in inseparable relation, so that the vision, language, and rhythms of the wayward shape and arrange the text" (xii).

6   On family abolition, see Lewis 2022 and O'Brien 2023.

7   I take inspiration on form from conversations with Claudrena Harold and from her collaborations with Kevin Jerome Everson. See for example, Harold and Everson (2014, 2016) (2014a, 2014b, 2017).

8   On errancy, see Hartman 2020.

WORKS CITED

Allen, James. 2000. *Without Sanctuary: Lynching Photography in America.* Santa Fe, NM: Twin Palms.

Brown, Kimberly Juanita. 2015. *The Repeating Body: Slavery's Visual Resonance in the Contemporary.* Durham, NC: Duke University Press.

Campt, Tina. 2017. *Listening to Images.* Durham, NC: Duke University Press.

Carby, Hazel. 2011. "Treason-Workers: Violators of Tradition and Other Unreasoning Women." Paper presented at the conference "The Idea of the Black Radical Tradition," Columbia University Institute for Research in African American Studies, April 22–23, 2011.

Damman, Catherine. 2020. "Saidiya Hartman on Insurgent Histories and the Abolitionist Imaginary." *Artforum*, July 14, 2020.

Davis, Angela. 1971. "Reflections on the Black Woman's Role in the Community of Slaves." *Black Scholar* 3 (4): 2–15.

Day, Iyko. 2021. "On Immanence and Indeterminacy: Black Feminism and Settler Colonialism." *Environment and Planning D: Society and Space* 39 (1): 3–8.

Finch, Aisha K. 2015. *Rethinking Slave Rebellion in Cuba: La Escalera and the Insurgencies of 1841–1844.* Chapel Hill: University of North Carolina Press.

Harold, Claudrena, and Jerome Everson, dirs. 2014. *Sugarcoated Arsenic.*

Harold, Claudrena, and Jerome Everson, dirs. 2016. *We Demand.*

Hartman, Saidiya. 1997. *Scenes of Subjection: Terror, Slavery, and Self-Making in Nineteenth-Century America.* New York: Oxford University Press.

Hartman, Saidiya. 2007. *Lose Your Mother: A Journey Along the Atlantic Slave Route.* New York: Farrar, Straus and Giroux.

Hartman, Saidiya. 2016. "Belly of the World: A Note on Black Women's Labors." *Souls: A Critical Journal of Black Politics, Culture, and Society* 18 (1): 166–73.

Hartman, Saidiya. 2019. *Wayward Lives, Beautiful Experiments: Intimate Histories of Social Upheaval.* New York: Norton.

Hartman, Saidiya. 2020. "Errant Daughters: A Conversation Between Saidiya Hartman and Hazel Carby." *Paris Review*, January 21, 2020.

Hunter, Tera. 1997. *To Joy My Freedom: Black Women's Lives and Labors After the Civil War.* Cambridge, MA: Harvard University Press.

Jaffe, Sarah. 2020. "Social Reproduction and the Pandemic, with Tithi Bhattacharya." *Dissent*, April 2, 2020. https://www.dissentmagazine.org/online_articles/social-reproduction-and-the-pandemic-with-tithi-bhattacharya.

Kaplan, Sara. 2021. *The Black Reproductive: Unfree Labor and Insurgent Motherhood.* Minneapolis: University of Minnesota Press.

King, Tiffany Lethabo. 2019. *Black Shoals: Offshore Formations of Black and Native Studies.* Durham, NC: Duke University Press.

Leroy, Justin. 2016. "Black History in Occupied Territory: On the Entanglements of Slavery and Settler Colonialism." *Theory and Event* 19 (4).

Lethabo King, Tiffany. 2018. "Black 'Feminisms' and Pessimism: Abolishing Moynihan's Negro." *Theory and Event* 21 (1): 68–87.

Lewis, Sophie. 2022. *Abolish the Family: A Manifesto for Care and Liberation.* New York: Verso.

Mays, Kyle. 2018. *Hip Hop Beats, Indigenous Rhymes: Modernity and Hip Hop in Indigenous North America.* Albany: State University of New York Press.

Mays, Kyle. 2021. *An Afro-Indigenous History of the United States.* Boston: Beacon.

Mays, Kyle. 2022. *City of Dispossessions: Indigenous Peoples, African Americans, and the Creation of Modern Detroit.* Philadelphia: University of Pennsylvania Press.

Morgan, Jennifer. 2007. *Laboring Women: Reproduction and Gender in New World Slavery.* Philadelphia: University of Pennsylvania Press, 2004.

Morrison, Toni. 1974. *Sula.* New York: Knopf.

O'Brien, M. E. 2023. *Family Abolition: Capitalism and the Communizing of Care.* New York: Pluto.

Shakur, Assata. 1987. *Assata: An Autobiography.* New York: Lawrence Hill.

Sharpe, Christina. 2010. *Monstrous Intimacies: Making Post-Slavery Subjects.* Durham, NC: Duke University Press.

Snorton, C. Riley. 2017. *Black on Both Sides: A Racial History of Trans Identity.* Minneapolis: University of Minnesota Press.

12

An Oceanic International in Catastrophic Times

Sharad Chari

Durban, South African Indian Ocean, 1972–1973: A Perfect Storm

In late 1972 and into 1973, the Port of Durban erupted in a strike wave that spread across apartheid South Africa's most important industrial port city. Of a different moment of political creativity, C. L. R. James argues that the concentrated, collective, and critical will of subjugated workers at key nodes in the dynamics of imperial accumulation can be the condition of possibility for revolution.[1] Before this, Durban's dockworkers had struck repeatedly: in 1874, at various points in the 1880s, through the racially mixed ("nonracial") Industrial and Commercial Workers Union of the 1920s and the Communist Party underground of the 1930s, and through the rural-urban ethnic politics in apartheid's first decade, the 1950s (Callebert 2017, 127–51). When a thousand stevedores struck in 1972, activist-intellectual Dave Hemson (1996, 86) argues, they launched "the beginnings of mass opposition to apartheid."

Over the subsequent year, the Durban strikes transformed into the "Durban Moment," an effervescence of political innovation linking a multiplicity of strands. A nascent Black student movement refused tutelage and drew on elements of Black theology and other sources to forge what would be called the Black Consciousness Movement. White students at the racially segregated University of Natal, Durban, linked up with trade union activists engaged in worker solidarity through survey research and strike support. Other young people of color, many of whom would embrace a coalitional conception of Blackness, joined in various ways with Black Consciousness–allied groups. Yet others joined a revived Natal Indian Congress, formed at the end of the nineteenth century through the efforts of the young M. K. Gandhi. These are only a few strands of what scholarly and popular historiography calls the Durban Moment.

In fact, there were many Durban Moments and many ways in which people participated in revising their conceptions of politics to spill out of the ivory tower or to infiltrate it properly, sometimes with deadly effects. Two figures epitomize these processes. While they are posed as rivals, they were also friends, with shared political and philosophical interests. Richard "Rick" Turner came to Durban from Paris in 1968, with its revisionist Marxism and utopianism in the street (Nash 1999). Bantu Stephen "Steve" Biko emerged from the Black student movement as the central figure of Black political self-expression, not just in the struggle for liberation, at a time when the leadership of the African National Congress and South African Communist Party were banned, jailed, or exiled (Biko 1978; Mangcu 2012). Like Frantz Fanon, Turner and Biko shared broader attempts in Africana radical philosophy that sought to bridge Marxism and existential phenomenology, and they saw liberation as also a process of radical transformation of the self, particularly the racial self.

There is too much to be said about Turner and Biko and the revolutionary situation emerging around them. People flocked to hear Turner's lectures at the university, including many in solidarity with the nascent independent Black trade union movement, like university students working on the Wages Commission to bolster worker demands for a living wage (Davie 2007, 2015). Bolton Hall became an important crucible for militant research. The relationship between Turner and Biko expressed intense questioning about the content of this militant politics, particularly in the early 1970s, drawing from New Left Marxism, existentialism, Africanism, and utopian Christianity (Macqueen 2011, 2–4). Their banning and subsequent murder by the apartheid state (Biko in 1977, Turner in 1978), added further intensity to their distinct and interrelated legacies. Their retrospective aura clarifies their importance not so much as exemplary figures, which they certainly were, but as ciphers of a collective effervescence emerging from the port, taking different and linked form as a wave of political invention washed across industrial Durban, differently affecting its racialized neighborhoods, churches, student groups, and dissident groups.

I engage this complex moment substantively elsewhere (Chari 2024, chapter 6). Here I point out some key aspects of its singularity. First, the Durban Moment was not in any way directed by the banned, jailed, and exiled liberation movements. Second, the study by Turner and his comrades of the 1973 strikes includes an exclamation from a worker: "This thing comes from God."[2] The volume's assertion that the strike was spontaneous was partly strategic, but the theological reference is important. Thinking with Walter Benjamin, I call the Durban Moment a "theologico-political moment," not just for its theological inspirations but because of the way in which, as Judith Butler puts it in their reading of Benjamin, the messianic flashes within historical time to express the transience of all worldly things: racial neighborhoods, racial selves, apartheid, even racial capitalism (Benjamin 1978; Butler 2016, 273, 276, 278). Third, it is important that this moment of possibility, a moment of actual abolition, emerged at a port city transformed in multiple ways through the legacies of the Indian Ocean.

The archives do not reveal whether and how traditions of maritime radicalism were part of this dockworkers' strike. Yet we should pause to consider that this dockworkers' strike set in train a set of struggles that would persist well after the assassinations of Biko and Turner. I am tempted to insist that the submerged legacies of the Indian Ocean rose to accompany the political cultures of the Black Atlantic, in an ensuing decade and more of struggle that would usher in apartheid's end and that might yet threaten its successive racial capitalism (Gilroy 1993; Hofmeyr 2007).

Yet this would be too teleological, and too ethereal an argument for the kind of evidence I marshal for it (Chari 2024). I find myself in a predicament parallel to Gilroy's when he finds, while revisiting his concept of the Black Atlantic in relation to the migrant crisis in the Mediterranean, the limits of "high altitude theorizing" from the vantage of an "anatomist of racial subordination, governmentality and conflict" who prefers to think "at sea level" (Gilroy 2017, 10). Gilroy does not actually mean, of course, that insight happens at a particular scale. That would be daft. Consider that in his Tanner Lectures, Gilroy similarly stretches the insights of *The Black Atlantic* (1993), but "as part of a plea that we consider, consistently and energetically, what it might mean to trace the refiguration of the human that has been articulated in opposition to the working of racial systems and to endow our alternative to those vexed formations with a largely forgotten lineage in which the contested relationship between the properly human and the racialized infrahuman loomed large" (Gilroy 2014, 23). Rather than a facile antihumanism in the face of transatlantic dehumanization, Gilroy turns to Fanon and Said to call for a new humanism emergent in differentiated relations between the properly human and the infrahuman (Gilroy 2014, 38). I supplement Gilroy's argument with a reading of Fanon as the thinker of a revolutionary humanism as well as of a revolutionary earthliness emergent in his bristling prose.[3] Fanon's revolutionary refusal of infrahumanity is twinned by his refusal of *la terre brûlée*, the scorched earths of our capitalist climate emergencies as well as of imperial war. Gaza remains directly in our line of sight.

"What, in such a world, is sanctuary?" ask Roy and Zablotsky in the introduction to this book. In a dialectical gesture that refuses the violence of humanitarian reason, they insist that *sanctuary* names an impossible political dream of freedom, an "assertion of solidarity in the face of incalculable loss of life, displacement, and disappearance." At sea level, for the political anatomist, this chapter offers the argument that there are many spaces in which a differently human-and-earthly solidarity is willed, fought for, lived through, and, too often, died with. These fragments of an emergent earthliness, rarely named sanctuaries though that is what they are, speak precisely to Roy and Zablotsky's prescient question. Thinking this emergent earthliness alongside the question of humanism that preoccupies Gilroy, Roy, and Zablotsky requires all the political imagination that courses through this book, reaching to the fragments of an emergent earthliness we cannot do without. And of course, this emergent Earth is still an oceanic planet, its oceanic currents central to the dissemination of the possibility of sanctuary for all.

Durban in 1972 was one shore of such political innovation, a temporary sanctuary within apartheid's crisis-ridden racial geographies that promised much more. We do not know whether and how maritime radicalism may have sparked the dockworkers' strike that may have been key to the unstoppable internal struggles against apartheid. Yet we do know that the sanctuary spaces forged in this moment of revolt allowed some people to fundamentally refuse infrahumanization and containment. I read this fleeting site of political sanctuary through an oceanic dialectical method that sublates and disseminates the possibility of sanctuary even as it ends in Durban by the late 1970s, a fleeting event that takes us to the ways in which oceans carry and link forms and fronts of struggle on an oceanic planet.

Oceanic Archives of Struggle

What we might playfully call the "human oceanography" of the oceanic world has given us a powerful set of imaginations and instruments of struggle, including the maritime origins of the strike, struggles for the abolition of the transatlantic slave trade and its differentiated aftermath, Third World lawyering on the determination of the Law of the Sea, and emergent critiques of oceanic ecocide central to the problematization of planetarity today, not least from Indigenous youth movements in the South Pacific.[4] The oceanic archives of struggle are never entirely in the past tense. They are activated in different ways across different seas. Collectively, they frame the *oceanic international*.

Writing on the origins of the strike by eighteenth-century seafarers, Marcus Rediker (1987, 111) argues that "the coexistence and integration of diverse types of labor, the coordination of efforts to combat a menacing laboring environment, the steady shifts of work as organized by the watch system, and the interdependence of the stages of production combined to produce a laboring experience uncommon to the first half of the eighteenth century. The seaman, in sum, was one of the first collective workers." From the archives of the British maritime world, this form of collective organizing emerged from a specific terraqueous labor regime in which, in 1768, British seafarers put out a call to "strike" their sails to halt maritime commerce in the Pool of London, joining the motley London working class of weavers, hatters, sawyers, glass grinders, coal heavers, and other artisans in a general strike (Rediker 1987, 110). The action of striking the sails was already part of cultures of seafaring, coded in the French word *affaler*, meaning "to fall," from Dutch and Flemish sailors bringing down their sails in high winds. During the seventeenth and eighteenth centuries, lowering the sails signified submission to conquerors or to superior ships; when seamen revolutionized the concept by setting down the means of production, they were very precisely refusing submission to a system that was no longer external to them but that had shaped their personhood and politics (Grandin 2014).

The strike has of course shifted and changed across a world of labor regimes, for instance in the mass refusal of Indian lascars in 1914 explored by Indian Ocean labor historian G. Balachandran, or indeed in the Durban Moment briefly explored here (Balachandran 2012). The strike has also taken wider forms across formations of land-labor-capital, from labor stoppages to the hunger strike, the debtors strike, the student strike, the feminist strike, the logistics strike, tenant strikes, and many other proliferating forms of interruption of capitalist and imperialist relations. The George Floyd rebellion and linked movements for Black lives in the United States may well be remembered as the strike against policing in defense of American apartheid, another front in the strike's oceanic transformations.

How do we understand what happened to the general strike? Did it mirror the hopes in the history of the category of abolition? Are their aftermaths inevitably the restoration of capitalism through the instruments of capitalism, or what Ruthie Gilmore calls, precisely, "using capitalism to save capitalism from capitalism"? If abolition has as its central reference the abolition of the transatlantic slave trade and of slave-based capitalist societies across the global plantation belt, the oceanic circulation of this category and its efficacy after formal abolition has been of signal importance. The aftermath of formal abolition was a primary concern for W. E. B. Du Bois (1935), as he diagnosed the complex sublation, or cancelation/ preservation, of racialized land-labor-capital relations rather than a more decisive "reconstruction" of society premised on Black proletarian self-determination, a "Black Reconstruction" that did not remake white power as property.

Kris Manjapra's (2022, 5) global history of abolition shows how, following Du Bois's insight, "when white societies actually began *implementing* their antislavery ideas, they did so in ways that prolonged and extended the captivity and oppression of black people around the world." We know from multiple shores that emancipation was transformed into the rationale for the elaboration of new regimes of unfree labor—for instance, through "blackbirding" in the Pacific, which provided new avenues for a variety of intermediaries to shift from Atlantic slave trading to kidnapping Indigenous people for plantation regimes in Fiji and the Australian colonies. Indeed, Du Bois was prescient in concluding his famous passage about an emerging color line with "the islands of the sea"; this was particularly apt in the South Pacific, as well as in the oceanic crossroads between the Black Atlantic and the Indian Ocean.

A key element in the restoration of capital across the global plantation belt was the reinvestment of reparations to slave owners in plantation systems in Guyana, Trinidad, Dominica, Honduras, South Africa, Sri Lanka, Malaysia, and Australia, through the shipping of indentured laborers across oceans, and in the shoring up of the sinews of nineteenth-century colonial capitalism through shipping, railways, finance, and so on—the logistics boom of an earlier era (Manjapra 2022, 107). The globalization of Jim Crow through circuits of expertise invested in limiting democratic self-government in settler colonies ensured that those colonies would at least retain the fantasy of forging "white men's countries," redrawing a transoceanic global color line and creating linked fault lines of anticolonial struggle (Lake and Reynolds 2008). By the early twentieth century, the long backlash against abolition utilized a new term and set of techniques of "segregation," from colonial Madras and Hong Kong to hill stations across colonial Asia and across the Indo-Pacific to South Africa and California, with the bubonic plague and public health as pretext (Nightingale 2012).

The spread of techniques of segregation brought into the public sphere Black and subaltern intellectuals thinking and linking struggles across seas. Any thought on this theme remains in debt to the late Julius Scott (2018), whose *The Common Wind* explored the clandestine web of communication across the eighteenth-century Caribbean and its dispersal of revolutionary ideas across the sea of islands before and after the Haitian Revolution. Scott's dissertation, and the book that emerged decades later, are founding texts, alongside Paul Gilroy's (1993) imaginative exploration of the slave sublime in *The Black Atlantic* and his reflections on the Mediterranean crisis more recently (Gilroy 2014, 2016, 2017). Another evocative engagement with radical oceanic circulation comes from Michael Denning's (2015, 38, 137) study of "the audiopoetics of a world musical revolution" through the sinews of imperialism in the early twentieth century, across "barrios, bidonvilles, barrack-yards, arrabales, and favelas of an archipelago of colonial ports, linked by steamship routes, railway lines, and telegraph cables" that joined plebian music and dance cultures to an emergent anticolonialism; as he puts it pithily, well before the making of anticolonial movements these dynamics forged "the decolonization of the ear and the dancing body."

Apart from the strike and abolition, the oceans have also been the site of debates about national rights to oceanic resources and what happens beyond their limits, in international waters. Samera Esmeir (2018) argues that Jeremy Bentham used the concept "international" in 1789, as in relation to the law of nations across a two-dimensional surface of the Earth, as "a distinct legal space for the regulation of inter-space relations." In contrast, Hugo Grotius conceived of the ocean as a traversed surface, but also much more than that; in Esmeir's (2018, 88, 95) words, Grotius saw the ocean as sharing "moisture with the skies, the clouds, and the stars. . . . It exceeded human cognition, human calculation. The earth, including its oceans, was not only a surface; it was also the seat of humankind, one planet among others." Here we see a nascent conception of planetarity that is not reducible to a resource for humans.

In contrast to this juridical itinerary of the concept "international," Esmeir (2018, 89) notes the concept's other—for instance, in the International

Workingmen's Association and itineraries through which "the adjective international gained a socialist revolutionary itinerary—one with experiences and horizons of expectation distinct from its juridical itinerary." Esmeir also notes that the noun form, as in the First and Second Internationals, was somewhat closer to Bentham's concept, but that the revolutionary conception of internationalism remained potent. A crucial moment was the Asian African Conference at Bandung in 1955.

One of the striking things about the Bandung conference, Esmeir (2017, 82) notes, was that Indonesian president Sukarno began by posing the oceanic sinews of empire as a poisoned gift through which "oceans and seas could transform into lifelines of other forms of human horror, domination, and destruction that would affect current and future generations." Bandung's possibility of solidarity was premised on refusing this ecocidal limit to the oceanic remains of empire. However, other forces were at work at Bandung, principally a conception of international cooperation premised on multiple sovereign nation-states. Sukarno could discern how the doctrine of the freedom of the seas had been an enabler of European colonization, but Bandung's capacities to rethink an anticolonial ocean were fundamentally constrained.

This would change through the mobilization of Third World lawyering in relation to the UN conferences leading up to the 1982 UN Convention on the Law of the Seas (UNCLOS). The movement Third World Approaches to International Law (TWAIL) sought to respond to the ways in which the emerging law of the seas would privilege powerful countries' will "to exploit the resource of the sea, to terrorize the world and to destroy the marine environment," as Ram Prakash Anand put it (Esmeir 2017, 86). Leaving the high seas to the "freedom of the seas" doctrine might shore up imperial power over international waters. There were several twists in these debates. India joined the bloc of "margineers," including the United States, the United Kingdom, Australia, New Zealand, and Canada, to argue for a six-hundred-mile limit to national jurisdiction of the seabed, rather than supporting Latin American arguments for a two-hundred-mile limit. The USSR joined its Cold War rivals in the First World to refuse demands to exploit the deep sea through an international body, "the Enterprise"; industrialized states argued that the deep seabed ought to be governed through the freedom of the seas, which, given the costs of deep sea exploration, would be exceedingly biased in their favor (Ranganathan 2021, 170–73).

The consequence of Third World lawyering was that several principles were codified into the Law of the Seas. The first was that coastal states could declare an "exclusive economic zone" (EEZ) to 200 nautical miles (230 miles) "as long as they did not overexploit living resources." The second was that "the sea bed, ocean floor and subsoil beyond the limits of national jurisdiction and consisting in an 'Area' that is the 'Common Heritage of Mankind'" and that this "area" would be adjudicated through the International Seabed Authority (Esmeir 2017, 87–88).

Esmeir (2017, 89) argues that the consequence of UNCLOS was to limit oceanic exploitation to some degree through exclusive economic zones and the concept of the "Common Heritage of Mankind," but that continuing "advocacy is required to preserve a more expansive marine environment, including its animate and inanimate lives." The more profound spatial division is between the oceanic surface and the undersea commons: "The sea is split into two: one where competing sovereigns can navigate the ocean's surfaces and project themselves onto them, and another where humankind can descend to preserve its heritage (while also failing to counter the destruction of the commons). Crucially, the former is the condition of possibility of the latter in the form of an outer limit; the heritage of humankind in the depths of the sea is conceivable only once its surface has been detached as a distinct but enlarged domain for sovereign states."

This dual legal structure sustains the illusion of an oceanic commons while also facilitating sovereignty over the sea and capitalist exploitation through it. Surabhi Ranganathan (2019, 590) adds that the division of seabed and seawater is further complicated by the fact that "the seabed up to 200 miles may be both the continental shelf and the EEZ of a state, but it is governed solely as the former. Furthermore, unlike in the case of the continental shelf, a state must expressly proclaim an EEZ. Absent such a proclamation, the waters beyond the territorial seas are treated as the high seas, although the bed remains the continental shelf" (Ranganathan 2019, 588). Despite the differentiation of the seabed from the seawater, "'sedentary' living resources are placed within the continental shelf regime . . . they include bottom-dwelling creatures such as clams, oysters, sponges and corals . . . [as well as] crustaceans, such as shrimps, prawns, lobsters and crabs, even though these can swim"; meanwhile, fish that breed on the seabed are part of the seawater regime, whether as part of the EEZ or in the high seas.

In this aftermath of Third World lawyering at sea, there are persisting questions of human/nonhuman relations in and through the oceans that refuse the hijacking of the oceanic international by sovereignty and capital, and that refuse oceanic ecocide for our collective planetary life. Esmeir turns to Sunil Amrith's wonderful environmental history of the Bay of Bengal for its thoughtful engagement with the strengthening of sovereignty across the bay at the expense of subaltern networks across it. Since these networks have long been key to the lives of subalterns, their loss is tragic at a moment when we face what Amrith (2013, 260) characterizes as the enclosure of the bay, which has intensified its exploitation and despoilation. The lessons of Amrith's study are clear, even if the paths to their realization are more difficult to discern.

The deepening tendency to ecocide is twinned by the zeal of contemporary oceanic extractivism, part of the broader problematic of extractive capitalism today. To return to Ruthie Gilmore, the impossible and yet dominant response to ecocide takes the form of using capital to save capital from capital, particularly in blue-green garb. In this vein, Ashley Dawson (2016, 83) critiques the UN Convention on Biological Diversity of 2008 for seeking to commodify environmental services and use offsets for "natural capital" in the face of ongoing species extinctions.

We have gone from a particular political conjuncture at a port city to the circulation of oceanic struggles. I would like briefly in the concluding section to turn to Black critical aesthetics that refuse the adage that it is possible to imagine the end of the world rather than the end of racial capitalism that has brought us to this planetary precipice.

Drexciyan Thoughts on the Planetary International

I turn in this final section to a constellation of Black artist-intellectuals, including the Drexciya electronica collective, artist Ellen Gallagher, geographer Katherine McKittrick, and historian Robin D. G. Kelley; together, they think with the possibilities of Black critical aesthetics as foundational to oceanic critique of our planetary predicament.

There is a renewed interest today in Drexciya, the Detroit electronica ensemble centered on James Stinson and Gerald Donald, who were fiercely anticommercial, refused to perform live, were anonymous for years, and emerged at different moments often under a variety of aliases. As Stinson puts it in one of their few interviews, "The basic idea is being spontaneous ... load up the equipment and start working ... there's nothing planned, no set course, the mystery of the unknown is basically what makes us tick ... it's like living on the edge with it." Stinson calls Drexciya's albums "storms" that will emerge in different places, with different record labels, to effect specific interventions. Asked if the places imagined by Drexciya exist, he responds, "Sorry, no! This planet's gonna have to be rearranged. . . . Somebody's gonna have to hit the restart button. . . . Somebody's opened up the Pandora's box and all hell's breaking loose, so that's why I'm pushing the gas; I'm putting out images and things to take people away from here. . . . I'm loading up the Drexciya ark and [have] a mind to take a trip away from here for a while."[5]

Drexciya's founding journey is recounted in the liner notes to *The Quest*. Pregnant African slaves thrown overboard gave birth underwater to babies who learn to breathe liquid oxygen. Katherine McKittrick (2021, 56) says of this submarine myth that "the cosmogony in the liner notes of *The Quest* provide a redoubled satisfaction: a legible neo-slave narrative that promises a future. But this future, as we know, has not arrived. We are still waiting." As she listens to the music, McKittrick (2021, 53–54) argues that instead of an aquatic Afrofuturism, "Drexciya offers anonymity as method and critique," and that it "briefly destabilizes the various surveillance systems that mark and make and weigh down black life." Elsewhere, I read Drexcyia's journey as forged within the ruins of Fordism in Detroit, in the undercommons of crisis-ridden American apartheid; it is curious that this journey goes first to an imagined undersea, then into outer space (Chari 2023), all the while offering a space of musical sanctuary for imagining liberation.

McKittrick (2021, 56) points out that Drexciya's synthesizers enable "collaboration, borrowing, sharing, removing, and rewriting," and that when "they played live into a predigital analogue recorder . . . what we are given, as listeners, is synthesized improvisation. They harness the storm and let it go." And this is also how McKittrick interprets the art of Ellen Gallagher.

Gallagher is an artist from Rhode Island, with part of her ancestry from Cape Verde, part of the whaling diaspora that brought Cape Verdeans across the oceans, and which she cites as her reason for being interested in *Moby-Dick* (Melville [1851] 2007) and things marine. She has been making artistic work for decades, often playing with racial forms and taxonomies, and for quite some time working with the possibilities of Drexciya. Works displayed at her 2018 solo show at Hauser and Wirth in Los Angeles, "Accidental Records," and at the 2022 Hayward Gallery show in London, "In the Black Fantastic," demonstrates the many techniques that Gallagher uses in painting the undersea.[6] McKittrick (2021, 53) says of Gallagher that "she storms us!," but in a specific non-martial interpretation of Drexciya that "draws attention to underwater life (plants, shells, seaweed, scales, watery circles) that are relational to the few almost-humanoids she details in her work . . . her undersea Drexciyans are constituted by, part of, within, fused with, and relation to nonhuman underwater lifeforms."[7] There is too much to say about Gallagher's work, but what is exciting is that she is also an avid reader who has long engaged sea stories and drawings, whether while drawing on a scientific ship in her youth or in what she calls her contemporary version of scrimshaw, seafarer carvings on whalebone. She calls Melville's *Moby-Dick* an Afrofuturist text, particularly through the enigmatic figure of Pip who has captured the attention of generations of Black critics (Miranda 2017, Chari 2022).

In Gallagher's "Whale Fall" a whale appears to fall on a ship; in "Whale Falls" other ships seem to join the scene, but are they on the precipice of catastrophe in the vein of *Moby-Dick*—or, perhaps more aptly, in C. L. R. James's reading of the book as an allegory of the United States on the precipice of authoritarianism?[8] But *Moby-Dick*, and the ruminations of the person who asks us to call him Ishmael, are far too meandering to suggest that catastrophe is inevitable. After all, the story begins as a queer love story between Queequeg, the expert harpooner from the South Sea Islands, who makes Ishmael his wife early on. And the life raft that enables this narrator's survival at the end is Queequeg's coffin, on which he has copied the tattoos from his body, the truths of his people of Oceania, truths that the narrator will not be able to read or appropriate. There is no essentialized oceanic indigeneity reappropriable by an imperialism in crisis.

Gallagher's "Sea Bed" paintings look like works of natural history, but closer inspection reveals faces folded into shades of brown.[9] But Gallagher doesn't just look over the edge of the boat. In her 2010 "Watery Ecstatic (Whale Fall)" Gallagher stays with the whale carcass as it slowly descends to the ocean floor, where it feeds a large number of organisms.[10] In the series "Ecstatic Draught of Fishes" from 2019, 2020, and 2021, shown in the exhibition "In the Black Fantastic" at London's Hayward Gallery in 2022, playful otherworldly Drexciyans, figures we cannot know, share the teeming life of the sea. I share Gallagher's fascination with the figure of Pip in *Moby-Dick*. Pip is a young Black cabin boy, perhaps still a slave, who falls into the ocean and is, for a time, left behind by the crew, and in the process he loses his mind. There is a lot to think about through Pip. Gallagher reads his fall like this: "It's like he's held up by these phantasmagoric terrors. The terror of drowning, the terror of the below you can't see. It's this portrait of the Middle Passage. His body has survived, but his mind has not" (Miranda 2017). But Gallagher's works offer us a political aesthetics that continues to see what Pip might have seen, a continuing undersea catastrophe that we must continue to think against.

Robin Kelley (2020), who has been writing about Gallagher's works for some time, reflects back on some of her early Drexciya-inspired work to say that what he had missed were the artistic elements that "mirror the regenerative qualities of coral, or the interdependent life forms of the sea—molluscs, crustaceans, exotic seaweed and the tentacles of jellyfish. And yet, despite the peaceful elegance of these life forms, regeneration does not occur outside of history. These are the bones of disembodied Africans, conscripts for the fields and factories, black bodies cannibalized by a racial capitalism and its scientific jaws. Even in the realm of myth, modernity never leaves her sights. Drexciya is not Utopia. It blooms under siege, which is precisely why regeneration is so essential."

Kelley's last lines are beautifully evocative as we try to draw together the lines of thought in this chapter. I began with a perfect storm in the Indian Ocean city of Durban, a dockworkers' strike that blossomed into a multiplicity of struggles that carried a Benjaminian messianic hope for the actual abolition of apartheid capitalism. This flashing of the possible within the crisis-ridden geography of apartheid's main industrial port city remains a story that is difficult to explain. I would like to think of it as a political complement to Drexciya's "storms," with a literal reference to oceanic maritime radicalism that has not left an archival trace.

Methodologically, a focus on oceanics helps us out of our hidebound terrestrialism and nation-centrism, even when we think about radical histories and geographies of movement, mobility, and fugitivity. Radical histories of the maritime origins of the strike and of abolition are helpful in this regard, but their political lessons have to be tempered by the historical geographies of the global color line and of the various forms that segregation, policing, and security have taken. The emergence of the general strike and of abolitionism, as we know, prompted a long and differentiated counterrevolution that sought to sublate radical possibilities, so much so that oceanic circuits themselves have been sites of intense struggle. This counterrevolution, in the differentiation of imperial power in direct response to the "age of revolution," took ideas of the general strike and abolition to a global scale, particularly across the imperial Indian and Pacific Oceans.

Debates over the idea of an oceanic international, or of oceanic internationalism, are particularly engaging for the possibilities that emerged through Third World lawyering, possibilities that quickly faced limits set by geopolitics, Third World nationalism, and capitalist thirst for the resources of the deep sea. The consequence has been a particular remapping of the deep sea as differentiated from the surface, a protection of sovereign state rights to territorial waters and an illusory oceanic commons that has intensified despoliation of the oceanic depths. And yet, another possibility lurks in negation in this pyrrhic victory, in the possibility of an oceanic internationalism that might include the teeming life of the sea itself, a Fanonian/Wynterian revolutionary internationalism beyond the earth, the human, and the international as we know these things. This is the sense in which a new conception of planetary sanctuary might be emergent in a necropolitical-economic world.

Sometimes, as in the musical cultures that spread across the oceans, subtle forms of struggle have perhaps been the most enduring and persistent in forging solidarities and protecting spaces of sanctuary. This takes us back to the relation between aesthetics and politics that the Black "aquafuturist" artist-intellectuals propose. I conclude with these artists, and with the work of Ellen Gallagher, to suggest that aesthetic circulations are vital for the fractal work of conserving and expanding sanctuaries for radical political hope, perhaps even of new forms of political kinship, as suggested by Mays, Smythe, and Roy and Zablotsky in their chapters in this volume. What is this form of "conservation," if we open our conception of the archives of global struggle to the oceanic as planetary sanctuary? This is what Kelley's interpretation of Gallagher's work invites us to ponder without rushing for an answer.

What might it mean to think of oceanic circuits as continuing to conserve conceptions of "the strike," "abolition," "the international," and the refusal of planetary ecocide, as well as of other conceptions of political regeneration yet to come? Drexciyan hopes point out that precisely in the face of imperiled planetarity, all these forms of political creativity remain with us, in different ways and combinations, and that they might storm us in ways we cannot yet know.

If the oceanic international is this planetary "storm" of multiple struggles, we must join Pip's madness as it faces the resurgence of socio-natural forces that "bloom under siege," as deep oppressions find new expressive articulation. Facing the madness cannot find partial redemption, only planetary sanctuary.

NOTES

1 Thanks to Ruthie Gilmore and Keith Hart for insisting on this point, in general and in James 1938.
2 *Daily News* (Durban), February 4, 1973, cited in Institute for Industrial Education 1977, 100.

3   Thanks to participants of my graduate seminar on "Marx, Colonialism, Planetarity" for thinking together about this, Berkeley, Fall 2024.
4   This and the next section draw from Chari 2023, chap. 4.
5   "James Stinson (Drexciya) 2002 Phone Interview w/Derek Beere (Future BPM)," YouTube, posted by Stephen Rennicks, November 15, 2018, https://youtu.be/yPZYisZJofo.
6   "Ellen Gallagher: Accidental Records [2018]," Hauser and Wirth, Los Angeles, https://www.hauserwirth.com/hauser-wirth-exhibitions/6185-ellen-gallagher-accidental-records; Gallagher, "Interview: Characters, Myths and Stories: Ellen Gallagher," Art21, November 2011, https://art21.org/read/ellen-gallagher-characters-myths-and-stories; "In the Black Fantastic," exhibition at the Southbank Centre, London, 2022, https://www.southbankcentre.co.uk/whats-on/art-exhibitions/black-fantastic.
7   "'In the Black Fantastic' | Curator Tour with Ekow Eshun | Hayward Gallery," YouTube, posted by Southbank Centre, July 25, 2022, https://youtu.be/a_L7tPG_pks, 2:45.
8   James 1953; "Ellen Gallagher: Accidental Records [2018]," Hauser and Wirth gallery, Los Angeles, https://www.hauserwirth.com/hauser-wirth-exhibitions/6185-ellen-gallagher-accidental-records.
9   "Ellen Gallagher: Accidental Records [2018]," Hauser and Wirth gallery, Los Angeles, https://www.hauserwirth.com/hauser-wirth-exhibitions/6185-ellen-gallagher-accidental-records.
10 "Ellen Gallagher in *The Tale*," Gagosian, n.d. https://gagosian.com/news/museum-exhibitions/ellen-gallagher-in-the-tale (accessed October 10, 2024).

WORKS CITED

Amrith, Sunil. 2013. *Crossing the Bay of Bengal: The Furies of Nature and the Fortunes of Migrants.* Cambridge, MA: Harvard University Press.
Balachandran, G. 2012. *Globalizing Labour? Indian Seafarers and World Shipping, c. 1870–1945.* New Delhi: Oxford University Press.
Benjamin, Walter. 1978. "Theologico-Political Fragment." In *Reflections*, edited by Peter Demetz, translated by J. Jephcott, 312–13. New York: Schocken.
Biko, Steve. 1978. *I Write What I Like.* San Francisco: Harper and Row.
Butler, Judith. 2016. "One Time Traverses Another: Benjamin's 'Theologico-Political Fragment.'" In *Walter Benjamin and Theology*, edited by Colby Dickinson and Stéphane Symons, 272–85. New York: Fordham University Press.
Callebert, Ralph. 2017. *On Durban's Docks: Zulu Workers, Rural Households, Global Labor.* Rochester, NY: University of Rochester Press.
Chari, Sharad. 2022. "Pip, Ellen Gallagher, and the White Whale: The Afrofuturism of *Moby-Dick*." Talk at Fort Mason Center for Arts and Culture, San Francisco, October 13, 2022.

Chari, Sharad. 2023. *Gramsci at Sea*. Minneapolis: University of Minnesota Press.
Chari, Sharad. 2024. *Apartheid Remains*. Durham, NC: Duke University Press.
Davie, Grace. 2007. "Strength in Numbers: The Durban Student Wages Commission, Dockworkers and the Poverty Datum Line, 1971–1973." *Journal of Southern African Studies* 33 (2): 401–20.
Davie, Grace. 2015. *Poverty Knowledge in South Africa: A Social History of Human Science, 1855–2005*. Cambridge: Cambridge University Press.
Dawson, Ashley. 2016. *Extinction: A Radical History*. New York: OR.
Denning, Michael. 2015. *Noise Uprising: The Audiopolitics of a World Musical Revolution*. London: Verso.
DuBois, W. E. B. 1935. *Black Reconstruction: An Essay Toward a History of the Part Which Black Folk Played in the Attempt to Reconstruct Democracy in America, 1860–1880*. New York: Harcourt, Brace and Company.
Esmeir, Samera. 2017. "Bandung: Reflections on the Sea, the World, and Colonialism." In *Bandung, Global History, and International Law: Critical Pasts and Pending Futures*, edited by Luis Eslava, Michael Fakhri, and Vasuki Nesiah, 81–94. Cambridge: Cambridge University Press.
Esmeir, Samera. 2018. "On Becoming Less of the World." *History of the Present* 8 (1): 88–116.
Gilroy, Paul. 1993. *The Black Atlantic: Modernity and Double Consciousness*. Cambridge, MA: Harvard University Press.
Gilroy, Paul. 2014. "Lecture I. Suffering and Infrahumanity. Lecture II. Humanities and a New Humanism." Tanner Lectures on Human Values, Yale University, February 21, 2014. https://tannerlectures.org/lectures/lecture-i-suffering-and-infrahumanity-lecture-ii-humanities-and-a-new-humanism.
Gilroy, Paul. 2016. "The Black Atlantic and the Re-Enchantment of Humanism: Suffering and Infrahumanity." In *Tanner Lectures on Human Values*, vol. 34, edited by Mark Matheson, 19–77. Salt Lake City: University of Utah Press.
Gilroy, Paul. 2017. "'Where Every Breeze Speaks of Courage and Liberty': Offshore Humanism and Marine Xenology, or Racism and the Problem of Critique at Sea Level." *Antipode* 50 (1): 3–22.
Grandin, Greg. 2014. *Empire of Necessity: Slavery, Freedom, and Deception in the New World*. New York: Metropolitan.
Hemson, David. 1996. "Beyond the Frontier of Control? Trade Unionism and the Labour Market in the Durban Docks." *Transformation* 30: 83–114.
Hofmeyr, Isabel. 2007. "The Black Atlantic Meets the Indian Ocean: Forging New Paradigms of Transnationalism for the Global South—Literary and Cultural Perspectives." *Social Dynamics* 33 (2): 3–32.
Institute for Industrial Education. 1977. *The Durban Strikes: "Human Beings with Souls."* Durban: Institute for Industrial Education and Ravan Press.
James, Cedric Lionel Robert. 1938. *The Black Jacobins: Toussaint Louverture and the San Domingo Revolution*. London: Secker and Warburg.

James, Cedric Lionel Robert. 1953. *Mariners, Renegades and Castaways: The Story of Herman Melville and the World We Live In*. Lebanon, NH: Dartmouth College Press.

Kelley, Robin D. G. 2020. "Blues Prints." In *Ellen Gallagher and Edgar Cleijne, Liquid Intelligence*. London: Walther König.

Lake, Marilyn, and Henry Reynolds. 2008. *Drawing the Global Colour Line: White Men's Countries and the International Challenge of Racial Equality*. Cambridge: Cambridge University Press.

Macqueen, Ian Martin. 2011. "Re-imagining South Africa: Black Consciousness, Radical Christianity and the New Left, 1967–1977." PhD thesis, University of Sussex.

Mangcu, Xolela. 2012. *Biko: A Biography*. Cape Town: Tafelberg.

Manjapra, Kris. 2022. *Black Ghost of Empire: The Long Death of Slavery and the Failure of Emancipation*. New York: Simon and Schuster.

McKittrick, Katherine. 2021. *Dear Science and Other Stories*. Durham, NC: Duke University Press.

Melville, Herman. (1851) 2007. *Moby-Dick*. New York: Vintage.

Miranda, Carolina. 2017. "Painter Ellen Gallagher's Tragic Sea Tales." *Los Angeles Times*, November 17, 2017. https://www.latimes.com/entertainment/arts/miranda/la-et-cam-ellen-gallagher-hauser-wirth-20171117-htmlstory.html.

Nash, Andrew. 1999. "The Moment of Western Marxism in South Africa." *Comparative Studies of South Asia, Africa and the Middle East* 29 (1): 66–81.

Nightingale, Carl H. 2012. *Segregation: A Global History of Divided Cities*. Chicago: University of Chicago Press.

Ranganathan, Surabhi. 2019. "Ocean Floor Grab: International Law and the Making of an Extractive Imaginary." *European Journal of International Law* 30 (2): 573–600.

Ranganathan, Surabhi. 2021. "Decolonization and International Law: Putting the Ocean on the Map." *Journal of the History of International Law* 23:161–83.

Rediker, Marcus. 1987. *Between the Devil and the Deep Blue Sea: Merchant Seamen, Pirates, and the Anglo-American Maritime World, 1700–1750*. Cambridge: Cambridge University Press.

Scott, Julius. 2018. *The Common Wind: Afro-American Currents in the Age of the Haitian Revolution*. London: Verso.

13

Black Mediterranean Freedom Dreams

SA Smythe

The Fascist Paradox of Diplomacy

Mere days before her visit to Ethiopia in April 2023, Italian prime minister Giorgia Meloni's cabinet declared a formal state of emergency over migration after yet another record-breaking influx of boats carrying people from the continent onto the shores of the European Union. This declaration allowed for the initial disbursement of more than €5 million in additional state resources that were reallocated from the national budget. These funds were set to be diverted to the further intensification of border management operations over the course of the next six months, specifically toward surveillance and detention centers—described across Europe's Orwellian political and media landscapes as "repatriation" facilities. As we have seen after such crackdowns, there is little deterrent to and no end in sight for this type of migration. But to the end of relatively safe and free migrations, some intended outcomes are achieved: the continued facilitation of physical, legal, and psychological violence meted out against displaced people traveling across the Mediterranean Sea and central European routes who are being rendered migrants, refugees, or asylum seekers as well as those non-state-sanctioned individuals and organizations who attempt to guide them to safe harbor, offer resources to support their journey, and defend their right to life free from borders and state repression (e.g., NGOs and humanitarian civilian rescue operations like Médecins Sans Frontières and Sea-Watch [MSF 2022; Sea-Watch n.d.]). This includes the progressive worsening of containment and border conditions that might appear to deter others in the short term, but which create an abjection that serves to produce and to deepen the border itself in the space between desire—for sanctuary or asylum for those who seek it and for state-crafted notions of security and property-oriented sovereignty for others—and the conditions of impossibility of its transgression (Walia 2021; Reid 2021).

This is hardly the first time that Italy has demonstrated callous redirection of resources away from migrants, Romani, or even its own citizens—purportedly the primary object of the narrow charge of the state's paternalistic care. The sleight of hand in claiming to benefit one's own people while instead consolidating power and subjecting the vulnerable to progressively worse conditions is not a new political phenomenon. Indeed, as the editors of this volume have parsed out in conversation with Nicholas De Genova, who describes the "ruse of asylum" (chapter 10), the related phenomenon under critique throughout this chapter may well be termed the ruse of citizenship, especially as the harbinger of rights or the dispenser of proportionately earned care. In recent memory, and under a similar pretense of crisis, cruise ships were commandeered by the Italian government beginning in summer 2020, at the height of the ongoing COVID-19 pandemic, and used for offshore quarantine housing for illegalized migrants. Italy was one of the earliest European states to enact travel bans to or from China. Still, it was one of the countries impacted by the highest infection and death rates during the first year of the global pandemic, following Iran and China's Hubei Province, whose capital, Wuhan, was identified as the epicenter for the pandemic's initial viral spread. In another instance of doublespeak, the ships—temporarily acquired from ferry vessel company Grandi Navi Veloci via the COVID state of emergency—were referred to as "accommodations" vessels. The rationale that enabled this was under the auspices of responding to the crises of both migration and the coronavirus under the guise of public health. Yet even the term *quarantine* reveals a paradox of investment, as migrants' offshore isolation (to reduce the spread of a novel airborne virus) was from the Italian citizenry, but not from each other. In some cases, they were crammed into small shared living quarters or huddled together on the deck of these ships, swaddled under Mylar blankets, and waiting for rations of food, word of when they might again set foot on land, and what would await them afterward. If any care operated in these literal scenes of subjection, the primary concern was for preserving borders at all costs. Or perhaps it was the serious attention to border logics and bare minimum humanitarianism over the necessary reinvention of humanism, which could portend its end. Meanwhile, migrants sojourned across increasingly militarized and more treacherous waters and disintegrating ships, only to be packed onto another container at sea, to languish in what journalists have described as purgatory (Urbina 2021).

This quarantine policy was first implemented under former prime minister Giuseppe Conte's leadership and was met with waves of dissent in and outside of Conte's second government. Meloni's current party, the Brothers of Italy, is in opposition to Conte's Five Star Movement, which he has presided over since stepping down as prime minister in 2021. Conte's successor, Mario Draghi, was given a mandate by President Sergio Mattarella to form a technocratic government in the wake of massive fallouts from policies mandating COVID-19 vaccination and restricting movement to hyperlocal community excursions with exemptions limited to travel to places of employment (commonly referred to as "lockdown"). These two policies spawned widespread outcries and large rallies from Italian citizens protesting the infringement of their rights to movement and bodily autonomy without irony and certainly without regard to the more accurately described lockdown and other carceral conditions of refugees and asylum seekers. Despite Italy's notorious recent history of rapid political transitions and its pretense of a multiparty political landscape featuring divergent ideologies, its policies coherently align to dispossess the most vulnerable and the usual non-normative suspects. The COVID-induced offshore quarantining of migrants was slowly sunsetted as the juridical limits on the state of emergency drew near, rather than through a principled break with an immoral and unjust policy.

This abhorrent mode of isolation is not the first instance of extraterritorial detention, with spatial jurisdictional cases like Gaza, the West Bank, and Guantánamo Bay and personal jurisdictional cases like with the Somali men deemed "pirates" off the Gulf of Aden coming to mainstream international consciousness at various points in recent years. In fact, legal scholars and practitioners of international law have included Italy in their studies of personal and spatial jurisdiction of national sovereignty (Milanovic 2011). They have referenced Italy's ongoing claims to just extraterritorial application through the policy of interdiction of migrant vessels in international waters as an attempt to preemptively reject asylum claims and to simultaneously skirt non-refoulement obligations, which is a principle under international law that, according to the UN's Office of the High Commissioner for Human Rights (OHCHR), prohibits "removing individuals from [any state's] jurisdiction or effective control when there are substantial grounds for believing that the person would be at risk of irreparable harm upon return, including persecution, torture, ill-treatment or other serious human rights violations" (OHCHR 2018), reinforcing the many legally codified and routinely disregarded decrees regarding migrant and refugee rights established from the 1951 Geneva Refugee Convention. What is striking about Italy's anti-migrant state of emergency is its coherent turn to border securitization and/as public health, through which we see increased consideration for "offshore processing" of asylum seekers and other people rendered undesirable or otherwise surplus. Indeed, the term *offshore* conveys a distant but charged proprietary relationship, used to mean a general sense of "not within the national confines of the nation in question." However, in May 2023, under the authoritarian leadership of an anti-migrant child of migrants, Suella Braverman, the United Kingdom's Home Office imported a carceral barge to Britain, the *Bibby Stockholm*. This was after months of opposition, which was responded to with calculated inspection of redundant cruise ships and large ferries like those used to travel locally between islands in Italy, Malta, and Greece, and by manufacturing consent with the aid of the mainstream media, who readily publicized right-wing prime minister Rishi Sunak's claims of a net benefit to "the British taxpayer." While some of the public outcry lambasted this move toward luxury because of how international cruises loom in the Western imaginary, as Aletha Adu reported in *The Guardian* on April 3, 2023, "ministers had not then said they would use barges instead of hotels, but said in time there could be 'hotels overflowing with people and barges overflowing with people until the government speeds up processing claims.'" The description "overflowing" only partially did this horror scene justice: after a mere five days of partial occupancy after 3 months and £300,000 a week, the *Bibby Stockholm* had to be evacuated due to the presence of the Legionella bacterium—which causes Legionnaires' disease—being discovered in the water supply. According to a subsequent editorial from *The Guardian* on October 12, 2023, scientists had previously determined this bacterium to be present even before the Home Office insisted on moving forward with its relocation notices served to additional migrants who were then housed in motels on land. *The Guardian* reported Braverman's defense of these actions and disappointment at not being able to maintain migrants' relocation due to the health crisis, mere weeks after publicly contemplating the UK's departure from the 1951 Geneva Convention due to migrants' "uncontrolled" and existential threat to Europe (*Guardian* 2023). As Adam Serwer's title-turned-rousing-mass-protest-slogan goes, "the cruelty is the point" (2018). This lesson underscores the cruelty of learning one's coerced place under colonial racial capitalism, intensified under the guise of border security and the inconsistent valuation of public health through an ongoing tyrannical apparatus within which the figure of the migrant is fundamentally a "nonperson" (Dal Lago 1999) and thereby counted out of any measured assessment of or in a "public." The figure of the migrant is therefore rendered a limit case of Western reason.

This was some of the immediate context surrounding Giorgia Meloni's visit to Ethiopia, a trip whose categorization as "diplomatic" meant to dissimulate the asymmetrical structure of (post)colonial relations from their fascist histories and their revitalizing sediments in the present conjuncture. While using brute force against illegalized migrants, Italy (like other Westernized nation-states) has continued its financialization of African states, such as in the case of Tunisia, which Italy pledged to support with at least €700 million in IMF funding and offers to send four thousand workers. This and other elements of a "comprehensive partnership package" were meted out with the understanding that the Tunisian government would protract Italy's borders, and thus Europe's, by violently repressing migrants—specifically Black migrants—from exiting through its own ports. In June 2023, a press statement was put out by the European Commission in relation to what was referred to by the public and some media as "an anti-migrant summit" featuring about twenty authoritarian African leaders, most of whom boasted bloody histories of dictatorial abuses of power specifically toward migrants and other vulnerable and minoritized populations. The opening words of European Commission president Ursula von der Leyen, flanked onstage by Italian prime minister Giorgia Meloni, Dutch prime minister Mark Rutte, and Tunisian president Kais Saied, were telling: "We are here as Team Europe." And on it goes: in the ecology of violence and subordination are things that get named "diplomacy," "mutual agreements," "peacekeeping missions," "public health advisories," "legalization," "citizenship," and "just following orders." As always, language is ideologically bound. The specter of responsibility that legal sanctuary evokes has been used to justify state actions of dispossession and the retrenchment of further harm. The radical reframing of what sanctuary is and who it is for—and when and where—necessitates attunement to the regimes of racialized capital and power, the ruse of citizenship, and other fascist paradoxes, not least because its juridical foundations began to disintegrate at the moment its legal fictions were initially set to paper.

While in Ethiopia, Meloni advanced her then incomplete Mattei Plan, linking Italy's energy aspirations with the pretense that interest in African development and infrastructure upgrade was for its own sake and out of goodwill. Several months later, in January 2024, Meloni unveiled the full plan at a summit in Rome. Stylized as the ItaliAfrica summit "A Bridge for Common Growth," the one-day event featured representatives from forty-six African states, international NGOs operating in Europe and Africa, international financial institutions, leaders of the European Union, and local Italian officials. The plan names five main policy pillars that overlap with soft-launched agreements with Tunisia, Libya, and Ethiopia in previous months as "areas of intervention": agriculture, energy, water, health, and education. The last includes vocational trade skills and teacher training "in line with labor market requirements." This strategic plan belies the bare truth of development as a project committed to extraction and consolidation of power. Diplomatic influence is also an asymmetrical exertion of power, in particular between the continents of Africa and Europe, whose imperial, colonial, and fascist relations still form ley lines that trace familiar conduits of subjugation, extraction, and abuse. The Ethiopian Italian Cooperation Framework, which formally existed between Ethiopia and Italy from 2017 to 2019 and which Meloni's government has sought to extend, has similarly followed this course of governance and control by financial intermediation named as development and growth. Much like her fascist icons of a previous generation, Meloni's forays into Africa also serve to establish Italy firmly as a once and future European power, despite its modern history as also a wayward, rural, and financially impoverished southern state within the European Union, a marginalized—that is, reinforcing the geographic margins—Mediterranean minor relative to states that wield more power and capital from northern and western Europe and the United States.

When Meloni offered to be a literal spokesperson for Ethiopia on the world stage, she said nothing of the conditions of her visit—the first visit by a Western head of government since the Pretoria agreements appeared to end the genocidal Tigray war in November 2022—merely two weeks after she ascended to the role of Italy's prime minister. She said nothing of necessary reparations or other structures of material accountability required of Italy, whose own militarized fascist and colonial histories include several Italo-Abyssinian wars and other failed occupations and incursions, the afterlives of which generated some of the ongoing conditions for migration that impact the region. Instead, of course, Italy's interest manifested as quid pro quo partnerships in fungibility—cash for stemming migration flows from Africa, energy for the externalization of borders and offloading the human cost of their maintenance. Like her predecessors, Meloni has mobilized the mutually beneficial disenfranchisement of asylum seekers and increased financial and geopolitical incentives for African heads of state like Ethiopian prime minister Abiy Ahmed to enable atrocities against their own people and to intensify violent crackdowns against illegalized European migration. As with Libyan and Tunisian officials, Italy strikes deals to mobilize African military forces and contracted or paramilitary mercenaries to perform public sensationalist acts of cruelty. As with coastal communities in Lampedusa and Tripoli and as rehearsed by Suella Braverman about the *Bibby Stockholm* offshore in Dorset, these mutually beneficial agreements serve to whip up dehumanizing anti-immigrant rhetoric while refusing to address the structural conditions undergirding migration, and further maintain a detached relationship to Europe's ethico-political responsibility (see Roy and Zablotsky's introduction to this volume). These are partnerships of dispossession shored up by tax dollars, Frontex Europe, and colonial amnesia (El-Tayeb 2008). The Mattei Plan has been likened to the European Recovery Program of 1948, which was a post–World War II US initiative popularly known as the Marshall Plan. The namesake of this plan, Enrico Mattei, was almost single-handedly responsible for restructuring the fascist energy monopoly Azienda Generale Italiana Petrolio (AGIP, or the General Italian Oil Company) beginning in 1945. He was a Christian Democrat and chief of Italy's state-owned oil and gas monopoly as well as founder and general director of Ente Nazionale Idrocarburi (ENI, or the State Hydrocarbons Authority) after that restructuring. Mattei would have been a staunch advocate of Meloni's purportedly "post"-fascist government and her neocolonial designs on African energy sources and other resources that would benefit "Italy First," a concept that clearly evokes contemporary white nationalist-populist sloganeering seen around the world, popularly with Trump's slogan "America First," which was mimicked by Jair Bolsonaro's slogan "Brazil First" and itself is an echo of Britain First, an avowedly fascist political party founded in the United Kingdom in 2011.

Under Meloni, Italy's extractive orientation toward the African continent is inevitable in its colonial continuity, rooted as it is in the necropolitical logics of surplus and subjugation. The Mattei Plan underscores the antagonistic pretense of false choice under colonial governance and the beast of racial capitalism that serves to suture deadly material and ontological realities into place. It does so here by masking the racial regimes and hemispheric asymmetries that bolster the plan without accounting for the a priori reality of colonial debt and the material reparations toward repair. This is the case with every plan for development (i.e., socioeconomic extraction of raw materials from life, minerals, and other natural resources) on the African continent by European forces, be they state-run operations or state-sanctioned corporate powers. As such, the Mattei Plan can do nothing but yield false claims of "support" through mechanisms of ruin and an influx of capital—€6.5 billion in the initial stages—set to reproduce a mythohistorical continuity of Italy and Italians as *brava gente* (good people) and as staunchly European (read: white) at that, through the same benevolent relational apparatus.[1] The presumption of this continuity follows a disavowal of the material underbelly constituting Europe's own cartographies of violence, which keep the African continent underdeveloped and render her inhabitants as surplus materials before and after migration to Europe even becomes a question (Rodney 1972). African and Afro-descendant folks are structurally held in an antagonistic purgatory in Europe. And Europe is always already in Africa now. Its specter haunts those lands, people, and waterways daily; most of us who know it feel the barometric pressure of that creeping shadow, and struggle to refuse continued conscription into its abject narrative.

Enter the Black Mediterranean

What is to be done in the face of a centuries-long catalogue of despair, in the wake of nonstop refinement of destructive stories (that is, *poiēsis* and programs of abstraction)? This chapter draws on lessons from griot culture, Black feminist internationalism and memory work, abolition geographies, and the Black radical tradition, in particular Robin D. G. Kelley's *Freedom Dreams*. Through these lessons, I am moved toward an ecology of thought, a relational poetics that offers radical (re)orientation to thinking blackness and belonging, dispossession and oceanic crossings. I locate my commitments within and beyond the Euro-African geographical space that physically harbors the Mediterranean Sea and to relational movements of people and culture despite borders and other ideological regimes of containment, crisis, and control. If the organizing conceit of this volume occasions us to consider reworlding humanism, in part through desires for a freedom beyond it, this chapter offers poetic intervention and analysis of what Black Mediterranean freedom dreaming might entail and engender, materially and otherwise. What conditions are required to mark one another as sanctuary and what can it look like to do so amid these colonial-fascist vestiges of a disregard that bares its teeth through juridical and liturgical rehearsals and other weaponized narratives of subjugation?

First, we must acknowledge the Mediterranean as geographically and ontologically more than the national and supranational borders that are being policed through Western impulses. The violence of Euro-African relations permeates what many activists, academics, writers, and artists have come to describe as the Black Mediterranean. The term is a proliferating framing analytic that speaks to the racial subordination, cultural syncretism, and geopolitical structuring of the Mediterranean region and its historical legacies across, within, and despite national boundaries. At first glance, the Black Mediterranean may appear analogous to the Black Atlantic and the contemporary categorization of the Black Pacific. In my own work, I try to consistently sit with the importance of avoiding hegemonic Western articulations of blackness that have over time reduced the generative containers for understanding Black life and its histories. The rationale is to refuse the inductive extrapolation or myopic shorthand that appears to serve as an equivalent basis for comparison to point to shared struggles. In reality, the mainstreaming of such attempts in relation to the Black Atlantic and the Black Mediterranean risks searching for superficial similarities and obscuring both geospecificity and ideological continuity despite the semblance of material, linguistic, or other mode of differentiation. While seductive in the slippages of the everyday, the shorthand of "blackness happens here" unhelpfully obfuscates through analogy. Further, the term "Black Mediterranean" increasingly appears alongside nationally bound terms like "Black Italy," "Black France," "Black Germany," "Black Europe," and so on, with varying degrees of critical success and common usage. In the tension generated by specificity about the stakes of collective liberation, we must struggle against the reinscription of what Jin Haritaworn, Adi Kuntsman, and Silvia Posocco termed "murderous inclusion" (2013), even as some of us endure (often coercively or with manufactured consent) the asymmetrical conscriptions of liberalism in search of sanctuary. Put another way, this cognitive pairing of "nation-state" or geographical region with blackness/Black life is one that both mirrors and demands distinction from Black America(ns). In colloquial, mainstream, academic and legal contexts, there persists a default assumption that Black US citizens or African Americans are the group being singularly hailed by that category, more than, say, any Black person dwelling in or forged through the United States: temporary visitors, international students, Indigenous Africans or (divergently) Afro-

Indigenous people, undocumented Black people, migrant workers, and so on. Further, recent work on hemispheric blackness/las Américas has taken great care to communicate the always already transnational dimensions of Black Americanness/es that resist competitive comparison (Hooker 2017 García Peña 2022); Afro-Indigeneities and Black-Indigenous relations (Pelaez Lopez 2023; López Oro 2020; Harvey 2020; Infante et al. 2020; Smythe 2020), afroamericanidad y amefricanidad (Barreto 2020; Gomez and Ramos 2022).

The categorical iterations spatio-legally bounding blackness in mainstream usage miss the true possibility of what is at stake and what is possible for black people in and across the site(s) in question, and despite the narrow conscription of geographic realities historically occasioned by fate, exigency, or fiat. With this in mind, I aim to resist the contiguity of metonymy (i.e., the proximal equation of "blackness/Black people" + "space" being addressed, which telegraphs inductive reasoning) and the perils of analogy from being cast onto the Black Mediterranean as a stand-in for any particular national formation(s). I aim to specify nation-states when they appear discrete, and—when hailing the Black Mediterranean—to engage the relational space, in the Glissantian sense, to communicate these tensions in relation to the contemporary state of black belonging against all terms and conditions of identity's elite capture, especially the nation (Táíwò 2022). Occasionally I reference the "Euro-African Mediterranean" to specifically refer to the states bordering the Mediterranean Sea, and to dislocate perceptions of Mediterraneanness from Europeanness, perceptions that have been central to various ethno-racial and racecraft projects in southern Europe at key historical junctures.[2] The Black Mediterranean, as Kelley noted, is indeed a precondition to the Black Atlantic (Kelley 2000, xix). Prior to their arrival along Africa's coasts, those ships thieving humans, other life, and raw materials came from somewhere, after all, and were transported along with the structuring forces of capitalist extraction and white supremacist monologics that have degraded and reorganized the current world order into/as the violence of modernity. The afterlives of slavery and ongoing realities of enslavement and dispossession persist in this space, and border ideology is one such weapon used to reinforce those aforementioned logics and regimes of racial meaning (Robinson 2012).

That is but some of the context organizing life in and across the Mediterranean, and it is one iteration of ongoing violence to which we must attend. Against this, inhabiting the poetics of the Black Mediterranean may seem insubstantial to those untrained in the black register of *poiēsis*—which is to say the *conditioning* and creation of possibility through invention, a metaphysical paradox in which black life is possible, it matters, and it truly means something more than its abstract negation serving as caulk for the cracked foundation of an antiblack world. I am interested in offering an otherwise orientation that does not look to any state for recognition but considers coalitional practices that can be thought littorally, shored up via the Mediterranean's seascape, peripheries, and stories/storytellers on the move rather than national European borders and the economics-driven valuation of human life. As I've mentioned elsewhere, "crisis" can be defined as a "turning point" (Smythe 2018). Cruelty may be the point within certain antagonizing ideological frameworks, but every day social movements and solidarity networks, race traitors, and the dispossessed convene across swaths of care and struggle to provide counterpoints, to sound out something else with one another. The real turning point is at hand; Fanon's ruptures are in sight. Before long, we are on the verge of Black Mediterranean freedom dreaming amid a sea of neglect.

We may think of the Caribbean, inspired by Glissant's Antillean space of relation that ebbs and flows across time and space and tongue. It is a site whose littoral spatial figuration is something that those of us committed to certain forms of liberation named prison and border abolition must consistently attend to and imagine. While there has been a concerted effort to address, historicize, and extend awareness about the analytic container of the Black Mediterranean, certain practices and principles get submerged in the name of speaking to the compounding atrocities of one of the deadliest sea and border crossings in the world. Those practices subtend the historico-material violence and offer many of us the tools to speak and act new realities into existence. So, I ask, what are the aesthetic contours of belonging in and to this region and its attendant terrains? What I come to is the poetics of abolition and the very material potentials within freedom dreaming. This concept comes from Robin D. G. Kelley's book *Freedom Dreams: The Black Radical Imagination*, whose 2002 publication and 2022 updated rerelease explore how Black Americans have used their imagination and creativity to resist oppression and envision better futures beyond linear approaches to progress. Kelley argues that these "freedom dreams" have played a critical role in shaping black social movements throughout history, and teaches us how those realities and tactics have reverberated throughout time and space—disrupting space-time itself, confounding the logics of liberal humanism and totalitarian governance alike, as they both undergird Western supremacy.

Antiblack Anti-Migrant Killings and the Eroding Economic Value of Black Life

The overt violences of borders and contemporary immigration apparatus are routine, state-mobilized, and historically bound to the mass rendering of refugees and other modes of dispossession. Indeed, experiences of interpersonal violence and harm are a regular occurrence for migrants, asylum seekers, and racialized peoples throughout the Euro-African Mediterranean. The necropolitical death drive of European border regimes is supranationally maintained by Frontex, the European Union's border management agency. Further, it is nationally reinforced by state coast guard operations, indentured African governments, local police, and (para)military forces. The last of these, who are non-European-state actors, are routinely guided by Frontex, continuing the scheme of lethal non-assistance and maintaining plausible deniability that enables state abdication of responsibility. "Team Europe," indeed. What emerges, then, is a collaborative transnational effort to preserve a consolidated nexus of power via the reification of a white supremacist and Western ethnonationalist global world order that entrenches antiblack and anti-Indigenous (e.g., anti-Roma, or anti-Imazighen) ideology.

The contemporary murders of racialized individuals throughout the Mediterranean (e.g., in Italy, France, and Libya) amplify reflections of this supranational necropolitical border regime that facilitates the deaths and disabling of thousands of migrants across the Mediterranean Sea annually. The examples of such interpersonal and widespread intramural violence are everywhere throughout the Mediterranean, and certainly beyond it. In Italy, as in France, Libya, Greece, Spain, Palestine, and elsewhere in the region, the issue of murdered Black, Indigenous, and migrant people has brought attention to the persistent antiblack, anti-African, and anti-migrant discrimination that plagues Europe and spreads like a contagion throughout the world. Too many incidents of state-sanctioned murder and border killings have emerged in recent years, raising alarms about the many who have been lost whose stories can never be specifically told, nor have their lives publicly mourned, either because they were rendered anonymous, suffering what I call death by numbers among the "possibly lost" in the sea, or because they fell prey to the cracks of the border injustice system, which has rampant human trafficking and enslavement as intentional side effects.

Let us stay with a few instances of some of the lives stolen and the ripples of loss of those other lives touched. In 2018 on Festa della Repubblica

(Republic Day, June 2), Soumaila Sacko was murdered. He was a twenty-nine-year-old Malian human rights defender, an agricultural worker who was collecting scrap metal when apprehended by an avowed white supremacist and shot in the head multiple times with a hunting rifle. Sacko was a union worker with Unione Sindacale di Base (USB), a trade union that fights to improve the atrocious working conditions of the farm laborers deployed in the citrus fields in the plains of Gioa Tauro, in Calabria. The steel he was collecting was intended to be repurposed for housing to improve the dismal conditions of the shantytown village where his comrades working in the citrus fields—many as seasonal migrant workers—took shelter. Sacko's brutal murder by an avowed white supremacist happened in broad daylight. It was at times deemed by media and the public as "overkill" and by his comrades in the union as a political assassination given his very public-facing work toward labor rights. The village or tent city that he navigated in San Ferdinando was first brought into being under then–prime minister Silvio Berlusconi in 2010 and has consistently experienced overcrowding, unhygienic living conditions, and hazards like toxic waste, outbreaks of fires, and disintegrating housing made from threadbare materials, like the one belonging to a comrade that Sacko sought to repair. In the meantime, local officials in the region of Calabria routinely threatened its dismantling as a "cleanup" operation, heightening the rhetoric during election times as their own seasonal occupation, with no regard for where the migrants would go in between their seasons of agricultural labor. This cycle remains unsurprising for Italy, and for every state that maintains capitalist and colonial valuation of life as undifferentiated from their labor productivity and the fluctuating need for it.

Ongoing citizenship struggles are taking place across nations that currently have an *ius sanguinis* policy (citizenship by descent, as opposed to *ius soli*, or birthright citizenship). In Italy, there have been several laws attempting to regulate immigration that linked migration to the national economy.[3] These increasingly bureaucratized and biopolitical practices are deeply entrenched in today's immigration landscape. The immigration process linked the right to enter and/or remain with economic prerequisites and set as a nationwide policy the devalued extraction of migrant workers' labor and lives, in particular by setting minimum wage requirements on (often feminized) domestic and subordinate health work (e.g., nurse's aides more so than doctors), which then of course led to further precarity. Unions like Sacko's were against many of these policies across the political spectrum.

On March 10, 2023, Italy's far-right government issued a new decree, once again expanding the carceral apparatus of its immigration policies.

This law restricted self-employment and family reunification, altering the special protections clause in Act No. 130/2020, which allowed migrants who could present evidence of integration into Italy in the form of biological progeny along with other verifiable social ties in Italy to have access to the right to remain when not eligible for asylum. It was Meloni doubling down on the far-right populist Matteo Salvini's initial 2018 introduction of the so-called Salvini Security Decrees and the development of additional tiers in the citizenship system. Until its forced but partial rollback, his system effectively abolished humanitarian protections for those two years, bringing in a swift process to strip naturalized citizens of their Italian citizenship upon conviction on charges of terrorism—provisions that did not apply to their non-naturalized counterparts. The now-rescinded Lamorgese Decree, named after the interior minister in Conte's second government, Luciana Lamorgese, (re)expanded the special protection considerations for minors, yet continued the trend of linking immigration to capacity for aesthetic/cultural use and potential for labor by offering a two-year special permit that could be converted to a work permit under specific categories like "sporting activities," "artistic work," and "calamity"—the last of which was readily used for Ukranians en masse, but not similarly available to those fleeing other comparable catastrophes or conflicts, as in Sudan, Gaza, Turkey, Nigeria, or Honduras. Poverty is explicitly excluded as a rationale for asylum, a telling lack of accountability given that the West's primary export is the impoverishment of the masses on a global scale, not least through the g(r)ift of aforementioned "development" and the further nebulous discourse of "rights."

The 2020 revision came in response to organized efforts by dozens of humanitarian rights groups, nongovernmental organizations, solidarity networks, Black-, Arab-, and Roma-led community groups, and activist cultural organizers (e.g., Italianə Senza Cittadinanza and QuestaèRoma) coming together around citizenship reform and linking it to the routinization of antiblack violence and dispossession in Italy and around the world. These voices reached a fever pitch during the summer of 2020, where the police killing of George Floyd converged with issues stemming from most governments' derelict responses to COVID-19 and other issues. In September 2020, after the summer of Black uprisings that touched the world and filled Italian piazzas with the signs of mass protest, a twenty-one-year-old recently naturalized Cape Verdean Italian named Willy Monteiro Duarte was brutally beaten and left to die in the streets of Colleferro, a town near Rome. Media again referred to his death as "disproportionate" and "overkill." Again, language is ideologically bound. It is necessary to ask what these words of scale and measure make manifest. The use of the term *disproportionate* implies that in some plane of existence lies a proportionate response to satisfy unbridled antiblackness.

The language of overkill has been theorized by Eric A. Stanley in the context of antiqueer violence and trans antagonism being surface-cast as practices that ought to be socially outlawed, on the one hand, but which are requisite for the maintenance of liberal democracy, on the other. Stanley notes that "*overkill* is a term used to indicate such excessive violence that it pushes a body beyond death" (Stanley 2011, 9). This could be said of the state-sanctioned and -facilitated murders, maiming, and incapacitation of migrants in the same year of Duarte's murder in Macerata, Florence, Calabria, Milan, and so on, and so on, and so on . . . the litany continues to insist itself onto our tongues and timelines. This is to say nothing about violence that appears even more illusory to the state and its agents, like purported suicides, such as those of Pateh Sabally, Mussie, and many others whose deaths I have described elsewhere as state-instigated self-inflicted death/suicide (Smythe 2018, 4).[4] The necropolitical harms are certainly more than death itself, beyond even the negatory abstract of the physical form via overkill and other mechanisms of excessive violence. A study conducted by the Italian National Institute of Statistics (ISTAT) found that Black immigrants are more likely to be unemployed and earn lower wages than their white counterparts. They also face significant obstacles in accessing education, housing, and healthcare services. The Italian government has been criticized for its inadequate response to these incidents and its lack of effective measures to address the root causes of racism and discrimination. In 2020, the Italian parliament proposed a new hate crime law that would impose penalties on perpetrators of hate crimes, for which there is no national legal definition. However, many advocates argue that more needs to be done to promote respect for human rights in Italy and beyond. The starting point is the problem, and vernaculars of liberation are curtailed when the antidote is alleged to have the same source as the poison—the law itself.

Black Mediterranean Freedom Dreaming and Abolition Poetics

The overlapping lifeworlds of surrealists, socialists, communists, Black nationalists, Third World activists, teachers, musicians, poets, and laborers discussed in Robin Kelley's *Freedom Dreams* hold impactful lessons. Between the first publication and its twentieth-anniversary expanded reprint in 2022, much has changed and much has remained the same. Indeed, across these last two decades we have continued to witness untold US- and other Western-driven, -cultivated, and -enacted wars, the uneven distribution of resources, and the proliferation of ethno-religious and other political orthodoxy furthering factionalism and genocide. Kelley shared the political insights of Amiri Baraka, one of the historian- and philosopher-poets of his era, who named for us the phenomenon of the "changing same" in a titular essay. The poem was written in the 1960s during the height of the intertwined civil rights and Black Arts movements, which itself renders a beautiful portrayal of the praxical simultaneity of organized struggle and poetical possibility toward the horizon of collective liberation.

In his poem, Baraka uses the phrase "the changing same" to describe the paradoxical experience of Black Americans' disidentification with the nation that gives them an old name: the feeling of being simultaneously different from and yet the same as white people (1967, 180). The essay describes the "primal impulse" of the idea that although Black Americans have their own distinct culture and history, they are also part of a larger American society that is characterized by racism and inequality. Baraka uses vivid and often confrontational language in "The Changing Same" to convey the dense level of intensity and regard for the Black experience in America, but also Black internationalism and political mobilization inherent across Black cultures. The essay is a powerful testament to the Black struggle for civil rights and social justice through detachment and disidentification with the state and is one of Baraka's most lauded works. We see that "primal impulse" that Baraka used to describe R&B and jazz as well what I would specify as "the anationality of black belonging," borrowing from Gerónimo Sarmiento Cruz's use of the term *anational* to describe "Baraka's complex and shifting, even contradictory, theorizations of community and self-determination describe the search for an aesthetic and political register of belonging" (Sarmiento Cruz 2022).

The organizing frame of the Black Mediterranean, I argue, does more than rehearse the litany of loss. Subtended therein are the cultures of resistance, the sounds of struggle against oppression, the relational poetics of possibility that anchor those practices. Thinking alongside Édouard Glissant's relational poetics (1997), the Black Mediterranean holds aesthetics and politics alike, and thus has the potential for anational orientation. This is not to place poetics and the literary register onto any sort of pedestal. Aesthetic containers like literature are ideological apparatuses that can yield a range of responses and political outcomes. After all, Meloni's reported obsession with the worlds of J. R. R. Tolkien has been described by turns as surprising for the choice of genre fiction and whimsy, and as indicative of the hermeneutic possibility of generations of neofascist youth in the Italian Social Movement (MSI) (Guerrin 2022).

The ways that we give language to these worlds are dynamic and contradictory, and therein lies our power. We know from radical visionary, teacher, and writer Toni Cade Bambara that "words set things in motion.... Words set up atmospheres, electrical fields, charges. Words conjure. I try not to be careless about what I utter, write, or sing. I'm careful about what I give voice to" (2000, 163). There are many words that we can and do give voice to in realization of collective and individual desires to be well and free, despite the available terrains and realities of necessary sites of struggle, like that of citizenship struggles in places like Italy. Rather than dwell in the master's house or aspirationally gaze upon it, deep attention to the literary/poetic allows us to acknowledge the ideological force of the everyday project of creating otherwise worlds.

Kelley offered remarks on the centennial commemoration of the Tulsa, Oklahoma, race massacre, a white supremacist campaign of terror whose lasting trauma and destruction of material wealth is one that reverberates to this day, locally and nationally, for Black people living in the United States: "How we proceed with repair depends on how we remember" (Yancy 2021). Through that interview, edited for publication in *Truthout*, we further understand that memory is tied to the imagination. A key part of who we are or will be is what we remember. Our dreams are more than a departure from our waking reality; they are the raw materials for our surreal futures, sinews and threads of which exist in our present. On the one hand, when images of migrant "swarms" and drowned children proliferate across the internet, mainstream media, and newsletters for nonprofit fundraising campaigns, those depictions attempt to trade on past vernaculars and codes, also serving as a chorale of a future-memory of those humans as harbingers of the fall of "civilized" Western life. Moreover, the figurative positioning communicated is that of an always-already dead thing. Perhaps, borrowing a term communally used to describe the use of a trans or gender-nonconforming person's name prior to social transition, we might recognize another form of deadnaming—that is to say, "naming as dead," in this case, those who were either already taking similar journeys or who were categorically linked to that migratized position, birthed from shared histories in/of the racial order.[5] But some of us know better. We continue to dream otherwise.

This would be the abolition poetics of Black Mediterranean freedom dreams, the ethico-political demand and desires of *poiēsis* in black (Judy

2020). It is the acknowledgment of the capacities and contours of words to change worlds when undergirded by action. In turning away from nationalist arguments and the limiting discourse of "rights," abolition poetics emerges from the streets and organizing practices; in memory events—from public memorials to meditation mindfulness techniques—as forms of wake work; in literary and cultural legacy; and in living archives of diasporic resistance. Capital circulates transnationally, and so do its antagonizing responses. Turning to the Black Mediterranean as a framework that pushes past national confines is a way to address those realities and to further acknowledge that our struggles extend beyond them and so, especially, does the joyous enterprise of our survival and bittersweet refuge in refusal and the capacity to mourn.

In the absence of physical sanctuary, wake work is being borne out by the people toward an affective, metaphysical refuge, the black poietic register of mattering beyond the confines of citizenship, one of the worst aspects of which, Kelley tells us, "is that it needs authorization or that its expression is tied to what is given by a governing (or, more precisely, ruling) body" (2022, 35). This is to suggest that it is contradictory to the *poiēsis* of possibility that I'm arguing has some purchase in the political and literary terrains of the Black Mediterranean, from political storytelling and literary traditions like *letteratura migrante*, postcolonial writing, and West African griots to "Say Her/His/Their Name" campaigns, internationalist staged manifestations, and transnational communal recovery projects aided on a pro bono basis by Euro-Mediterranean forensic identification teams like the Forensic Missing Migrant Initiative (primarily based in Greece and the Netherlands) and other iterations of "forensic care work" that Amade M'charek and Sara Casartelli state "has allowed the dead migrants to become part of the collective of humanity, one that overflows the borders of nation states" (2019, 753).

Much of this creative, surrealist, and antifascist work is highly gendered, with the most well-regarded writing and art in and around the Black Mediterranean including texts like Gabriella Ghermandi's griot-inspired Atse Tewodros Project music and performance collaboration and her first novel, *Regina di fiori e di perle* (Queen of flowers and pearls); Maaza Mengiste's *The Shadow King*; Igiaba Scego's *Adua* and *Oltre Babilonia* (Beyond Babylon); Fatou Diome's *Le Ventre de l'Atlantique* (The belly of the Atlantic); Diriye Osman's *Fairytales for Lost Children*; the reclamatory music of Buika (Concha Buika), who returns flamenco to its Black and Maghrebi context; and the transcendent ritual performances and musical practices of *stambeli*, to be heard echoing throughout the streets of Tunisia. This is a non-exhaustive set of examples from Black women and Black gender-nonconforming people across the Mediterranean who have chosen to respond to the centuries of harm from imperialism-colonialism-fascism, neoliberalism and African financialization in the 1980s and 1990s, various Third World liberation movements and Western-inflected or otherwise funded conflict, and so on. It is particularly salient to note the relevance of this tendency in the wake of Black Lives Matter's mainstreaming (not the movement, but the mainstream projection that its branding and sloganization translated to material political gains for Black people). The invisibilization of Black women, girls, and gender-nonconforming people who are also full targets of suffering under the same regimes of gendered racial capitalism are optics that are routinely refused here. That refusal is affirmation, opting into the kind of care that is opting *into* belonging rather than coerced into it, echoing the dreams of a surrealist philosopher who observed in a conversation with Haitian poet René Depestre that "it's true that superficially we are French, we bear the marks of French customs; we have been branded by Cartesian philosophy, by French rhetoric; but if we break with all that, if we plumb the depths, then what we will find is fundamentally black" (Césaire 2000, 84). The pull of reorienting the dead, the dead things, and the living together into an otherwise possible configuration beyond a guarantee of authority beyond self-determination and making sure the lights of our kin do not go out, or that they do not do so unaccounted, can be seen in the short recitation "Soumaila Sacko: Story of the Good Life" (Kan 2021). The title, Djarah Kan adds in an author's note, "echoes Salvini's statement on the day of Sacko's murder: *Per i clandestini è finita la pacchia* ('For illegals, the party is over'). His rhetoric implied that people who migrated to Italy had it good." This is the same implication observed throughout this chapter about the right-wing rhetoric around "accommodations" for migrants in Britain, Germany, and France. Kan's performance of this piece took place one month after Sacko's murder. A voice for the people through his union organizing, immigration, and agricultural labor, Sacko's physical silencing was interrupted when Kan channeled his spirit's rageful mourning into her performance, which begins: "Now that I'm dying, my face becomes everyone's." Kan's Sacko (a dreamed rendition of the people's Sacko) insists on his humanity and dispels the perceptions, the projections, and the usual channeling under mainstream white supremacist logics: that he was a thief, that all Black people and all migrants are thieves, that their purpose is to be pitied and used. The character Sacko insists on his own humanity in a world that demands his unliving, supplanting his personhood into the figure of the migrant (that is to say, not a migrant "person," but rather explicitly a "nonperson"):

> Because the skin that I leave on this land will become separated from my flesh and blood sooner or later. Time will make it happen; death already has. And then what? People will forget what it meant to mourn for a migrant who isn't rooted to any place—just as the word implies—and who hears his life described as an obscure, weightless cloud, empty and irrelevant. A migrant is like a cloud that's pushed by a wind that blows from afar. It gets stuck and lands, but never grows roots anywhere. So, I was not a migrant. None of us are.

Thus, Kan writes and performs meditations that the young Sacko can no longer give. Through her characterization and demands for "Revenge. Revenge. Revenge" in the closing of his diatribe/her performance, we hear loud and clear that the language of migrancy and migratizing that the state uses and the language that we are coerced to adopt do not share the same significations, as they are born from divergent value systems. It is as Césaire said to the racist critics in 1943: *Nous ne parlons pas le même langage* (we do not speak the same language). The disruptive remembering work and shared languaging persists on this other side. For example, in March 2023, the Cantiere community center in Milan hosted a two-day memorial service, "Due Giorni per Abba!" (Two days for Abba) to honor the life of Abdul William Guibre, a nineteen-year-old Black Italian from Burkina Faso who was beaten to death with lead pipes by a father-son team of assailants in 2008 after being accused of stealing a biscuit, which Kan's spirit of Sacko also protests in his denunciation of presumptions of guilt and accusations of criminality (Cantiere 2023).

Those of us who study racialization, migration, and inequity beyond the North American context have long observed that the international dimensions of abolition are either underaddressed or hailed only in dependent and comparative ways, although nothing could be further from the truth. The demonstrations in summer 2020 throughout Italy under the banner of Black Lives Matter recognized the lives of migrants (overwhelmingly of black African descent), including those struggling for their lives on their journeys across the Mediterranean. Names of immigrants, refugees, and Black Italian citizens without papers like Mussie, Emmanuel Chidi Nnamdi, and others were listed on posters in Rome alongside George Floyd's and Breonna Taylor's. Across cities like Paris and Marseille in France, George Floyd's name was shouted and painted on murals alongside the names of

Adama Traoré and Lamine Dieng. Before 2020, collectives such as Ferguson in Paris were founded and connections between the global dimensions of carcerality emphasized. In Germany, Black people and non-Black supporters struggle for justice for Christy Schwundeck and Oury Jalloh, linking the struggle against border regimes, neocolonial extraction, superexploitation, and policing to what happened to Sandra Bland and Breonna Taylor. The End SARS movement in Nigeria renders scandalous and struggles to end the history of colonial policing in and from Europe, also by mobilizing beyond/despite national borders. In Palestine, freedom fighters agitating for the sovereignty of their people since the first Nakba began in 1948 made calls for liberation from Ferguson to Palestine in solidarity with Black residents of the US South expressing righteous rage and uprising again the colonial afterlives of slavery after the police murder of Mike Brown in the summer of 2014. Six summers later, in 2020, Palestinians in Palestine began calling out that they (also) couldn't breathe as the settler-colonial state of Israel rained down tear gas and bombs; their calls evoked the brutal death of Eric Garner suffered at the hands of New York police, connecting what Vanessa E. Thompson has referred to as "unbreathing" to the colonial-carceral conditions of these contexts and many others (2020). Time and time again, we have seen activists and organizers make intentional references and connections between Oakland and Haiti, Berlin and Bahia, Moria and Tripoli to Lagos. We know well that they are more than arbitrary sites of anticolonial, decolonial, black radical critique and struggle.

So, on the one hand, there is "nothing new" about the deeply historical and poetic movement work toward collective liberation, even as many of us have been witnessing the acceleration and intensification of a painful rupture within our current conjuncture, and which I'm hailing within the Black Mediterranean. "When movements have been unable to clear the clouds, it has been the poets—*no matter the medium*—who have succeeded in imagining the color of the sky, in rendering the kinds of dreams and futures social movements are capable of producing" (Kelley 2022, 56, emphasis added). The medium is not the message here, but agential poetics is.

How do we give language to the realities of this moment, especially as they often become routinely flattened, excoriated, and undermined in their mainstream retellings, or in service of simplifying deep-nuance struggle and envisioning? Audre Lorde famously taught us that "poetry is not a luxury" (1984). However, it is in the subsequent words that we find convergence with the intention of internationalist and feminist liberation struggles. Lorde insists that "[poetry] is a vital necessity of our existence. It forms the quality of the light within which we predicate our hopes and dreams toward survival and change, first made into language, then into ideas, then into more tangible action" (37). The connective tissue between and within movements across the world and the language of abolition is the clarion call of liberation: language, naming, and action form the sinew of collective politics and work to consistently build power through meaningful and material performances of solidarity and social transformation. These are Black Mediterranean freedom dreams. Thus, freedom dreaming—reorienting from noun to verb—has emerged in translingual ways, meaning through/across and beyond shared literal tongues into a shared language of what is collectively yearned for as that which is ultimately possible.

Keep Dreaming of Better Ships

The ache here is for the birthing of something else as possible. Or, as my comrade and fellow author in this book, Vanessa Eileen Thompson, told me during one of our many critical dreaming sessions, the desire is to sound out "breathing into the struggle itself." The political pluripotential of a motley formation is one that we see on the ground throughout the Black Mediterranean in recent years, and one that may yet revolutionize us anew into a coalitional groove that makes every border tremble and shatter.

Kelley goes on to say that he dreams of a kind of citizenship where "we acknowledge our attachment to each other, desire to be attached to one another, in relations other than property relations. Where serving the other is a way of serving the self. It sounds romantic, but isn't that the origin of all the things we want to make and bring into the world? The power of the love letter that is written without a guarantee of a response?" (2022, 35).

In Calais, mutual aid networks proliferated within and beyond the barbed-wire fences that bordered Camp de la Lande, known as "The Jungle," with all of its dehumanizing nomenclature and service as antiblack geo-ideological container as it rendered black people and other asylum seekers as refuse(d)—the camp was literally located on a landfill containing nuclear waste and other hazardous waste. Despite being consistently on the verge of complete spiritual and material destruction fomented by violent and dehumanizing policing, intercultural and interclan conflict between people homogenized under a Western gaze, and alarming public and personal health conditions without treatment, love is; friendship and deep solidarity exist. Groups such as Calais Migrant Solidarity and Human Rights Observers, a volunteer welfare monitoring project within L'Auberge des Migrants at Calais–Grand-Synthe and across the France-UK border (Calais Migrant Solidarity 2010) and others within the anarchist No Borders movement organized (with and as) migrants against abandonment by the carceral state and the (dys)calculated ideologies of disregard that Ruth Wilson Gilmore described as a geographic sight of abolitionist concern (Gilmore 2022, 359).

As we organize ourselves across imaginative landscape and take up the mantle of memory work, storytelling, and other poetic liberation technologies, I turn briefly to the opening scenes of this chapter. In a sense, they are rehearsals of a litany of colonial violence, fascist antagonism, and threats of first-generation gatekeeping by foot soldiers of empire. These are devastatingly thriving narratives as the creep of fascism inches forth and intensifies climate catastrophe and the acceleration of racial capitalism to what may seem like a planetary rupture at the end of the Anthropocene. And yet, we must acknowledge that the current conjuncture holds slivers of the possible, and thus cannot have failed. As Kelley notes, "Too often, our standards for evaluating social movements pivot around whether or not they 'succeeded' in realizing their visions rather than on the merits or power of the visions themselves. By such a measure, virtually every radical movement failed because the basic power relations they sought to change remained pretty much intact. And yet it is precisely these alternative visions and dreams that inspire new generations to struggle for change" (2022, 43).

In the added coda to the reissue of *Freedom Dreams*, Robin Kelley opens with an epigraph from poet Octavio Paz's "'When History Wakes': A New Beginning": "When History wakes, image becomes deed, the poem is achieved: poetry goes into action" (213). Here we are in the world of the "changing same," with internecine conflict and warfare plaguing the world. Africa's underdevelopment—fueled by the power-hungry complicity of her own heads of state or faction leaders—portends the ongoing dispossession of a people from their humanity, land, and self-determination. There is contemporary resurgence of fascist and ethnonationalist interpersonal relations. And ecocidal impulses are spurred by the West. It's not that everything old is new again, but rather, as Fanon impressed upon us, "each generation must, out of relative obscurity, discover its mission, fulfill it, or betray it" (1963, 206). The real turning point, which is to say the real revolution, is ongoing and outstretched before us, in an echo of that moment (itself an echo of centuries of antiblack dispossession and racial capitalist-colonial subordination via the transatlantic slave trade).

In all these contexts, Black people rendered migrants, migratized, or refugees, alongside Black people who were born or otherwise lay claim within these contexts, are all asymmetrically subjected to liberal notions of citizenship and its traumatic seductions. They not only struggle collectively but also necessarily push the struggles beyond their respective contexts. This is strategic and urgent in the midst of maritime "pushback" and other coercive structures of ideological and demographic containment. Many had to cross the necropolitical routes of the Black Mediterranean, were abjected through Europe's neoimperial externalization of borders to Libya, and experienced policing and other carceral conditions, from urban centers to so-called domestic spaces, from the land to the shores and the sea. The responses to these transnational struggles are not simple reactions but reconstructions, ruptures into new horizons anchored by abolitionist traces, on abolitionist routes that are shaped by the movement and mediation of Black people. The abolition poetics inherent in Black Mediterranean freedom dreams invites us to imagine—which is also to translate the dreams of how our communities could look different if we focused on taking care of each other, rather than on punishment. If we breathe collective life into what Ashon Crawley has described as "otherwise possibilities" rather than orienting ourselves to courting authorizing terminology and overburdening nationalist dreams with semantic meaning that is a rearticulation of a desire to belong (2017, 6). What would it mean if we took up a defense of these new visions, these internationalist Black Mediterranean freedom dreams of abolitionist poetics transporting the conversations around abolition and their spatialized/racialized/temporalized contexts in the Mediterranean and beyond? What would it take for us to let go of certain authorizing words of containment to get to the sanctuary of belonging beyond them? We need not "know" the answers to those questions so much as we need to be open to a transformed orientation that would make some inkling of those ideas manifest. In search of home, in search of freedom, in search of better ships than citizenship—which Kelley tells us "include friendship, relationship, or even a pirate ship" (2022, 35), to disrupt notions of capital and authorization via state governance—what if we dwelled within an inquisitive primary orientation to one of the most ideologically weighted terms there is? Who, that is to say, is "we" at all?

NOTES

1 The phrase "Italiani brava gente" references the persistent revisionist myth of Italian fascist and colonial benevolence. The term's initial use regarded perceptions of Italy's populace accepting the propaganda of its fascist government

that claimed little to no intervention or complicity during the Holocaust, and the further atrocities surrounding and subsequent to World War II. Today it remains a persistent aphorism, extending to Italy's response to the influx of migration and asylum seekers from the Middle East, Africa, and the Indian subcontinent. The framing of "Italians are good people" is similarly revisionist here and serves to absolve contemporary Italy from its own destabilizing colonial endeavors—and those of Europe writ large—which are directly contributing factors to the current state of migration into Europe from the Global South. For more in-depth historical analysis, see Del Boca 2011 and Hom 2019.

2 For one prime example, see Sergi 1901. Giuseppe Sergi was an anthropologist who in the early twentieth century contributed theories of the Mediterranean race to the Southern question, describing Mediterraneans as a "pure" racial category that is both a subcategory of the Caucasian race and the "greatest" race responsible for civilizing the world through empire (e.g., Carthage, Rome). His constructions of race were adapted under fascist ideology to support their revisionist irredentist policies, reclamation of the legacy of the Roman Empire, and colonial forays into Africa.

3 Preliminary laws marking citizenship in Europe include Act No. 39/1990, the Martelli Law, which specified migration quotas based on immigrants' countries of origin; Act No. 40/1998, the Turco-Napolitano Law, introduced by a center-left government, which sought to integrate migrants into the labor market and also introduced specific, but at the time extended, processes for deportation and thus further precarity and exposure to a carceral system from which it was difficult to escape; and Act No. 189/2002, the right/center-right government's Bossi-Fini Law, which further expanded the carceral and administrative apparatus—specifically allowing fingerprinting of individuals even for being "under suspicion" by the police of being an illegalized migrant. This law would go on to terrorize migrants regardless of their status, including children under the age of eighteen as well as most racialized people presumed to be of non-Italian or non-ethnic-Italian origin and therefore without the legal or cultural right to remain.

4 In my forthcoming monograph, *Where Blackness Meets the Sea: On Crisis, Culture, and the Black Mediterranean*, I talk more about the relationship of migrant and refugee suicides/suicidality, the geographic terrain of possibility, and the urgency for which we need to organize for the world we truly want, rather than the best option out of a miserable and skewed sample set.

5 See Tudor 2018, where they explain that their suggested term "Migratisation . . . foregrounds the ascription of migration to certain bodies, and the construction of certain people as 'at home' . . . while others are constructed as migrants."

WORKS CITED

Adu, Aletha. 2023. "Home Office to Announce Barge as Accommodation for Asylum Seekers." *Guardian*, April 3, 2023. https://www.theguardian.com/uk-news/2023/apr/03/home-office-to-announce-barge-as-accommodation-for-asylum-seekers.

Bambara, Toni Cade. 2000. "What It Is I Think I'm Doing Anyhow." In *The Writer and Her Work*, edited by Janet Sternburg, 153–68. New York: Norton.

Baraka, Amiri [LeRoi Jones]. 1966. "The Changing Same (R&B and New Black Music) (1966)." In *Black Music*, 180–211. New York: William Morrow.

Barreto, Raquel. 2020. "Amefricanity: The Black Feminism of Lélia Gonzalez." Translated by Rafael Mófreita Saldanha. *Radical Philosophy* 209: 15–20.

Calais Migrant Solidarity. 2010. "Who Are We? وی کوخ رِنوم ؟ ام یک ھ سِت یم .؟ 2010." February 16, 2010. https://calaismigrantsolidarity.wordpress.com/who-are-we-؟-ام-یک-ھ سِت یم-؟-وی-کوخ-رِنوم-؟.

Cantiere. 2023. "25 e 26 marzo: due giorni per Abba!" March 22, 2023. https://www.cantiere.org/44610/due-giorni-per-abba.

Césaire, Aimé. 2000. *Discourse on Colonialism*. New York: Monthly Review Press.

Crawley, Ashon T. 2017. *Blackpentecostal Breath: The Aesthetics of Possibility*. New York: Fordham University Press.

Dal Lago, Alessandro. 1999. *Non-persone: l'esclusione dei migranti in una società globale*. Milan: Feltrinelli.

Del Boca, Angelo. 2011. *Italiani, brava gente? Un mito duro a morire*. Venice: Neri Pozza.

El-Tayeb, Fatima. 2008. "The Birth of a European Public: Migration, Postnationality, and Race in the Uniting of Europe." *American Quarterly* 60 (3): 649–70.

Fanon, Frantz. 1963. *The Wretched of the Earth*. Translated by Constance Farrington. New York: Grove.

García Peña, Lorgia. 2022. *Translating Blackness: Latinx Colonialities in Global Perspective*. Durham, NC: Duke University Press.

Gilmore, Ruth Wilson. 2022. *Abolition Geography: Essays Towards Liberation*. New York: Verso.

Glissant, Édouard. 1997. *Poetics of Relation*. Ann Arbor: University of Michigan Press.

Gomez Menjivar, Jennifer, and Hector Nicolas Ramos Flores. 2022. *Hemispheric Blackness and the Exigencies of Accountability*. Pittsburgh: University of Pittsburgh Press.

Guardian. 2023. "The Guardian View on Bibby Stockholm: Behold, the Great Floating Fiasco." Editorial. *Guardian*, October 12, 2023. https://www.theguardian.com/commentisfree/2023/oct/12/the-guardian-view-on-bibby-stockholm-behold-the-great-floating-fiasco.

Guerrin, Michel. 2022. "'For Giorgia Meloni, 'The Lord of the Rings' Is Not Just a Beloved Novel but an Agenda.'" *Le Monde*, October 3, 2022.

Haritaworn, Jin, Adi Kuntsman, and Silvia Posocco. 2013. "Murderous Inclusions." *International Feminist Journal of Politics* 15 (4): 445–52.

Harvey, Sandra. 2020. "Unsettling Diasporas: Blackness and the Specter of Indigeneity." *Postmodern Culture* 31 (1–2).

Hom, Stephanie Malia. 2019. *Empire's Mobius Strip: Historical Echoes in Italy's Crisis of Migration and Detention*. Ithaca, NY: Cornell University Press.

Hooker, Juliet. 2017. *Theorizing Race In the Americas: Douglass, Sarmiento, Du Bois, and Vasconcelos*. New York: Oxford University Press.

Infante, Chad, Sandra Harvey, Kelly Limes Taylor, and Tiffany King. 2020. "Other Intimacies: Black Studies Notes on Native/Indigenous Studies." *Postmodern Culture* 31 (1–2).

Judy, R. A. 2020. *Sentient Flesh: Thinking in Disorder, Poiesis in Black*. Durham, NC: Duke University Press.

Kan, Djarah. 2021. "Soumaila Sacko: Story of the Good Life." Translated by Candice Whitney. *Words Without Borders*, July–August 2021. https://wordswithoutborders.org/read/article/2021-07/july-2021-afro-italian-women-writers-soumaila-sacko-djarah-kan.

Kelley, Robin D. G. 2000. "Foreword." In *Black Marxism: The Making of the Black Radical Tradition*, by Cedric J. Robinson. Chapel Hill: University of North Carolina Press.

Kelley, Robin D. G. 2022. *Freedom Dreams: The Black Radical Imagination*. Boston: Beacon.

López Oro, Paul Joseph. 2020. "Garifunizando Ambas Américas: Hemispheric Entanglements of Blackness/Indigeneity/AfroLatinidad." *Postmodern Culture* 31 (1–2).

Lorde, Audre. 1984. *Sister Outsider: Essays and Speeches*. New York: Quality Paper Book.

M'charek, Amade, and Sara Casartelli. 2019. "Identifying Dead Migrants: Forensic Care Work and Relational Citizenship." *Citizenship Studies* 23 (7): 738–57.

Milanovic, Marko. 2011. "Models of Extraterritorial Application." In *Extraterritorial Application of Human Rights Treaties: Law, Principles, Policy*. Oxford Monographs in International Law, 118–28. Oxford: Oxford University Press.

MSF. 2022. "Sauver les gens de la noyade: une année à bord du Geo Barents." Médecins Sans Frontières, July 11, 2022. https://www.medecinssansfrontieres.ca/sauver-les-gens-de-la-noyade-une-annee-a-bord-du-geo-barents.

OHCHR. 2018. "Technical Note: The Principle of Non-Refoulement Under International Human Rights Law." Office of the United Nations High Commissioner for Human Rights, July 5, 2018. https://www.ohchr.org/en/documents/tools-and-resources/technical-note-principle-non-refoulement-under-international-human.

Pelaez Lopez, Alan. 2023. *When Language Broke Open: An Anthology of Queer and Trans Black Writers of Latin American Descent*. Tucson: University of Arizona Press.

Reid, Nicky. 2021. "Borders Are a Weapon of Mass Destruction." *Counterpunch*, March 26, 2021.

Robinson, Cedric. 2012. *Forgeries of Memory and Meaning: Blacks and the Regimes of Race in American Theater and Film Before World War II*. Chapel Hill: University of North Carolina Press.

Rodney, Walter. 1972. *How Europe Underdeveloped Africa*. London: Bogle-L'Ouverture.

Sarmiento Cruz, Gerónimo. 2022. "Amiri Baraka's Changing Same as Anational Sociality." *Post45*, June 28, 2022.

Sea-Watch. n.d. "Über Uns—Wer Wir Sind." https://sea-watch.org/ueber-uns (accessed December 2022).

Sergi, Giuseppe. 1901. *The Mediterranean Race*. London: Walter Scott.

Serwer, Adam. 2018. "The Cruelty Is the Point." *Atlantic*, October 3, 2018.

Smythe, SA. 2018. "The Black Mediterranean and the Politics of the Imagination." MERIP 286 (Spring): 3–9.

Smythe, SA. 2020. "Unsettle the Struggle, Trouble the Grounds." *Postmodern Culture* 31 (1–2).

Stanley, Eric. 2011. "Near Life, Queer Death: Overkill and Ontological Capture." *Social Text* 29 (2)(107): 1–19.

Táíwò, Olúfẹ́mi O. 2022. *Elite Capture: How the Powerful Took Over Identity Politics (and Everything Else)*. Chicago: Haymarket.

Thompson, Vanessa Eileen. 2020. "Unbreathing and the Possibility of Abolition." Lecture as part of "American Chameleon: The Living Installments," August 29, 2020.

Tudor, Alyosxa. 2018. "Cross-Fadings of Racialisation and Migratisation: The Postcolonial Turn in Western European Gender and Migration Studies." *Gender, Place and Culture* 25 (7): 1057–72.

Urbina, Ian. 2021. "Purgatory at Sea." *Atlantic*, May 6, 2021.

Walia, Harsha. 2021. *Border and Rule: Global Migration, Capitalism, and the Rise of Racist Nationalism*. Halifax: Fernwood.

Yancy, George. 2021. "Robin D. G. Kelley: The Tulsa Race Massacre Went Way Beyond 'Black Wall Street.'" *Truthout*, June 1, 2021.

14

Dispossession and Its Aftermath

The Sites of Black and Indigenous Fugitivity

Kyle Mays

I am Black and Saginaw Chippewa. I want to begin with a recent ancestor. My great-grandmother Esther Shawboose Mays, on my father's side, was a Saginaw Chippewa woman who traveled from the reservation to Detroit at sixteen years old in 1940. Detroit is on Anishinaabe aki, or the land of Ojibwe people, which is in the current Great Lakes region. After a short time, she married my great-grandfather, who was African American; she received a great deal of hate from Detroit's Indigenous community, especially men, for doing so. But as one of my Sault Ste. Marie professors, Dr. George Cornell, told me when I was a sophomore at Michigan State, "Your grandma didn't take shit from nobody!"

Why did she travel from the Saginaw Chippewa reservation, which is about two hours northwest of Detroit? It seems as if she sought refuge. From what? My family doesn't know. She and my great-grandfather produced nine Afro-Indigenous children. My mother's side of the family is from Cleveland, Ohio, via Georgia and South Carolina. They came to Cleveland in the 1920s and 1930s during the Great Migration, where millions of African Americans relocated from the South to northern and western cities seeking better opportunities and to escape the brunt of white supremacy in the South. They were seeking refuge.

Why did I introduce myself via family? Because it is one way to show my positionality as well as how I relate to these communities. While reading one of the most important books to come out on reparations in years, I was struck by philosopher Olúfémi Táíwò's statement "We should think about our ancestors. But we will win and lose our own ethical battles based on what we do for our descendants. We are defined by what kind of ancestors we choose to be" (Táíwò 2022, 206). We talk about the future we desire, but looking back on the work of our relatives is often a useful way to measure not failures or successes but the desire to be a good ancestor—in the present, but mostly for the future descendants. I want to live in a world free of antiblackness and anti-Indigenous bigotry. I want my descendants to experience this world, even as it's not likely I ever will, and I believe that to get there we should recall historical examples and imagine new possibilities of spaces for our collective freedom from dispossession, or the sites of Black and Indigenous fugitivity.

Black and Indigenous fugitivity on stolen and occupied land is a refusal to capitulate to settler-colonial capitalism. It is a recognition that our futures center on land and our shared responsibilities to one another. This combined fugitivity is a direct confrontation with colonial systems with the intention to incapacitate them, to build more relationality, and to put into practice alternative, liberatory imaginaries through art, through activism, through a retelling of history, for our collective futures. Fugitivity is a part of the process that moves us toward our end goal: the aftermath of settler colonialism and white supremacy.

Black and Indigenous fugitivity requires briefly unpacking why their struggles should be compared in the first place. For too long, activists and thinkers have thought of their struggles as inherently separate. The formulation goes something like this: Black people experience white supremacy and Indigenous peoples experience settler colonialism, and, as a result, they should struggle for freedom separately. Thus, if Black people were only given more rights under this so-called democracy, they would be free. For Indigenous peoples, if the United States only honored the treaties, all would be good. However, in a settler-colonial, racial-capitalist society, thinking separately will only reproduce unequal forms of justice and limit the possibilities of Black and Indigenous co-resistance and co-belonging. Nor does it account for the fact that we share occupied land, and until the land is returned to Indigenous nations, until that land is decolonized, none of us will be free. In other words, the land is key. But what does centering the land mean?

What does this have to do with the current Land Back movement?

Mainstream mentions of Land Back focus on the US government returning land out of the kindness of their colonial heart. If history has taught us anything, colonial nation-states do not return land because they are kind. Land returns under US democracy won't fundamentally change the colonial politics of recognition. It will not create a sanctuary space void of the inherent antiblackness and anti-Indigenous racism within this society. Centering the land means creating relationships rooted in kinship for freedom. It means creating, imagining, and putting into practice shared Afro-Indigenous spaces of co-resistance and co-belonging; it means amplifying our collective voices for liberation against settler colonialism and racial capitalism. Black and Indigenous fugitivity in a shared space of co-resistance is a vision for the future.

I admit, it is hard to imagine a future in the aftermath of settler colonialism and white supremacy. Why? Because ongoing dispossession from land and personhood under racial capitalism requires a social system that sees little value in collaboration that leads to freedom. I define dispossession as a process that includes displacements and removals and occupation; narratives and stories used to justify ongoing colonization; and the memorializing of the colonial space (Mays 2022, 1). Why are narratives important to dispossession? Palestinian scholar Edward Said wrote, "There is no doubt that imaginative geography and history help the mind to intensify its own sense of itself by dramatizing the distance and difference between what is close to it and what is far away" (1979, 55). Settlers use narratives not only to justify violent, unending colonization and to create distance between themselves and it, but also to rewrite history as if it was their God-given right to be the original people of a land (O'Brien 2010, xiii).[1]

There is also the matter of whether we should even compare Black and Indigenous experiences in the first place. While we can assume that we should, I think it is important to spend time on the question. Of course, settler capitalists have deliberately set up this system to work as such.

The questions that undergird my approach and analysis on this topic are simple: What is the relationship between Blackness and indigeneity? What has been the impact of settler colonialism, white supremacy, and racial capitalism on Black and Indigenous peoples? And what kind of world do we want to build and be a part of in the aftermath of settler colonialism and white supremacy? This is my attempt to explore these questions, to ponder our futures, and to move toward collective freedom.

The Site

Detroit is a part of the historical territory of Anishinaabe peoples. It is Anishinaabe aki, or Ojibwe land. They called it Waawayeyaattanong, "the place where the water bends." It was one of the seven sacred stops for the Anishinaabeg, where the Creator (Gitchi-Manidoo) said they would find food growing on water; that food was manoomin (wild rice). The French first occupied the territory in 1701, when the Frenchman Antoine de la Mothe Cadillac landed. The French wanted to participate in the fur trade and sought refuge from the Haudenosaunee, historical enemies of the Anishinaabe. They renamed the place Detroit, meaning "the straits." The British took over Detroit in 1760 as a part of negotiations to end the Seven Years' War with the French. The Odawa, led by the war chief Pontiac, tried to recapture the fort in 1763 but were unsuccessful. By 1807, William Hull, the governor of Michigan Territory, negotiated a treaty with Indigenous nations to cede land in present-day southeastern Michigan and northwestern Ohio to the United States. Detroit was also a place deeply invested in enslavement.

Detroit is a place rooted in multiple forms of antiblackness and anti-Indianness. For example, a law enacted in 1827 was designed to halt Black settlement in Detroit unless those coming in showed papers that said they were free or that provided proof of birth. Black and Indigenous peoples, along with increased white settlement, shaped the city into a manufacturing giant, including the automobile industry. It became the Motor City, a place squarely in the middle of American modernity. During World War II, President Franklin Roosevelt called Detroit the "arsenal of democracy" because it was the epicenter of American production for the war. By the 1950s and 1960s, with the migration of African Americans and Indigenous peoples to the city, the landscape changed. While mainstream narratives persist about Detroit's demise after the 1967 rebellion, historian Thomas Sugrue has long demonstrated that decline in the manufacturing industry and local policies was the root of Detroit's problems in the 1950s, with industry having suffered four recessions, reducing the workforce and the number of plants in the area (2014, 126).

For my great-grandmother to find refuge in the big city might seem fascinating, even challenging, for a sixteen-year-old—and surely it was. But she was migrating within the lands of her ancestors, which they had occupied for centuries prior to European colonization. She would witness and participate in the transformation of the city.

She did everything she could to create a here and now for the future of Indigenous youth. She founded a nonprofit to work on behalf of Indigenous children who were without other family members for a host of reasons. As my aunties have told me, she had children in her house all the time. She believed that Indigenous children regardless of circumstance should grow up in the cultural milieu of Indigenous peoples. She also co-founded Detroit's Indian Educational and Cultural Center in 1974. She, like most of Detroit's Indigenous community, believed that for Indigenous youth to have a future in a city like Detroit, education was the way to go. Their version of education was meant to be a hybrid. It was to be pancultural, meaning having many Indigenous perspectives with a focus on urban futures. It was also meant to be holistic, meeting the intellectual, cultural, and basic needs of the children. They had elders in residence to provide counseling, and they made sure the children had cultural projects, like beading, as well as Western education (Mays 2022, 140–44).

Esther and her children lived in various parts of the city while the children were growing up, but one of the residences was in Garden Homes, which is in the northwestern part of the city. Eight Mile Road borders the north, which is where the official city limits end before entering Royal Oak, a working-class suburb. It is bordered by Pembroke Avenue to the south, Wyoming Street to the west, and Livernois to the east. She continued her advocacy for children, including testifying before Congress in April 1974, along with many others, to comment on the issue of Indigenous children in the foster care system. This culminated in the passing of the Indian Child Welfare Act (ICWA) in 1978. At the time of this writing, the Supreme Court is considering whether that act is constitutional; a decision in the negative would be a threat to tribal sovereignty.

In the early 1990s, my aunt Judy Mays founded the third-ever public school with an Indigenous curriculum, called Medicine Bear American Indian Academy. it is important to highlight this school as another space for Indigenous and Black possibilities (Mays 2022, 135–64). The school's creation was supported by the Black political class because they knew the significance and importance of a culturally relevant school. Medicine Bear was created to meet the specific needs of urban Indigenous youth. Like Esther before her, Judy believed that unless the Indigenous community created educational and cultural spaces to meet young people, they would not survive into the future.

Medicine Bear was open from 1994 until 2005. It was quite a run. But the forces of educational dispossession and neoliberal austerity policies decimated education in Detroit. As I have argued elsewhere, Detroit's eventual bankruptcy was preceded by the Detroit public schools takeover in 1999 (Mays 2022, 160).

Finding spaces to imagine liberation is a significant response to dispossession, but these efforts will never be easy and they are not without contradiction. The possibility of freedom is a dream that can quickly turn into a nightmare. Everyday forms of surveillance, police brutality, and colonization weigh on our hearts and spirits, and without the ability to think, to breathe, to plan our escape in fugitive spaces, that existence can be difficult. A major component of finding space to imagine liberation is to unpack the historical contradictions of land and reparatory justice.

The Contradictions of Our Freedom

One of the major contradictions we must address in our move toward the aftermath of settler colonialism and white supremacy is the relationship between Black freedom and Indigenous sovereignty, or we might say Black belonging on Indigenous land. As an Afro-Indigenous person, as someone deeply invested in these groups' liberation, I contend that if we do not think seriously about the contradictions, then we won't really get anywhere. The paradox I want to explore entails calls for reparations and decolonization, specifically the question of land. As we move toward the aftermath of settler colonialism and white supremacy, we might critically interrogate the meaning of justice, freedom, and reparatory justice. We must think as creatively and judiciously as possible regarding Black freedom and its relationship to Indigenous sovereignty. The person who had this right was Stokely Carmichael, who would change his name to Kwame Ture. But first, let's explore the idea of land as it relates to African Americans.

The era of Reconstruction was a pivotal moment for Black freedom, a momentary possibility of abolition-democracy. Black people were able to vote and serve in the government, and some were able to secure land. For example, Black people in South Carolina and the islands off the coast acquired land taken from former plantation owners during the Civil War, though it was later taken from them during Reconstruction.

The United States did several things to capture southern plantation owners' land. The US Revenue Act of 1862 seized land from southern landowners who did not pay taxes to the Union. After President Abraham Lincoln issued the Emancipation Proclamation, formerly enslaved people had the opportunity to purchase that land sold at auction. On January 16,

1865, Union Army general William T. Sherman declared Special Field Orders No. 15. This order planned out that redistribution of seized Confederate lands in Florida, Georgia, and South Carolina to formerly enslaved people. That land extended about 245 miles from Charleston, South Carolina, to Jacksonville, Florida. Formerly enslaved people were given forty-acre sections from 400,000 acres (the basis for the "forty acres and a mule" promise). For a short time, the land redistribution offered some form of self-determination. As the order stated, "The sole and exclusive management of affairs will be left to the freed people themselves, subject only to the United States military authority and the facts of Congress" (Sherman 1865). During Reconstruction, however, President Andrew Johnson quickly returned that land to former southern owners.

Three years before Sherman's order, the United States had also passed the Homestead Act of 1862. This act provided 160 acres to any individual willing to farm that land. While not equal in practice, Sherman's order stated, "Whenever a Negro has enlisted in the military service of the United States, he may locate his family in any one of the settlements at pleasure, and acquire a homestead, and all other rights and privileges of a settler" (Sherman 1865). In other words, Sherman's proclamation not only provided land, a source of Black self-determination, but actively invited them to participate in the settler-colonial project as settlers. I don't consider formerly enslaved people settlers because their ancestors were forcibly removed from their own indigenous homelands. Indigenous scientist Jessica Hernandez succinctly sums it up this way: the United States was built "on stolen lands and built by stolen Indigenous peoples from the continent of Africa" (Hernandez 2022, 3). However, we should think about the meaning of Black freedom in this context of who was removed, and we should consider the relationship between Black freedom, the expansion of democracy, and the further dispossession of Indigenous peoples.

That short-lived moment of democracy coincided with further restrictions on Indigenous peoples and their removal. Even during the Civil War, when Black people fought valiantly to secure their freedom, the United States committed acts of genocide, including the hanging of thirty-eight Dakota men in 1862 as well as opening millions of acres for settlement to whites in the Western United States. Even W. E. B. Du Bois takes land for granted in *Black Reconstruction*, arguing, "It was a war to determine how far industry in the United States should be carried on under a system where the capitalist owns not only the nation's raw material, not only the land, but also the laborer himself; or whether the laborer was going to maintain his personal freedom, and enforce it by growing political and economic independence based on widespread ownership of land" (1935, 29).

My aim here is not to invalidate what Du Bois is formulating in that passage, which reiterates the point of how important land was both to the capitalist class and to Black and white laborers. But securing that land came at a cost to Indigenous peoples.

Du Bois articulates the importance of land at various levels during Reconstruction, from Black folks to Radical Republicans like Charles Sumner and Thaddeus Stevens to the planter class trying to reclaim land confiscated from them during the war. "Again and again, crudely but logically, the Negroes expressed their right to land and the deep importance of this right," opines Du Bois (1935, 368). He shows how Stevens and Sumner unequivocally advocated for land being gifted to Black people, which would be paid by taxing the former planter class because of the treason they committed by separating and forming the Confederate States of America. Du Bois takes up this argument: "For 250 years the Negroes had worked on this land, and by every analogy in history, when they were emancipated the land ought to have belonged in large part to the workers" (1935, 368). Du Bois understood, though, that the planter class knew that "land was the key to the situation and they tried desperately to center thought on labor rather than land ownership" (1935, 379). Afro-Indigenous historian Alaina Roberts shows that while Sumners and Stevens might have advocated for this, most whites, even those who supported Black emancipation, could not fathom "the idea of separating white men from their private property, one of the most hallowed protections in the Constitution" (2021, 77).

The struggle for land continued to be a key part of the African American experience during the Black Power era.[2] For example, in a speech Ture gave in St. Paul, Minnesota, in the winter of 1975, titled "The Red and the Black," he argued that Black people must center land in their struggle for freedom: "If you do not own land or control land you will be under the power of he who does own and control land." He further contended, "If you don't own land you cannot have a nation." He believed in the power of nationalism to change the conditions of Black people throughout the diaspora. He further argued, "When people fight a revolutionary struggle, they must be fighting for land." While he centered land in his analysis, he was quick to point out that the land that became the United States was Indigenous land. He is perhaps one of the few Black radicals who understood and argued this point. He did not want a future in a world without land being returned to Indigenous peoples. "The land in America belongs to the red man," he said;

"his struggle is for his land" and "it can only be his land" (Carmichael 1975). Ture argued for reparatory justice rooted in revolution—and that revolution centered land. But he was one of the few.

Other Black liberation groups like the Republic of New Afrika, founded in Detroit in 1969, argued that the United States owed them land for their exploitation and as a reparatory compensation for enslavement. Claiming that they were a nation within a nation, they desired five southern states. It is not clear whether they advocated for a future with Indigenous nations.

Indigenous peoples were not always committed to Black liberation. For example, Standing Rock Sioux intellectual Vine Deloria Jr., in *Behind the Trail of Broken Treaties: An Indian Declaration of Independence*, argued that "minority groups were often astounded to learn that the Indians were not planning to share the continent with their oppressed brothers once the revolution was over. Hell, no. The Indians were planning on taking the continent back and kicking out all the black, Chicano, Anglo, and Asian brothers who had made the whole thing possible" (1985, 2–3). I don't think Deloria was antiblack or harbored any negative sentiment toward Black people. In other works, including *Custer Died for Your Sins: An Indian Manifesto* (1969), he offered legitimate critiques of the liberal civil rights movement, showing some love to Stokely Carmichael and the power of the promises of Black Power toward social justice. Deloria even argued that "Black power, as a communications phenomenon, was a godsend to other groups. It clarified the intellectual concepts which had kept Indians and Mexicans confused and allowed the concept of self-determination suddenly to become valid" (1969, 180). Here Deloria suggested that Black people should seek self-determination based on nationalism, not integration into the burning house of the United States.

The discourse around mainstream reparations has remained limited in its imagination. A discussion of reparations as monetary value is a useful example. William Darity and Kirsten Mullen have argued that the United States would have to pay the descendants of enslaved Africans $15–20 trillion (Darity and Mullen 2022). We know they ain't paying that! What, then, are our other options? I also think that while cash compensation is worth calculating, it reifies racial capitalism. I don't think we should seek compensation under capitalism. We should demand something else, something radically different from capitalism. I don't want back wages; I want justice, and that demands the end of racial capitalism and settler colonialism.

Another issue with mainstream reparation lacks a critical reckoning with the fact that the United States is a settler-colonial society. Enslaved

Africans were exploited on Indigenous land. In a report on reparations researched and written by a collection of people in the state of California, the authors argue that those who can prove they had an ancestor enslaved in the nineteenth century should be eligible for some compensation, though they are still figuring out how that might work. Another recommendation is to "create forms of expression, acknowledgement, and remembrance of the trauma of state-sanctioned white supremacist terror, possibly including memorials, and funding a long-term truth and reconciliation commission" (California Task Force 2022, 19). I agree with these outcomes. However, my major concern is that these suggestions and discourses on reparations don't even mention land. The development of California, from the missions to its statehood, is fundamentally a settler-colonial project, based on a genocide committed against Indigenous peoples in the nineteenth century.[3] In other words, what can a discourse and ideology of reparations that includes a return of land mean for both Indigenous peoples and people of African descent whose ancestors were exploited in the United States?

Philosopher Olúfémi Táíwò argues that we need a more expansive philosophical position on reparatory justice. In his view, a global distributive idea of justice is one in which "the just world we are trying to build is a better distribution system, by apportioning rights, advantages, and burdens in a better manner than the one we've inherited from the global racial empire" (2022, 74). The move toward distributive justice requires us to continue to build, organize, and center the land based on our shared responsibility to humans and nonhumans.

Conclusion: Where We Find Fugitivity

I find it difficult to imagine our collective future without understanding land and responsibility, and collective responsibility through kinship is where Black and Indigenous peoples can be in fugitivity together. Kinship as a formative part of our fugitivity not only is about resistance—though that is a part of it—but also concerns developing new ideas of self, nations, and communities based on Indigenous relationalities, not colonial ones. Kinship is not only human relationships, but if we were in better kinship relations we would develop better relations with the nonhuman, including land. If we center kinship in our fugitive practices, then we develop the necessary love to wade through the tides of ongoing colonial violence.

I mentioned earlier that I am Black and Saginaw Chippewa. But I am also a member of the Bear Clan, or Makwa Dodem. Historically, we were the healers and protectors of the people. The clan system exists in many Indigenous nations and explains the relationship and responsibility we have to others in our clan, in our nations. We should pursue mino-bimaadiziwin, which means "the good life." It means maintaining relationships built on reciprocity and care for all living things—humans and nonhumans (Nightingale and Richmond 2022, 1). I would apply this Anishinaabe philosophy specifically to Black and Indigenous communities, for it means being in kinship with one another. Pursuing mino-bimaadiziwin requires also that we center land. For Anishinaabe people, land is an inseparable part of identity. We are part of the land, and the land is a part of us. Centering land is also about kinship—and it is through kinship that we might find solidarity.

The work of solidarity for our collective futures requires a rethinking of how we relate. But this will not be easy. As queer Black feminist Audre Lorde reminds us, "Any future vision which can encompass all of us, by definition, must be complex and expanding, not easy to achieve" (2007, 136). I want to sit with the expanding part. For me, that means we must constantly reevaluate, bring in new ideas and people, and find new ways to relate. Perhaps it will build on Black and Indigenous radical traditions; it might also require creating and developing new traditions.

I propose we consider kinship as solidarity. As I mentioned above, Anishinaabe people have a clan system that tells you how you relate to other people and what your responsibilities are. It defines your responsibilities to those people. What if tribal nations, in exercising sovereignty, began incorporating, for example, Black people into their nations using the clan system? We can quibble about resources, practicality, and so on, but what better way than to build kinship? If sovereignty means anything, it must include our bodies, our epistemologies, and "the ability to regenerate Indigenous languages, philosophies, legal systems, and intellectual systems and to nurture and continue those systems for the land" (Betasamosake Simpson 2015, 21). I would add that regeneration might also look like building new forms of kinship. Sometimes imagining our futures requires creating something new, but often our established practices of kinship already exist, and it might be worth contemplating.

Our desire for liberation cannot be tied up with the destiny of the United States. We have to imagine our lives and the spaces we create outside of the United States. And not just the nation-state, either. One of my beefs with, for example, Indigenous sovereignty is not that Indigenous nations can do for themselves. It's that some see their destinies tied to the United States.

I'm grateful for Grand Traverse Band of Ottawa and Chippewa Indians law professors such as Matthew Fletcher, who remind me that this doesn't have to be the case (2022). But I think even notions of tribal sovereignty can be simply liberal and not transformative. I'm not the only one. Yellowknives Dene theorist Glen Coulthard has convincingly argued that we should reject the colonial politics of recognition (2014, 3), which for me also means rejecting the terms of the game that the United States has set for Indigenous nations to play. It's time to change the rules or reject them altogether.

Solidarity can be a difficult term, and I understand. Just because we might share the same historical experience, that doesn't automatically mean we are kin. I ain't rooting for everyone Black and Indigenous. I want to live in a world with shared histories and interactions rooted in love and similar ideologies. We don't have to agree on every little thing. But for me, we must share basic critiques: that racial capitalism harms most of us, that settler colonialism is a foundational part of US democracy; and that getting more rights from this nation-state is not enough, nor will it ever be. In the reissue of *Freedom Dreams: The Black Radical Imagination*, historian Robin D. G. Kelley asks, "But is it possible to reconcile reparations for slavery and structural racism with decolonization?" (2022, xxxv). He answers the question, but does so by explaining the meaning of decolonization that I understand as an example of solidarity in motion: "Decolonization means ending capitalism and returning the land, not as 'property' but as the source of life to be stewarded by its original inhabitants and where animals, plants, and humans can coexist and thrive together" (2022, xxxvi). Reparations and decolonization can indeed be reconciled, but it will take a sustained effort of difficult conversations, searing critiques, and constant reevaluation.

Amber Starks, my comrade and Afro-Indigenous sister in struggle, is one person I look to for speculative futures. She argues, "I fundamentally believe our arrival at Black Liberation and Indigenous Sovereignty will certainly require us to remember who we are outside of our oppressors' institutions, ideologies, and imaginations" (2021). I appreciate the temporal position she articulates here. It involves remembering our pasts, understanding our present, and projecting ourselves into a future outside the settler-capitalist imaginary, and that is scary. She further contends, "It is a future that will ask us to internalize and embody the notion that subjugation is neither our birthright nor our inheritance. It will demand that we forfeit any loyalties to our current positioning and divest from any misguided belief that this is our lot. It is not! Our destination of freedom will also challenge us to see ourselves and one another as worthy of something better than this" (2021).

Our birthright is not subjugation, nor do we have to pass it on to the next generation. Our position moving forward should be the creation of spaces where all our kin can not only survive but flourish and be who they be—that is, live to their fullest human potential without the limits of a patriarchal, settler-colonial society. My great-grandmother did the best she could with limited resources to change society. My aunt Judy tried to take it up a notch by creating safe spaces in schools. They did the best they could within the context of their lives, and we need to create those spaces for our future as well. As Amber would say, we need to imagine our possibilities outside of what might seem possible within a white supremacist society and beyond. My great-grandmother did her part; so too did my aunt Judy. Now it's up to us to build and do something better. We can do it; we must.

NOTES

1. Deloria makes an astute point: "The contradictions embedded in noble savagery have themselves been the precondition for the formation of American identities. To understand the various ways Americans have contested and constructed national identities, we must constantly return to the original mysteries of Indianness" (2022, 4).
2. See Rickford 2017. I also want to point out that these conversations around land began much earlier, including in W. E. B. Du Bois's *Black Reconstruction* (1935). Indeed, the first Reconstruction was not only about Black freedom but also about how and where Black people could belong.
3. For books on the California Indian genocide, see Madley 2017 and Lindsay 2012.

WORKS CITED

Betasamosake Simpson, Leanne. 2015. "The Place Where We All Live and Work Together." In *Native Studies Keywords*, edited by Stephanie Nohelani Teves, Andrea Smith, and Michelle Raheja, 18–24. Tucson: University of Arizona Press.

California Task Force. 2022. "Interim Report." California Task Force to Study and Develop Reparation Proposals for African Americans. https://oag.ca.gov/system/files/media/ab3121-reparations-interim-report-2022.pdf.

Carmichael, Stokely. 1975. "The Red and the Black." Speech presented at the *Akwesasne News*.

Coulthard, Glen Sean. 2014. *Red Skin, White Masks: Rejecting the Colonial Politics of Recognition*. Minneapolis: University of Minnesota Press.

Darity, William A., and A. Kirsten Mullen. 2022. *From Here to Equality: Reparations for Black Americans in the Twenty-First Century*. 2nd ed. Chapel Hill: University of North Carolina Press.

Deloria, Philip J. 2022. *Playing Indian*. New Haven, CT: Yale University Press.

Deloria, Vine. 1969. *Custer Died for Your Sins: An Indian Manifesto*. New York: Macmillan.

Deloria, Vine. 1985. *Behind the Trail of Broken Treaties: An Indian Declaration of Independence*. 1st University of Texas Press ed. Austin: University of Texas Press.

Du Bois, W. E. B. 1935. *Black Reconstruction: An Essay Toward a History of the Part Which Black Folk Played in the Attempt to Reconstruct Democracy in America, 1860–1880*. New York: Harcourt, Brace.

Fletcher, Matthew L. M. 2022. "The Dark Matter of Federal Indian Law: The Duty of Protection." SSRN Scholarly Paper.

Hernandez, Jessica. 2022. *Fresh Banana Leaves: Healing Indigenous Landscapes Through Indigenous Science*. Berkeley, CA: North Atlantic.

Kelley, Robin D. G. 2022. *Freedom Dreams: The Black Radical Imagination*. Boston: Beacon.

Lindsay, Brendan C. 2012. *Murder State: California's Native American Genocide, 1846–1873*. Lincoln: University of Nebraska Press.

Lorde, Audre. 2007. *Sister Outsider: Essays and Speeches*. Berkeley, CA: Crossing.

Madley, Benjamin. 2017. *An American Genocide: The United States and the California Indian Catastrophe, 1846–1873*. New Haven, CT: Yale University Press.

Mays, Kyle T. 2022. *City of Dispossessions: Indigenous Peoples, African Americans, and the Creation of Modern Detroit*. Philadelphia: University of Pennsylvania Press.

Nightingale, Elana, and Chantelle Richmond. 2022. "Reclaiming Land, Identity and Mental Wellness in Biigtigong Nishnaabeg Territory." *International Journal of Environmental Research and Public Health* 19 (12): 7285.

O'Brien, Jean M. 2010. *Firsting and Lasting: Writing Indians Out of Existence in New England*. Minneapolis: University of Minnesota Press.

Rickford, Russell. 2017. "'We Can't Grow Food on All This Concrete': The Land Question, Agrarianism, and Black Nationalist Thought in the Late 1960s and 1970s." *Journal of American History* 103 (4): 956–80.

Roberts, Alaina E. 2021. *I've Been Here All the While: Black Freedom on Native Land*. Philadelphia: University of Pennsylvania Press.

Said, Edward W. 1979. *Orientalism*. New York: Vintage.

Sherman, William T. 1865. "Special Field Orders, No. 15, Headquarters Military Division of the Mississippi." Freedman and Southern Society Project. http://www.freedmen.umd.edu/sfo15.htm.

Starks, Amber. 2021. "Envisioning Black Liberation and Indigenous Sovereignty." US Department of Arts and Culture, September 22, 2021. https://usdac.us/news/2021/9/21/envisioning-black-liberation-and-indigenous-sovereignty.

Sugrue, Thomas J. 2014. *The Origins of the Urban Crisis: Race and Inequality in Postwar Detroit*. Princeton, NJ: Princeton University Press.

Táíwò, Olúfẹ́mi O. 2022. *Reconsidering Reparations*. New York: Oxford University Press.

15

Freedom's Revenge, or Toward Liberation

Rinaldo Walcott

The question of what constitutes freedom in the post-Columbus world is a question of both epistemology and power. Freedom animates the foundation of all of our struggles, and the idea of freedom is one that is furnished as the most salient element of what it means to inhabit the category of the human, or the species more broadly. In this essay, I turn to an idea of freedom that draws from the Enlightenment and post-Enlightenment tradition—which I recognized was not intended for the subjects whose lives animate my thinking—to offer a revision of what freedom might be as a way to reorient the ongoing catastrophe that is the post-Columbus world. For the subjects who were never intended to claim freedom, claiming freedom is to seek a kind of revenge from the past that undoes Euro-American white supremacist logics of what it means to be human, to be a life-form, to be speciated. Freedom in its unfolding logics requires a new accounting of what it means to live a life, and this new accounting must grapple with the very history of why and how freedom has come to be important as an idea, desire, wish, and demand for practice in a world where life has been often sorted into those who are free and those who are not, and therefore into those who deserve to live and those who do not.

The idea of freedom that I attempt here is one that enacts a break with captivity or the scene of the crime of unfreedom, since captivity is the very ground from which freedom as we utter it has grown. In fact, captivity is the theft of freedom. Indeed, it is my intention that freedom might mean something beyond post-Enlightenment, late modern articulations of a perfected human self that can only be imagined as white and thus beyond the reach of the rest of the species. Therefore, when not-white people assert the desire for freedom, they seek revenge on a narrative that has rendered their speciation not just suspect but of an entirely different order. As Toni Morrison (1990) has taught us, European ideas of freedom are always caught up in some project of conquest. It is my argument that the achievement of something called freedom is the achievement of a different world, a different rhythm of movement, an entirely new order of life. The order of life bequeathed to us from the post-Columbus moment is one where freedom's possibility is held hostage by multiple modes of unfreedom. A Euro-American insistence on freedom being authored only by and through its perspective, its partiality—enforced as universal—is what is at stake in a world seeking to decolonize and reanimate what speciation might mean and how it might be lived in the world. It is with the idea that Euro-American freedom is a fiction of its own violence unleashed on the rest that I argue for a different order of knowledge that might usher in a possible freedom yet to come.

In what follows in this chapter I uncouple freedom from democracy. Instead I see freedom as an antagonist of representative democratic institutions insofar as those institutions promise to produce or ensure freedom while actually doing otherwise. Those institutions tasked with demonstrating freedom and its reach are in fact the poisoned fruit of the expansive terrain of post-Columbus ideological and material colonization and cannot be taken as sites for the possibility of freedom. In short, those institutions marked as democratic manage unfreedom. By this I mean that what freedom might be is entirely constrained by a narrative that has it unfold from post-Columbus European expansion as an outcome of coming to terms with the violences that produced the Americas and then the globe as a space for conquest, exploitation, subjugation, and the transformation of people in exploitable and extractive forms of social life. The editors of this collection point out in their foreword that sanctuary is a "problem of liberal democracy." And they are clear that Europe, its borders, and its fortress mentality are foundational to how unfreedom makes its mark in the world. Freedom, then, must be untethered from Europe for its possibilities to actually arise. The only name we have for that untethering is decolonization. It is not democracy or sovereignty or any of the other euphemisms that are used to assert how one group might more skillfully dominate another. Decolonization, as foundational to the kind of freedom I want to articulate, is an overthrow of a dominant and violent register of global being. Of course, the central figure of this problem of freedom that I am narrating here is that of chattel slavery, a form of slavery introduced through the transatlantic slave trade in African flesh—a system of attempted total domination of the slave figure, and a system that in the post-emancipation period continues to order relations of life and speciation. And in accord with transatlantic slavery is the theft, genocide, and near genocide of Indigenous peoples. These acts inaugurate a way of life and a form of being or speciation that makes the quest for freedom a form of revenge against the imposition of the Euro-American account of what a life might be. I am particularly interested in the epistemological aspect of this problem. In fact, I believe that the ideas that underpin the material extractive practices are more significant in prohibiting the possibility of freedom than the unequal distribution of extractive wealth is.

There is a significant tension between ideas of freedom, emancipation, and liberation. Writing in the context of the work of Saidiya Hartman, Fred Moten, Sylvia Wynter, and David Marriott, I am concerned to delimit an idea of freedom that does something more than renovate Euro-American humanism. These thinkers have furnished us a grammar that allows us to pay attention to that which is structurally maintained by recourse to marking Black being as both the foundation and the opposite of what life might be. Their broad theoretical interventions organize my thinking here. Requiring that we do more than notice blind spots and/or work toward an inclusion or unfinished project of freedom, these thinkers ask us to think the unthought and the thought of Black life as an undoing of claims of a universal. In this way these thinkers have offered us multiple theoretical routes toward risking a Black animation of freedom. The critique provided of Euro-American humanism is not one in search of a space, a gap, or a position to enter it, but rather one that demolishes its edifice. What these thinkers have in common is not a theoretical unity but a political project that writes us toward freedom beyond Euro-American humanism.

Olaudah Equiano (1789, 39), in his attempt to both critique European humanism and push toward an account of freedom beyond it, put it this way: "When you make men slaves you deprive them of half their virtue, you set them in your own conduct an example of fraud, rapine, and cruelty, and compel them to live with you in a state of war; and yet you complain that we are not honest or faithful." Equiano's assertion is one that reverses the claim of who is corrupt and without virtue; it is the enslaver. Once we contend with the idea that Equiano had an experience and understanding of freedom well before his captivity, we read his narrative differently. Thus, Equiano becomes "free" in the context of Enlightenment logics of freedom, not free in the context of the ideological system he was initially born into. In this instance, European conceptions of "freedom" remain a kind of captivity because it expunges other conceptions of the world. Or as Wynter (2003, 268) puts it, "What I have defined (on the basis of Quijano's founding concept of the coloniality of power) as the Coloniality of Being/Power/Truth/Freedom, with the logical inference that one cannot 'unsettle' the 'coloniality of power' without a redescription of the human outside the terms of our present descriptive statement of the human," is the central dilemma of the problem of the human and the problem of freedom. Indeed, it is crucial to note that in Black studies/study the concern of a new humanism and its possibility or the entire refusal of the category of the human as worthy of remaking has come to occupy one of the fundamental ideological differences in the field. My own thinking on this question, influenced by Fanon and Wynter but subtended by David Marriott's significant interventions, is to nonetheless take the leap toward a new humanism with the pessimism of its always potential failure. What animates my in-between position here is how I understand the work that a potential freedom yet to come might do for speciation.

David Marriott (2018, xv), writing of Fanon and freedom, states: "I became completely convinced that Fanon wishes the colonized to be absolutely free, but that this is a freedom that has nothing to do with political sovereignty; instead, for Fanon, each citizen should stand on their own feet and be able to look the enemy in the eye without trembling." While Marriott uses the language of the citizen, his is not an appeal to the nation-state and/or the previously mentioned democratic institutions that manage and distribute the conditions of unfreedom. Instead, Marriott alerts us to a kind of confrontation with the limits of European humanism as a route toward being free. The ability to "look the enemy in the eye without trembling" is the acknowledgment of another mode of being, one that must be at least fought for. Marriott (2018, 48) further alerts us that, in thinking about how we might arrive at decolonization, we might consider that "the moment of liberation, of decolonization, without which, in fact, freedom is not possible, is always a complex network of displacements and valorizations, and to suggest otherwise is to forget the psychotherapeutic terms in which colonialism is to be transvaluated." Again, we see that freedom is not an end but a process in which a move toward decolonization is the route toward its achievement.

Marriott's reading of Fanon and his critique of revolutionary teleological thought in Fanon helps us to scaffold a way of moving toward decolonization that acknowledges the various stages of its unfolding. We might do well to understand Fanon as having arrived at the site of the anticolonial, but death stalled his thinking at the decolonial on the way to decolonization. Indeed, as a theorist and a practitioner of a coming decolonization, Fanon provided for us in *The Wretched of the Earth* a kind of map toward freedom and how the move toward it would be interrupted. In some recent scholarship the debate concerning the poignancy of the anticolonial versus the decolonial has positioned these as belonging to different conceptual and even geographical spaces and languages, and one is given primacy over the other, as if such primacy legitimates correct process for or toward decolonization. In my reading, both terms function as stages toward decolonization, which for me are the stages toward a possible freedom.

I attempt to put into contention Europe's expansion as a project of unfreedom rather than one of freedom. This essay seeks most emphatically to argue for an understanding and idea of freedom as one that ends Euro-American global rule. Writing with the backdrop of ongoing coloniality, ecological disaster, carceral practices of all kinds, fascism, and the ever increasingly late-modern primitive capitalist accumulation, I argue that taking freedom seriously as a mode of reorganizing the world is freedom's revenge on Euro-American forms of unfreedom. Freedom's revenge then is the rebound of Europe's idea of freedom, but only as it undoes Euro-America as the site where liberation might be inaugurated globally.

Raoul Peck's *Exterminate All the Brutes* (2021) is an important example of the ways in which narratives of freedom, liberation, and decolonization can remain inchoate even as the material being presented points toward a demand for the eventual enactment of decolonization. *Exterminate* is a four-part documentary series that runs for a little under four hours and traces Europe's post-Columbus global expansion and its accompanying ideas. Peck narrates the documentary for the most part, drawing on multiple archives and enactments to tell a five-hundred-year history of Europe's reign. The background source texts for the documentary are *Silencing the Past* by Michel-Rolph Trouillot, *Exterminate All the Brutes* (from which it draws its title) by Sven Lindqvist, and *An Indigenous Peoples' History of the United States* by Roxanne Dunbar-Ortiz—three acclaimed books that have had tremendous impact on anyone who has encountered them. In the very first episode of the series, Peck tells us that the documentary is about three things: civilization, colonization, and extermination.

Exterminate All the Brutes has been described in headlines and reviews as "a vast, agonizing history of white supremacy," "a masterpiece," and "one man's odyssey in the heart of darkness and the origins of European genocide"; it "rewrites a brutal history" and demonstrates "the courage to understand and draw conclusions." The tenure of the reception is like this:

> Part personal essay, part investigation, the docuseries "Exterminate All the Brutes" is a striking piece of nonfiction work that has the intellectual rigor of an advanced history course, and asks that viewers keep up with its many ideas and horrors over the course of its four hours. Raoul Peck picks and pulls at every connecting fiber throughout history, finding several lines through the ages of how hateful dogma begat public policy, systemic murder, and cultural genocide. If you finish "Exterminate All the Brutes" without re-examining the hundreds of hours spent in history classes, then you didn't pay attention to Peck's lesson. (Castillo 2021)

Mike Hale, the *New York Times* television reviewer, shifts course with a surprising, quite balanced review:

> But throughout "Exterminate All the Brutes," the specific drifts into the general and the historical into the personal without, perhaps, the effect that Peck is hoping for. He closes with a reproving phrase that echoes through the film: "It's not knowledge we lack." But he declines to say what it is we lack—compassion? Willpower? If there is something we possess that could have made history different, either he doesn't know or he's not telling. (Hale 2021)

So why am I dissatisfied with the unfolding of the material and the argument of the documentary? Hale's commentary begins to point us there. Peck represents what is already known by many, and even those who might not articulate it in similar fashion know that the conditions they live and experience every day are not simply their doing. So, what work does Peck's representation do, and what work should we expect it to do?

Exterminate gathers the important evidence to demonstrate how Euro-American reign has produced the deeply troubled world we have inherited and now inhabit. Peck's narration, with its personal touches reflecting his background as Haitian, adds a certain sentimental but important quality to this retelling of world history. And yet *Exterminate* does not break with the narrative that Europe has furnished the world. Instead, it takes Europe's universalism, especially France's, as the core of its argument and as the ideal to achieve. But as one of Peck's interlocutors, Trouillot (2021, 237), has written in another context, "France itself is not as universalist as it sometimes seems from this side of the Atlantic"—a caution that is worth holding in mind as one views Peck's documentary. Trouillot is of course making this commentary in the context of debates in the humanities and social sciences, riffing off Marcel Detienne's position on the disciplinary, interdisciplinary and multidisciplinary debates. I, however, think it is important to note the ideological position from which the retelling of Euro-American colonialist expansion occurs and consider whether such a retelling can break out of the very narrative it seeks to call into question. Indeed, Wynter's call has been for us, the damned, to produce a new narrative of the world we inhabit by renarrating the consequences of Euro-American expansion. It is the problem and the hold of Euro-American universalism that troubles and indeed undermines what would otherwise be a powerful critique and undoing of Euro-American reign.

Because Peck's documentary is a popular representation of important arguments, insights, and debates concerning European expansion and imperialism, it is crucial to engage it. It popularizes important histories that can and must be mobilized to produce a substantively different kind of planetary life. And yet Peck fails in reorienting and mobilizing those histories beyond Euro-American humanism. Peck continually returns to the Shoah as the most brutal evidence of Europe's and thus the West's violence. The very last images of this four-part series are a long and continuous shot of Auschwitz. This image, I argue, undoes much of what Peck can achieve with various segments of the series. While a close read of the series reveals various contradictions, one can overlook those contradictions if a more robust critique of European humanism as an ever-evolving progress toward freedom is offered. Indeed, Peck's conclusion signals a neat packaging that immediately invoked the Declaration of Human Rights. A more robust account from Peck would have recognized that the Declaration of Human Rights has as its foundation the fight against transatlantic slavery, as Paul Gilroy has elegantly and powerfully demonstrated and argued in *Darker than Blue* (2010). It is to these contradictions in our resistance to, refusal of, and counter-imaginary to Euro-American humanism and a progressive unfolding freedom that I now turn.

Why am I exercised by Peck's series? Its content accords with the accumulated knowledge of what we already know of European expansion and its further Euro-American instantiation as a brutal genocidal white supremacist project. So my aim is not to quibble with the content of the documentary but rather to probe what art can do. Sylvia Wynter has long taught us that art, or rather aesthetics, does something. And it is this something that one wishes Peck's powerful yet ultimately failed documentary would do. I am not asking for the artist to set out a program of liberation for us, but I am asking for something like it to be at least approached. Indeed, we know these stories, as they have been repeated over and over again. When is it that we might move from the telling and retelling to another mode of enactment? Writers, artists, intellectuals and others are now tasked with moving beyond the repetition of our subject to risk articulating what it might mean to bring into account a new order of knowledge that might inaugurate new modes of thought and thus new modes of living together.

In the essay "On Disenchanting Discourse," Sylvia Wynter (1990) offers us analysis of Black literature in which she proffers that it produces a counter-novel. In Wynter's argument, the counter-novel is not merely a different or Black-inflected novel but rather an entirely new apparatus that makes visual the brutal work of the novel and then transforms that work into a new account of what life might be—a counternarrative. Caribbean intellectual Kamau Brathwaite (2006) has called this counter-novel the literature of catastrophe, and I have extended this to the culture of catastrophe. In any case, if we take Wynter and Brathwaite together, we might think of their interventions as constituting the demand for a counter-imaginary in an ongoing culture of catastrophe. In Wynter's (1990, 459) articulation of the counter-novel she calls for a "counter-exertion," "one that will entail the transformation both of literary scholarship and of our present organization of knowledge." Similarly, Brathwaite (2006) argues for a literature of catastrophe, against the danger of forgetting that the "omens of catastrophe that originate in the explosion out of which the Caribbean came" should guide our intellectual project. Riffing off Wynter and Brathwaite, I am interested in the articulation of a counter-imaginary and a culture of catastrophe in which a different and new account of how we might live differently together is possible.

Given the texts that Peck was working with, one might have expected to experience or see unfolding a counter-cinema in his retelling of global history from the view of the subaltern. Instead with Peck we get the nadir of the Holocaust, or rather the Shoah, as the lasting image of European and by extension Euro-American genocide. Now, I am not suggesting that Peck must furnish us a program for liberation; rather, I am saying that Peck cannot even approach liberation because he remains tethered in his cinematic pedagogy to a French universalism that is in fact a product of the very terms of engagement he seeks to untangle. In Peck's cinematic lens we have a powerful re-presentation of the history and the problem, but what is missing in that re-presentation is the counter-imaginary, one that might point us toward liberation.

In the late stages of global postmodern culture, narratives of liberation have been reduced to the horizons of capital, sovereignty, self-determination, land, and representative democracy. These are all post-Enlightenment ideas of European expansion and how the globe should be ordered. Even more specifically, in a post-1989 world with the collapse of communism and the triumph of Western capitalist democracy, opposition to the existing social arrangements is often ridiculed as impossible, and what is offered are adaptations inside capitalist democracies. It is my argument that a counter-imaginary is urgently needed. In fact, one might say that the accumulated evidence that Peck's film provides requires, if not demands, that we risk articulating what a counter-imaginary of living together might look like. In my view such a counter-imaginary unhitches its liberation of the species from humanist accounts of what it is, can be, and might be. Instead, we start to use the accumulated evidence of European and Euro-American reign as the detritus out of which we begin to imagine anew other modes of living lives. We begin this process not just with a refusal of Euro-American humanism but also with a profound knowledge that Euro-American humanism is itself an act of profound speciated violence.

In Aimé Césaire's (2000, 74) critique of Europe, he identifies Man and the nation as two things that Europe "launched throughout the world." Those two things remain the most significant bulwarks against something we might call freedom. The continued demand for freedom nonetheless is the evidence of the brutality of those categories of ruling. In essence, then, we must liberate ourselves from Man and the nation-state.

The move from colonial to anticolonial to decolonial represents the phases of how we might get free, a process toward freedom rather than different conceptions of freedom. I argue that anticolonialism is one moment or phase of the freedom struggle in which the desired outcome is a decolonial present and a decolonized future.[1]

Therefore, I write against the logic that these are all different, not a part of a continuum, not phases that fold back onto and into each other. Indeed, a decolonial present and a decolonized future would be one in which Euro-American humanism is not the central mechanism through which life is organized globally; such a profound refusal would radically shift our relationship to what is now called nation and state, tethered together as the nation-state and ordering how planetary life is organized. Fanon had already taught us in *The Wretched of the Earth* that the anticolonial struggle becomes a decolonial present and that decolonization is usurped by the anticolonial elites, thereby foreclosing decolonization. Fanon's analysis demonstrates clearly the phases of decolonization and how in each stage or phase the struggle toward freedom can be interrupted and even stolen. Indeed, the differences that seem to matter are ones of translation rather than genealogy, insofar as these three terms (anticolonial, decolonial, and decolonization) are meant to point toward struggles for freedom from and against Euro-American humanism and to author new modes of being.

If we are to approach something that we might imagine as freedom, we will have to risk saying what that something is. Increasingly for me, that something rests in refusing the post-Enlightenment categories that Euro-American modernism has bequeathed us. By this, I mean that even as the historical weight of those categories shapes how we experience the world, we also know that there is something beyond them—in fact, something beyond them that is in relation to them and even partially produced by them but also exceeds them. And it is the sober reality of the hybrid nature of our experience that demands the invention of new forms of sociality. These new inventions of sociality will take as their foundational structure and refusal the historical brutality of our encounters to fashion new modes of being together and thus to invent a *new being-ness*. The earlier insistence that anticolonial practices are in service of a decolonial present and a decolonized world—which, to restate, is a world without the practice of domination—points toward the freedom that is to come, but only if we can break the brutal and seductive hold that Euro-American humanism has locked us into. Indeed, Peck is not able to do so in *Exterminate*.

There is an appeal being continually made to a humanism that can never contain the black monster of its own creation. And Peck's film falls prey to this appeal. Even among our best articulators of "the problem" we remain incapable of risking articulating what its demise might be. Our imaginations are so profoundly corrupted by European humanism as the only game in town that to imagine ourselves as life-forms after it and before it continually eludes our intellectual pursuits. I want to insist that our contemporary intellectual tasks are to break out of the repletion syndrome and risk invention. And to risk invention will require something more from all of us.

Hazel Carby in a generous review of *Exterminate* writes that Peck's film resurfaces the links of solidarity and cooperation of Indigenous and Black refusals of Euro-American colonial violence. And indeed, the film dramatizes such refusal and community-making and the violence it is greeted with. Carby further demonstrates how the film's aesthetics produces this relation:

> The camera zooms in slowly on a headshot of Osceola, a male warrior of the Seminole Nation, played in the film by a woman. We are told "her story reaches deep into the history of this continent." The portrait is intercut with two brief glimpses of the future, in which Osceola is shot and scalped while fighting alongside her Black allies. Osceola's face dissolves into that of Peck's mother, Gisèle, as a young woman in Haiti, an intertwining of resemblance and difference that tells a global story of the greed and destruction of European imperialism and a particular story of Black and Indigenous solidarity. (Carby 2022)

Carby's excellent reading of the scene is attuned to the film's limits as a counter-cinematic and counter-imaginary work. Indeed, the film does demonstrate these solidarities, and that is one of the important elements of its intervention. However, the final shot of the film is a long, persistent, and steadied shot of an empty and eerie Auschwitz. It is my argument that Peck's cinematic decision undermines the other strengths of the documentary series because of an inability to break with Euro-American humanism as the central dynamic through which to arrive at an account of the historical past that might point toward freedom. What Peck achieves with *Exterminate* is the re-presentation of the accumulated injuries, displacements, violences, and other modes of Euro-American global expansion, colonizations, imperialism, and extermination, without recourse to providing an accounting that might do something more. Am I asking for something more? Yes.

If the Shoah is the singular nadir of the accumulated violences of post-Columbus expansion, then we can adequately make sense of the ongoing violences of that expansion and, most importantly, the thought and ideas that continue to underpin such violence. For example, we can then adequately think the settler-colonial ethnic cleansing of Palestinians by the Israeli state now, which gives us another register with which to address the unfolding violence of late modern life. Of course, *Exterminate* does not approach this question of what is to be understood in the aftermath of the Shoah, how a state morphs into one of tremendous violence that mimics that from which it too arose. Locked in the logic of a Euro-American humanism that does not produce a counter-imaginary, Peck's film ends with a powerful and moving image that recalls the violence of the Shoah, and thus the film does not approach the possibility of arriving toward freedom. The conclusion of Peck's film actually highlights the dangers of entering the category of Man and how entering that category through the nation-state reproduces not just the echo of violence but the foundational violence of European expansion. The abolition of Man and the nation-state therefore lies as central to the proposition of arriving at freedom.

What does it mean to work toward something, something like freedom? For me, to work toward freedom is to understand and apprehend past and present violences as constituted within the domain of a Euro-American humanism that prohibits others from benefiting from it while making it the standard of what living and achieving a life might be. It is the skilled ideological prohibition of achieving a life for some of us that profoundly demonstrates the violence of Euro-American humanism and its ongoing accumulations of who might live and who might die. It is thinking beyond this paradigm that allows us to begin to fashion something like freedom—freedom beyond humanism.

The short film *Without a Whisper—Konnon-Kwe* (2020) is an interesting counterpoint to *Exterminate*. This documentary is what I call a straight doc—showing talking heads, following its principal personality doing their work, and offering expert commentary. That is, the filmmaker does not innovate much with form. It is a documentary that describes itself as "the hidden history of the profound influence Indigenous women [had] on the beginnings of the women's rights movement in the United States," and it follows Louise Hern as she reclaims this history and importantly extends it into the present and (dare we say) future. In the recognition that the film is future-oriented—even while its documentary mode is utterly within the cinematic norm—the film breaks open the possibility of another way of being and living in the world, and not only because of Hern's profound commitment and charisma. The film works as a counter-imaginary that exceeds the cinematic frame. It is the thought of the film that makes a future-present. In fact, in watching the film one encounters what Françoise Vergès (2021, 20) calls "a decolonial feminism whose objective is the destruction of racism, capitalism, and imperialism." The stance is not merely rhetorical in the documentary; as Hern moves around and engages others, viewers witness a living and in-motion reassertion of a mode of life prior to and beyond Euro-American humanism. It is in noticing and experiencing Hern as living something in excess of or beyond Euro-American humanism that one sees the potential for another account of freedom not dissimilar to what

Hern's ancestors would have known and lived, and analogous to the earlier claim made about Equiano.

Of course, history has intervened, as Stuart Hall has taught us so well. We must now carve out and invent a freedom that is unshackled from Euro-American humanism—a freedom that emerges from the encounters of European expansion, and one that exceeds its ideological formations. To do so means we will have to encounter each other within and against the world-orienting forces of Euro-American humanism. It is a task worth pursuing. The late Caribbean novelist, essayist, and activist George Lamming (1995, 25) understood the task as one of invention. He is writing of the Caribbean region, but I think his idea is bigger than the region. He theorizes what decolonization might be, and then says, "And that is the most urgent task and the greatest intellectual challenge: how to control the burden of this history and incorporate it into our collective sense of the future."

NOTE

1 I draw from Mignolo, who writes, "The decolonial paradigm struggles to bring into intervening existence an-other interpretation that brings forward, on the one hand, a silenced view of the event and, on the other, shows the limits of imperial ideology disguised as the true (and total) interpretation of the events" (2005, 33). This is why I see anticolonial and decolonial as phases or stages toward decolonization and thus freedom or liberation.

WORKS CITED

Brathwaite, Kamau. 2006. *Middle Passages: A Lecture*. Toronto: Sandberry.
Carby, Hazel V. 2022. "We Must Burn Them." *London Review of Books*, May 26, 2022. https://www.lrb.co.uk/the-paper/v44/n10/hazel-v.-carby/we-must-burn-them.
Castillo, Monica. 2021. Review of *Exterminate All the Brutes*. RogerEbert.com. https://www.rogerebert.com/reviews/exterminate-all-the-brutes-tv-review-2021.
Césaire, Aimé. 2000. *Discourse on Colonialism*. Translated by Joan Pinkham. New York: Monthly Review Press.
Equiano, Olaudah. 1789. *The Interesting Narrative of the Life of Olaudah Equiano, or Gustavus Vassa, the African*. https://www.gutenberg.org/files/15399/15399-h/15399-h.htm.
Fanon, Frantz. 1963. *The Wretched of the Earth*. Translated by Constance Farrington. New York: Grove.

Gilroy, Paul. 2010. *Darker than Blue: On the Moral Economies of Black Atlantic Culture*. Cambridge, MA: Belknap Press of Harvard University Press.

Hale, Mike. 2021. "Review: 'Exterminate All the Brutes' Rewrites a Brutal History." *New York Times*, April 6, 2021. https://www.nytimes.com/2021/04/06/arts/television/review-exterminate-all-the-brutes.html.

Lamming, George. 1995. *Coming, Coming Home: Conversations II: Western Education and the Caribbean Intellectual*. Philipsburg, St. Martin: House of Nehesi.

Marriott, David. 2018. *Whither Fanon: Studies in the Blackness of Being*. Stanford, CA: Stanford University Press.

Mignolo, Walter. 2005. *The Idea of Latin America*. Malden, MA: Blackwell.

Morrison, Toni. 1990. *Playing in the Dark: Whiteness and the Literary Imagination*. Cambridge, MA: Harvard University Press.

Trouillot, Michel-Rolph. 2021. "Discipline and Perish." In *The Michel-Rolph Trouillot Reader*, edited by Yarimar Bonilla, Greg Beckett and Mayanthi L. Fernando, 235–38. Durham, NC: Duke University Press.

Vergès, Françoise. 2021. *A Decolonial Feminism*. Translated by Ashley J. Bohrer. London: Pluto.

Wynter, Sylvia. 1990. "On Disenchanting Discourse: 'Minority' Literary Criticisms and Beyond." In *The Nature and Context of Minority Discourse*, edited by Abdul JanMohamed and David Lloyd, 432–69. New York: Oxford University Press.

Wynter, Sylvia. 2003. "Unsettling the Coloniality of Being/Power/Truth/Freedom: Towards the Human, After Man, Its Overrepresentation—An Argument." *CR: The New Centennial Review* 3 (3): 257–337.

INTERLUDE

Codeswitch

The Transborder Immigrant Tool

Veronika Zablotsky

Developed by the artivist collective Electronic Disturbance Theatre (EDT) 2.0 while in virtual residency with the Sanctuary Spaces Sawyer Seminar, "Code*s*witch: The Transborder Immigrant Tool" is a choral reading of excerpts and *switches* that mobilizes "transborder algo-rhythms against caging algorithms" across multiple sites—including a live broadcast from the US-Mexico border—through readings of poetry, queer-feminist analysis, statistical records, haunting lamentations, prerecorded audio and video fragments, images, historical maps, and source code.[1] It is based on "Codeswitch: The Transborder Immigrant Tool" (2014), a collection of poetry, prose, and source code designed to guide border crossers to safety sites across the Sonoran Desert with a GPS-enabled Android mobile device. Inviting the audience to reflect on the ethics of witnessing in relation to border surveillance, "undocumentation," and physical/virtual capture, the virtual play constellates into a political gesture of solidarity with people on the move who are forced into hostile terrain by the US Customs and Border Patrol's 1994 "Prevention Through Deterrence" policy.

Featuring micha cárdenas, Amy Sara Carroll, Ricardo Dominguez, Elle Mehrmand, and Brett Stalbaum, the five members of EDT 2.0, this "play-performance-app-poem-song-essay" exposes the necropolitical violence of liberal humanism/humanitarianism and generates aesthetic strategies of disruption that facilitate flight. By inserting the register of the poetic and experimental arts to "ghost" the border and disappear *it*, rather than migrants, EDT 2.0 hails the "glitch" (Russell 2020) as a crack in the hegemonic status quo that opens onto different worlds of political being—or "androidism"—beyond "Man as the Rational Self and political subject of the state" (Wynter 2003, 281).

NOTE

1 The convening "Codeswitch: The Transborder Immigrant Tool" can be viewed at https://challengeinequality.luskin.ucla.edu/codeswitch-the-transborder-immigrant-tool.

WORKS CITED

Electronic Disturbance Theatre 2.0 and b.a.n.g. lab. 2014. "Codeswitch: The Transborder Immigrant Tool." University of Michigan, Ann Arbor.

Russell, Legacy. 2020. *Glitch Feminism: A Manifesto*. New York: Verso.

UCLA Luskin Institute on Inequality and Democracy. 2021. *Codeswitch: The Transborder Immigrant Tool*. Featuring micha cárdenas, Amy Sara Carroll, Ricardo Dominguez, Ella Mehrmand, and Brett Stalbaum. April 23, 2021. https://challengeinequality.luskin.ucla.edu/codeswitch-the-transborder-immigrant-tool.

Wynter, Sylvia. 2003. "Unsettling the Coloniality of Being/Power/Truth/Freedom: Towards the Human, After Man, Its Overrepresentation—An Argument." CR: *The New Centennial Review* 3 (3): 257–337.

CONCLUSION

Sanctuary and the Praxis of Solidarity

*Gaye Theresa Johnson
and Leisy J. Abrego*

On the evening of March 27, 2023, a fire at a detention center in Ciudad Juárez run by the Mexican National Migration Institute (INM) killed forty people. The victims—Central and South American migrants who were aiming to seek asylum in the United States—were protesting the overcrowded conditions and lack of access to water in the facility. Videos released later showed that Mexican migration agents did nothing to free the men—guards are recorded walking away—even when the smoke from the fire thickened and flames were visible. Mainstream news offered differing accounts of what happened and who was to blame. Yet this was not an isolated incident. One person died and fourteen were injured in a 2020 fire at a Tabasco detention center. In Dessau, Germany, in 2005, Guinean migrant Oury Jalloh died while tied to a mattress in a suspicious fire in a holding cell (see chapter 4). In Guatemala City in March 2017, a similarly horrific incident killed forty girls in a state-run home. And in 2024, a three-month-old migrant girl died of cardiac arrest in a migrant shelter in Queens, New York. Her family and thousands of other migrants faced below-freezing temperatures in an ongoing housing crisis imposed by Mayor Eric Adams. In each of these cases, government-run institutions—whether in the country of birth, transit, or destination—demonstrated an abject disregard for human life.

Over and over, governments fail to provide refuge for migrants or would-be migrants and to members of the most marginalized communities.

In a world where hoarding wealth and prioritizing profits over human beings is normalized, nation-states dehumanize those who do not produce financial value. Especially in countries that fashion themselves as emblematic of Western humanism, the disidentification from humanity is so pervasive that immigration authorities and government agents at every level of authority feel permitted—indeed, empowered—to look away from suffering and ignore anguish. People desperate for refuge and sanctuary from the political, environmental, and economic consequences of neoliberal capitalism in their own homelands find, therefore, the opposite of safety and human regard on the shores of Greece, on the riversides of Germany, in the towns of Mexico, and in the urban centers of Guatemala. While mainstream news sources blamed migrants and would-be refugees for their own deaths, the people around them, their families and fellow migrants, name the truth: #FueElEstado (the state is to blame).

Like those truth-tellers, the authors in this book look beneath the surface of mainstream messaging to document the conditions of precarity that force people to risk their lives for a chance at life; they describe instances of deep resistance in multiple moments and contexts; they call us to rethink what is possible when we work collectively to see ourselves in each other's humanity; and they inspire us to build our own forms of sanctuary in radically reimagined practices of solidarity.

Western humanism suggests that countries and their governments are the torch-bearers for protection, refuge, and sanctuary. Politicians exhort settler-colonial laws and systems of order as the only ones that will keep us safe; subjects are asked to imagine themselves into those frameworks of human rights. Yet as scholars of gendered colonial racial capitalism, we know that the promise of democracy under these terms of order is an illusion. Ananya Roy along with Maite Zubiaurre and Veronika Zablotsky in the foreword and introduction to this volume invite us to consider insightful questions, and we insist on finding answers: Who counts as human in the language of human rights? What is sanctuary? How can sanctuary also be liberatory? And how do we, as scholars, seed and nourish academic rebellion within the imperial university? Indeed, these are the questions at the core of each of the chapters in this volume. Each author grounds their piece in a unique yet complementary vision of how we are already learning, how we can experience, create, and sustain liberation through reimagined practices of refuge and sanctuary.

Power, Wealth Hoarding, Borders, and Sanctuary

We commenced our Sawyer Seminar in 2019, just before the global COVID-19 pandemic. Since then, the landscape of what we understand as sanctuary and who we understand refugees to be—and especially what nation-states understand their responsibility to them to be—have changed drastically. The pandemic came to provide yet another "boogeyman," as De Genova (chapter 10) so clearly labels the War on Terror and the Cold War before it. Illness as another type of boogeyman requires more extreme closing off from a growing set of "others." It is what has allowed for the new spectacle at the border. Drawing on language that centers the protection of qualifying national subjects (those with citizenship, those with employment, those who are able-bodied, those who are white, and acceptable minoritized communities—and even when they are not actually protected, as Smythe underscores in chapter 13), administrations have changed refugee and asylum practices, often in egregiously illegal ways, to block most immigrants from entering the United States. National and international refugee and asylum policies notwithstanding, migrants are denied their legal claims to enter. The settler-colonial legal order will not save us.

And yet masses of people continue to flee for various complex reasons, needing safety from petty crime, but also from state securitization practices. Those masses are forced to live in encampments on the street, photographed and shown around the world, to teach others to stay away. In 2023, the Biden administration asked the US Congress to increase the budget for the US Customs and Border Protection and the US Immigration and Customs Enforcement agencies by about $800 million to a record high of nearly $25 billion in a single year. Similarly, in the European Union, the border and coast guard agency, Frontex, has a higher budget than any other single EU agency (Akkerman 2023). Such a rise in immigration enforcement suggests a move toward greater tightening of borders, keeping out the most marginalized and doubling down on an abject disregard for human life (chapters 10 and 13). At the time of this writing, Israel is committing genocide in Palestine. By October 2024, the Israeli invasion of Gaza, in the aftermath of the October 7, 2023, attack by Hamas and other armed groups, had killed over 41,000 people—many of them children. Biden's support for Israel, Ukraine, and Taiwan is itself a blatant effort to consolidate US power abroad and to align it with various neocolonialist projects. He urged Congress to grant him $100 billion in supplementary military aid for all three countries, and his promise, in exchange for this aid, was to shut down the US-Mexico border if granted emergency authority to do so. Borders continue to work efficiently in the service of colonial racial capitalism, not just at the physical borders but in every interior pocket of nation-states.

Indeed, borders played a key role during the pandemic, when the world bore witness to the unprecedented transnational wealth-building for the richest nations—and individuals. As capital moved freely across borders, the justification of wealth accumulation in the midst of such widespread human suffering necessitated a reification of the hegemonizing project of national belonging that has been so central to what Walcott terms "Euro-American humanism" (chapter 15). In the United States, attacks on labor, immigrants, Black people, reproductive rights, trans rights, unhoused people, and those otherwise living in poverty increased exponentially as the right sought to solidify its power ahead of the fall 2020 presidential election. A characteristic strategy of wealth accumulation on this scale requires a changing and escalating vilification of the "other" in multiple forms.

By the middle of 2020, the world bore witness to the creation of an atmosphere of fear and xenophobia so pervasive that the right could justify without qualification the denigration of immigrant lives and rights in the name of border security. Black and Brown people were being killed for doing nothing more than being in their own homes and places of work (Smythe, in chapter 13); women's and trans people's autonomy came into serious peril. All of this occurred amid the forging of new alliances among elites of nations that prize globalized finance over human life. Destabilizing the welfare state was justified as the necessary cost of solidifying our place in a highly dynamic and unstable international marketplace. Meanwhile, at the border, because they are fleeing governments headed by self-proclaimed socialists, Venezuelans and Nicaraguans are allowed to enter to apply for asylum within the United States. Their numbers on the rosters of asylum seekers add strength to US tropes about capitalism's global superiority and necessity.

Border regimes produce death and various spectacles of violence (De Genova, chapter 10), but not for everyone. At their core, these processes are also informed by structures of and affinities with white supremacy. That is, as solid as the metaphorical border wall is when it blocks Haitian, Honduran, Maya Guatemalan, and Cameroonian immigrants from entering, it is equally open for Ukrainian immigrants and their pets (Laurel 2022). While Haitian and Central American asylum seekers languish in Mexico for months and years, displaced white refugees from allied nations are instantly legible to the world as refugees. Black refugees on the US-Mexico border are made to run from the whips of mounted Border Patrol agents, and those in ships in the Mediterranean Sea run out of fuel and go adrift while European nations debate about who should be forced to accept them (Haq, Magee, and Nadeau 2023). But white immigrants from friendly nations are placed on the "fast track" for asylum resources and vast social and economic support from the most patriotic US and EU citizens.

What is the function of sanctuary in this context, when not everyone is perceived or treated as having full humanity? And, as De Genova articulates, "for all those who don't die, what's the consequence of that trauma?" Is it possible, as Smythe invites us to do, to develop a "Black poietic register of mattering beyond the confines of citizenship," as full human beings who resist joyously outside of state authority and settler logics? Collectively, in this volume, we are also interested in the possibilities for living a poetics and politics of true sanctuary (chapters 1, 6, 11, 12, and 13).

Fugitivity and Sanctuary, Abolition and Liberation

In the face of these ongoing and long-standing problems, the practices of fugitivity and sanctuary that inspire the chapters in this book dwell in the inspired intersections of migrant imaginaries, prison abolition, and Land Back. The convening of artists and public intellectuals around visions of freedom and liberation in this book illuminates languages and affinities across historical moments, spaces, struggles, and communities of resistance and refusal. Drawing from their work, we sketch here what we believe to be the collective "diagnosis" of this moment, as well as the collective statement made by this group of scholars, and why it is so vital in this historical era.

The first thread that comes alive across the chapters reveals that this moment is not unlike others in many respects. World history is riddled with examples of abject humanity. Antiblackness and anti-Indigeneity have been central to the global project of gendered colonial racial capitalism (see chapters 2, 3, 14, and 15) and imperialism (chapters 8 and 12). Their consistency over so much of modern history means that current approaches to democracy, peace, or justice will simply not suffice. Fighting for rights within the settler-colonial legal frameworks of Western humanism has always and will only continue to reproduce new, adapted versions of white supremacy (chapter 13). As Walcott argues (chapter 15), Europe's purported project toward freedom has always actually been a project toward "unfreedom"; instead, the establishment of a true program of liberation requires us to name "Euro-American humanism" as a form of "profound speciated violence" that must end for a new "being-ness" to be imagined and practiced.

This option for radical solidarities first names the violence of colonial racial capitalism (chapters 3 and 15) and then rejects Western humanism's logics of supposed freedom through democracy (chapter 13).

The authors collectively move us to consider that decolonial solidarities from below are the most promising paths to real liberation. In moments of crisis, whether in refugee encampments that are the very legacies of colonial history (chapter 7) or in the midst of political and legal violence that happens during shifts in administrations (chapter 5), those who are most directly and negatively impacted are also the most visionary in their organizing. Today's refugee camps, made up of white standardized boxes in Greece or small bare tents in northern Mexico, serve to produce "totalitarian environments for controlling the 'other' (of whatever origin)" (chapter 7). Yet despite such production of bare life, these conditions of unfreedom and carcerality cannot entirely break the human spirit. There are always the potentialities of survival, creativity, agency, and solidarity. Forced outside of the purported protections of nation-states, members of marginalized communities are often able to execute powerful, even if sometimes makeshift, political projects in the face of vast challenges (chapters 6, 11, and 13). In seeking survival, they effectuate reimagined notions of home that are only possible through wide-ranging solidarities across national and racial groups, over expansive geographies (chapters 4, 12, and 13) often rooted in multiple forms of love (chapters 1 and 5). Radical mutualities can be forged in refuge, even in the barest of circumstances and even across diverse groups (chapter 9)—and that gives us hope.

As the authors in this volume demonstrate, radical solidarities can be rooted in multiple approaches and take various forms. One powerful path is through the Black radical tradition, which takes a materialist abolitionist perspective that considers the "prisons and the detention centers, the migrant boats, borderscapes, and the urban concentrations of houseless people and working-poor classes" as those who have been left out of capitalist possibilities for survival and makes their un-breathing the target for change, as Thompson writes (chapter 4). Breathing, as a central, necessary act of life for any human, is also what allows us to be in the world and in relation with one another, Thompson argues. Breathing, in this sense, offers a path of relationality that leads to solidarity as a method out of carcerality and away from the chokehold that is racial capitalism.

In the both/and project of abolition that requires us to both attend to the crisis and dismantle the structures that produce ongoing crises (Davis et al. 2022), we need creative spaces to envision pathways to abolition. Rooted in acknowledgment and repair (chapter 1), abolition is possible through a radical reimagination of our present moment, particularly through creative conceptions and artistic production. While Zionist and other imperial projects use (often unimaginative) art to convey their messages (chapter 8), artistic creation is vast and allows for endless possibilities of resistance and refusal that move us toward liberation. When nation-states legislate and impose erasure and forgetting to deny the violent consequences of their regimes, artists remember and make victims whole by representing them anew. While mainstream messaging and logics that sustain gendered colonial racial capitalism are always already stacked against justice (chapters 8 and 11), art and creative reimaginings both remind the world of marginalized people's humanity and create new worlds and practices that are not centered around profit-making (chapters 5, 6, 9, and 12) or under the rules of the state (chapter 13).

Beyond the possibilities available through the imagination, Indigenous cosmologies also open up immense and important possibilities for solidarity and peace (chapters 2 and 14). Being in good relation with people and the world around us forces us to move outside of the rules and structures of gendered colonial racial capitalism and its ills. That is, to build solidarity, we must maintain "relationships built on reciprocity and care for all living things—humans and nonhumans," as Kyle Mays writes (chapter 14). This requires that we begin to live as "good ancestors," as "guests," as Sepulveda states; this, he argues, "invites everyone to radically imagine a future based on mutual obligation, reciprocity, responsibility, and healthy human-land kinship(s). Becoming kuuyam is a way of living in this world for the generations yet to come—as good ancestors—beyond the social death of conquest" (chapter 2).

In broad strokes, the current political climate in the Global North can be characterized by a right that has weaponized the concept of sanctuary to deem it immoral and unacceptable while the institutionalized left has idealized and depoliticized it in response. To counter such erasures, the conversations made possible through the Sawyer Seminar in the series of videos and the chapters in this book travel across time, lingering in spaces and moments that take up the actions and imaginaries of Black radicalism, Indigenous sovereignty and land rights, and migrant poetics. Contributing participants and authors theorize hospitality and fugitivity in ways that move us toward freedom. Taken together, these convenings are an incitement, an invitation to make worlds that not only acknowledge and repair but do so in expansive, meaningful, and sustainable ways because they are committed to abolition, mutuality, solidarity, and joy.

The speakers and authors teach us that commitment to abolition, mutuality, and alternative traditions of humanism, especially those rooted in colonial relationalities and histories of fugitivity, are to be mobilized and enacted. Abolition and "mino-bimaadiziwin, which means 'the good life'" in Anishinaabe (chapter 14), can flourish through intellectual mobilities and artistic interventions. Like this book, the process is messy and complex, filled with ideas that are grounded in similar but very particular contexts. The book is not intended to solve or resolve the issues we face when we begin to think together about these intersecting (and often competing) issues. Instead, the collection provides generative starting points and a call to come together to build a liberated world. The practices of sanctuary and marronage that inspire the chapters in this book dwell in the imaginative intersections of prison abolition and Land Back, made possible through the convening of artists and public intellectuals around visions of freedom and fugitivity. Through the creation of new languages and affinities across historical moments, spaces, struggles, and communities of resistance and refusal, the authors in this volume collectively and resoundingly declare: we are the ones who imagine the terms of our freedom, and we are the ones who will bring freedom into being. More than merely describing the potentialities of radical sanctuary, the authors bring into being new communities and epistemologies that make radical humanism possible in the present moment.

Using This Volume as a Liberatory Pedagogical Tool

As social justice researchers and professors, it is critically important for us to consider questions about how we engage in our work in liberatory ways, including how we might teach a volume such as this in the present moment. Teaching about the deeply held meanings of cultural and political work in impacted communities requires us to work, listen, and learn alongside organizers and artists, and in solidarity with those whose lives are directly shaped by the forces created in opposition to their humanity. As teachers engaging the legacies of colonial violence and conditions of unfreedom that variously impact our students and communities of learning, as scholars who ground our curricula in the radical solidarities and Indigenous cosmologies that provide the visions and practice for the world we want, we are compelled to use these videos and essays as more than intellectual interventions, but rather as instructions on how to write community practices into our work.

In studying the grounds of dispossession that underpin migration regimes (introduction), we endeavor to understand not only the material evidence of colonial legacies but also the insidious persistence of hidden forms of oppression infinitely more damaging for the morale and trust-building necessary for our communities to maintain opposition to its totalizing possibilities. This volume invites us to train our ears and eyes to understand how creating sanctuary on occupied lands can sometimes and alternately be a radical act of home-making or an act of complicity in the capitalist logics of humanitarianism. As teachers who treat our classrooms and learning spaces as communities, we are at once creating the trust we know we need for radical new understandings of what freedom entails, and we are also deeply committed to teaching ways of both doing and being. Without radical self-reflection about our own identities and complicities in this historical moment, and without the radical love and reciprocity required to sustain the alliances necessary for resistance, we are simply teaching words and ideas.

The essays in this book remind us that there are situated knowledges indispensable to understanding the mutuality and interrelatedness of antiracism and Indigenous sovereignty, and that the theory we are waiting for has been within and waiting for us in the ancestral knowledges of hospitality (chapter 2), theater pedagogies of the Electronic Disturbance Theater (chapter 9), and the organized and spontaneous resistance to logics of containment in Europe, Mexico, Brazil, the Mediterranean, and the United States. It is in Achille Mbembe's reminder that we have power to imagine and enact more democratic futures. It is in Robin D. G. Kelley's call to "acknowledge our attachment to each other . . . in relations other than property relations . . . [in a] love letter that is written without a guarantee of a response" (Kelley 2022, 35). Therefore, to teach this book, one must begin with the fact that as students and researchers, we may not have all the answers, but as community members, we can be fully resourced in networks of reciprocity and mutual learning. When we begin from this place, we can no longer believe the lie that anyone but the people themselves are experts in and designers of the world in which they want to live.

Students exposed to this ontology as the premise for radical scholarship need to see it enacted, more than merely described. As we ask them to question and trouble normative assumptions, we must also demonstrate a fearlessness and frankness about the role of the academy in acts of displacement and disenfranchisement, policing and surveillance, carceral investment, and the perpetuation of generational wealth. This can result in innovative assignments that ask students to notice and research where those things are concretely occurring in the life of the university, as a way to understand the web of complicity woven by capitalist institutions. Tracing wealth, liberating and imaginatively redirecting resources such as research funding and services provided for university students, help students to understand the ways that wealth and privilege operate, even for those of us who feel marginalized by the institution.

All of this requires frank conversations about the role of the institution, the ethics of community-engaged scholarship, and the most grounded modes of being in community with organizers and artists in ways that respect long-established relationships and networks. In the spirit of collaboration with fellow professors and students using this volume, we offer the following narrative of our own experiences over the past few years that we hope will inspire you to consider how to use these ideas in your classrooms.

> *Gaye: In January 2017, I returned to the classroom after a one-quarter teaching leave. I recall feeling relieved that I had been spared teaching during the tumultuous presidential election of fall 2016. I knew the content I was accustomed to teaching would be more relevant and charged than ever, so I welcomed the time away from the classroom to process these events. Naively, I figured that by January, the United States would have settled into the new reality and my students and I would watch this historical moment unfold with at least some detachment.*
>
> *More than six hundred students were enrolled in my course, and I commenced as I had for many years, by introducing students to concepts of social justice and systemic power. When I teach courses like Introduction to Chicana/o Studies or Introduction to Race and Racism, my process is to expand students' understandings of how power works in the world by getting them to see systemic oppression over centuries of colonization and racism. By the fourth week of the course, I introduce them to a new way of seeing history: from the perspective of those who are not simply subjects of oppression, but agents of change. We linger on the social movements and cultural practices that have sustained marginalized communities. I introduce them to community organizations and organizers who show how this is being done. I had no reason to think this wouldn't work in January 2017. I enjoyed wonderful reviews of my instruction for as long as I had followed this process. But within a few weeks, something unexpected happened that profoundly expanded my teaching and philosophy about civic engagement.*
>
> *On January 25, President Trump signed an executive order that directed the US government to begin constructing a wall along the southern*

border with Mexico. The order also increased and prolonged jailing of asylum seekers, and permitted expedited deportation procedures. Many of my students were immigrants, many of them undocumented or the children of undocumented parents. Some of them were waiting for a family member to return from a trip to their home country. Two days later, President Trump signed a second executive order that became known as the "Muslim ban," prohibiting foreign nationals from seven predominantly Muslim countries from visiting the country for ninety days. It suspended entry to the United States of all Syrian refugees indefinitely, and refused any other refugees from coming into the country for 120 days—a stretch of time that could mean the difference between life or death for someone fleeing to the United States for political or health reasons. In less than a week, my Muslim and Latinx immigrant students were living a very different reality.

As I stood on the stage of my classroom, I could see the fear in their eyes and hear it in the questions they asked. Because we were in the first few weeks of the class, we were studying how structural oppression has historically resulted in dispossession, vulnerability, poverty, and family separation. I pushed on, knowing there was no more relevant moment for this material. But the next week I faltered. When I looked out at my students, I saw that I wasn't just expanding their sense of historical context; I was contributing to the growing terror they were feeling. I had always known that many of my students don't have the privilege of studying these issues from a "safe" distance. But now it was much worse: they felt anguish and fear for themselves and their families in a very different way. Students visited me during office hours; some cried, and others quietly wondered if I could tell them what would happen next.

By the time of the next class session, the new government administration was threatening prolonged and indefinite detention of asylum seekers. That day I paused in mid-lecture, unsure of how to continue. I realized that what I was teaching was not aligned with how students needed to learn in this historical moment. For the first time in my career, I was at a loss. What did we need? After all these years of successful teaching, it was clear I needed to change my approach. But how? What was my role and purpose as a faculty member at this moment?

Standing silently on the classroom stage in January 2017, I decided to be transparent. I told my students about the confusion I was having.

I had been a professor for fifteen years, and the way I taught my courses had been transformative for many students who had never seen their communities reflected in their classrooms. Students had often left my classes feeling hopeful and inspired. But it didn't feel that way now, and I needed to know more about why.

I realized that before that humbling moment on my classroom stage, the foundation of my community-engaged work was mostly about a commitment to the application and liberation of resources in public-facing institutions, which I believe are meant to serve the public. I invited organizers and artists to speak in my classes. But now I realized I was saying one thing and doing another: I was lifting up the situated knowledge of folks on the ground, but I wasn't showing students how to listen to what community folks needed, and to trust them. Everywhere we looked, we saw broken branches. But there is a forest of possibility that the history of community resilience and movement building offers us. No wonder we felt despair and a sense of lost purpose about the usefulness of our studies and skills—most of them gained through privileges that most people don't have. I needed to show my students what happens when we listen to what organizers, advocates, and artists know and practice better than academics: that the work goes on, that people keep going, as long as they have each other. Students need a way to create a strong connection between the usefulness of our studies and skills and the methods that movement building offers.

I started asking different questions about the role and purpose of community engagement. My questions changed from "What can we do for movement organizers?" to "How does our work change when we trust those who know?" This was a powerful and humbling shift for me as a professor in a research institution who was used to being "the expert," and it was due to the accountability made possible by my students and community partners in the early months of 2017. For the rest of that course, organizers, artists, and members of community-based organizations came into my classroom and shared a more empowering vision of the present moment. Together, my students and I discovered that the antidote to the despair we were experiencing was to meaningfully connect to movements that we profess to study. Students learned from organizers that movement work also has its challenges, that there are many toxic practices within struggle, and that movement dynamics can also cause harm. But we created and committed to an ever-

changing system of deeply caring for each other, with the hope that some piece of it would endure, reincarnate, and live again when we needed it.

Since then I have shared about the power of this experience with Leisy, and before the start of any new class we reach out to people whose work aligns with the course learnings. Our community partners over the years include Hunger Action LA, California Latinas for Reproductive Justice, the California Coalition for Reproductive Freedom, Los Angeles Co-op Lab, Mateo25 (a network of ecumenical asylum workers), the Downtown Women's Action Coalition, Healing Hearts Restoring Hope, the Central American Resource Center, and the National TPS (Temporary Protected Status) Alliance. Our students have studied the city and history of Los Angeles through the lenses of asylum work, hunger, reproductive justice, houselessness among women and children, worker co-ops, and restorative justice. By being responsible for projects that include mapping public reproductive-health services for low-income communities across Los Angeles County and developing media kits for immigrants' legislative visits, they have learned about the extreme disparity in care and opportunities for pregnant women and young families, and about the kind of collective care needed to support legally vulnerable immigrants.

Students learned from organizers that it was better for women to approach unhoused women and children to conduct surveys and for those who identified as men to take notes, a different perspective on work and gender for many involved. As part of their research paper, this same group wrote about witnessing how profoundly women and children are affected by eviction, which fundamentally changed their views on gender and the power of rent stabilization. They realized that anyone can ask, "Why do women who are poor continue to have children?" but students who learn from reproductive-health and housing-justice workers will ask more humane and productive questions: "How strong are the resources for women of color and poor women in our society? What kind of access is available for birth control, prenatal care, and postnatal care?"

Some students in our classes couldn't have imagined feeling compassion and understanding for an incarcerated person who had been released early from prison for participating in a restorative justice group. Yet they watched organizers refuse to simply discard community members who had harmed others, and they learned that prison is not the

> *answer. Students became curious about why most of the people who are in prison are from poor and marginalized communities. One group learned from food justice organizers that stable housing and effective transportation are fundamental to food security. When they completed their assignment for Hunger Action LA, students asked if there was anything further they could do. The executive director shared that one reason seniors didn't use their food stamps at farmers markets might be that they had low vision and needed a ride or assistance with shopping. The next Saturday, many of my students were walking beside elders as they chose organic produce.*

All of the research produced in these classes is offered to our community partners to use in grant applications, resource mapping, social media platform design, fundraising, social media training, video content generation, updating of their own research, and refining the language around their roles in the communities they serve. Today, before we begin writing a syllabus for a civically engaged course, we meet with activists to understand what they need and want and we craft the course toward that end. In Gaye's first lecture to students, she reframes what it means to be a community-engaged scholar in a public institution, emphasizing foundational points she learned from her own mentors, specifically in the scholarship and teaching of George Lipsitz:

- Learning about community from community members requires focus and discipline.
- There is fascinating research to conduct, not statements to proclaim or victims to save.
- Realizing freedom entails what might seem like a lot of ordinary work.
- We are empowered to take stock of the actual skills we have, many of them the result of privileges that have often been denied to marginalized communities.

All of this work has led Gaye to a greater capacity to lead diverse and dynamic groups of students in reimagining who they are and what they can be together. For both of us, teaching at a university opens up one of our many communities of activism, as researchers and teachers finding ways to bring these areas of work into common conversation.

The chapters in this volume help us to further strengthen our vision and practice in the classroom. Because we study the ways that colonial and state violence impact the communities with whom we wish to think and work alongside toward freedom, we often encounter what feels like overwhelming stories of organized white supremacy designed to humiliate, subordinate, and destroy our communities. As we attend to the multiple crises of late capitalism in community with front-line movement leaders, we might become confused, imagining the ground littered with broken promises to our people and those with whom we remain in solidarity. We might imagine that the most impactful things worth teaching are the stories designed to shock our students into action. But history and humanity have shown us that the greatest motivation for change is sourced not only from being sick and tired but also from believing deeply in the power and potential of our beloved communities and knowing that they are entitled to freedom, sovereignty, and safety. The antidote to broken promises is to meaningfully connect to movements and lived conditions that we profess to study. There is no shortage of resilience, fortitude, leadership, nor plans in radical teaching and public intellectualism. In the work toward collective liberation, if despair and anger are all we feel, we are looking in the wrong places.

WORKS CITED

Akkerman, Mark. 2023. "Global Spending on Immigration Enforcement Is Higher Than Ever and Rising." Migration Policy Institute, May 31, 2023. https://www.migrationpolicy.org/article/immigration-enforcement-spending-rising.

Davis, Angela Y., Gina Dent, Erica R. Meiners, and Beth Richie. 2022. *Abolition. Feminism. Now.* Chicago: Haymarket.

Haq, Sana Noor, Caolán Magee, and Barbie Latza Nadeau. 2023. "Europe's Migration Policies in Chaos as Arrivals Surge." CNN, April 16, 2023. https://www.cnn.com/2023/04/16/europe/europe-migration-chaos-boat-arrivals-intl/index.html.

Kelley, Robin D. G. 2022. *Freedom Dreams: The Black Radical Imagination.* Boston: Beacon.

Laurel, Anna. 2022. "San Diego Humane Society, CDC Partner to Help Pets of Ukrainian Refugees Cross Border." CBS 8, May 3, 2022. https://www.cbs8.com/article/life/animals/san-diego-humane-society-cdc-help-pets-ukrainian/509-69eb15c2-b417-4a58-abb2-8a00b05a670e.

ACKNOWLEDGMENTS

The Sanctuary Spaces endeavor, and now this book, *Beyond Sanctuary*, was made possible by a Mellon Foundation Sawyer Seminar grant for which Ananya Roy was PI along with co-PIs Leisy J. Abrego, Gaye Theresa Johnson, Maite Zubiaurre, and postdoctoral fellow Veronika Zablotsky. Unfolding in the midst of a global pandemic as well as the Trump regime, the project was both urgently necessary and yet difficult to convene. We wish to thank the tireless and creative efforts of the staff at the UCLA Luskin Institute on Inequality and Democracy, where the Sawyer Seminar was housed, notably deputy director Marisa Lemorande and former programs manager Vania Sciolini, as well as graduate student researchers Zachary Mondesire and Kali Tambreé and dissertation fellows AnMarie R. Mendoza and Rosanna Simons. We are grateful for the editorial vision and support provided by Elizabeth Ault at Duke University Press. Andrew Ascherl compiled the index for this book.

CONTRIBUTORS

Names listed per the order of the table of contents

Ananya Roy is professor of urban planning, social welfare, and geography and the Meyer and Renee Luskin Chair in Inequality and Democracy at the University of California, Los Angeles. She is founding director of the UCLA Luskin Institute on Inequality and Democracy, which advances scholarship concerned with displacement and dispossession in Los Angeles and elsewhere in the world. Ananya's work has focused on urban transformations and land grabs as well as on global capital and predatory financialization. Her current scholarship, organized through insurgent research collectives, is concerned with "racial banishment," the expulsion of working-class communities of color from cities through racialized policing and other forms of state-organized violence. Ananya was named a Freedom Scholar by the Marguerite Casey Foundation in 2020.

Maite Zubiaurre has a PhD in comparative literature from Columbia University, New York, and is presently a professor in the humanities at UCLA. Before joining UCLA, she taught at UT Austin, UNAM (Mexico), ITAM (México), and USC, Los Angeles. She has been deeply involved with the study and teaching of migration and borderland cultures during her whole academic career and at various institutions both in the United States and in Mexico. Zubiaurre is the author of numerous publications, and the co-director, co-producer, and co-writer, with Kristy Guevara-Flanagan, of *Aguilas* (2021), an Oscar-shortlisted and multiple-award-winning short documentary on migrant death at the US-Mexico border and the search and rescue efforts of the volunteer group Aguilas del Desierto / Desert Eagles. Filomena Cruz is Zubiaurre's nom de plume as a visual artist and the creator of the Venice Beach, California–based art practice and artistic urban intervention "The Wall That Gives / El Muro Que Da."

Veronika Zablotsky is a political theorist with an interest in interconnected histories of migration and empire; feminist and postcolonial studies; transnational social movements; Armenian diaspora studies; and postsocialism in the SWANA region. She teaches in the Department of Philosophy at Freie Universität Berlin and held visiting professorships in politics and gender studies at Justus-Liebig-Universität Gießen and Universität Koblenz in Germany. Previously she served as Andrew W. Mellon Postdoctoral Fellow in the Sawyer Seminar "Sanctuary Spaces: Reworlding Humanism" at the UCLA Luskin Institute on Inequality and Democracy. She holds a PhD in feminist studies, politics, critical race and ethnic studies, and history of consciousness from the University of California, Santa Cruz. Among her co-edited publications are the anthologies *Decolonize the City!* (Unrast, 2017) and *Transforming Solidarities* (Adocs, 2025). At the University of Pennsylvania she co-founded the Critical Armenian Studies Collective. She also organizes with the scholar activist collective Abolition Beyond Borders (www.abolitionismus.org).

Gaye Theresa Johnson is an associate professor of Chicana/o, Central American, and African American Studies at UCLA. A historian of freedom struggles and cultural politics, she is also a lead facilitator and trainer in healing justice. Johnson's first book, *Spaces of Conflict, Sounds of Solidarity: Music, Race, and Spatial Entitlement* (University of California Press, 2013), is a cultural history of political coalition-building and spatial struggles among Black and Brown freedom seekers in Los Angeles. Johnson's second book, *Futures of Black Radicalism* (co-edited with Alexander Lubin), is animated by and in tribute to the Black radical tradition. In its third edition, *Futures of Black Radicalism* (Verso, 2017) has been translated into German, and selected chapters into Japanese. Johnson is an award-winning scholar and community-engaged teacher, and an advocate for grassroots organizing and policy advocacy in reproductive justice, farmworkers' rights, and ethnic studies. She has written curriculum and provided ethnic studies teacher training. Johnson has been board president of the Central Coast Alliance United for a Sustainable Economy (CAUSE) and is a member of the board of California Latinas for Reproductive Justice.

Her proudest achievement is being a mother and a part of the circle of friends and family that constitute the core of her life.

Damon Azali-Rojas was born and raised on Tongva/Kizh land, also known as South Central Los Angeles. He is co-director and co-founder of Coaching for Healing, Justice, and Liberation, a nonprofit school that trains Black, Indigenous, and people of color social justice movement leaders to be liberatory coaches. Damon comes to this work as an experienced community organizer, a Babalawo (Ifá priest), a prison abolitionist, a parent of a neurodivergent child, a coach, a coach trainer, and a Black surfer. Damon is co-author (with Sarah Jawaid) of the book *Love Letter to the Movement: Using a Coach Approach for Healing, Justice, and Liberation* (2022). The textbook is an invitation for movement leaders to reach back to gather the seeds of ancestral intelligence and wisdom, cultivate authentic communication, reciprocal relationships, and spirit-led purpose. From this place we can harvest the dreams of both the "BIG Liberation" we are building for our descendants and the "little liberation" that we have access to every single day. Damon is co-founder of Destiny Coaching and Consulting (with his partner, Cynthia Azali-Rojas), a member of the Change Elemental Governance Team, and a board member of Organizing Roots.

Charles A. Sepulveda is an Assistant Professor of ethnic studies at the University of California, Riverside. His research on California Indian histories includes missionization, slavery, genocide, dispossession, ecological devastation, rematriation, and resistance. His research centers on relationality and often includes genealogy to document the violence of conquest. His first manuscript, *Native Alienation: Spiritual Conquest and the Violence of California Missions*, was published in 2024. Dr. Sepulveda is an active member of his communities and a board member of the Tongva Tarahat Paxaavxa Conservancy, the Acjachemen Tongva Land Conservancy, and the Sacred Places Institute for Indigenous Peoples.

Moon-Kie Jung teaches sociology and antisociology at the University of Massachusetts, Amherst.

João H. Costa Vargas is professor in the Departments of Black Study and Anthropology at UC Riverside and, with Moon-Kie Jung, editor of *Antiblackness* (Duke University Press, 2021).

Vanessa E. Thompson is an assistant professor and distinguished professor in black studies and social justice in the Department of Gender Studies at

Queen's University, Canada. Before she moved to Ontario, she was a lecturer at the Institute of Sociology at Goethe University Frankfurt and at the Faculty of Social and Cultural Sciences at European University Viadrina, Germany. Her scholarship and teaching focuses on critical black studies (especially black social movements), anticolonialism, racial capitalism and state violence, abolition and abolitionist internationalism, and critical ethnographies. She has co-edited *Abolitionismus: Ein Reader* (Suhrkamp, 2022, with Daniel Loick) and a special issue on black feminisms for the journal *Femina Politica* (2021, with Cristine Löw and Denise Bergold-Caldwell), and her book *Black Socialities: Urban Resistance and the Struggle Beyond Recognition in Paris* is forthcoming from Manchester University Press. Vanessa has further published on black social movements in Europe, policing and abolition, and Fanonian thought. Vanessa organizes with abolitionist feminist movements in Europe and globally and is a member of the International Independent Commission on the Death of Oury Jalloh.

Lorgia García Peña is a writer, activist, and scholar who specializes in Latinx studies with a focus on Black Latinidades. Her work is concerned with the ways in which antiblackness and xenophobia intersect the Global North, producing categories of exclusion that lead to violence and erasure. She is the author of three award-winning books, *The Borders of Dominicanidad: Race, Nation, and Archives of Contradictions* (Duke University Press, 2016), *Translating Blackness: Latinx Colonialities in Global Perspective* (Duke University Press, 2022), and *Community as Rebellion* (Haymarket, 2022). Peña is also a co-founder of Freedom University Georgia, a school that provides college instruction to undocumented students, and the co-director of Archives of Justice, a transnational digital archive project that centers the life of people who identify as Black, queer, and migrant. She has been widely recognized for her public-facing work: in 2022 she received the Angela Davis Prize for Public Scholarship, in 2021 the Margaret Casey Foundation named her a Freedom Scholar, and in 2017 the Massachusetts Institute of Technology presented her with a Disobedience Award. García Peña received a PhD in American culture from the University of Michigan, Ann Arbor, and a master's in Latin American and Latino literatures from Rutgers University.

Charalampos Tsavdaroglou is a scholar in critical urban studies, and his work specializes in migrants' urban and housing commons, refugee camps, and newcomers' right to the city. He is currently principal investigator in the HFRI research program Refugees' Solidarity City: Institutional Policies and Commoning Practices in Athens, Mytilene and Thessaloniki (RECITY) at Aristotle University of Thessaloniki and Postdoctoral Researcher in the Horizon H2020 program Arrival Infrastructures as Sites of Integration for Recent Newcomers (REROOT) at University of Thessaly. He is visiting professor in human geography at the School of Humanities, Hellenic Open University, and lecturer on urban planning at the Department of Planning and Regional Development, University of Thessaly. Tsavdaroglou holds a PhD in urban and regional planning from the School of Architecture, Aristotle University of Thessaloniki. During the academic years 2017–2023 he was Marie Skłodowska-Curie Fellow at the University of Amsterdam and postdoctoral researcher at the University of Thessaly, University of the Aegean, and the National Hellenic Research Foundation. His research interests include critical urban theory; autonomy of migration; approaches to urban commons and mobile commoning practices; intersectional, decolonial, and affective geographies; and urban social movements.

Maria Kaika is director of the Centre for Urban Studies and chair in urban regional and environmental planning at the University of Amsterdam. She is recipient of the 2017 Jim Lews Prize for the most innovative academic publication (with L. Ruggiero) and of the 2021 European Award of Excellence in teaching in the humanities and social sciences. Her research focuses on urban political ecology, the relation between economic crisis and environmental and housing marginalization, and the embodied politics of infrastructures. She is author/editor of *Turning Up the Heat: Urban Political Ecology for a Climate Emergency* (Manchester University Press, 2023, with R. Keil, T. Mandler, and Y. Tzaninis), *The Political Ecology of Austerity* (Routledge, 2021, with R. Calvario and G. Velegrakis), "Urbanizing Degrowth: Five Steps Towards a Radical Spatial Degrowth Agenda for Planning in the Face of Climate Emergency" (2023, special issue of *Urban Studies*, with A. Varvarousis, F. Demaria, and H. March), *In the Nature of Cities: Urban Political Ecology and the Metabolism of Urban Environments* (Routledge, 2006, with N. Heynen and E. Swyngedouw), and *City of Flows: Modernity, Nature and the City* (Routledge, 2005).

Saree Makdisi is professor of English and comparative literature at UCLA. His recent books include *Tolerance Is a Wasteland: Palestine and the Culture of Denial* (University of California Press, 2022) and *Making England Western: Occidentalism, Race, and Imperial Culture* (University of Chicago Press, 2013). He also writes occasional pieces for the *Los Angeles Times,* the *Nation, n+1,* and other publications.

Amy Sara Carroll's books include *Secession* (San Diego State University Press, 2012); *Fannie + Freddie / The Sentimentality of Post-9/11 Pornography* (Fordham University Press, 2013), chosen by Claudia Rankine for the 2012 Poets Out Loud Prize, and *Remex: Toward an Art History of the NAFTA Era* (University of Texas Press, 2017), which received honorable mentions for the 2017 MLA Katherine Singer Kovacs Prize, the 2018 Latin American Studies Association Mexico Section Best Book in the Humanities, and the 2019 Association for Latin American Art–Arvey Foundation Book Award. Since 2008, she has been a member of Electronic Disturbance Theater 2.0, co-producing the "Transborder Immigrant Tool." She co-authored *[({ })] The Desert Survival Series / La serie de sobrevivencia del desierto* (The University of Michigan Digital Environments Cluster Publishing Series, 2014) which was published under a Creative Commons license and widely redistributed. Recently her work has appeared in the *Boston Review, Michigan Quarterly Review, Panorama: Journal of the Association of Historians of American Art*, and *Aztlan: A Journal of Chicano Studies* and in the exhibitions *Below the Underground: Renegade Art and Action in 1990s Mexico, Cuánto tiempo lleva todo esto derramándose sin desbordarse*, and the 2022–2023 MexiCali Biennial. Previously she taught at the New School in New York City; currently she's an associate professor of Literature and Literary Arts at the University of California, San Diego.

Ricardo Dominguez was a member of Critical Art Ensemble and a co-founder of Electronic Disturbance Theater (EDT) 1.0 with Carmin Karasic, Brett Stalbaum, and Stefan Wray, a group that developed Virtual Sit-In technologies in 1998 with the Zapatista communities in Chiapas, Mexico. With EDT 2.0 (Brett Stalbaum, micha cárdenas, Amy Sara Carroll, and Elle Mehrmand) he co-created the "Transborder Immigrant Tool," a GPS cell phone safety net tool for wandering over the Mexico–US border. EDT 3.0 presented at the 2022–2023 MexiCali Biennial *Land of Milk and Honey*, available at https://edt30.ucsd.edu and on YouTube. He is a Creative Capital awardee, a Hellman Fellow, a Society for the Humanities Fellow at Cornell University, a Rockefeller Fellow (Bellagio Center, Italy), and a UCLA Luskin Institute on Inequality and Democracy Fellow. Dominguez is a professor in the Department of Visual Arts and a principal investigator at CALIT2/QI at UCSD.

Nicholas De Genova is professor of the Department of Comparative Cultural Studies at the University of Houston. He previously held teaching appointments in urban and political geography at King's College London and in anthropology at Stanford, Columbia, and Goldsmiths, University of London, as well as visiting professorships or research positions at the Universities of

Warwick, Bern, and Amsterdam. He is the author of *Working the Boundaries: Race, Space, and "Illegality" in Mexican Chicago* (Duke University Press, 2005), co-author of *Latino Crossings: Mexicans, Puerto Ricans, and the Politics of Race and Citizenship* (Routledge, 2003), editor of *Racial Transformations: Latinos and Asians Remaking the United States* (Duke University Press, 2006), co-editor of *The Deportation Regime: Sovereignty, Space, and the Freedom of Movement* (Duke University Press, 2010), editor of *The Borders of "Europe": Autonomy of Migration, Tactics of Bordering* (Duke University Press, 2017), co-editor of *Roma Migrants in the European Union: Un/Free Mobility* (Routledge, 2019), co-editor of *Europa/Crisis: Nuevas Palabras Claves en "la Crisis" en y de "Europa"* (Catarata, 2021), co-editor of *The Borders of America: Migration, Control, and Resistance across Latin America and the Caribbean* (Duke 2026), and co-editor of *Border Abolitionism: Migrant Struggles and the Law* (Duke University Press, forthcoming).

Sarah Haley's research areas include US gender history, carceral history, Black feminist and queer theory, prison abolition, and feminist historical methods. She is the author of *No Mercy Here: Gender, Punishment, and the Making of Jim Crow Modernity* (University of North Carolina Press, 2016), which earned honors in the fields of history, gender studies, American studies, and African American studies and was selected for the 2020 National Book Foundation's Literature for Justice Reading List. Her writing has appeared in journals including *Signs: Journal of Women in Culture and Society*, the *Journal of African American History*, GLQ: *A Journal of Lesbian and Gay Studies*, *Souls*, and *Women and Performance*, and she is working on a book titled *The Carceral Interior: A Black Feminist Study of American Punishment, 1966–2016*. In 2022, Haley was named a Marguerite Casey Foundation Freedom Scholar. She is associate professor of gender studies and history at Columbia University and has been active in prison abolition, gender justice, and labor movements. She currently organizes with Scholars for Social Justice.

Sharad Chari is faculty at the Department of Geography and Program in Critical Theory at the University of California at Berkeley and affiliated to the Wits Institute for Social and Economic Research and the Marxist Institute for Research. His recent publications include *Apartheid Remains* (Duke University Press, 2024), *Gramsci at Sea* (University of Minnesota Press, 2023) and the co-edited *Ethnographies of Power* (Wits, 2022). He is currently at work on a book with South African queer activist and thinker Beverley Palesa Ditsie titled *Beverley Ditsie's Fearless Speech*, a book that bends an account of her life in the critique of sexuality at apartheid's end. He has also been engaged in multisite research in Mauritius, Reunion, and the South African east coast on various engagements with the "ocean economy" at the interface of the Black Atlantic and the Southern African Indian Ocean. He is also, with Carolien Stolte, editing the fifth volume of the *Cambridge History of Colonialism and Decolonization*, preliminarily titled *The Colonial Present and the Planetary Demand*.

SA Smythe is a critical theorist, transmedia storyteller, and educator committed to cartographies of Black belonging beyond geographies, genders, genre, and other borders. They are assistant professor of Black studies and the archive in the Faculty of Information and director of the Collaboratory for Black Poiēsis at the University of Toronto. They are a senior fellow at the Center for Applied Transgender Studies and serve on advisory boards for the Center for Critical Internet Inquiry, punctum books, Black Artists' Networks in Dialogue, Italian Culture, and the book series Imagining Black Europe and MFI Momentary Futures in Black Studies. Smythe is editor of *Transnational Black Studies* (Liverpool University Press, forthcoming) and the two-volume special issue "Troubling the Grounds: Global Configurations of Blackness, Nativism, and Indigeneity" of the journal *Postmodern Culture*. They are author of *Where Blackness Meets the Sea: On Crisis, Culture, and the Black Mediterranean* (forthcoming) and the poetry-collection-cum-multimedia-installation and nine-movement sound-performance suite titled *[proclivity]*. For decades, Smythe has organized with literary, abolitionist, and migrant support collectives across Turtle Island, Europe, and the Mediterranean. Winner of the 2021–22 Rome Prize for Modern Italian Studies, the 2023–24 MacDowell Fellowship in Multimedia Installation, and other international composer/artist fellowships and residencies, Smythe's transmedia artworks have been featured in collaborative and solo exhibitions, installations, and festivals.

Kyle Mays (he/him) is an Afro-Indigenous (Saginaw Chippewa) scholar of Afro-Indigenous studies, urban studies, and contemporary popular culture. He is an associate professor in the Departments of African American Studies, American Indian Studies, and History at UCLA. He is the author of four books, including *An Afro-Indigenous History of the United States* (Beacon, 2021), *City of Dispossessions: Indigenous Peoples, African Americans, and the Creation of Modern Detroit* (University of Pennsylvania Press, 2022), and, with Sam Hitchmough, *Rethinking the Red Power Movement* (Routledge, 2024).

Rinaldo Walcott is professor and Carl V. Granger Chair of Africana and American Studies at the University at Buffalo. He is the author of *The Long*

Emancipation: Moving Toward Black Freedom (Duke University Press, 2021) and *On Property: Policing, Prisons, and the Call for Abolition* (Biblioasis, 2021).

Leisy J. Abrego is professor in the Department of Chicana/o and Central American Studies at UCLA, always in search of liberatory spaces in the classroom, in community with colleagues, and in accompaniment of immigrant communities and movements in research. She is a member of the first large migration of Salvadorans who arrived in Los Angeles in the early 1980s. Her research and teaching interests—inspired in great part by her family's experiences—are in Central American studies and law and society. She writes about the intimate consequences of US empire and immigration policies for Central American migrants and Latinx families in the United States. Her books include *Sacrificing Families: Navigating Laws, Labor, and Love Across Borders* (Stanford University Press, 2014), *Immigrant Families* (co-authored with Cecilia Menjívar and Leah Schmalzbauer, Polity, 2017), and *We Are Not Dreamers: Undocumented Scholars Theorize Undocumented Life in the United States* (co-edited with Genevieve Negrón-Gonzales, Duke University Press, 2020). She also supports and advocates for refugees and immigrants by writing editorials and pro bono expert declarations in asylum cases.

INDEX

Note: page numbers followed by *f* refer to figures.

abandonment, 98, 102, 110–11, 286; of migrants, 21
abjection, 22, 86, 267
Abolish Frontex, 107–8, 110
abolition, 54–56, 68, 96–98, 124, 251, 254, 285, 330–32; abolition-democracy, 299; of apartheid capitalism, 261; Black, 27; of borders, 107, 276; decolonization and, 28; family, 246n6; as feminist project, 106, 119; of Frontex, 107; geographies, 97, 102, 132, 273; language of, 287; as love, 30, 119–20; of Man and the nation state, 320; of migration regime, 108; minobimaadiziwin and, 332; movement leaders, 48; poetics, 276, 282–83, 289; of police, 105, 131; politics, 55; practical, 5–6, 10; of prisons, 28, 55, 131, 276, 329, 332; as rehearsal of life, 4, 60, 73; sanctuary and, 5, 29; scholars of, 46; on stolen land, 4, 52, 131; strike and, 254–55, 261–62; of transatlantic slave trade, 14, 253–54; university and, xi, 56, 120

Abolition on Stolen Land convening, xi, xivn2, 4, 14, 30n2, 45, 58n1
abolitionist movements, xii, 97–98
Abrego, Leisy J., xii, 28
academic rebellion, xi, xiii, 326
accommodation, 155, 161, 163–64. *See also* camps
accompaniment, xii–xiii, 29, 210; ethics of, 231
Achiume, E. Tendayi, 2, 14
activism, 53, 118, 218, 295; ACT UP's, 1; communities of, 338; community, 122; Indigenous cross-border, 19; migrant worker, 109; "Mujer Migrante Memorial (MMM)" and, 140; performative, 184; squatting and, 17
Afghanistan, 13, 157, 166, 181, 219
Africa, 10, 16, 102, 167, 181, 207, 273, 290n2; Clooney Foundation and, 180; French imperialism and, 110; Meloni and, 271–72; migrants from, 155, 290n1; North, 189; Portuguese colonization of, 61–62; United States and, 330

African Americans, 274, 294, 297, 299. *See also* Black Americans; Black people
Afro-Indigenous people, 48, 274–75, 294, 299
Agamben, Giorgio, 26, 157. *See also* bare life
Algeria, 8, 157, 168
Amrith, Sunil, 257–58
Anduril, 11, 208–9
Anishinaabe peoples, 297, 304; land, 294, 297; philosophy, 304
antiblackness, x, 5, 63, 92, 244, 295, 329; in Detroit, 297; Freedom University Georgia and, 123–24; genocide and, 15, 80, 90–91, 245; indigeneity and, 296; Indigenous displacement and, 48; Indigenous people and, 50; land return and, 296; language and, 280; migrant lives and, 23; racial capitalism and, 104 ; in the United States, 123, 231
antisemitism, xiii, 187
Anzaldúa, Gloria, 17, 210
apartheid, 251; American, 254, 259; capitalism, 261; in Israel, 15, 177, 179, 182–84, 187, 191; in South Africa, 249–50, 252
Arizona, 2–3, 11, 135, 137–41, 143, 145–50, 198, 203; State Bill 1070, 121, 129n5. *See also* Pima County Office of the Medical Examiner (PCOME)
asylum, 3, 8, 27, 41, 267–68, 337; for Central Americans, 125; church, 17–18; cities of, 7; in Europe, 10–13, 17–18, 24, 162, 215–17, 219–20; in Italy, 279; ruse of, 3, 7, 10, 26, 267; sanctuary as, 23; in the US, xii, 6, 11, 203, 206, 325, 327–29
~~Asylum~~: *At the Borders of Humanitarianism*, 27–28, 31n11, 41, 214
asylum seekers, 11–13, 103, 161, 170n1, 211, 214–17, 266, 268–69, 272; Camp de la Lande and, 287; COVID-19 pandemic and, 212n3; Italy and, 290n1; lawyers and, 18–19; United States and, 6, 203–7, 328, 335; violence and, 277
Atlantic Ocean, xiii, 6, 12, 18, 20, 315; slave trade and, 254. *See also* Black Atlantic

Australia, 254, 256
Azali-Rojas, Damon, xi, 14, 29

Baraka, Amiri, 281
bare life, 10, 57, 70, 156–57, 330
Benjamin, Walter, 179, 251
Bentham, Jeremy, 92n5, 255–56
Biden, Joseph, xivn1, 50, 178, 210, 212n5; administration of, 204–5, 327
Biko, Steve, 250–51
Black Americans, 124, 276, 281. *See also* Black people
Black Atlantic, 97, 251, 254, 274–75
Black death, 15–16, 82–83, 91, 241
Black diaspora, 79, 84, 299
Black knowledge, 24, 120
Black life, 20, 23, 47, 90, 237, 241, 243, 274, 311
Black Lives Matter, 51, 98, 131, 284–85
Black Mediterranean, 5, 10, 20–24, 101, 276, 283, 285–87; Black Atlantic and, 97, 274–75; freedom dreaming, 273, 276, 282, 287, 289; necropolitical routes of, 289; non-assistance and, 21; *poēsis* of, 29; poetics of, 275, 281–82, 289
Black Mediterranean Collective, 10, 23
blackness, 112n1, 274–75; coalitional conception of, 248; political, 110; relational poetics and, 273; radical, 111n1
Black people, 51, 80–82, 84–87, 89–92, 123–24, 254, 275, 282, 288–89, 328; anti-Indigeneity and, 50; Black Lives Matter and, 284; Camp de la Lande and, 287; Deloria and, 302; enslavement of, 59; forced labor and, 49; genocide and, 21, 78–80, 89–90; in Germany, 286; indigeneity and, 70; kinship and, 304; land and, 301; in Los Angeles County, 72; rape and, 86; Reconstruction and, 299, 306n2; relation and, 238; terror against, 15, 81–82, 85; undocumented, 275; violence against, 23, 80; white supremacy and, 295. *See also* Jim Crow; slavery
Black Power, 301–2
Black radical tradition, 4, 47, 123, 273, 330
Black studies, 60, 312

border enforcement, 11–12, 86, 136
borders, 15, 41, 196, 198, 224–26, 228, 267–68, 328; abolition of, 97, 109, 119; capitalism and, 102; closure of, 159; crossing of, 217, 219, 224; of Europe, 2, 12–13, 29, 31n8, 107, 276, 310, 327 (*see also* Frontex); exteriorization of, 11–12; externalization of, 2, 272, 289; housing commons and, 167; interiorization of, x, 13; international, 204; Italy's, 270; maritime, 31n8; Mediterranean and, 273–74; militarization of, xi, 107; national, 29, 274, 286; social, 168; state, 221, 282; surplusification and, 14; violence and, 277. *See also* US-Mexico border
borderscapes, 100–101
Brathwaite, Kamau, 316
Braverman, Suella, 269, 272
Brazil, 18, 333
breathing, 30, 96, 98–101; combat breathing, 30, 99–101; un-breathing, 30, 98–101, 286, 330
Brothers of Italy, 10, 268
Bullock, Sandra, 184, 190
Burkina Faso, 108, 285
Bush, George W., 201–2
Butler, Judith, 9, 251

caging, 2; algorithmic, 209, 323
California, 59–60, 63–65, 70–71, 303; Angel Island detention center, 197; Drone Valley, 209; Indian genocide in, 306; mission system, 59–60, 63–64, 66–68, 74n3; sanctuary laws in, 3; segregation in, 253; Venice Beach, 135, 143
camps, 163–64, 166; abolition of, 102; colonial legacies of, 158, 162, 169; dehumanization in, 18; detention, 11; EU-funded, 12; fractal geography of, 3, 206; Nazi death, 88, 157; protests against, 109; refugee, 2–3, 17, 157, 330; resistance in, 107; state-run, 17, 155–62, 168–69; suicides in, 103; surplus populations in, 105. *See also* container camps
Campt, Tina, 27, 246n2

Canada, 50–51, 256; border with US, 20
Canary Islands, 61–62
capital, 42, 228, 254, 258, 271, 273, 283, 289, 328; accumulation, 100; class struggle and, 109–10; global, 17; labor and, 196, 226–28, 253–54; land and, 196, 253–54; liberation and, 317; moral, 182, 184; oceans and, 257; racial, 55, 101; racialized, 269
capitalism, 30, 111, 118, 136, 254, 302, 328, 339; apartheid, 261; carceral, 105; colonial, 220, 226, 254; crisis of, 104; decolonial feminism and, 320; decolonization and, 305; extractive, 258; geographies of, 110; global, 97; Indigenous sovereignty and, 19; industrial, 238; neoliberal, 18, 100, 326; philanthrocapitalism, 161, 169; policing and, 96, 100, 102, 105; settler-colonial, 295; social reproduction and, 241; un-breathing and, 100. *See also* racial capitalism
captivity, 23, 51, 237–38, 241, 254, 309–10, 312
Carby, Hazel, 318–19
carcerality, 18, 106, 286, 330
carceral system, 29, 46, 48, 290n3
Card, Claudia, 80, 87–90, 92n6
Carmichael, Stokely (Kwame Ture), 297, 301–2
Carroll, Amy Sara, 11, 17, 323
Centers for Disease Control and Prevention (CDC), 204–5
Central America, 19, 143, 210
Césaire, Aimé, 285, 317
Chari, Sharad, 14, 29
Christianity, 62–65, 89, 250
citizenship, 159, 210, 270, 278–79, 283, 287, 327, 329; in Europe, 290n3; French, 8; Italian, 279, 282; liberal notions of, 289; rights, 20; US, 88; ruse of, 267, 269
civilization, 47, 59, 63–64, 313
Civil Rights Congress (CRC), 78–79, 81–82, 84, 89–91; *We Charge Genocide*, 15, 78–86, 90–91, 92n7
climate justice, 54–55
Clooney, Amal, 180, 184

Index   355

Clooney, George, 176–84, 186, 190, 193
Cold War, 215, 221, 256, 327
colonial amnesia, xiii, 9, 272
colonialism, 60, 62, 105, 126, 158, 225, 284, 312; Derrida and, 8; European, 6, 181, 214, 220; founding violence of, 239; neo-colonialism, 110; nineteenth-century, 187; Spanish, 70; Taraaxam and, 66, 72; visitors and, 67; Western, 192. *See also* settler colonialism
coloniality, 5, 313; postcoloniality, 220; of power, 312
colonization, 5, 45–47, 63, 296, 299, 310, 313, 334; of Africa, 61; of California, 63; European, 256, 297; of Palestine, 178, 189–90, 192
commons, 165, 241; housing, 17, 159, 164–70; mobile, 24, 165; oceanic, 257, 261; urban, 18, 156, 165, 170
communism, 54, 317
conquest, 2, 28, 30, 59–73, 220, 310
consent, 27; manufactured, 269, 274
container camps, 30, 155–56, 158–59, 162–63, 164 *f*, 166
containerization, 10, 22, 163
containers, 202, 268
containment, 3, 22–23, 51, 73, 252, 267, 289; ideological regimes of, 273; of Indigenous communities, 197; logics of, 333; refugee camps and, 158; sexual terror and, 86; white supremacy and, 70
Conte, Giuseppe, 268, 279
cosmopolitanism, 4, 24; Derrida's, 9–10; Kantian, 8
Coulthard, Glen, 72, 305
COVID-19 pandemic, xii, 12, 41, 125, 205, 233, 267–68, 279, 327; asylum seekers and, 214n3; borders and, 328
criminalization, 3, 21, 46, 108; Black, 87; of homelessness, 1–2; of justice work, 103; of labor migration, 104; of migrants, 7, 217, 231 (*see also* illegalization); of sanctuary, 28; of solidarity, xiii
critical refugee studies, 4, 47
Critical Resistance, 54–55
crossings, 2, 14, 16, 21, 23, 276; fractal geography of, 3, 206; oceanic, 273
Cuba, 157, 205, 244, 246n1

Darfur, 180–83
Davis, Angela Y., 18, 119, 123
death, 5, 22, 64, 89, 118–19, 126–27, 137, 150, 224, 285, 335; accounting of, 3; borders and, 11, 327; civil, 128n3; COVID-19 pandemic and, 267; humanitarian reason and, 9; invisibilization of, 21; maps, 136, 150; by numbers, 277; overkill and, 279; premature, 65, 85, 101, 105, 107, 241; of settlers, 67; sites, 143, 145, 147; social reproduction and, 238; spaces of, 2; US immigration system and, 231. *See also* Black death; migrant death; social death
decolonization, 26, 131, 255, 310–12, 318, 321; abolition and, 27–28; migrant justice and, 20, 42; migration as, 2, 14; reparations and, 29, 299, 305
De Genova, Nicholas, 7, 10–11, 13, 21, 214, 267, 327–29
dehumanization: of Black people, 23, 87; of homeless people, 1; of migrants, 18, 48; transatlantic, 252
Deloria, Vine, 302, 306n1
democracy, 15, 91, 124, 185–89, 300, 310, 317, 326, 329–30; abolition and, 299; Black death and, 15; Detroit as arsenal of, 295; US, xiv, 65, 80, 91, 295–96, 305; Zionism and, 22. *See also* liberal democracy
deportability, 224–25
deportation, 20, 107, 121, 123, 203, 205, 222–23, 229, 290n3; expedited, 335; fast-track, 12; humanitarian reason and, 9; mass, xiv; regimes, 13, 104, 109; sanctuary and, 7, 13; sanctuary laws and, 3; of undocumented immigrants, x, 126; United Kingdom and, 10; universities and, xi; US immigration system and, 231
Derrida, Jacques, 7–10
detention, 48, 107, 196–97, 202, 222–23; of asylum seekers, 11–12, 335; extraterritorial, 268; labor and, 13; logics of, 9; migrant, 10, 197, 201, 203; of refugees, 108; of unaccompanied minors, 19; of undocumented immigrants, x; universities and, xi

detention centers, 100, 109, 266, 325, 330; migrant, 3, 197, 203; mylar blankets and, 17, 210f; suicides in, 103; unbreathing and, 101
Detroit, 236, 258–59, 294, 297–99, 302
development, 72, 273, 279; African, 10, 271; of California, 303; of Los Angeles, 68; of US Sunbelt, 196
De Waal, Alex, 180–81
dignity, 146, 193; human, 22, 185–87, 189–91
discrimination, 1–3, 280; against Black workers, 85; anti-migrant, 148, 277
displacement, xiii, 2–6, 41, 72, 312; academy and, 333; dispossession and, 296; *Exterminate* (Peck) and, 319; forced, 23; Indigenous, 48; mass, 97, 136; settler colonialisms and, 196; solidarity and, 4, 252. *See also* permanent displaceability
dispossession, 5, 47, 54, 196, 235, 272–73, 277, 288; breathing and, 99; colonial technologies of, 20; citizenship reform and, 279; consent and, 27; educational, 298; freedom from, 27, 293, 299; genocide and, 50, 89; grounds of, 26; histories of, xiii, 41; hospitality and, 8–9; Indigenous, 6, 27, 51, 59, 62, 68–70, 72, 300; internationalist politics and, 102; land, 60, 63, 296; migration regimes and, x, 332; of Palestinian people, 187; resistance to, 6; slavery and, 275; state, 30, 270; structural oppression and, 335; violence of, 189; women and, 118
disruption, xiii, 230, 323
diversity, xi, 53, 117, 188
Doctrine of Discovery, 46, 61–62, 73
domicide, 2–3, 22
Dominguez, Ricardo, 11, 17, 323
Drexciya, 258–61
drones, 198–99, 208–9, 211
Du Bois, W. E. B., 80, 252, 300–1, 306n2

ecocide, 14, 258, 262; oceanic, 14, 253, 257
education, 50, 107, 117, 165, 271; abolition, 119; access to, 124, 160, 280; Indigenous youth and, 298–99; political, 17–18, 131–32; public college, 121; scholars of, 67

Egypt, 21, 108
Electronic Disturbance Theater 2.0 (EDT 2.0), 17, 323, 333
El Salvador, 6–7
El-Tayeb, Fatima, 9, 41
encampments: border, 206; refugee, 327, 330; unhoused, 22–23, 26, 30
Enciso, Álvaro, 144, 149–52
enclosure, 6, 41, 241–42, 258; camps and, 169; racialized, 244
enslavement, 47, 60–61, 63–64, 112n2, 275, 277; of Black people, 59, 62; Detroit and, 397, 302; Indian, 65–66, 70
Equiano, Olaudah, 311–12, 321
equity, xi, 120, 188
Esmeir, Samera, 255–57
Estes, Nick, 14, 46–47, 50–52
ethics: of accompaniment, 233; aesthethics, 140; of community-engaged scholarship, 334; as hospitality, 8; love as, 119; of love, 127; of witnessing, 323
Ethiopia, 266, 270–71
ethnicity, 71, 158–59, 167
ethnic cleansing. *See* Palestine: ethnic cleansing of
Eurocentrism, 9, 24
Europeanness, 220, 275
European Union (EU), 2, 12–13, 208, 271; asylum and, 215; border regime, 107; citizens, 329; maritime borders of, 31n8; migrants to, 155; migration policies of, 161–62; security apparatus of, 21, 105. *See also* Frontex
evictions, 2, 168, 337
exclusion, 23, 41, 125–27, 225; of Black people, 79; of economic migrants, 14; places of, 160, 169; of undocumented immigrants, 128n3; zone, 13
expulsion, 23, 222
Exterminate All the Brutes (Peck), 313–20
extermination, 313, 319
extraction, 219–20, 23840–41, 271, 278; capitalist, 275; migration and, 41; neocolonial, 286; socioeconomic, 273
extremism, 105, 185, 187

Index 357

Fanon, Frantz, 5, 9, 64, 250, 252, 276, 288, 312–13; *A Dying Colonialism*, 99; breathing and, 30, 98–99; *The Wretched of the Earth*, 25, 313, 318
Farrow, Mia, 180–81
fascism, 18, 82, 105, 284, 288, 313; antifascism, 7; Islamic, ix
femicides, 145–46, 149
feminism, 143; abolition, 120; Black, 47, 234; border, 7; decolonial, 320
(F)empower, 131–32
Ferreira da Silva, Denise, 21, 42
financialization, 108–9, 270, 284
Finch, Aisha, 26, 235, 243, 244, 246n1
Floyd, George, 50, 98, 101, 131, 254, 2779 285
France, 12–13, 101, 106, 108, 117, 277, 285; accommodations for migrants in, 284, 288; Black, 274; Derrida and, 8; police in, 104; racism in, 99; universalism of, 315
freedom, 5, 25–27, 47–48, 124, 305, 309–13, 317–21, 329–30, 332–33, 338–39; academic, xiii, 118; Black, 29, 81, 123, 236, 299–301, 306n2; carceral regimes and, 56–57; decolonization and, 312, 321n1; democratic, 161; from dispossession, 295; dreaming/dreams, 273, 274, 282, 287, 289; fighters, 286; freedom-making, 118, 126; fugitivity and, 4, 46, 51, 61, 331–32; hospitality and, 331; humanism and, 273, 311, 315, 320–21; Indigenous, 236; land and, 296; learning in, 120; love and, 119; of movement, 18, 107–8, 227–28; sanctuary and, 30, 252; of the seas, 256; seekers, 52; slavery and, 60; United States' notion of, 65. *See also* unfreedom
Freedom University (FU) Georgia, 118–20, 122–24, 126, 128
Freeman, Morgan, 184, 190
Frontex, 107, 207–8, 272, 277, 327; agents, 211; Italian coast and, 12; Polytechnic of Turin and, xi. *See also* Abolish Frontex
fugitivity/fugitivities, 10, 14, 16, 47, 261, 329, 331–32; Black, 20, 28–29, 295–96, 303; freedom and, 4, 26, 46, 61; Indigenous, 28–29, 295–96, 303; kinship and, 30; mass, 51; relation and, 245; social reproduction and, 238; Western archive and, 25
futurity, 27, 60, 68; decolonial Indigenous, 29; grammar of, 16

Gallagher, Ellen, 258–60, 262
García Peña, Lorgia, xi, 29–30
Garner, Eric, 101, 286
Gaza, xiii, 178, 252, 268, 279; genocide in, xiii, 15–16, 21, 193; Israeli bombardment of, 180, 182; Israeli invasion of, 327
Gehry, Frank, 184–85, 188
gender, 65, 139, 235, 241–42, 337; Black politics and, 124; carcerality and, 106; conquest of California and, 71; nonconformity, 282, 284; studies, 47, 246n1; violence, 140, 143, 145, 149
genocide, 15, 22, 47, 50–51, 77–81, 85–91, 92n6, 281; antiblackness and, 245; beyond genocide, 21, 25, 80, 90; Black, 81–82; conquest and, 59; in Darfur, 182–83; Euro-American, 316; European, 314; in Gaza, xiii, 15–16, 21, 193; of Indigenous people, 6, 57, 62, 303, 306n3, 311; in Namibia, 15–16; Ottoman, 16; in Palestine, 118, 178, 327; UN Convention on, 78–79, 81–82; in the United States, 300. *See also* Card, Claudia; Civil Rights Congress (CRC): *We Charge Genocide*; social death; United Nations Convention on the Prevention and Punishment of the Crime of Genocide
geography, xi, 3, 17, 22, 208, 261, 296; abolition, 97, 102
Georgia, 117–19, 121–24, 126, 294; HB 87, 121–22; redistribution of land in, 300
Germany, xii, 18, 101–5, 108, 284, 286, 326; asylum and, 12; Berlin Wall and, 204; Black, 274; Dessau, 325; Namibia and, 15–16; Nazi, 77, 179, 205
Gilets Jaunes (Yellow Vests), 13, 108
Gilets Noirs (Black Vests), 13, 108–11
Gilmore, Ruth Wilson, 4, 28, 46–47, 54–55, 60, 97, 132, 254, 258, 288; on racism, 85; on surplus populations, 100

Gilroy, Paul, 9, 22, 24–25, 251–52, 255, 315. *See also* Black Atlantic
Glissant, Édouard, 276, 280
Global North, 16, 108, 331
Gordon, Neve, 190–91
governance, 22, 271; of Alta California, 63; of asylum, 215; colonial, 272; faculty, 118; of human mobility, 219; Indigenous modes of, 20; liberal, x–xi, 2–3, 41; policing as mode of, 98; state, 289; totalitarian, 276
Greece, 207, 269, 277, 326; Athens, 17, 155–56, 158–60, 163–66, 168–70; Forensic Missing Migrant Initiative, 283; immigration policy and, 161–62, 169; migrant camps in, 158, 330 (*see also* container camps); migrant housing projects in, 155; migrants and, 12, 21; Moria camp, 17, 107, 286; Thessaloniki, 155, 157–60, 162–70
Guatemala, 6–7, 140, 325–26
guest, 8, 67, 73; guest worker program, 201

Haley, Sarah, xi, 26–27, 46–47, 55, 57
Hall, Stuart, 23, 321
Hartman, Saidiya, 235–36, 240, 242–45, 246n1, 311; on afterlife of slavery, 246n3; on errancy, 246n8; "Freedom and Fugitivity," 26, 235, 237, 244; *Lose Your Mother*, 238–39, 246n1; *Scenes of Subjection*, 25, 92n5; *Wayward Lives*, 238, 242–43, 246n1, 246n5
Herzl, Theodor, 191–92
Hier, Marvin, 186, 188
Hollywood, 179–80, 182–84, 190, 193
Holocaust, 215, 290n1, 316; survivors, 189
homelessness, 54; mass, 1–2
Honduras, 6, 254, 279
hooks, bell, 29, 118–20, 124, 126–28
hospitality, x, 5–6, 8–9, 169, 219, 331; ancestral knowledges of, 333; ethics of, 8; Indigenous, 28; liberal logics of, 18
host, 8, 18
"Hostile Terrain 94" (De León), 11, 31n4, 150, 152
housing, 8, 108–9, 119, 163, 167, 206, 278, 280, 338; companies, 161; crisis, 109, 325; justice, 337; projects, 17–18, 155–58, 164–66, 168–69; offshore quarantine, 267; public, 107; right to adequate, 2. *See also* commons: housing; squats; squatting
humanitarianism, xiv, 3–4, 16, 24, 268, 333; language of, 177, 191; liberal, 17, 97, 323; military, 159, 162, 169
humanitarian reason, xiii, 9, 16, 22, 41, 214n5, 252; sanctuary as, 3; Western humanism and, 26
human rights, 1–3, 12, 21, 23, 50, 54, 177, 183–84, 193, 326; abuses, 79, 182; activists, 179, 190, 278; bare humanity of, 26; causes, 181; discourse of, 22, 190–91; in Italy, 280; Jewish, 192; lawyers, 18, 180, 184; liberal mobilizations for, 107; organizations, 179, 183, 191; violations, 191, 231, 269

illegality, 48, 223; migrant, 216–17, 223
illegalization, xii, 1, 13, 214–15, 217, 222
immigrants, 122, 124, 129n5, 166f, 201, 209, 290n3, 327–29, 335, 337; Black, 280; dehumanization of, 48; names of, 285; undocumented, x, 123, 128n3; United States as nation of, 28; Western categorizations of, 167
immigration, 197–98, 227, 277–79, 284; authorities, ix–x, 326; enforcement, 136, 231, 327 (*see also* Prevention Through Deterrence); law, ix, 129n5, 227–28, 278; to Palestine, 178; policies, 124–25, 162, 202, 205; status, 121; in the United States, 205, 216, 231
imperialism, 255, 260, 284, 319–20, 329; border, x–xi, 7, 105, 231; critique of, 24; European, 315, 319; French, 110; free-market, 180; neo-imperialism, 107; US, 182, 219; Western, 7, 18
incarceration, 48, 55, 97, 123, 126, 197, 202
inclusion, xi, 16, 117, 188, 311; horizontal, 170; migrant justice movements and, 20; migration policies and, 169; murderous, 274; sanctuary as, 4; selective, 13; universities and, 120
incorrigibility, 214, 227–28
indigeneity, 52, 59, 64, 70–72, 74n4, 191, 242; anti-indigeneity, 50, 329; Blackness and, 296; oceanic, 260

Indigenous land, 66–67, 299; Black belonging on, 299; defense of, 20; enslaved Africans on, 303; theft of, xi

Indigenous peoples, 27, 48, 55, 57; Black liberation and, 302; Black people and, 49–51; in California, 63; conquest and, 59; in Detroit, 297–98; dispossession of, 300; forced assimilation of, 88; forced removal of, 6; genocide of, 6, 303, 311; kidnapping of, 254; kinship and, 303; land and, 50, 67–68, 72, 301, 303; Mexican and Central American, 201; settler colonialism and, 295–96. *See also* Afro-Indigenous people; Taraaxam

Indigenous sovereignty, 19–20, 47, 60, 303–5, 331; antiracism and, 333; Black freedom and, 29, 299; Indian Child Welfare Act (ICWA) and, 298

Indigenous studies, 4, 47

Indigenous youth, 298; movements, 253

infrastructures, 108, 156, 206; abolitionist, 111; arrival, 164; capital, 110; migration, 215; solidarity, 13, 18, 107, 155

internationalism, 54–55, 97, 102, 108, 219; abolitionist, 97–98, 111; Black, 281; Black feminist, 273; oceanic, 261–62; revolutionary, 101, 256

International Organization for Migration (IOM), 161, 207

International Parliament of Writers (IPW), 7–8

invisibilization, 21, 137, 157, 169, 284

Iran, xivn1, 18, 157, 267

Iraq, 157, 181–82, 219

Israel, xiii, 15, 22, 178, 184–86, 191, 286, 319; apartheid in, 182; bombardment of Gaza, 180, 193; invasion of Lebanon, 177, 184; love of, 185, 187, 191; as Zionist state, 178, 186–87, 189, 191. *See also* genocide; Palestine; Peres, Shimon

Jabotinsky, Vladimir, 191–92
Jalloh, Oury, 103–4, 286, 325
James, C. L. R., 249, 260
Jim Crow, 77, 89–90, 254
Johnson, Gaye Theresa, xi–xii, 14, 28–29
Jung, Moon-Kie, 15–16, 21, 23, 92n3, 92n8

justice, 15, 68, 329, 331; antiracism and, 120; climate, 54–55; demands for, 3, 5; food, 338; housing, 337; love and, 119; migrant, 7, 17, 19–20, 26–27, 42, 107, 232; reparatory, 29, 299, 302–303; reproductive, 131, 337; restorative, 337; social, 52–53, 219, 281, 302, 332, 334; spatial, 1–2; system, 103; transformative, xii; unequal forms of, 295

Kaika, Maria, 10, 17–18
Kan, Djarah, 284–85
Kaplan, Bettina, 119, 122
Kelley, Robin D. G., 23, 51, 258, 260–62, 275, 281–83; *Freedom Dreams: The Black Radical Imagination*, 273, 276, 280, 287–89, 305, 333. *See also* revolt: Black
King, Tiffany Lethabo, 26–27, 235, 238–40, 244–45, 246n1
kinship, 5, 27–30, 59–61, 63–64, 69, 239, 303–4; human-land, 73, 331; kuuyam and, 68; land and, 296, 303; political, 262; sovereignty and, 243
kuuyam, 28, 60, 66–68, 73, 331

labor, 57, 70, 99–100, 196, 226–28, 278–79, 301; abolitionist internationalism and, 98; affective, 240; agricultural, 278, 284; attacks on, 328; capital and, 226, 228, 253–54; disposable, 197; domestic, 240, 242; enslaved, 42, 92n5; exploitation, 102, 109; force, 217; forced, 23, 49; gendered division of, 106; illegalized, 223–24, 228; of Indians, 66, 72; market, 112n2, 271, 290n3; migration, 104, 112n2, 214–15, 218; politics of, 218; regimes, 13, 101, 107, 253; rights, 108–9, 278; training, 161; unfair practices of, 116; unfree, 254
land, 29, 49–50, 59, 64, 71–72, 295–96, 299–305, 306n2; acknowledgments, xi, 67, 120; art, 149–50; borders, 13; defense, 14, 20, 232; dispossession of, 60, 63, 288, 296; Indigenous, xi, 14, 20, 28, 60, 63, 67–69, 191–92, 297, 299, 301, 303; kinship and, 29, 73, 304, 331;

liberation and, 315; Ojibwe, 294, 297; Palestinian, 177; public, 137; relationships, 29, 46, 63, 69, 73; repatriation of, 55–56; rights, 331; theft, 48, 57; toxic, 54. *See also* stolen land
Land Back, 28, 18–51, 55–56, 296, 329, 332; Indigenous, 46
law enforcement, 87, 204; agencies, 202; local, ix; officers, 121–22
Law of the Sea, 14, 253, 256
Lemkin, Raphaël, 77–80, 88, 90, 92n7
liberal democracy, x, 3, 15, 26, 280, 310; Western, 10, 41, 214
liberalism, xiv, 188; nineteenth-century, 187; sanctuary and, 274
liberation, 3, 46, 193, 259, 287, 296, 304, 311–13, 321n1, 326, 329–31; abolition and, 97, 276; Black, 1, 111–12n1, 132, 243, 299, 302, 305; Brown, 132; co-liberation, 236–37, 243; collective, xiii, 274, 281, 286, 339; Durban Moment an, 250–51; *Exterminate All the Brutes* (Peck) and, 313, 316–17; Indigenous, 19, 22, 132, 232, 243, 299; national, 192–93; Palestinian, xiii, 22, 286; politics of, 101; of resources, 336; struggles, 18, 123, 286; technologies of, 288; theology, 6; Third World, 284; vernaculars of, 280
Libya, xivn1, 12, 18, 181, 207, 271, 277; Europe's borders and, 289; refugees in, 101, 108, 110
Lipsitz, George, xii, 338
local governments, ix, 2, 168
Lorde, Audre, 286, 304
Los Angeles, 3, 11, 68–73, 143, 335; airport, 27; artivist movement building in, 52–53; Hauser and Wirth, 259; homelessness in, 2; Latinx communities in, 135; Stop LAPD Spying Coalition, xi; surveillance in, 209; unhoused people in, 1, 26. *See also* Mission San Gabriel; Museum of Tolerance; Simon Wiesenthal Center; Taraaxam
Los Angeles County, 72, 337
love, 118–20, 123, 126–28, 287, 303, 305; abolition as, 30, 120; familial, 236; home and, 328; of Israel, 185–87, 191;
for land, 72; liberatory, 5; of Palestine, 192; radical, xi, 119, 333; sanctuary and, 124–26
lynching, 84, 92n1, 235; photographs, 246n3

McKittrick, Katherine, 30, 258–59
Makdisi, Saree, 22
Malta, 12, 269
Mamdani, Mahmood, 182–83
Mamilla Cemetery, 176, 184
Man, 4, 324; nation and, 317; obsolescence of, 211; universal, 26
"Map of Migrant Mortality," 145–50, 152
marginalization, 23, 162, 164, 169
Marriot, David, 30n11–13
marronage, 5, 20, 28, 47, 332
Matsipa, Mpho, 16, 41
Mattei Plan, 271–73
Mayorkas, Alejandro, 205–6, 212n5
Mays, Esther Shawboose, 235–37, 294
Mays, Judy, 236, 298
Mays, Kyle, 26, 28–29, 48–49, 236–37, 246n1, 262, 331
Mbembe, Achille, 14–15, 25, 333
Mediterranean, 2, 20–23, 29, 31n8, 147, 224, 266, 273–77, 284–85, 329; Black Lives Matter and, 98; containment in, 333; maritime disaster and, 207; migrant crisis in, 251, 255; weaponization of, 208. *See also* Black Mediterranean
Meloni, Georgia, 10, 266, 268, 270–72, 279, 281
Mexico, 11, 69–71, 117, 121, 143, 180, 192, 205, 216; Border Industrialization Program (BIP), 196; Central American asylum seekers in, 326; Ciudad Juárez, 145–46, 149, 325 (*see also* femicides); containment in, 333; economies of, 203; maquilization, 201; Piedras Negras, 204; refugee camps in, 330; smart security and, 210; Tijuana, 19, 145, 198, 201, 209
Mignolo, Walter, 24, 321n1
migrant death, 135–39, 141, 148–49, 152, 224; female, 140, 147; invisibility of, xii; maps, 150
migrant detention centers, 3, 197, 203

migrant justice, 19; groups, 107; movements, 7, 17, 20, 26–27; struggles, 42
migrant movements, 4–5, 10, 26
migrant remains, 11, 137–41, 149–50, 152, 203; female, 143, 145, 147
migrants, 4, 10–13, 20–22, 97, 103, 136–41, 149–50, 152, 166–69, 170n1, 203–7, 210–11, 215, 219, 225–26, 266–70, 278–80, 290n3, 290n5, 325–27; accommodations for, 284; Black Lives Matter and, 285; criminalization of, x, 7; dead, 283; economic, 12, 14–15; female, 135, 139–41, 143–48; housing and, 17, 166 (*see also* camps; squats; squatting); illegalized, 3, 13, 109, 214, 216–17, 223–24, 228, 267, 270; Indigenous, 147–48; justice, 42; Mexican, 218; missing, 2; murder of, 105; naval blockade against, 10; the poetic and, 322; racialized, 231; rights of, 31n8; sanctuary for, 232; solidarity with, 5, 18–20, 288; spatiotemporality of, 222; surveillance of, 107; undocumented, 109, 141; violence against, 277; whiteness and, 163
migration, 2, 10, 13, 41, 137, 198, 205, 214–15, 218–22, 225–28, 236, 266–67, 271–73; abolition and, 285; control, 107; critique of, 23; decolonial, 15; Europe and, 21, 290n1, 290n3; Great Migration, 294; housing and, 155; illegalization of, 217; labor, 104, 112n2, 214; Mexican, 216, 218, 325; migratisation and, 290n5; national economy and, 278; necropolitics of, 136; policies, 161, 168–70; politics of, 218, 229; regimes, x, 5, 13–14, 108, 112n2, 215, 332; women and, 140
missionaries, 65–66
Mission San Gabriel, 66, 68–71, 74n5
mobility/mobilities, 14, 15–16, 26, 261; African, 16; counter-cartographies of, 16–17; forced, 2–3, 12, 136, 204, 222 (*see also* deportation); human, 214, 216–17, 227–28; intellectual, 332; kinship and, 30; migration and, 41; sanctuary and, 10; Western archive and, 25

mobilization: anti-imperialist and feminist, 7; Black, 281; against border imperialism, 231; collective, 86; in France, 13; of geographic space, 202; liberal, 107; by migrants, 4; popular, 81; of Third World lawyering, 256
Moby-Dick (Melville), 259–60
modernity, 23, 261; American, 297; Black people and, 80, 90, 92; containers and, 158; postcolonial, 9; violence of, 275; Western, 239
Moreton, Bethany, 119, 122
Morocco, 108, 157
Morrison, Toni, 45–46, 310
movement, 17, 89, 162, 237, 261; of Black people, 289; breath and, 101; control of, 14; freedom of, 18, 107–8, 227–28; migratory, 215, 217; restriction of, 268; rhythm of, 310; rights to, 268
"Mujer Migrante Memorial (MMM)," 11, 135–36, 140–50, 152
Museum of Tolerance, 176–79, 183–86, 189, 191–93
Muslim ban, ix-x, 27, 335
mutual aid, 108, 245; networks 6, 13, 287

Nakba, 177–78, 184, 286
Namibia, 15–16, 157
nationalism: Black Power and, 301–2; methodological, 97, 102, 214; Third World, 261; white, x, xiii, 28, 51
National Socialist Underground (NSU), 105–6
nation-state/nation-states, 221, 275, 331; belonging and, 27; blackness/Black life and, 274; borders and, 283, 328; city and, 8; colonial, 296; decolonization and, 318; dehumanization and, 326; empire-building and, 65; freedom and, 312, 317; internationalism and, 111; land and, 301; Man and, 317, 320; protections of, 330; racialization and, 48; sanctuary and, 327; Westernized, 270
Native people. *See* Indigenous peoples
nativism, 224–25
necro-art, xii, 136, 140, 149
necropolitics, 135, 152; Europe as, 20; of migration, 136

Netherlands, 108, 283
Never Stop Dreaming, 176, 179
newcomers, 68, 155–65, 167–70
Nigeria, 101, 279, 286
nongovernmental organizations (NGOs), 18, 159, 161, 191, 202, 267, 271, 279
No One Is Illegal, 18, 26

occupation, 99, 102, 168, 296; of the Pantheon, 109; of Tovaangar, 67–68, 72. *See also* Palestine: occupation of
oceanic international, 14, 29, 253, 257, 261–62
O'odham people, 19–20
otherness, 25, 189–90
overkill, 278–80

Paik, A. Naomi, x, 7, 28
Palantir, 11, 208–9
Palestine, 18, 177–80, 183–85, 191–92, 277, 286; colonization of, 189–90, 192; exception, xiii; ethnic cleansing of, 177; genocide in, 118, 327; humanitarian racism and, 22; human rights and, 183; occupation of, xiii, 15, 22, 183; sanctuary and, 5. *See also* Gaza; Nakba
Palestinians, 124, 184–85, 187, 191–92, 219, 286; ethnic cleansing of, 22, 177–79, 187, 190–91, 193, 319; genocide of, xiii, 15, 193; *Never Stop Dreaming* and, 178
patriarchy, 30, 65, 118; heteropatriarchy, 65–66, 69, 71, 126
Patterson, Orlando, 23, 60, 65, 87–89. *See also* social death
Patterson, William, 79–82, 84–85, 91
Peres, Shimon, 176–78, 183–84, 186, 190, 193
Perugini, Nicola, 190–91
permanent displaceability, 2–3, 159, 298
Pima County Office of the Medical Examiner (PCOME), 137–39, 145, 147, 149, 152n2
planetary sanctuary, 14, 262
police, 17, 101, 103–6, 168, 277, 290n3; abolition of, xii, 48–49, 119, 131; Black death and, 83; border, 12 (*see also* Frontex); brutality, 86, 299; camps and, 160; colonies and, 98–99; immigration checks and, 129n5; murder, 104, 131, 279, 286; Palantir and, 209; state, x, 3, 89; violence, 104, 110
policing, 96–100, 103, 105–7, 197, 254, 261, 286–87, 289; academy and, 333; border, 227; capital and, 109; capitalism and, 100, 102, 112n2; colonialism and, 70; in Germany, 104–5; Indigenous land and, xi; labor and, 65; of oceans, 101, 105; olfactory, 206
possession, 8, 30, 59–60, 62–63, 66–68; paradoxes of, 235; settler logics of, xi
poverty, 2, 279, 328, 335; line, 124
Power, Samantha, 79–80, 90
praxis: abolitionist, 132; love as, 119, 123–24, 126–28; pedagogical, xii; of relationality, 68; of solidarity, 28
Prevention Through Deterrence, 11, 139, 141, 198, 202–3, 205, 208, 321
prisons, 28, 48, 54, 100–103, 112n2, 119, 197, 330; abolition of, 48–49, 55, 57, 97, 131; migrants in, 18. *See also* carcerality; carceral system; incarceration
private property, 45, 54, 209, 301
protection, 3, 6, 27, 214, 326–27; border, 207; of migrants, x, 12, 20–21, 211n1, 216; for minors, 279; sanctuary and, 4–5, 23, 25; water, 14, 261
public intellectuals, 55, 329, 332

Quintanilla, Alyssa, 150, 152

race, 45, 78, 88, 90, 112n1, 220, 290n2; class relations and, 100; conquest and, 62; critical race studies, 117; critical race theory, 163; division, 158; politics of, 218, 220, 222; traitors, 276; in the US, 79
racial capitalism, xi, 46–47, 60, 124, 201, 251, 272, 296, 305; Black people and, 261; colonial, 270, 326, 328–30; critiques against, 51; end of, 258, 302; fascism and, 288; gendered, 238, 241, 245, 284, 331; global, 5, 14; humanitarianism and, 3; land and, 296; negation of the negation of, 132; policing and, 98; reparations and, 302; sociality and, 239; US, 196

Index 363

racism, 6, 14, 30, 80, 105, 220, 320, 334; antiblackness and, 91; anti-immigrant, 124; anti-Indigenous, 296; antiracism, 91, 220, 333; Black and, 23; carceral, 104; colonial, 99; environmental, 54; humanitarian, 22, 177, 187, 190–91, 193; immigration system and, 205; in Italy, 280; liberal discourse and, 188; premature death and, 85; sexual terror and, 86; state, 103, 105; structural, 305; systemic, 117; un-breathing and, 100; in the United States, 79, 281; Zionism and, 190

Ramos, Nicole E., 19, 31n7, 231

rape, 66, 86–87, 140, 178, 224, 236

Reagon, Bernice Johnson, 56

reciprocity, 25, 56, 73, 165, 304, 331, 333

recognition, 9, 16, 26–27, 88; Black people and, 89–90; colonial politics of, 296, 305; of Israel as Jewish state, 189; kinship and, 29; liberal, 28, 236; migrants and, 21; political, 245; politics of, xi, 16, 27; radical blackness and, 111n1; selective, 237; by the state, 276; of suffering, 10

reconstruction, 289; Black, 254; in the United States, 51, 197, 202, 299–301, 306n2; white, x; of the world, 42

refuge, 15, 122, 127, 152, 211n1, 214, 283, 294, 297, 326; cities of, 5, 8; Darfur and, 182; hegemonic formations of, x; Indigenous communities and, 20; as postcolonial apology, 27; radical mutualities and, 330

refugee movements, 18, 214, 227–28

refugees, 22, 97, 103, 108, 162, 170n1, 201, 204, 209–10, 214–17, 219, 324–26; abolition and, 119; Black, 288, 328; carceral conditions of, 268; Central American, 6–7, 125; in Europe, 11–12, 266; housing and, 166–68; Indigenous people as, 6; in Italy, 285; Jewish, 179; in Libya, 101; mass rendering of, 277; Moria camp and, 17; race and, 220; solidarity with, 5, 19; Syrian, ix, 335; Trump administration and, 231; Ukranian, 13

Refugees in Libya, 18, 108, 110

refusal, 46–47, 107, 180, 236, 246n2, 283, 318; abolitionist, xi, 7, 55, 57; as affirmation, 284; artistic creation and, 331; Black feminist, 55, 243; of Black humanity, 84; communities of, 329, 332; of ecocide, 262; of Eurocentrism, 24; everyday, 245; Fanon and, 252; fugitivity and, 51, 295; of the human, 312; of humanism, 27, 315, 317; lascars and, 253; of liberal governance, 3; of violence, 319

religion, 5, 167; Catholic, 71

removal, 6, 69, 161, 296, 300

reparations, 49–50, 254, 271, 273, 299, 303; decolonization and, 29, 305; mainstream, 302; transnational, 15

Requerimiento, 62, 64

resistance, 14, 46–47, 103, 106, 110, 315, 326, 331; abolitionist strategies of, 231; alliances and, 333; anticolonial, 19; antifascist, 7; black, 24; in camps, 107; communities of, 329, 332; co-resistance, 29, 295–96; cultures of, 281; diasporic, 283; Indigenous, 6; Indo-Chinese, 99; institutionalized, 220; kinship and, 303; Palestinian, xiii; politics of, 23; racial capitalism and, 3; Reconstruction and, 51; refugee, 18; sanctuary and, 125; sanctuary as, 7; subalterns and, 164; of surplus populations, 101

revolt, 4, 17, 25, 244, 252; Black, 23, 26, 84; global, 29

Rigg, Sean, 101, 106

right to the city, 159, 161, 168–70

rights, 2, 117, 211, 267–68, 295, 303, 305, 329; citizenship, 20; civil, 53, 122, 124, 212n5, 281, 302; discourse of, 279, 283; environmental, 1; equal, 13, 15; Indigenous, 72, 193, 331; labor, 108–9, 278; language of, 191; migrants', 31n8, 328; national, 255; Palestinian, 184, 187; of refugees, 168, 269; reproductive, 328; of settlers, 230; sovereign state, 261; trans, 328; workers', 54; women's, 177, 320. *See also* human rights

Rodríguez, Dylan, x, 64, 69

Roma people, 105, 277, 279

364   Index

Romanus Pontifex, 61–62
Roy, Ananya, x, xii, 24, 46, 214, 235, 272, 326; on humanism, 236, 252; political kinship and, 262
Rushdie, Salman, 7–8

Said, Edward, 252, 296
Salvini, Matteo, 279, 284
Samudzi, Zoé, 16
sanctuary cities, x, 24
sanctuary jurisdictions, ix–xi, 4
sanctuary movements, 5–7, 126
Sanctuary Spaces Sawyer Seminar, 14, 17, 26–28, 131, 323
San Diego, 63, 65, 198, 201–2, 207–9
Schwundeck, Christy, 101, 286
Scott, David, 5, 25
Scott, Julius, 255
security, 11, 91, 261; border, 270, 328; EU and, 21, 105; food, 336; guards, 166; human, 179; job, 109; migration and, 169; national, 21, 198; radical ontological, 90, 92n8; smart, 210; state and, 267
Sepulveda, Charles, 28, 30, 45–49, 55–56, 331
Serra, Junípero, 59, 63, 68
settler colonialism, 18, 22, 28, 46, 49, 57, 196, 239, 243, 245; aftermath of, 29, 295–96, 299; end of, 302; of Los Angeles, 69; racial, 193, 255; as a structure, 67; US democracy and, 305; Western, 193; Zionist, 190–91
Sharpe, Christina, 20, 23, 118
Shoah, 315–16, 319–20. *See also* Holocaust
Simon Wiesenthal Center, 176, 179, 183–84
Simpson, Audra, 27
slavery, 23, 25, 59, 63–65, 73, 123–24, 237; abolition of, 51; afterlife of, 124, 236, 242, 246n3, 275, 286; Black, 48; conquest and, 61; fugitives from, 19; Jim Crow and, 89; legacies of, 2; perpetual, 61; racial, 90, 92n8; reparations for, 305; as social death, 87–88, 90; transatlantic, 311, 315
slave trade, 62, 180; founding violence of, 239; transatlantic, 6, 14, 251–52, 288, 311

Smythe, SA, 10, 22–23, 29, 262, 327, 329
Snorton, C. Riley, 241–42
social death, 15, 22–23, 25, 119, 126; Black, 91; of conquest, 28, 60, 70, 73, 331; genocide as, 80, 87–90, 92n6; slavery as, 87–90
social media, 18, 117, 127, 206, 338
social movements, xii, 117, 276, 286, 288, 334; black, 276
social reproduction, 238, 240–41, 246n4; Black feminist, 245; creative, 27, 236; errant, 240–41, 245
social welfare, 101, 217, 328; dependency, 161
solidarity, 4, 6, 17–20, 22, 24, 46–47, 49, 150, 287, 323, 331–32, 339; abolitionist, 97, 233; Bandung conference and, 256; breathing and, 330; community, 52; criminalization of, xiii, 169; cross-border, 17–18, 26; decolonial, 18, 20, 155–56; decolonization and, 305; *Exterminate All the Brutes* (Peck) and, 318–19; formations, 108; housing, 155, 165; Indigenous cosmologies and, 331; infrastructures, 13, 107, 155; international, 7, 193; kinship and, 29, 304; multi-racial, 105; networks, 276, 279; Palestine and, 286; praxis of, 28; religion and, 5; reparations and, 50; sanctuary and, 6, 252, 326; university as, xiii; worker, 250
Soltis, Emiko, 120, 128n4
Sonoran Desert, 17, 135, 140, 144, 147, 150, 203, 323; Prevention Through Deterrence and, 11, 139
South Africa, 15, 157, 247, 254–55; Durban, 249–53, 259. *See also* apartheid
sovereignty, 24, 243, 245, 310, 339; European, 169; narratives of liberation and, 317; national, 268; over the sea, 257; in Palestine, 286; political, 312; property-oriented, 267; state, 8, 14, 73; subaltern networks and, 256. *See also* Indigenous sovereignty
Spain, 61–62, 70, 108, 146, 277
Special Anti-Robbery Squad (SARS), 101, 286
Spillers, Hortense, 238, 241

Spivak, Gayatri, 24–25
squats, 17, 160, 166; migrant, 24, 26, 156, 166–68
squatting, 17, 165
Starks, Amber, 305–6
state, 100, 178, 211, 331; Baraka and, 281; civil murder and, 120, 123, 128n3; deindustrialization and, 201; deportation and, 223; Derrida on, 8; displacement and, 2; housing, 18; kidnapping of Indigenous children and, 236; migrants and, 285; minor figure and, 237; paternalism, 267; police, x, 3, 89; political subject of, 324; refugees and, 326; violence, 104, 106, 109, 280. *See also* nation-state
Stewart-Ambo, Theresa, 67
stolen land, 5, 54–55; abolition and, 4, 46–47, 52, 131; border imperialism and, 243; sanctuary and, xi, 29; United States and, 300
stranger, 169, 237–40, 242; racialized, 163; suffering, 9
Streisand, Barbara, 184, 190
strikes, 47, 102, 108–10, 262; Durban, 249–51, 253, 261; general, 253–54, 261; hunger, 189, 253; maritime, 14, 253, 261; oceanic, 26, 255; against policing, 254; refugee, 17–18; student, 116, 253
Sudan, 108, 179–80, 183, 279
suffering, 106, 152, 326, 328; Black, 81–82, 284; necro-art and, 136; racial capitalism and, 3; sanctuary and, 9–10
superexploitation, 99, 108, 110, 112n1, 286
surplusification, 14, 22, 100, 109–11
surplus populations, 14, 100–101, 105
surveillance, 3, 11, 17, 50, 266, 299, 333; Black life and, 23, 259; border, 323; Libyan coast guard and, 12; migrant, 10, 107; sexual terror and, 86–87; slavery and, 92n5; US-Mexico border and, 202, 208–9
Syria, xivn1, 21, 157, 162; asylum seekers from, 13; refugees from, ix, 155, 167, 335

Táíwò, Olúfémi, 295, 303
Tambreé, Kali, 235, 237, 242, 246n1

Taraaxam (Tongva/Gabrielino), 28, 60, 66–73, 74n5. *See also* kuuyam
Taylor, Breonna, 101, 131, 285–86
terror, xiii, 65, 73, 80, 82, 89, 91, 260, 335; against Black people, 81–82, 84–85; carceral, 57; colonial, 57; of conquest, 59; racial, 9, 15, 178, 237; racial colonial, 47, 49; sexual, 72, 86–87; slavery and, 92n5; of Western humanism, 27, 236; white supremacist, 282, 303. *See also* War on Terror
terrorism, 66, 105, 221, 279
Texas, 117, 137–38, 206
Third World lawyering, 14, 251, 256–57, 261
Thompson, Vanessa E., xii, 13–14, 30, 286–87, 330
Title 42, 204–7, 210, 212n4
tolerance, 22, 176, 178, 184–91, 193. *See also* Museum of Tolerance
Tongva. *See* Taraaxam
torture, 187, 224, 269
Traoré, Adama, 101, 286
Trouillot, Michel-Rolph, 313, 315
Trump, Donald J., ix-xiv, 4, 272, 334–35; administration, 11, 19, 27, 203, 233; cut-outs of, 206; election of, 125–26; regime, 339. *See also* Muslim ban
Tsavdaroglou, Charalampos, 10, 17–18
Tunisia, 108, 270–72, 284
Turkey, 106, 159, 279
Turner, Richard "Rick," 250–51

Ukraine, 13, 327
unfreedom, 6, 26, 309–10; conditions of, 312, 330, 332; Europe and, 313, 329; relative, 240
unhoused people, 1, 328
United Kingdom, 106, 108, 256; Britain First, 272; deportation agreement with Rwanda, 10; Home Office, 269; Initiative in Remembrance of Oury Jalloh and, 104
United Nations Convention on the Law of the Seas (UNCLOS), 256–57
United Nations Convention on the Prevention and Punishment of the Crime of Genocide, 79, 81–85, 87

United Nations High Commissioner for Refugees (UNHCR), 22, 161, 163
universities/university, the, xii-xiii, 116-17, 150, 201, 333; abolition and, xi, 120; decolonization of, 120; love and, 126; Palestine and, xiii, 118; public, 120-21; sanctuary and, x-xi, 117, 125-26; state, 122
University of California, Los Angeles, x-xi, xiii; Promise Institute for Human Rights, 1
University of Georgia, 120, 122
US Border Patrol, 19, 136-37, 202, 204, 207-8, 323, 328
US Customs and Border Protection (CBP), 11, 202-6, 209, 321, 327
US Department of Justice, 202, 205
US Holocaust Memorial Museum, 183, 189
US Immigration and Customs Enforcement (ICE), 11, 121, 202, 211, 327
US-Mexico border, 135-37, 139-40, 197, 201, 203-4, 208, 216, 323, 335; Biden and, 327; Black refugees at, 328; Border Research and Technology Center (BRTC) and, 202; death and, 150, 224; female migrant death and, 146-47; homeless camps and, 2; human rights violations and, 231; mobility and, 17; necro-art and, 149; sanctuary and, 11; violence and, 196. *See also* "Mujer Migrante Memorial (MMM)"; Prevention Through Deterrence

Vargas, João H. Costa, 15-16, 21, 23, 92n3
Vargas, Karla Marisol, 205-6
Venezuela, xiv, 205
violence, 15, 22, 48, 52, 59, 86, 119, 216, 238-39, 244; against Black people, 23, 48, 80, 84, 242, 279; antiqueer, 280; border, 18-19, 23, 96, 107, 196, 224, 228, 328; of capitalism, 330; carceral, 109; cartographies of, 273; colonial, 9, 16, 18-19, 98-99, 288, 303, 319, 332, 339; of colonial land relations, 73; as cultural object, 190; of dispossession, 189; domestic, 54; ecology of, 270; of EU border regime, 107; of Euro-African relations, 274; Euro-American freedom and, 310; excessive, 280; external spaces of, 6; extralegal, 11, 98; gender, 140, 143, 145, 149; historico-material, 274; of humanism, 27, 317, 320, 323, 329; of humanitarian reason, 252; against Indigenous people, 48, 61-62, 68; institutional, 126; interpersonal, 277; against migrants, 146, 268; of modernity, 275; narco-violence, 203; necropolitical, 323; police, 104, 110; racial, 9, 30, 178, 187-88, 193; sanctuary and, 125; of settlement, 67; sexual, 18, 66, 68, 71; of the Shoah, 319-20; of slavery, 63; state, 2, 30, 98, 103-5, 109-11, 140-41, 152, 339; structural, xii, 7, 137, 212n3; of White Being, 69; of the West, 136, 315; white supremacist, 237; women and, 118; of Zionism, 178, 190, 193. *See also* domicide; genocide; rape; terror
violent conflict, 2-3, 179
Voekel, Pamela, 119, 122

Walcott, Rinaldo, 25-26, 29, 328-29
"The Wall That Gives / El Muro Que Da" (Cruz), 135, 141, 143
War on Drugs, 197, 201
War on Terror, 221-22, 237
West, the, ix-x, 6, 26; asylum and, 27, 41; capitalism and, 136; ecocide and, 286; hospitality and, x; humanism and, 25; humanitarian reason and, 22; imperial vision of, 6; Islam and, ix; Judeo-Christian, x; liberal democracies of, 41, 214; media platforms of, 21; moral standing of, 22; refuge and, 27; reworlding and, 24; sanctuary and, 4, 24, 26-27, 214; universities of, xiii
West Bank, 183, 268
Western humanism, 23-24, 26-27, 236-37, 326, 329-30
whiteness, 163; embodying, 64-65; epistemic system of, 59; Europeanness and, 220; genocide and, 16; privilege and, 117; *razón* and, 70-71; Ukraine and, 13

white supremacy, 47–49, 55, 57, 69–70, 86, 294–96, 339; aftermath of, 29, 295–96, 299; border regimes and, 328; border violence and, 18; colonialism and, 220; *Exterminate All the Brutes* (Peck) and, 314; institutions and, 126; multiculturalist, x, 69; Western humanism and, 329

women, 77, 82, 123, 208, 235, 242, 328; Afghan, 182; Black, 48, 86, 236, 238, 240, 246n4, 284; of color, 18; enslaved, 242; Indigenous, 19, 65–66, 68, 71, 236, 320; leaders, 65; love and, 118; migrant, 11, 140, 146; unhoused, 337; white, 86; women's rights, 177, 320; working-class, 106

World War I, 83, 157

World War II, 189, 217, 290n1

Wynter, Sylvia, 4–5, 24–25, 64–65, 311–12, 315–16

xenophobia, 121, 170, 227, 328

Yang, K. Wayne, 67

Yazzie, Melanie, 22, 27–28

Zablotsky, Veronika, xii, 46, 214, 252, 262, 272, 326

Zionism, 179, 187, 189–93. *See also* Israel

Zionist project, 22, 190–91

Zubiaurre, Maite, x, xii, 11, 326; *Talking Trash: Cultural Uses of Waste*, 137. *See also* "Mujer Migrante Memorial (MMM)"